A HISTORY OF THE

SIKHS

VOLUME I: 1469-1839

A HISTORY OF THE
SIKHS

BY KHUSHWANT SINGH

VOLUME I: 1469-1839

PRINCETON, NEW JERSEY
PRINCETON UNIVERSITY PRESS
1963

Publication of this book
has been aided by the Ford Foundation program
to support publication, through
university presses, of works in the humanities
and social sciences

Printed in the United States of America by
Westview Press, Boulder, Colorado

Reissue, 1984
First Princeton Paperback Printing, 1984
ISBN 0-691-03021-9
ISBN 0-691-00803-5 (pbk.)

To my Parents
Sardar Bahadur Sir Sobha Singh
and Lady Viran Bai

PREFACE

EVER since its publication in 1849, Captain Joseph Davey Cunningham's *History of the Sikhs* has been considered the standard work on the religion and history of the Sikhs. Since then extensive research has been done on different aspects of Sikh history: large portions of their scriptures have been translated; records bearing on the building of the Sikh church and community have been unearthed; the founding of an independent Punjabi state under Sikh auspices and its collapse after the death of Ranjit Singh have been explained. However, no attempt has been made to revise Cunningham's work in the light of these later researches; nor, what is more surprising, has any one undertaken to continue Cunningham's narrative beyond the end of the First Sikh War and the partial annexation of the Punjab by the British in 1846.

This work is the first attempt to tell the story of the Sikhs from their inception to the present day. It is based on the study of original documents in Gurmukhi, Persian, and English available in the archives and libraries of India, Pakistan, the United Kingdom, Canada, and the United States. It also gives an account of the Sikh communities scattered in different parts of the world—Great Britain, the United States, Canada, China, Malaya States, Burma, and South and East Africa—and of the way they are facing the challenge of modern times in alien surroundings.

The story of the Sikhs is the story of the rise, fulfilment, and collapse of Punjabi nationalism. It begins in the latter part of the 15th century with Guru Nanak initiating a religious movement emphasising what was common between Hinduism and Islam and preaching the unity of these two faiths practised in the Punjab. By the beginning of the 17th century the movement crystallised in the formation of a third religious community consisting of the

· vii ·

disciples or *sikhās* of Nanak and the succeeding teachers or *gurus*. Its mysticism found expression in the anthology of their sacred writings, the *Ādi Granth*, comprised of the writings of the Sikh gurus as well as of Hindu and Muslim saints. The next hundred years saw the growth of a political movement alongside the religious, culminating in the call to arms by the last guru, Gobind Singh. Within a few years after the death of Gobind Singh, the peasants made the first attempt to liberate the Punjab from Mughal rule. Under the leadership of Banda they defied the authority of Mughal governors and kept the imperial armies at bay for a full seven years. Although Banda and his followers were ruthlessly slaughtered, the spark of rebellion that they had lighted smouldered beneath the ashes and burst into flame again and again in different parts of the province. The period which followed witnessed a renewal of invasions of Northern India by Afghan hordes led by Ahmed Shah Abdali, which gave a further impetus to the growth of Punjabi nationalism. Peasants grouped themselves in bands (*misls*), harassed and ultimately expelled the invaders.

The movement achieved its consummation with the liberation of Lahore and the setting up of the first independent Kingdom of the Punjab under Ranjit Singh in A.D. 1799—by a curious coincidence exactly one hundred years after Guru Gobind Singh's call to arms (1699), just a little under two hundred years after the compilation of the *Adi Granth* (1604), and three hundred years after the proclamation of his mission by Guru Nanak (1499). Under Ranjit Singh, the Punjabis were able not only to turn the tide of invasion back into the homelands of the traditional conquerors of Northern India, the Pathans and the Afghans, but also to make their power felt beyond the frontiers—northwards across the Himalayas; across the Khyber into Afghanistan; in Baluchistan, Sindh, and in Northern India as far as Oudh. The Sikhs became the spearhead of the nationalist movement which had gathered the parent communities within its fold. The achievements were those of all Punjabis alike, Hindus, Muslims, and Sikhs. It was in the fitness of things that in the crowning successes of Punjabi arms, the men who represented the state were drawn from all communities. In the victory parade in Kabul in 1839 (a few months after Ranjit Singh's death) the man who bore the Sikh colours was Colonel Bassawan, a Punjabi Mussalman. And the man who carried the Sikh flag across the Himalayas a year later was General Zorawar Singh, a Dogra Hindu.

This is the theme and substance of Volume I and the first part of the projected second volume. The rest of the next volume will continue the narrative and tell how the nationalist movement, having run its course, began to peter out and finally collapsed in a clash of arms with the British in 1848-1849. It will also recount how the Sikhs, who, within a couple of centuries of their birth, had evolved a faith, outlook, and way of life which gave them a semblance of nationhood, have had to fight against the forces of dissolution to preserve their identity. It will deal with the political and social movements that took place during British rule, the fate of the Sikhs in the partition of their homeland in 1947, their position in independent India, and the demand for an autonomous Punjabi state within the Indian union.

Acknowledgments

I would like to express my gratitude to Dr. Percival Spear of Selwyn College, Cambridge, Dr. Sir Gokul Chand Narang, Sardar Sardul Singh Caveeshar, and Sardar Bahadur Ujjal Singh for reading the manuscript and making valuable suggestions; to Krishna Shungloo for his assistance in translating the hymns published in the appendix; to V. S. Suri, Curator of the Punjab Government Archives, Patiala, for placing unpublished material on Ranjit Singh at my disposal; and above all to Miss Yvonne Le Rougetel, who collaborated with me in the research.

I would also like to place on record my deep sense of gratitude to the Rockefeller Foundation, which made it possible for me to travel extensively and devote myself exclusively to this work for three years.

KHUSHWANT SINGH

Muslim University,
Aligarh

CONTENTS

Preface   v

PART I. THE PUNJAB AND THE
BIRTH OF SIKHISM

Chapter 1. The Sikh Homeland   3

Chapter 2. Birth of Sikhism   17

Chapter 3. Building of the Sikh Church   49

Chapter 4. The Call to Arms   63

Chapter 5. From the Pacifist Sikh to the
Militant Khalsa   76

PART II. THE AGRARIAN UPRISING

Chapter 6. The Rise and Fall of Banda Bahadur   101

Chapter 7. Persecution of the Sikhs and the
Reorganisation of the Khalsa Army   120

Chapter 8. Ahmed Shah Abdali and the Sikhs   131

Chapter 9. From the Indus to the Ganges   169

PART III. PUNJAB MONARCHY
AND IMPERIALISM

Chapter 10. Rise of the Sukerchakia Misl   187

Chapter 11. Maharajah of the Punjab   196

Chapter 12. Suzerain of Malwa   210

Chapter 13. British Annexation of Malwa:
Treaty of Lahore, 1809   219

Chapter 14. Consolidation of the Punjab   232

Chapter 15. Extinction of Afghan Power in
Northern India   246

Chapter 16. Europeanisation of the Army   258

CONTENTS

Chapter 17. Dreams of Sindh and the Sea   268

Chapter 18. Across the Himalayas to Tibet   278

PART IV. APPENDICES

Appendix 1. Janamsakhis and Other Sources of
Information on the Life of Guru Nanak   299

Appendix 2. Adi Granth or the Granth Sahib   304

Appendix 3. Bhai Gurdas   310

Appendix 4. Dasam Granth   313

Appendix 5. Hymns from the Adi Granth   319

Appendix 6. Treaty of Lahore, 1809   378

Appendix 7. Tripartite Treaty of 1838   380

Bibliography   385

Index   399

ILLUSTRATIONS

PLATES

PAGES

Guru Nanak and His Companions, Mardana and Bala   210

Guru Gobind Singh, last of the Sikh gurus   211

Ranjit Singh, with his favorite Muslim wife,
  Bibi Gulbahar Begam   242

Harimandir, the Golden Temple of the Sikhs
  at Amritsar   243

The plates are used through the courtesy of
M. S. Randhawa

MAPS

General Map of the Punjab   3

Northern India at the Birth of Ranjit Singh, 1780   186

The Punjab in 1809   218

Northern India at the Death of Ranjit Singh, 1839   290
  From *Ranjit Singh*, by Khushwant Singh. Used by
  permission of George Allen and Unwin, Ltd.

PART I
THE PUNJAB AND THE BIRTH OF SIKHISM

CHAPTER 1

THE SIKH HOMELAND

THE PUNJAB has a geographical unity distinct from the neighbouring countries and the rest of India. It is shaped like a scalene triangle balanced on its sharpest angle. The shortest side is in the north and is composed of the massive Himalayas, which separate it from the Tibetan plateau. The western side is bounded by the river Indus from the point it enters the plains to another point 1,650 miles downstream, where it meets the confluence of the Punjab's rivers at a place appropriately named *panjnad*, the five streams. Westwards of the Indus runs a chain of rugged mountains, the Hindu Kush and the Sulaiman, pierced by several passes like the Khyber and the Bolan which have served as inlets for the people of the countries which lie beyond, Afghanistan and Baluchistan. The eastern boundary of the Punjab's triangle is not clearly marked, but from a point near Karnal where the Jumna plunges southeastwards a jagged line can be drawn up to Panjnad, which will demarcate the state from the rest of Hindustan and the Sindh desert.

The Punjab, except for the salt range in its centre, is an extensive plain sloping gently down from the mountains in the north and the west towards the desert in the south. Across this monotonously flat land flow six large rivers: the Indus, Jhelum, Chenab, Ravi, Beas, and the Sutlej. In the intra-fluvial tracts or *doābs*[1] between these rivers

[1] The intra-fluvial tracts or mesopotamias are known in the Punjab as *doābs*—two waters. Except for the doabs between the Indus and the Jhelum and the Sutlej and the Jumna, they are known by a combination of the names of the two rivers between which they lie. These names were coined in the time of Emperor Akbar, presumably by his minister, Todar Mal.

a. The Sindh Sagar Doab, between the Indus and the Jhelum.

b. The Chaj Doab between the Chenab and the Jhelum. This doab was also known as Dhanni-Gheb, Chinhat-Chenab, and Behat (which is another name for the Jhelum).

and in the western half of the tract between the Sutlej and the Jumna live people who speak the Punjabi language and describe themselves as the people of the Punjab. The

c. The Rechna Doab between the Ravi and the Chenab. At one time this area was known as Dharpi.

d. The Bari Doab between the Beas and the Ravi. The tract on either side of the Ravi south of Lahore was at one time called Nakki.

e. The Bist Doab or the Bist-Jullundur Doab between the Beas and the Sutlej. This area is also known as Seeroval because of the many hill torrents (sīrs) which intersect it.

f. The Cis-Sutlej Doab between the Sutlej and the Jumna. Only the northwestern portion of this doab is strictly in the Punjab.

Since the river Sutlej runs through the middle of the zone of the main concentration of Sikh population, historians refer to the region west of the river as the Trans-Sutlej and that east of the river as the Cis-Sutlej. This division corresponds roughly to the traditional division of the Punjab into Majha and Malwa explained later in this footnote.

In addition to these divisions, the following Punjabi names for different regions have been (and in some cases still are) used:

a. Pothohar or Dhanni Pothohar for Rawalpindi district including a part of Jhelum district.

b. Majha or the middle, for the Bari Doab. The people living in Majha are known as Majhails. (Also spoken of as Manjha and Manjhail.)

c. Doab for the Bari Doab or Jullundur Doab. The inhabitants are known as Doabias.

d. Malwa for the Punjabi-speaking zone between the Sutlej and the Jumna. The people are known as Malwais. (The Malwa of the Punjab should not be confused with the Malwa of Central India north of the river Narbada.) Malwa is sometimes referred to as Sirhind.

e. Kurukshetra, between the rivers Sarasvati and Drisadvati (probably the present-day Ghaggar). In this region somewhere between Karnal and Jind was fought the famous battle between the Kurus and Pandavas mentioned in the Mahābhārata which occasioned the sermon by Krishna and the theme of the Bhagavad Gītā. Because of its association with Krishna, this land was reputed to be free of sorrow—nirduḥkha. It was also the brahmāvarta, the land of the holy singers where many of the great classics of Sanskrit literature were written. Manu refers to it as the land frequented by gods (ii,17). The Chinese traveller Hsüan Tsang, who visited the Punjab in the 7th century A.D., refers to it as the sukhabhūmī, the land of contentment.

f. Bhatiana, area in southwestern Punjab extending from Hissar to Bikaner, which was the home of Bhatti Rajputs; hence bhaṭiānā, the land of the Bhattis.

g. Hariana, comprising Hissar, Rohtak, and the southern parts of the old states of Jind and Patiala. This tract of desert was at one time irrigated by the Sarasvati and was very green; hence hariānā, the green land.

homeland of the vast majority of the Sikhs is in the doabs between the Chenab and the Jumna.

The Name: Punjab

When the Aryans came to India there were seven rivers in the Punjab, so they named it Sapta Sindhva, the land of the seven seas. The Persians took the name from the Aryans and called it the Hafta Hindva. Sometime later, after the seventh river, the Sarasvati, had dried up, people began to exclude the Indus from the count (since it marked only the western boundary of the province) and renamed it after the remaining five rivers as Pentopotamia or the *panj-āb*, the land of the five waters.[2]

Climate and Landscape

The climate of the Punjab ranges from bracing cold in the winter to scorching heat in the summer. Extremes of temperature and the two monsoons produce a variety of seasons and a constantly changing landscape.

The spring is traditionally ushered in on *Basant Pañcamī*, which falls early in the month of February. It is the Punjab's blossom time, when, in the words of Guru Nanak, "all is seemly; the woodlands are in flower and loud with the humming of bumble bees."[3] The countryside is an expanse of mustard yellow, broken by solid squares of green sugar cane with its fluffy pampas plumes. If the winter monsoon has been good, a crop of wheat, barley,

---

[2] Two other names by which parts of the Punjab were known in ancient times were:

a. Madra Desha, the land of the *madras*. So named after Madri, the mother of the Pandavas. Madra Desha extended from the Beas to the Chenab or the Jhelum. Its capital was at Sakala, probably present-day Sangla. In the *Bicitra Nāṭak*, Guru Gobind Singh also speaks of the Punjab as the Madra Desha. (J. Dowson, *Classical Dictionary of Hindu Mythology and Religion*, p. 183.)

b. Uttarapath, or the northern country. This name appears in Buddhist literature.

[3] The descriptions of the seasons in this chapter are taken from Guru Nanak's *Bārā Māhā* (The Twelve Months). See Appendix 5.

gram, oil-seeds, and tobacco will cover the land with lush abundance. Peasants supplement the rain by canal water, or, where there are no canals, by Persian wheels turned by bullocks or camels. Around the wells grow vegetables: carrots, radishes, cabbages, and cauliflower. Branches of Jujube trees sag under the weight of their berries. In springtime, the sounds that pervade the countryside are the creaking of Persian wheels, the call of partridges, and the monotonous *kooh, kooh,* of flour mills.[4]

The sugar cane is cut, its juice squeezed out, boiled in large cauldrons, and solidified into dark brown cakes. The canary yellow of the mustard is replaced by newly sown cotton and the golden-brown of ripening wheat—and we know that spring has given way to summer.

Trees shed their leaves and after a short period of barrenness come into blossom. While the margosa is still strewing the earth with its brittle ochre leaves, the silk cotton, the coral and the flame of the forest burst into flowers of bright crimson, red, and orange. Even the thorny acacia, the commonest tree of the Punjab, is covered with tiny pale pom-poms. Persian wheels and the partridges are silent: instead there is the screaming of the koils in the mango groves and the crying of barbets.

The wheat is cut and winnowed in the warm breeze. In the words of Guru Nanak: "The sun scorches . . . the earth burns like an oven. The waters give up their vapours, yet it burns and scorches relentlessly." The temperature rises to a fever heat. The parched earth becomes an unending stretch of khaki with dust devils spiralling across the wastes. Even the stolid *pīpal* and the tamarisk are shorn of their leaves and the only green that meets the eye are bushes of camel-thorn, prickly cactus, and the *ak—* calotropis. The succession of hot days and shimmering mirages is occasionally broken by fierce storms which spread layers of dust and sand over everything. All through

---

[4] The blasts are produced by an empty pitcher placed on the mouth of the exhaust pipe of the diesel engine.

the torpid afternoons comes the call of the brain fever bird[5] in a rising crescendo, *peeooh peeooh*. On moonlit nights one can see the wavering arrow-head formations of geese honking their way northwards to the snowy Himalayas.

The blazing inferno lasts from the end of April to the end of June. Then come the rains.

The monsoon makes a spectacular entry. It is heralded by the monsoon bird[6] which fills the dusty plains with its plaintive cries. The colourless grey sky suddenly fills with dense masses of black clouds. There are flashes of lightning and the earth shakes with the rumble of thunder. The first big drops of rain are swallowed by the dust and a heavenly fragrance rises from the earth. Then it comes in torrents, sheet upon sheet, and continues for several hours. Thereafter the skies are frequently overcast; clouds and sunshine contend for dominion; rainbows span the rain-washed landscape; and the setting sun fires the bulbous clouds in hues of red and purple. Two months of incessant downpour turn the land into a vast swamp. Rivers fill up and become a mass of swirling, muddy waters. Punjabis, who have to live through many months of intense heat every year, love the monsoon. It is the time for lovers' trysts and the reunion of families. Guru Nanak went into raptures over it: "The season of the rains has come and my heart is full of joy . . . river and land are one expanse of water. . . . The nights are dark. Frogs croak in contentment. Peacocks cry with joy. The *papīhā* calls *peeooh, peeooh*. The fangs of serpents and the stings of mosquitoes are full of venom. The seas have burst their bounds in the ecstasy of fulfilment." Life begins afresh. There are

---

[5] The hawk-cuckoo (*hierococcyx varius*). Its cry is rendered as "brain fever, brain fever" in English; in Punjabi and Hindustani as *peeooh* or *pi kahāṇ*, "where is my beloved?"

[6] The pied-crested cuckoo (*clamator jacobinus*) takes advantage of the monsoon winds and flies from the East African Coast ahead of the clouds. It usually reaches the coast of India a day or two before the monsoon breaks; hence the name, monsoon bird.

new leaves on many trees and grass covers the barren ground. Mangoes ripen. The clamour of the koils and the brain fever bird is drowned in the song and laughter of girls on swings in the mango groves.

By the time the monsoon is over, it is cool again. The dust has settled and the countryside is green once more. If the summer monsoon has been good—neither too sparse to create a drought nor too heavy to cause floods—all is well. A new crop of rice, millet, maize, indigo, and pulses of many kinds is sown. The peasants wind brightly coloured and starched turbans round their heads, put on waistcoats covered with mother-of-pearl buttons, tie bells round their ankles, and dance the *bhaṅgrā* to the beat of the drum. From October to the festival of the lamps (*Divālī*) in November there is a succession of fairs and festivals.

There is little rest for the peasant. Cotton is to be picked and the land ploughed again for sowing wheat and gram. Persian wheels begin to turn. The *kooh, kooh* of the flour mills is heard in every village. Partridges call in the wheat fields. And at night one hears the honking of geese on their way back to the Punjab.

Once more it is wintertime. The starlit nights are cold and frosty, the days full of blue skies and sparkling sunshine. The mustard is in flower, the woodlands are loud with the humming of the bumble bees, and all is seemly once again.

The Punjab is essentially a rural state made up of innumerable mud and brick villages built on the ruins of older villages. At one time most of them were fortified. Even today one comes across remains of baronial castles and ancient battlements that rise out of the rubble or the village dung heap. Until the 15th century the Punjab had only two important cities, Lahore, which was the seat of most governments, and Multan in the south, which had a busy market dealing with commerce coming up the rivers

from Sindh and caravans from Baluchistan and Persia.
There were also several towns like Rawalpindi, Jhelum,
Wazirabad, Gujarat, Gujranwala, Sheikhupura, Saidpur
now called Eminabad, Pak Pattan, Kasur, Sialkot, Ludhiana, and Sirhind, whose various fortunes rose and fell
with those of their feudal overlords (or, as in the case of
Pak Pattan, with the popularity of the religious order of
which it was the centre). Nothing remains of the extensive
forests which once covered large parts of the Punjab. Up
to the 16th century there were jungles in the north where
rhinoceros[7] (and probably elephants) were found. In
Central Punjab there was the notorious *lakhī* (the forest
of a hundred thousand trees),[8] which gave Sikh outlaws
refuge from their oppressors. There were equally dense
forests in the Jullundur Doab and one long belt of woodland stretching from Ludhiana to Karnal. Up to the middle of the 19th century these forests teemed with wild life:
lions, tigers, leopards, panthers, bears, wolves, hyenas, wild
boars, *nīlgāi*, and many varieties of deer. The flora and
fauna survived the incursions of foreign armies but succumbed to the indiscriminate felling of trees and slaughter
of game in the 19th and the present century. The desert
with its camels and goats—the only animals which can
thrive on cacti and thorny scrub—are a phenomenon of
recent times.

Antiquity

Indologists are not agreed on the age of Indian civilisation except that it is among the oldest in the world and
that its cradle was in the Punjab.

Near Rawalpindi, spears and hatchets made of quartzite

[7] In the *Bābar Nāmā* the Mughal conqueror Babar who invaded India
in A.D. 1526 writes of hunting rhinoceros in the Punjab.

[8] In the *Khulāsat-ut-Tawārikh*, Sujan Rai, who lived in the latter part
of the 17th century, described the *lakhī* in the following words: "Every
year the floods overspread the land far and wide, and when the water
subsides so many jungles spring up all over this country owing to the great
moisture, that a pedestrian has great difficulty in travelling. How then can
a rider?" (J. N. Sarkar, *Fall of the Mughal Empire*, I, 104.)

have been found which date human habitation in the region to between 300,000 and 500,000 years ago.[9] Agricultural implements made of copper and bronze have been found in mounds on both sides of the river Indus which prove the existence of fairly organised rural communities between 25,000 to 20,000 B.C. Nothing more is known about these communities, nor would it be right to describe them as civilisations. We are, however, on surer ground when we come to the archaeological remains of Mohenjodaro in Sindh and Harappa in Southern Punjab, both of which were unearthed in the 1920's. From the sculpture, pottery, jewellery, fabrics, and other relics (particularly seals bearing extremely beautiful figures of bulls, rhinoceros, and other animals) found among the ruins of baked-brick buildings in these cities (and subsequently in many other places) it can be presumed that the people of the Indus Valley had attained a high degree of civilisation. They lived in multi-storeyed houses with marble baths; their craftsmen made goods which were sold as far away as Mesopotamia; and they had evolved some form of religion around the worship of a mother-goddess and her male consort. Neither the hieroglyphics nor the relics found in these cities have yet revealed all their secrets; archaeologists and historians are still disputing the identity of the people who made them. The generally accepted view is that these cities flourished between 2500 B.C. and 1500 B.C. and that they were destroyed by a people known as the Aryans who began to infiltrate into Sindh and the Punjab about fifteen centuries before the birth of Christ.[10]

The Aryans, who were tall and fair, drove out the darker-skinned inhabitants and occupied most of Northern Hindustan. The newcomers were a pastoral people with a religion and a language of their own. Both of these were further developed in the land of their domicile. It was in

[9] S. M. Ikram and Percival Spear, eds., *The Cultural Heritage of Pakistan*, pp. 20-24; Sir R. E. Mortimer Wheeler, *The Indus Civilization*.
[10] A. L. Basham, *The Wonder That Was India*, p. 28.

the Punjab that Vedic Hinduism was evolved, and many
of the great works of Sanskrit literature written.

The Aryans were followed by other races. The Persians
under Darius (521-485 B.C.) conquered Northern Punjab,
and for a hundred years his successors ruled over Peshawar, Taxila, and Rawalpindi. In 326 B.C. Greek armies
under Alexander the Great crossed the Indus and swept
on as far as the Beas. Although the Greeks left behind by
Alexander were deprived of power by the Indian Mauryas a few years after his death, they left a permanent impress on the face of the Punjab. In Peshawar, Taxila, and
perhaps in some other towns as well, Greek artists produced some of the greatest works of sculpture found any-
where in the world.[11]

Maurya power was extinguished by Bactrian invaders.
Menander is believed to have gone across central Punjab
and beyond the Beas. The Bactrians were followed by
many Scythian tribes. When the dust raised by the invading armies had settled, the Indian Guptas spread their
benevolent rule over the country. For some centuries they
were able to block the gaps in the mountains and keep
out other invaders. By A.D. 500, the pressure from Central
Asia became too great and once more the sluice gates were
forced open to let in the Mongoloid Huns. The Huns
were subdued and expelled by Vardhana. His son Harsha
was the last great Indian ruler of the Punjab. After Harsha's death in A.D. 647, Vardhana's empire disintegrated
and races living across the Sulaiman and Hindu Kush
mountains began to pour into Hindustan. The new conquerors who came belonged to diverse tribes but had one
faith: they were Muslims.

In A.D. 1001 came Mahmud of Ghazni. Thereafter the
Afghans came like the waves of an incoming tide, each
column advancing further inland into Hindustan. The

11 Examples of the Gandhara School can be seen in Museums at Peshawar, Taxila, Lahore, Delhi, Mathura, and many other cities.

Ghaznis were followed by other Afghan tribes: the Ghoris, Tughlaks, Surs, and Lodhis.

Between the succession of Afghan invasions came the terrible visitation in 1398 of the Mongol, Taimur, an invasion from which northern India did not recover for many decades. A hundred years later Babar, who was one of Taimur's descendants, started dreaming of an empire in India. His opportunity came with the decline of the Lodhi dynasty. After a few unsuccessful attempts, he finally defeated and slew the reigning Afghan, Ibrahim Lodhi, on the field of Panipat in 1526, and set up the most powerful and long-lived dynasty in the history of India.

People of the Punjab

The ethnic pattern of the Punjab has changed with every new conquest. At the time of the birth of Nanak (A.D. 1469) it was somewhat as follows:

In the northwest stretching along both sides of the Indus were Pathans and Baluchis—the former on the upper and the latter on the lower reaches of the river. These people, like their neighbours (Gakkhars, Awans, Janjuas, and others who settled between the Indus and the Jhelum) were divided into innumerable warring tribes, jealously preserving their traditions and way of life but united in their fierce loyalty to the Islamic faith. On the northern fringe of the country in a narrow belt running along the foothills of the Himalayas were the domains of Hindu princes who had fled the plains in front of the Muslim onslaughts. In this sub-montane region intersected by mountain streams and deep ravines, made impassable by entangled bushes of lantana, vasicka, and ipomea[12] they built chains of forts which defended them from further inroads of Muslim invaders. Here they burnt incense to

[12] These three flowering bushes are found all over India. The adhatoda vasicka is used to make medicinal syrup; the ipomea is grown to reinforce canal banks. Since it blossoms most times of the year it is known in Punjabi as sadā suhāgaṇ (ever-in-marital-bliss).

their gods and preserved their inegalitarian society in which the Brahmin and Kshatriya exploited the lesser castes. In the rest of the Punjab, consisting of the vast champaign stretching to the Jumna and beyond, the countryside was inhabited by Jats and Rajput agricultural tribes, the cities by the trading Banias, Mahajans, Suds, and Aroras. In all cities, towns, and villages there were the dark and somewhat negroid descendants of the aboriginals who were considered beyond the pale of the caste-system, forced to do the dirtiest work and then condemned as untouchables. In addition to all these were nomadic tribes of gypsies wandering across the plains in their donkey caravans, with their hunting dogs and herds of sheep and goats.

Birth of Punjabi Nationalism

The Punjab, being the main gateway into India, was fated to be the perpetual field of battle and the first home of all the conquerors. Few invaders, if any, brought wives with them, and most of those who settled in their conquered domains acquired local women. Thus the blood of many conquering races came to mingle, and many alien languages—Arabic, Persian, Pushto, and Turkish—came to be spoken in the land. Thus, too, was the animism of the aboriginal subjected to the Vedantic, Jain, and Buddhist religions of the Aryans, and to the Islamic faith of the Arabs, Turks, Mongols, Persians, and Afghans. Out of this mixture of blood and speech were born the Punjabi people and their language. There also grew a sense of expectancy that out of the many faiths of their ancestors would be born a new faith for the people of the Punjab.

By the end of the 15th century, the different races who had come together in the Punjab had lost the nostalgic memories of the lands of their birth and begun to develop an attachment to the land of their adoption. The chief factor in the growth of Punjabi consciousness was the evolution of one common tongue from a babel of languages.

Although the Punjabis were sharply divided into Muslims and Hindus, attempts had been made to bring about a rapprochement between the two faiths and a certain desire to live and let live had grown among the people. It was left to Guru Nanak and his nine successors to harness the spirit of tolerance and give it a positive content in the shape of Punjabi nationalism.

It is significant that the spirit of Punjabi nationalism first manifested itself in Majha, the heart of the Punjab, and among a people who were deeply rooted in the soil. Although the founders and many of the leaders of the movement were not agriculturists, its backbone was the Jat peasantry of the central plains.

There are as many conjectures about the etymology of the word Jat[13] as there are of the origin of the race. It is

[13] Cunningham followed Tod and other European scholars in believing that Jats were of Scythian stock. (See Appendix I of his *History of the Sikhs.*) The origin of the Jats has been exhaustively dealt with by K. R. Qanungo, who states emphatically that the Jats are of Aryan stock who migrated from Rajasthan into the Punjab. He estimated the number of Jats to be 9 million in 1925, of whom one-third were Muslims, one-fifth Sikhs, and the remaining Hindus. (K. R. Qanungo, *History of the Jats*, pp. 1, 2, 5-23 and Appendix A, pp. 323-30.) Qanungo's figures include Jats of Rajasthan, Delhi, and Uttar Pradesh.

According to the Hindu caste system, the Jats, being Vaisyas (workers), are of lower caste status than the Brahmin and Kshatriya.

There are many sub-tribes of Sikh Jats, of whom the following are the most prominent: Sidhu (including Sidhu-Brar), Sandhu, Gill, Garewal, Sekhon, Dhillon, Man, Her, Virk, Bhuttar, Bal, Punnun, Aulak, Dhariwal, Sara, Mangat, Chahl, Randhawa, Kang, Sohal, and Bains. There are other Sikh agricultural tribes like the Labana, Kamboh, Sansi, and Mahtam who are not Jats by race.

Prominent among the "untouchable" village communities converted to Sikhism and living in Jat villages are the Mazhabi, Ranghreta, and Ramdasia.

In present-day speech, the Sikh Jat is called *jat* (to rhyme with gut) while the Hindu, particularly of Hariana (Gurgaon, Hissar, Rohtak) and Bharatpur remains a *jat* (to rhyme with the British pronunciation of "start").

For a detailed account of the Jats of the Punjab see "Punjab Castes," by Sir Denzil Ibbetson (reprint of a chapter on the subject in the Census of 1883). According to Ibbetson, the Jats and Rajputs form 28 percent of the population of the Punjab. In the 1883 census the Jats numbered 4,432,750

now generally accepted that the Jats who made the northern plains of India their home were of Aryan stock. They brought with them certain institutions, the most important being the *pañcāyat*, an elected body of five elders, to which they pledged their allegiance.[14] Every Jat village was a small republic made up of people of kindred blood who were as conscious of absolute equality between themselves as they were of their superiority over men of other castes who earned their livelihood as weavers, potters, cobblers, or scavengers. The relationship of a Jat village with the state was that of a semi-autonomous unit paying a fixed sum of revenue. Few governments tried to assert more authority, and those which did soon discovered that sending out armed militia against fortified villages was not very profitable. The Jat's spirit of freedom and equality refused to submit to Brahmanical Hinduism and in its turn drew the censure of the privileged Brahmins of the Gangetic plains who pronounced that "no Aryan should stay in the Punjab for even two days" because the Punjabis refused to obey the priests.[15] The upper caste Hindu's denigration of the Jat did not in the least lower the Jat in his own eyes nor elevate the Brahmin or the Kshatriya in the Jat's estimation. On the contrary, he assumed a somewhat condescending attitude towards the Brahmin, whom he considered little better than a soothsayer or a beggar, or the Kshatriya, who disdained earning an honest living and was proud of being a mercenary. The Jat was born the worker and the warrior. He tilled his land with his sword girded round his waist. He fought more battles for the defence of his homestead than the Kshatriya, for unlike the martial Kshatriya the Jat seldom fled from his village when the invaders came. And if the Jat was mal-

---

and the Rajputs 1,677,569. In the last detailed census of the Punjab prior to partition (census of 1931), the figures were: Jats, 4,855,426; Rajputs, 1,874,325.

[14] *Pañc men parmeśvar.* There is God in the five (elected men).

[15] *Mahābhārata,* VIII, verses 2063-2068 (*Karna Parva*).

treated or if his women were molested by the conqueror on his way to Hindustan, he settled his score by looting the invaders' caravans on their return journey and freeing the women he was taking back. The Punjabi Jat developed an attitude of indifference to worldly possessions and an instinct for gambling with his life against odds. At the same time he became conscious of his role in the defence of Hindustan. His brand of patriotism was at once hostile towards the foreigner and benign, even contemptuous, towards his own countrymen whose fate depended so much on his courage and fortitude.

CHAPTER 2

BIRTH OF SIKHISM

EVERY new religious movement is born out of and shaped by existing faiths, and like offspring bears likeness to them. Sikhism was born out of a wedlock between Hinduism and Islam after they had known each other for a period of nearly nine hundred years. But once it had taken birth, it began to develop a personality of its own and in due course grew into a faith which had some semblance to Hinduism, some to Islam, and yet had features which bore no resemblance to either. In order fully to understand Sikhism and its contribution to the religious thought of the world, we have to be acquainted with early Hinduism, its reaction to Muslim invasions, and the compromises it effected in its tenets to meet the challenge of Islam. We also have to know something of the way Islam developed as it travelled away from its desert home in Arabia and domiciled itself in India. We will then know how the two rival faiths extended the hand of friendship towards each other and evolved rules of good neighbourliness in order to be able to live together in peace.

The Background: Hinduism

It is difficult to define Hinduism with any precision.[1]

[1] "To many, Hinduism seems to be a name without any content. Is it a museum of beliefs, a medley of rites, or a mere map, a geographical expression? Its content, if it has any, has altered from age to age, from community to community. It meant one thing in the Vedic period, another in the Brahmanical, and a third in the Buddhist. It seems one thing to the Saivite, another to the Vaishnavite, a third to the Sakta." S. Radhakrishnan, *The Hindu View of Life.*

"The question what is Hinduism is one to which no one is likely ever to be able to give a simple or quite intelligible answer. It has no creed summing up authoritatively its tenets. It has no historical personality as its centre whose life dates its beginning that can be discerned. It may be described rather as an encyclopaedia of religion than as a religion, a vast

It has three aspects: its pantheon of gods and goddesses with the legends that are attached to them, the social order of the caste system, and the poetry and philosophy of its Sanskrit classics. The first two were the direct outcome of the Aryan impact on India's aboriginal people and their culture. The third was the work of Aryan scholarship, some brought from the Aryan's original homeland, much of it produced in India.

It appears that when the Aryans came, the inhabitants of northern India had no defined religion of their own. They worshipped a variety of gods and goddesses (like the female and male deities of Mohenjodaro) which frequently symbolised the things they dreaded. They offered sacrifices to images of reptiles and animals, and propitiated epidemics like smallpox and plague. The Aryans were worshippers of the beautiful in nature. They chanted hymns to the sky and to the rising sun, to thunder and lightning, and they raised goblets of soma juice to the full moon. Out of the frightened faith of the animists and the rapturous faith of the lovers of nature was created the Hindu pantheon. The aboriginal gods were either pushed into the background or reincarnated in Aryan garb. The relationships between the gods themselves underwent many changes until there came to the fore the triumvirate of Brahma the Creator, Vishnu the Preserver, and Shiva the Destroyer, the three facets of the One God who was Ishvara. Thus out of the polytheism of the pantheon had emerged the idea that the ultimate power to create, keep, or kill resided in the one Supreme Being.

Another result of the Aryan settlement in India was the birth of the caste system. The tall, blonde, and blue-eyed invaders devised this system to maintain the purity of their race and reduce to servitude the dark-skinned inhabitants

---

conglomeration, comprehensive in the widest sense, an amalgam of often contradictory beliefs and practices, held together in one by certain powerful ideas and by a system of social regulations." N. MacNicol, *Indian Theism.*

among whom they had come to live. They divided the populace into four classes which reflected the degree of racial purity, and assigned specific functions to them. On top naturally were the creators of this social system, the Brahmins. They reserved for themselves the exclusive monopoly of priesthood: the reading of the sacred texts and the imparting of knowledge. After them in descending order were Kshatriyas, or warriors, who had to defend the country; Vaishyas, or tradesmen, and Shudras, who were the workers. The pure aboriginal had no social privileges. He was pushed out in the wilderness or utilised to do the most unpleasant jobs. To prevent his coming in by the back door, he was made an outcast whose very touch could pollute. The caste system has been rightly described as Brahmanical Hinduism, for it was the Brahmins who moulded this pattern of social order to suit their own ends.

The most important aspect of Hinduism was neither its pantheon nor its social order, but the philosophy and poetry of the Vedas and the commentaries written about them. While the gods gained or lost in stature and the social order of the caste system was criticised and condemned, the sacred texts remained inviolate. The hymns of the Vedas gave spiritual sustenance, the Upanishads the philosophical justification, and the epics the ethical code of behaviour to the Hindu masses. These texts gave Hinduism the strength to face the challenge of other religions, such as Jainism, Buddhism, and Islam.

It was obvious that a religion which was a confusion of gods and which degraded a large section of the people by treating them as sub-human would not go unchallenged for long. The first to revolt against Brahmanical Hinduism were Mahavira (5th cent. B.C.) and Gautama the Buddha (567-487 B.C.). Within a hundred years of the death of the Buddha, his teaching had swept Hinduism off its feet and spread all over northern India. At the birth of Christ and for seven hundred years or more, the predominant faith of India was Buddhism.

The renaissance of Hinduism began in the south of India some time after the 9th century A.D. Two groups of saintly orders, the Alvars and the Adyars, took up its cause and struck at the weakest point of Buddhism and Jainism— the absence of emotional content in their code of ethics. The Alvars championed the cause of Vishnu, the Adyars of Shiva. But both gave their respective deity the status of the One Supreme God. They relaxed the rigours of the caste system and allowed members of the lower orders to join in worship. They spread their message through hymns of love and praise of God. The millions who, because of their inability to understand the high moral tone of the Jain and Buddhist ethics, had been left in cold isolation, felt the warm enveloping embrace of a new Hinduism which believed in One God, the equality of mankind, and worship through community hymn singing. The tide began to turn. Buddhism fled from the shores of India and Jainism was submerged. Just when Hinduism had come back into its own, it was faced with the challenge of Islam, which had firmly planted its green standard in the soil of India.

The Background: Islam

Commercial intercourse between Arabia and India had been going on from times immemorial. Every spring as the monsoon clouds gathered over the Arabian sea, Arabs loaded their dhows with dates and aromatic herbs produced in their oases. When the winds turned eastwards they unfolded their sails and let the sea breezes waft their boats to the shores of India. A few days before the rains broke over the Western Ghats, Arabian vessels were safely moored in Indian ports and their cargo stored in the warehouses of merchant princes. The people living on the western coast of India, stretching from the mouth of the Indus along the Gulf of Cambay and the Western Ghats right down to the southernmost tip of Cape Comorin, were as familiar with the annual coming of Arab traders as they were with the flocks of monsoon birds which flew ahead of the rain clouds coming from East Africa. Both were almost as ancient a phenomenon as the monsoon itself. The only difference was that whereas the monsoon birds flew back to Africa after a sojourn of a few months, not all Arab traders returned to their homes in the desert. Many married Indian women and settled down in India.

The advent of Mohammed (A.D. 569-632) changed the idolatrous and easy-going Arabs into a nation unified in faith and fired with a zeal to spread the gospel of Islam to every shore. The merchant seamen who had brought dates and frankincense year after year now brought a new faith with them. From the year A.D. 636 onwards, scattered settlements of Arab Muslims sprang up in Western India, particularly in Malabar. The new faith was well received by the people of South India. Muslims were allowed to build mosques, those who were single found wives, and very soon an Indo-Arabian community came into being.[2] Early in the 9th century, Muslim missionaries gained a notable convert in the person of the King of Malabar. The Muslim community grew and spread to the Tamil regions on the east coast. Then Islam spread northwards and more colonies of Muslims grew up on the coast of Cambay.

The peaceful spread of Islam was suddenly checked when Muslim armies began to invade India. In A.D. 672 the seventeen-year-old Mohammed-bin-Qasim marched through Baluchistan and overran the whole of Sindh. The Muslims began to be looked upon as foreign invaders who had to be resisted, and conversions to Islam ceased for some time. There was a lull after Qasim's invasion. The storm burst in all its fury with the invasion of Mahmud of Ghazni (A.D. 971-1030), who swept across Northern India down to Gujarat, annihilating all opposition and destroying Hindu temples wherever he went. Thereafter

[2] In Malabar, the Arab came to be known as *māpilla*, meaning "the great child" or "bridegroom"—the ancestor of the present-day Moplah. (Tara Chand, *Influence of Islam on Indian Culture*, p. 35.)

invasions by Muslim armies became a regular feature of life in Northern India. But neither the succession of victories by Muslim armies nor the massacre of Hindus and the destruction of their temples brought many Hindus into the fold of Islam. On the contrary, as would be natural in the circumstances, conquest only built up Hindu resistance, and the conversions that were made by force were followed by reconversions back to Hinduism. The battles of Islam were not won by Muslim iconoclasts but by peaceful missionaries.

Hinduism's Compromise with Islam: The Bhakti Movement

The Hindu renaissance, started by the Alvars and the Adyars of South India, suddenly found itself confronted with Islam. The Muslim scimitar could be matched with the Hindu sword, but someone had to produce an answer to the argument of Islam. This was supplied by a philosopher whose main concern was not Islam but the refutation of heresies of the Jains and Buddhists, but who in so doing started a movement of renaissance and reformation which had a decisive bearing on Hinduism's attitude towards the new faith. This was Shankara (c. A.D. 800), a Brahmin of Malabar.

Shankara exorted return to the Vedas for inspiration. His Hinduism was an uncompromising monotheism and a rejection of idol worship, for his God was one, indefinable and all-pervasive.

> O Lord, pardon my three sins.
> I have in contemplation clothed in form
>   Thee who art formless.
> I have in praise described Thee who art ineffable,
> And in visiting temples I have ignored Thine
>   Omnipresence.

Shankara was essentially a metaphysician, and, although he provided protagonists of Hinduism with debating points, he did little to forward the mass movement started by the Alvars and the Adyars. This was done by Ramanuja (A.D. 1016-1137), who disagreed with Shankara's purely logical approach to religious problems and advocated the path of *bhakti* (devotion) recommended many centuries before by the *Bhagavad Gita* and revived by the Alvars and the Adyars as the best way to salvation. Ramanuja travelled extensively throughout Northern India as far as Kashmir and left a large number of disciples at every place to propagate his teaching.

The Bhakti movement owes its influence to the Alvar and Adyar saints, the exponents of their creed (Madhva, Vishnu Swami, Vallabha, and others), and, above all, to Ramanuja. The main points of the teaching of the Bhaktas were that God was one, and though He was indescribable He was the only reality; the rest was *māyā* (illusion). The best way to serve God was by absolute submission to His will. The way to approach Him was through meditation and through the chanting of *mantras* and the singing of hymns. This could best be achieved under the guidance of a spiritual mentor, a guru.[8]

The cult of Bhakti was popularised in Northern India by Ramananda. He allowed Hindus of lower castes and Muslims to join him in worship and become his followers. It was his disciple Kabir[4] (A.D. 1440-1518) who, more than any other, spread the message of Bhakti across the Indo-Gangetic Plain.

[8] The house of the Bhakta was said to rest on four pillars: *bhakti, bhakta, bhagvanta,* and the *guru*—worship, the worshipper, God, and the teacher.

[4] A Hindi couplet sums up the history of the spread of the Bhakti movement

> *Bhakti drāvar ūpjī uttar Rāmānanda*
> *pargat kiyo kabīr ne sapt dvīp nav khaṇḍ*

(Bhakti was born in the Dravida country—Tamilnad—brought to the north by Ramananda; Kabir spread it over the seven seas and nine continents.)

Hymns of Ramananda's disciples Dhanna, Pipa, Sain, and Ravi Das are found in the *Adi Granth*.

The spirit of religious ferment was at work all over the country; people who knew little or nothing of each other felt the pull of the *zeitgeist* and were saying the same sort of thing in their own languages in distant parts of India. There was Chaitanya in Bengal; Ramananda and Kabir in Uttar Pradesh; Mira Bai in Rajasthan; Tukaram, Nam Dev, Trilochan, and Parmanand in Maharashtra; Vallabha Swami in Telegana; Sadhana in Sindh. By the end of the 15th century, the influence of the Bhakta orders was far greater than that of orthodox Brahmanical Hinduism. What was more important, many of the Bhaktas had taken positive steps towards a rapprochement with Islam.

The chief protagonist of an understanding between Hindus and Muslims was Kabir, who described himself as "the child of Rama and Allah." He said: "The Hindu resorts to the temple and the Mussalman to the mosque, but Kabir goes to the place where both are known. . . . Kabir has taken the higher path abandoning the custom of the two. If you say that I am a Hindu then it is not true, nor am I a Mussalman. I am a body made of five elements where the Unknown plays. Mecca has verily become Kasi, and Rama has become Rahim."[5] Kabir, though born a Muslim, found no difficulty in worshipping as a Hindu. He believed that there could be only one God and he refused to bow before idols. "If God is a stone, I will worship a mountain," he said. He did not believe that Mohammed was the only guide in spiritual matters, but like other Bhaktas he believed in the necessity of every person attaching himself to a guru. He believed in the singing of hymns of praise. He accepted the Hindu theory of rebirth after death in preference to the Islamic one of a purgatory and paradise. Being a Muslim, he did not mince his words in condemning the Hindu caste system which made him an outcast.

To sum up, what the different Bhaktas achieved in the realm of religious speculation was this: there was only one

[5] Tara Chand, *Influence of Islam on Indian Culture*, p. 150.

God. He was the only reality; the rest was illusion. God could not be represented in the form of an idol, for He was indefinable and all-pervasive. The best way to approach God was by resigning oneself to His will. The easiest way to find God's will was by becoming a disciple and seeking the guidance of a guru, as well as by meditation and singing hymns of love and praise (*kīrtan*). The caste system was not divinely ordained, for all human beings were born equal. Spiritual life did not demand an ascetic denial of food, company, and sex, for a citizen discharging his obligations to his family and society had as good a chance of attaining salvation as a hermit or a monk.

Unfortunately, not many of the Bhaktas practised what they preached. Despite their proclamations of the unity of God, they continued to worship one or the other reincarnations of Vishnu or Shiva, more often than not represented by stone idols. And their pronouncements on the equality of mankind seldom meant more than allowing men of lower castes to become their followers and an occasional symbolic acceptance of food from their hands. What was wanted was a man who would gather the teachings of the Bhaktas into one comprehensible system and set an example by putting his precepts into practice.

Islam's Compromise with Hinduism: The Sufi Mystics

It has been noted how the peaceful spread of Islam was arrested by the conquest of Northern India by Mussalman armies. The Hindus were defeated and many of their temples were razed to the ground. This could not, nor did it, succeed in bringing them around to the faith of their conquerors. But following in the train of the invaders were men of peace who came with the specific purpose of spreading the gospel of Mohammed. In order to equip themselves for the task, they studied other languages, cultures, religions, and ways of life. They learned about Christianity and Buddhism, about Greek and Hindu philosophy. They tested the religion of the Prophet in the light of their new knowledge and emphasised those aspects which suited their mission and temperaments. These men were known as Sufis.

The Sufis did not form a definite sect nor did they have a uniform doctrine. But many of them gained renown as scholars or godly men, and communities of admirers grew about them and came to be known after the leaders.

The Koran and the Hadith (traditions based on the life of Mohammed) gave the Sufis all they wanted. As orthodox Muslims they believed in the One God whose presence was, as the Koran said, all-embracing—"Whichever way you turn, there is the face of Allah." Like Mohammed, they set store on poverty. And like him they fasted and meditated to achieve the sort of mystical experience which had first illumined the Prophet's mind with the vision of God. They came to the conclusion that an easier way of inducing a mystic experience (*hāl*) was through *dhikr*—repeating the name of Allah or a short litany with so much concentration that the worshipper's own personality was merged with that of God. The Sufis, like the Hindu Bhaktas, came to believe that singing and dancing were also a means of inducing a state of divine exaltation where thoughts of self were destroyed (*fanā*), the restless wandering of the mind was stilled, and one surrendered oneself in absolute entirety to God.

The most significant aspect of Sufism, and one which had the greatest impact on the people, was the way of life adopted by the Sufi leaders and their immediate disciples. Whereas the Muslim conquerors had tried to destroy nonbelievers and their places of worship, the Sufis welcomed them into their homes and embraced them as brothers. One of the cardinal principles of their belief was *talīf-i-kulūb*—the stringing together of hearts. Hindus, who had been terrorised by the Mussalman soldiery, now found a body of Muslims wanting to befriend them. The Sufis did not need to do very much more to win over large numbers of converts. Most of the proselytes were from the lower classes who had been denied equal rights by the upper-caste Hindus. In the treatment of the lower orders the Sufis scored over the Bhaktas because they gave what they promised. Hindu untouchables accepting Islam no longer remained pariahs. They were given titles of honour like *Šaikh*, *Malik*, *Khalifā*, or *Mu'min*, and, at least in the earlier stages, enjoyed equal social privileges and inter-married with the most aristocratic of Muslim families.

By the beginning of the 15th century there were over a dozen orders of Sufis in Northern India. Of these, four, the Chisthi, Qadiri, Suhrawardi, and presently the Naqsh-bandi, were the most important.

The influx of large numbers of Hindus to the Muslim fold radically changed Islam, as it came to be practised in India. The converts adapted their new faith to suit the way of thinking and life to which they had been accustomed. Not many could afford to travel to Mecca and yet they wanted to go on pilgrimage. They made the tombs of Sufi saints their lesser Meccas, the Sufis their gurus, the *nāt-i-rasūl* and *qavālī* (songs in praise of the Prophet) their *kīrtan*. Since immigrants were considerably outnumbered by the Hindu converts, they too accepted the religious practices of Muslims and the way of living of their Indian co-religionists. In this way the Muslims of India came close to the Hindus. In dress, food, customs, speech, music—in fact everything except the place of worship—the two communities became identical. All they needed was someone who could bridge the gap between the temple and the mosque.

There are many famous names in the long list of Sufis who settled in the Punjab. Among the earliest was Ali Makhdum Hujwiri (d. A.D. 1092), who, because of his great generosity came to be known as Data Ganj Baksh, God's treasure house.[6] The most important Sufi name in the

---

[6] His mausoleum was rebuilt in marble by the Sikh ruler Ranjit Singh and his daughter-in-law, Rani Chand Kaur, wife of Maharajah Kharak

Punjab is that of Shaikh Farid Shakarganj (13th century) of the Chishti order. He lived at Pak Pattan, which became the centre of Sufism in the province.[7] Another centre was opened at Multan by the Suhrawardiyas, Bahauddin Zakarya and Ruknuddin Zakarya, and in the 15th century the Qadiriya order set up a centre in Sindh.[8]

Religious and Political Climate in
Fifteenth-Century Punjab

Taimur's invasion in A.D. 1398 was the end of organised government in Northern India. Local governors threw off allegiance to the Sultan at Delhi and set themselves up as independent monarchs. Thereafter there was constant strife between the king and his provincial satraps, and lawless elements began to raise their heads in defiance. The ruling class, which was largely Muslim, found its authority circumscribed and its coffers denuded and turned to robbing the wealthier Hindu trading community by imposing illegal taxes and denying it justice. Protests were met with severe persecution, massacre of "infidels," and destruction of their places of worship. Thus the work done by the Sufis who had preached tolerance towards Hinduism and of the Hindu Bhaktas who had advocated a sympathetic understanding of Islam was undone.

Political turmoil affected the religious practices of the masses. For the Muslim, the most meritorious act became the conversion or destruction of infidels. For the rest, he

---

Singh. The tomb of Data Ganj Baksh in Lahore was venerated by members of all communities. The Sikh ruling family gave generously for the upkeep of many Sufi tombs. Ranjit Singh paid homage every year at the tomb of Madho Lal-Hussain, which was rebuilt by Ranjit's Muslim wife, Bibi Mohran.

[7] Moinuddin Chishti of Ajmer and Nizamuddin Auliya of Delhi, who spread Islam in Central India and Rajasthan, also belonged to the Chishti order.

[8] Mian Mir, the famous divine of Lahore who became a personal friend of the fifth guru, Arjun, and laid the foundation stone of the Harimandir at Amritsar, was a member of the Qadiriya order.

simply had to be circumcised, refrain from eating flesh forbidden by the Koran, and fast during the month of Ramadan, to pass off for a good Mussalman. Hindus reverted to the worship of idols, to washing away their sins in holy rivers, to the wearing of caste marks and "sacred" threads, as well as to fads like vegetarianism and cooking food in precisely demarcated squares.[9] The caste system came back into its own.

Guru Nanak described the times in many of his writings: "The age is like a knife. Kings are butchers. Religion hath taken wings and flown. In the dark night of falsehood I cannot see where the moon of truth is rising." (*Mājh kī Vār*) And again: "Modesty and religion have disappeared because falsehood reigns supreme. The Muslim Mulla and the Hindu Pandit have resigned their duties, the Devil reads the marriage vows. . . . Praises of murder are sung and people smear themselves with blood instead of saffron." (*Tilaṅg*)

The reigning dynasty at the time were the Lodhis, who according to Nanak had "squandered away the priceless heritage" that was Hindustan and allowed it to be ravaged by Babar's Mughal hordes. The tumult of hate and falsehood had made the songs of love of the Sufis and the Bhaktas almost inaudible.

Guru Nanak

Nanak was born on April 15, 1469.[10] His father, Mehta Kalian Das Bedi, was an accountant in the village Tal-

[9] The order of Hindu ascetics which drew Nanak's attention most of all were the *Kanphaṭā* (pierced ear) Yogis who were the followers of Gorakhnath (15th century). The *Kanphaṭās* were the Shaivites who had imbibed some elements of Buddhism. To Nanak the *Kanphaṭās* represented Hinduism in its most decadent form. He had many encounters with leaders of this order, and some of his philosophic tenets were propounded in discoursing with them. They are referred to as the *sidhas* and the dialogue with them as *sidhagoṣṭ*.

[10] The guru's birthday is celebrated on the full moon night of the month of November. This is based on the *janamsākhī* (biography) by Bala Sandhu, which is considered by most scholars to be spurious. But for the

wandi Rai Bhoe, now named Nankana Sahib, about forty miles from Lahore. It is likely that Nanak, like his elder sister, Nanaki, was born in the home of his mother, Tripta, and like her, named after his maternal home, Nanake.[11]

Nanak was a precocious child; at the age of five he started asking questions about the purpose of life. At seven he was sent to a pandit to learn the alphabet and numerals, and two years later to a Muslim mullah to learn Persian and Arabic. He took little interest in his studies and began to spend his time discoursing with holy men or in solitude, "without confiding the secrets of his heart in any one."[12]

At the age of twelve he was married to Sulakhni, the daughter of Mool Chand Chona of Batala. Even the marriage did not turn his mind towards mundane matters. "He began to do worldly tasks, but his heart was never in them; he took no interest in his home. His family complained: 'These days he wanders out with the fakirs.'"

Nanak was nineteen when his wife came to live with him. For some time she succeeded in turning his attention

---

sake of continuity of a tradition, no change has been made in the date of the celebration. There is no doubt that the correct date is April 15, 1469. The more reliable janamsakhis agree that "in Sambat 1526 in the month of Baisakh on the third day of the first quarter of the moon, in the early hours of the dawn, three hours before sunrise, was born Baba Nanak." This is confirmed by the *Mahima Prakās* and all other accounts, which are agreed on the exact span of his life and the date of his death—which, worked backwards, fixes the date of his birth as April 15, 1469.

11 The janamsakhis and the *Mahima Prakas* state the place of birth to be "in the house of Mehta Kalu Bedi of Talwandi Rai Bhoe." This statement need not be taken literally. The custom of returning to the maternal home for confinement was well-established in Hindu families. The choice of the name confirms the fact of the birth taking place in the mother's parental home, which was in the village of Kahna Katcha. Cunningham supports this view and bases it on an old manuscript, but without giving its reference. Mehervan's janamsakhi mentions Chahleval near Lahore as Nanak's place of birth.

12 The janamsakhi quotations in this chapter are taken from the *Purātan Janamsākhī* edited by Dr. Bhai Vir Singh and published by the K̲h̲ālsā Samā Cār in 1948. It is a compendium of all the other janamsakhis. See Appendix 1 on sources.

to herself and two sons were born to them, Sri Chand in
A.D. 1494 and Lakhmi Das three years later. They also
probably had a daughter or daughters who died in infancy.
Then Nanak's mind went back to spiritual problems and
he again sought the company of wandering hermits for
guidance. His father tried his best to get him to tend his
cattle or to set up as a tradesman, but it was of no avail.
His sister brought him over to her home in Sultanpur,
and through her husband's influence got him a job as an
accountant with the Nawab Daulat Khan Lodhi, a distant
kinsman of the reigning Sultan of Delhi. Although Nanak
took over the post with some reluctance, he discharged his
duties diligently and won the affection of his employer.

At Sultanpur a Muslim minstrel, Mardana, joined
Nanak and the two began to organise the singing of hymns
in the town. The janamsakhi describes their life in Sultanpur: "Every night they sang hymns. . . . They fed
everyone who came. . . . An hour and a quarter before
sunrise he would go to the river to bathe, by daylight he
would be in the durbar doing his work."[13]

During one of these early morning ablutions by the
river, Nanak had his first mystic experience. The janamsakhi describes it as communion with God, who gave him
a cup of *amrit* (nectar) to drink and charged him with
the mission in the following words:

"Nanak, I am with thee. Through thee will my name
be magnified. Whosoever follows thee, him will I save. Go
into the world to pray and teach mankind how to pray.
Be not sullied by the ways of the world. Let your life be
one of praise of the Word (*nām*), charity (*dān*), ablution
(*iśnān*), service (*sevā*), and prayer (*simran*). Nanak, I give
thee My pledge. Let this be thy life's mission."[14]

Nanak's voice rose in praise of his Maker:

> There is One God.
> He is the supreme truth.

[13] *Janamsākhī*, p. 16.   [14] *Janamsākhī*, p. 17.

He, the Creator,
Is without fear and without hate.
He, the Omnipresent,
Pervades the universe.
He is not born,
Nor does He die to be born again.
By His grace shalt thou worship Him.

Before time itself
There was truth.
When time began to run its course
He was the truth.
Even now, He is the truth
And evermore shall truth prevail.

(Japji)

The Mysterious Voice spoke again:
"Nanak, he whom you bless will be blessed by Me; he to whom you are benevolent shall receive My benevolence. I am the Great God, the Supreme Creator. Thou art the Guru, the Supreme Guru of God."[15]

Nanak is said to have received the robe of honour from the hands of God Himself.

He was missing for three days and nights and it was assumed that he had drowned. He reappeared on the fourth day. The janamsakhi reports his dramatic return:

"People said, 'Friends, he was lost in the river; from where hath he emerged?' Nanak came home and gave away all he had. He had only his loin cloth left on him and kept nothing besides. Crowds began to collect. The Khan also came and asked, 'Nanak, what happened to you?' Nanak remained silent. The people replied, 'He was in the river and is out of his mind.' The Khan said: 'Friends, this is very distressing,' and turned back in sorrow.

"Nanak went and joined the fakirs. With him went the musician Mardana. One day passed. The next day he got up and spoke. 'There is no Hindu, there is no Mussal-

---

[15] *Janamsākhī*, p. 18.

man.' Whenever he spoke, this is all he would say: 'There is no Hindu, there is no Mussalman.' "[16]

This incident probably took place in A.D. 1499 when Nanak was in his thirtieth year. It marks the end of the first phase of his life: the search for the truth was over; he was ready to go forth to proclaim it to the people of the world.

There is some uncertainty about the exact itinerary of Nanak's travels in the years following.[17] All sources are, however, agreed that he did travel extensively to different parts of India and abroad as far west as Baghdad. Wherever he gained adherents he set up a centre of worship. In all probability the first extensive tour was to the east, when he went through Hindu places of pilgrimage like Mathura, Benares, Gaya, and on to Bengal and Assam.[18] On the way back he stopped at Jagganath Puri.

He spent some years travelling in the Punjab, paying more than one visit to the Sufi establishment at Pak Pattan. His next tour was southwards through Tamilnad down to Ceylon. He is said to have come back along the western coast through Malabar, Konkan, Bombay, and Rajasthan.[19] The third tour was in the Himalayan regions as far as Ladakh.

[16] *Janamsākhī*, pp. 18, 19.

[17] The janamsakhis and the evidence of tablets found in Baghdad are at variance on the subject.

[18] See *Dacca Review*, October/November 1915, pp. 224-32; January 1916, pp. 316-22; February/March 1916, pp. 375-78. Articles by Gurbaksh Singh on the relics commemorating Guru Nanak's visit to Bengal and the evidence of his tours in Bihar and Assam.

[19] There is reason to doubt the extent of this journey. The janamsakhis are unanimous in stating that the King of Ceylon was a Hindu. This is historically incorrect. Besides, there is very little direct reference to Buddhism in Guru Nanak's compositions; only Buddhist nomenclature like *nirvāṇa*, *saṅgat*, etc., which was also used by the Hindus, appear in his hymns. This is fairly conclusive evidence that he had little or no contact with Buddhism in practice. There is also absolutely no mention of Christ or Christianity in any of Nanak's hymns or in the janamsakhis. It is hardly likely that this would have happened if Nanak had visited Malabar, where there was a thriving Christian community at the time. It must, however, be admitted that there are some aspects of Sikhism which bear close re-

The Guru's last long journey was his pilgrimage to Mecca and Medina. He went farther westwards to Baghdad, where he spent some time with the local fakirs.[20] On his way back home he passed through Saidpur when the town was sacked by Babar.[21] He went around preaching in different towns of the Punjab, and then settled down with his family in a new township that he had built earlier on the banks of the Ravi and named Kartarpur (the abode of the Creator).

Although there is some uncertainty about the exact itinerary, the janamsakhis are agreed about the incidents that took place during the travels. They go into great detail about the outlandish garb that Nanak wore on his journeys. It was always a combination of styles worn by Hindu Sadhus and Muslim fakirs. The people were constantly asking him: "Art thou a Hindu or a Mussalman?" On two of his long journeys, he took the Muslim Mardana as his companion. On the others he was accompanied by Hindus of the lesser castes. While visiting Hindu places he had long discourses with the local pandits. He also spent many days with Shaikh Sharaf, Shaikh Ibrahim, and other Sufi saints at Pak Pattan and Multan. The substance of these discourses was later put in verse by the Guru. The follow-

---

semblance to Christianity, e.g., the doctrine of Grace (parsād). Rev. C. H. Loehlin has pointed out how some of the poetry of the *Adi Granth* resembles the Psalms, Proverbs, Job, and especially the Song of Solomon (*The Sikhs and Their Book*).

[20] A tablet with the following inscription was discovered in Baghdad in 1916: "In memory of the Guru, the holy Baba Nanak, King of holy men, this monument has been rebuilt with the help of seven saints." The date on the tablet is 927 Hijri, i.e. A.D. 1520-1521 (*Loyal Gazette*, Lahore, January 1918).

[21] In the *Bābar Vānī*, the Guru speaks of the Mughal invasion: "They who had beautiful locks and with vermilion dyed the parting of their hair, have their tresses shorn with scissors and dust thrown on their heads. They who dwelt in palaces cannot find a place in the streets." (*Āsā*)

According to the janamsakhis, the Guru was imprisoned by the Mughals and released on the personal intervention of Babar. There is no reference to this in the *Bābar Nāmā*.

ing incident illustrates Nanak's method in conveying his message. He wanted to prove to the pilgrims bathing in the Ganges the absurdity of making offerings to dead ancestors:

"One day the holy Guru came to Hardwar and went to the eastern part of the city. He saw a vast multitude bathing in the river and praying by offering water to the Sun. The holy father had divine vision whereas the others saw only with their eyes. Although the world came to bathe in the sacred Ganges, in the eyes of the holy father not one was pure. The Guru entered the Ganges, and whereas the others were offering water to the rising Sun, he offered it in the opposite direction. The people questioned: 'Man of God, why offerest thou water in that direction?' The holy father asked, 'To whom do you offer the water?' They replied: 'We offer it to our ancestors.' The holy father asked: 'Where are your ancestors?' They replied: 'Our ancestors are in the land of the Gods.' The holy Guru asked: 'Brothers, how far is the land of the Gods from the land of mortals?' They replied: '49.½ crore *kos*.' The father asked: 'Will it get there?' They replied: 'Sir, the *Sāstras* assure us it will.' The father heard, and instead of offering a few drops started throwing up a lot of water. The people asked him again: 'Brother, to whom dost thou offer this water?' The holy Guru replied: 'Brothers, I have a farm which is dry. Even when there is much rain, there not a drop stays on my land: that is why I am sending the water.' They asked: 'How will it ever reach there?' Then the holy Guru replied: 'Brothers, your ancestors are a long way away, my farm is much nearer. The land of your ancestors is far and also high up, and if water can reach there, my farm is only 250 *kos*, why shouldn't it get there?' When they heard this, they said in their own minds: 'This man is not crazy, he is a great man,' and they fell at his feet."[22]

Another incident took place when Nanak was on his way

[22] This incident, for some inexplicable reason, does not appear in the *Janamsākhī* edited by Bhai Vir Singh. It is, however, mentioned in the others and in almost the same words.

to Mecca: He was staying in a mosque and fell asleep with his feet towards the *Kā'bā*—an act considered of grave disrespect to the house of God. When the mullah came to say his prayers, he shook Nanak rudely and said: "O servant of God, thou hast thy feet towards *Kā'bā*, the house of God; why hast thou done such a thing?" Nanak replied: "Then turn my feet towards some direction where there is no God nor the *Kā'bā*."[23]

Nanak spent his last years at Kartarpur, where large crowds flocked to hear him preach. He made them observe a strict routine, which set the pattern of daily life for his followers, who by then had come to be known as his Sikhs (presumably derived ultimately from the Sanskrit *śiṣya*, disciple, or *śikṣā*, instruction—Pali, *sikkhā*), i.e., disciples. People were roused a watch before daybreak. They bathed in cold water and foregathered in the temple, where they recited the morning prayer and sang hymns. The service was over a watch and a quarter after sunrise. People were then free to attend to their worldly affairs. They foregathered again in the evening for congregational prayers and hymn-singing. After the evening service they dined together at the temple. Another short prayer was said, and they went to their homes for the night.

The same routine was followed by communities of Sikhs in other towns. Nanak's hymns were copied and sent to them. Every centre had a leader to instruct newcomers.

Among the disciples who attached themselves to the Guru at Kartarpur was one Lehna, a Khatri of the Trehan sub-caste, who impressed Nanak by his devotion and qualities of leadership. The Guru's elder son, Sri Chand, had become an ascetic and Nanak disapproved of asceticism. The younger son, Lakhmi Das, turned the other way and showed no interest in spiritual matters. Consequently, Nanak chose Lehna to carry on his mission, giving him the name Angad (of my own limb).

---

[23] *Janamsākhī*, pp. 116-17. This incident took place during the fourth of the Guru's long voyages.

Guru Nanak died on September 22, 1539 in the early hours of the morning, the time of the day he loved most and described as *amrit-velā*, the ambrosial hour. His end was in a manner most befitting a man who had made the bringing together of Hindus and Muslims the chief object of his ministry. "Said the Mussalmans: 'we will bury him'; the Hindus: 'we will cremate him'; Nanak said: 'You place flowers on either side, Hindus on my right, Muslims on my left. Those whose flowers remain fresh tomorrow will have their way.' He asked them to pray. When the prayer was over, Baba pulled the sheet over him and went to eternal sleep. Next morning when they raised the sheet they found nothing. The flowers of both communities were fresh. The Hindus took theirs; the Muslims took those that they had placed."[24]

Nanak is still remembered in the Punjab as the King of holy men, the Guru of the Hindus, and the Pir of the Mussalmans:

> *Bābā Nānak śāh fakīr*
> *Hindū kā guru, musalmān kā pīr*

In his forty years as a teacher, Nanak set up centres in many places stretching from Assam in the east to Iraq in the west. But the centres in these distant places did not last very long after his departure. Since what the Guru had to say was said in Punjabi, it was in the Punjab that his message really took root in the minds of the people and that his hymns began to be sung. It is unlikely that in his lifetime his numerous admirers formed a distinct sect; they were at best people who dissented from both Hinduism and Islam and became his disciples because they agreed with what he said. His teaching appealed specially to the politically downtrodden Hindus of the lower castes and the poor of Muslim peasantry. The ground had, no doubt, been prepared by the Sufis and the Bhaktas. But

---

[24] *Janamsākhī*, p. 129. A similar version is given of the death of Kabir.

it was Nanak's own personality, in which he combined gentleness with great courage, that endeared him to the masses. He defied convention and lived the life of a non-conformist in a highly conformist society. He was convinced that the people would see his point of view if it were put to them without anger, sarcasm, or ridicule. His great standby was his kindly sense of humour, which he did not hesitate to turn against himself:

> When I am quiet, they say I have no knowledge;
> When I speak, I talk too much they say.
> When I sit, they say an unwelcome guest has
>   come to stay;
> When I depart, I have deserted my family and
>   run away.
> When I bow, they say it is of fear that I pray.
> Nothing can I do that in peace I may spend
>   my time.
> Preserve Thy servant's honour now and
>   hereafter, O Lord sublime.
>
> *(Prabhāti)*

Nanak was a poet of uncommon sensitivity who could turn his pen from gentle satire to rapturous praise. He loved the Punjab and painted its landscape as it had never been done before. The ripening of the cornfields, the flight of deer in the woodlands, the chirping of cicadas when the shadows lengthen, the pitter-patter of raindrops during the monsoon, are drawn with the consummate skill of an artist with a feeling for the music of words.[25] Nanak's poetry was in great measure responsible for his popularity.

The theologian Bhai Gurdas described Nanak's achievements in the following words:[26]

> The true Guru, Nanak, was then born
> The fog and mist evaporated

---

25 See Appendix 5, especially the *Bārā Māhā*, p. 351.
26 Bhai Gurdas, *Vārāṇ*.

And light shone on the earth.
As the rising Sun dispels the dark
    and outshines the Stars
As flee the herd of deer when the lion roars
Without pause, without turning back for assurance
(So fled evil from the world).

The Teaching of Nanak

Nanak not only founded a new religion and started a new pattern of living, he also set in motion an agrarian movement whose impact was felt all over the country. To get a comprehensive picture of his achievements, it is necessary to know the religious and secular aspects of his teaching.

We will first refer to some salient points of his faith.

CONCEPTION OF GOD. Nanak was a strict monotheist. He refused to accept any compromise on the concept of the unity of God. In this he disagreed with the Bhaktas, who, despite their profession of monotheism, believed in the reincarnations of God and of His Avatars. Since God was infinite, argued Nanak, He could not die to be reincarnated, nor could He assume human form which was subject to decay and death. Nanak disapproved of the worship of idols because people tended to look upon them as God instead of symbolic representations. Nanak believed that God was *sat* (both truth and reality), as opposed to *asat* (falsehood) and *mithyā* (illusion). He thus not only made God a spiritual concept but also based principles of social behaviour on the concept. If God is Truth, to speak an untruth is to be ungodly. Untruthful conduct not only hurts one's neighbours; it is also irreligious. A good Sikh therefore must not only believe that God is the only One, Omnipotent, and Omniscient Reality, but also conduct himself in such a way towards his fellow beings that he does not harm them: for hurtful conduct like lying, cheating, fornication, trespass on a person or on his property, does not conform to the truth that is God. This principle is stated categorically by Nanak in the opening lines of his most celebrated morning prayer, the *Japjī*, and is the *mūl mantra* or the basic belief of Sikhism.[27]

Nanak believed that the power that was God could not be defined because God was *nirankār* (formless). All of his descriptions of God were consequently admissions of an inability to define Him.

> Thou hast a million eyes, yet no eye hast Thou.
> Thou hast a million forms, yet no form hast Thou.
> Thou hast a million feet, yet no feet hast Thou.
> Thou art without odour, yet millions of odours
>   emanate from Thee.
> With such charms, O Lord, hast Thou bewitched me.
> Thy light pervades everywhere.
>
> *(Dhanāsarī)*

Despite the difficulty of definition, Nanak used a variety of names for God. He was the Father *(Pitā)* of all mankind; He was the Lover *(Prītam)* and Master *(Khasam)* of his devotee; He was also the Great Giver *(Dātā)*. Nanak did this to show human dependence on God rather than invest Him with anthropomorphic qualities. Although Nanak used both Hindu and Muslim nomenclature for God, *Rām, Govinda, Harī Murārī, Rab*, and *Rahīm*, the attribute he usually ascribed to Him was that of the True Creator *(Sat Kartār)* or The True Name *(Sat Nām)*.[28]

In equating God with the abstract principle of truth, Nanak avoided the difficulty met by other religious teachers who describe Him only as the Creator or the Father: if God created the world, who created God? If He is

---

[27] Quoted on pp. 31-32.

[28] The word *nām* is usually translated as name, whereas in fact it means much more: it is the adoration of God. At a later stage in the evolution of Sikhism, *Vāhiguru* became the Sikh name for God. *Vāhiguru* literally means "Hail Guru" and is very close to the Muslim *Subhān Allāh*. It has been suggested that the word is a combination of different Hindu names for God: *Vāsudev, Harī, Govinda*, and *Rāma*. There is no basis for this suggestion. None of the Sikh commentators support this view.

the Father, who was His father? But Nanak's system had its own problems. If God is truth, what is the truth? Nanak's answer was that in situations when you cannot decide for yourself, let the guru be your guide.

THE GURU. The Bhaktas and the Sufis had emphasised the necessity of having a spiritual mentor; Nanak went further and made the institution[29] of the guru the pivot of his religious system. Without the guru, said Nanak, there could be no salvation. He was the guide who prevented mankind from straying from the straight and narrow path of truth; he was the captain of the ship which took one across the fearful ocean of life. But the guru, insisted Nanak, was to be regarded as a guide and not a god. He was to be consulted and respected but not worshipped. Nanak accepted for himself the status of a teacher but not a prophet;[30] in his writings he constantly referred to himself as the slave or servant of God.

THE IDEAL OF LIFE: PURITY AMONG THE WORLD'S IMPURITIES. Nanak did not approve of ascetic isolation or torturing of the flesh as a step to enlightenment. His ideal was to have the detachment of the yogi while living among one's

[29] Dr. Sher Singh has not exaggerated the importance of the institution of guruship in saying that "the belief of unity in the plurality of the gurus served as a useful purpose in the development of Sikhism. But for this belief there would have been no Sikh nation." (*Philosophy of Sikhism*, p. 46.)

The concept of a continuing spiritual succession was known to the Buddhists and is current to this day in the succession of the Lamas.

Nanak believed that the personality of the guru could pass to the disciple and raise him to a status of equality: "As one lamp can light another without losing any of its light, so can a teacher impart wisdom to his disciple and elevate him to equality."

[30] The following dialogue took place between the guru and Mian Mitha.
MIAN MITHA: The first name is that of God, the second of the Prophet.
  O Nanak, if you repeat the creed, you will find acceptance in God's court.
NANAK: The first name is that of God; how many prophets are at the gate!
  O Shaikh, if your heart be pure, you will find acceptance in God's court.
  At God's gate there is no room for a prophet. God alone dwells there.

fellow beings—*rāj men jog* (to achieve enlightenment in civic life):

> Religion lieth not in the patched coat the yogi wears,
> Not in the staff he bears,
> Nor in the ashes on his body.
> Religion lieth not in rings in the ears,
> Not in a shaven head,
> Nor in the blowing of the conch shell.
> If thou must the path of true religion see,
> Among the world's impurities, be of impurities free.[31]
>
> *(Sūhī)*

Nanak, who had often to leave his family to propagate his mission, always came back to his home and lived among the common people as one of them.[32] His religion was for the householder *(grihastha dharma)*, and he strongly disapproved of monastic other-worldliness sustained by charity. "Having renounced *grihastha*, why go begging at the householder's door?" he asked. He believed that one of the essential requisites for the betterment of individuals was *sādh sangat* (the society of holy men),[33] and righteous conduct towards one's neighbours.

[31]   The lotus in the water is not wet
        Nor the water-fowl in the stream.
        If a man would live, but by the world untouched,
        Meditate and repeat the name of the Lord
                                  Supreme.
                                  (Sidhagost)

[32] Nanak was frequently questioned by Hindu ascetics and Sufis, who lived in hermitages, as to how he combined the obligations of a householder with spiritual pursuits. In a meeting with Shaikh Ibrahim (tenth successor of the famous Farid Shakargunj) at Pak Pattan, the following dialogue took place. The Shaikh said to the guru: "Either seek worldly gain or the way of God. Put not thy feet in two boats, lest thou losest both thy life and thy cargo." Nanak replied: "It is best to place your feet in two boats and trade with two worlds. One may founder, and the other take thee across. But for Nanak there is neither water, nor boat, nor wreck, nor cargo to lose, for his merchandise and capital is truth, which is all pervading and in which he finds gentle repose." *(Janamsākhi*, p. 48.)

[33] In a sermon delivered at Kurukshetra, Nanak said there were four ways by which, in addition to the repetition of God's name, one could

Sacoṇ ore sabh ko
Upar sac ācār

Truth above all,
Above truth, truthful conduct.

CASTELESS SOCIETY. The Bhaktas had paid only lip service
to the ideal of a casteless society; Nanak took practical steps
to break the vicious hold of caste by starting free community kitchens—*guru kā laṅgar*—in all centres and persuading his followers, irrespective of their castes, to eat
together. Nanak's writings abound with passages deploring
the system and other practices which grew out of caste
concepts, particularly the notion held by Brahmins that
even the shadow of a lower-caste man, on a place where
food was being cooked, made it impure. Said Nanak:

Once we say: This is pure, this unclean,
See that in all things there is life unseen.
There are worms in wood and cowdung cakes,
There is life in the corn ground into bread.
There is life in the water which makes it green.
How then be clean when impurity is over the
    kitchen spread?

Impurity of the heart is greed,
Of tongue, untruth,
Impurity of the eye is coveting
Another's wealth, his wife, her comeliness.
Impurity of the ears is listening to calumny.
                              (*Āsā dī vār*)

THE GENTLE PATH OF NAM AND SAHAJ. The Hindus had advocated three alternative paths to salvation: that of action
(*karmamārga*), of knowledge (*gyānamārga*), and of devotion (*bhaktimārga*). Guru Nanak accepted the path of

---

reach God: "in the company of holy men, by being absolutely truthful,
by living in contentment, and by keeping the senses in restraint."

bhakti, laying emphasis on the worship of the Name (*nā-mamārga*).[34] "I have no miracles except the name of God," he said.[35]

> As hands or feet besmirched with slime,
> Water washes white;
> As garments dark with grime,
> Rinsed with soap are made light;
> So when sin soils the soul
> The Name alone shall make it whole.
>
> Words do not the saint or sinner make.
> Action alone is written in the book of fate.
> What we sow that alone we take;
> O Nanak, be saved or forever transmigrate.
>
> *(Japjī)*

Nanak believed that by repetition of the *nām* one conquered the greatest of all evils, the ego (*haumain* = literally, I am), because the ego also carries in it the seed of salvation which can be nurtured to fulness by *nām*.[36] Once

---

[34] Sher Singh, *Philosophy of Sikhism*, pp. 51 and 213.

[35] An exhortation to repeat the name (*nām japo*) was the main theme of the teaching of Nanak. Its vulgarised and popular form was repetition *ad nauseam* of a litany, as if it had some magical potency to overcome evil. This is not what Nanak meant by *nām*. He considered the mere mumbling of prayer of little consequence. "When you take rosaries in your hands and sit down counting your beads, you never think of God but allow your minds to wander thinking of worldly objects. Your rosaries are therefore only for show and your counting of beads only hypocrisy." (*Srī.*) To Nanak, *nām* implied not simply the repetition of prayer but prayer with the understanding of words and their translation into action. See Sher Singh's *Philosophy of Sikhism*, Chapter xvi, where he states that *nāmamārga*—the path of *nām*—required three things: realisation in the heart (*hride gyān*), its expression in prayer (*mukh bhakti*), and detachment in all one's actions (*vartan vairāg*), pp. 84 and 248.

[36] This was summed up by Guru Angad, when he said:

> *haumain dīragh rog hai dārū bhī is mānh*
> *(Āsā)*
> Ego is a foul disease;
> but it carries its own remedy.

the power of the ego is properly canalised the conquest of the other five sins—lust, anger, greed, attachment, and pride—follows as a matter of course. The wanderings of the restless mind are stilled and it attains a state of divine bliss (*vismād*). It is in that state of super-conscious stillness (*divya driṣṭī*) that the tenth gate, the *dasam dvār* (the body having only nine natural orifices), is opened and one receives a vision of God and merges one's light with the light eternal.[37] For such a one the cycle of birth, death, and rebirth is ended and he attains salvation.[38]

Nanak believed in the triumph of human will over fate and predestination. He believed that all human beings have a basic fund of goodness which, like the pearl in the oyster, only awaits the opening of the shell to emerge and enrich him. But most human beings are as ignorant of the goodness in them as the deer is of the aromatic *kastūrī* in its navel; and just as the deer wanders about in the woods to fall in the snares of poachers or becomes a victim of the hunter's darts, so man falls in the snares of *māyā* (illusion). The chief task of the Guru is to make men aware of the treasure within him and then help him to unlock the jewel box.

A method advocated by Nanak was the gentle one of *sahaj*.[39] Just as a vegetable cooked on a gentle fire tastes

[37] In the fort of the body
God has fixed nine windows for the use of the senses.
It is through the tenth that the Unseen shows
Himself in His Greatness.
(*Mārū*)

[38] In the *Japjī*, Nanak mentions four successive steps towards salvation. These are *dharam khaṅd, gyān khaṅd, karam khaṅd,* and *sac khaṅd,* corresponding to discipline, knowledge, action, and ending with the blissful merger in God. These steps follow very closely the four stages of the spiritual progress of the Sufis.

[39] *Sahaj* is both a method and a state of being. The method is one of gentle discipline, the state *sahaj avasthā,* a mystic fulfilment. It is the state of which Wordsworth spoke in the "Lines composed a few miles above Tintern Abbey":

"That blessed mood,
In which the burthen of the mystery,

best because its own juice gives it the proper flavour, so a
gradual training of the body and mind will bring out the
goodness that is inherent in all human beings. There is no
general rule applicable to everyone; each person should
discipline himself according to his physical capacity and
temperament. Ascetic austerity, penances, celibacy, etc.,
had no place in Nanak's religion. In addition to self-im-
posed discipline of the mind, he advocated listening to
kīrtan (hymn singing). Nanak's verses were put to music
in *rāgas* or modes best suited to convey their meaning. He
advised his followers to rise well before dawn and listen
to the soft strains of music under the light of the stars. He
believed that in the stillness of the ambrosial hours (*amrit-
velā*) one was best able to have communion with God.

What Nanak taught was not startling in its originality.
Different Bhaktas and Sufis had stressed one or another aspects in their writings. Some had condemned polytheism
and idolatry; some castigated the caste system and the monopoly of the priestly Brahmins over spiritual matters.
Most of them had talked of the fundamental unity of all
religions, and regretted that form and ritual should have
created rifts between people of different religious professions. They had composed and sung hymns in praise of
God and advocated the love of one's neighbours. Nanak
alone made all these into one system and started institutions with traditions to nurture this eclectic creed.[40] In

In which the heavy and weary weight
Of all this unintelligible world,
Is lightened—that serene and blessed mood,
In which the affections gently lead us on
Until, the breath of this corporeal frame
And even the motion of our human blood
Almost suspended, we are laid asleep
In body, and become a living soul;
While with an eye made quiet by the power
Of harmony, and the deep power of joy,
We see into the life of things."

[40] Did Nanak have anything new to say? He believed he had. During one
of his journeys he happened to visit Multan. The holy men of the city

addition, what he said was said with utter simplicity which could be understood by the rustic as well as by the sophisticated. He himself summed up his message in three commandments: *kirt karo, nām japo, vaṅḍ cako*—work, worship, and give in charity.[41] That is why the names of other saints of the time passed into the pages of history books while that of Nanak was kept alive by a following which increased day by day.[42]

The way of life adopted by Nanak's disciples was some-

---

were alarmed that their meagre living would be jeopardized by the arrival of this famous Saint. Nanak was still on the outskirts when they sent him a bowl of milk full to the brim to indicate that there was no more room for holy men in the city. Nanak placed the petal of a jasmine flower on the milk and sent back the offering. The symbolic gift received a symbolic reply: even though the bowl was full there was room enough for fragrance; even though the world was loud with the clamour of religions there were some who would listen to his gentle voice.

[41] *khat ghāl kich hathon de*
Nānak rāh pachāne se.

(Sāraṅg Kī Vār)

He who toils and earns,
Then with his hand gives some away
He, O Nanak, has discovered the real way.

Nanak, who was fond of rural similes, used them with telling effect in conveying his message that the way to salvation was not predestined but could be found by effort:

As a team of oxen are we driven
By the ploughman, our teacher,
By the furrows made are thus writ
Our actions—on the earth, our paper.
The sweat of labour is as beads
Falling by the ploughman as seeds sown.
We reap according to our measure
Some for ourselves to keep, some to others give.
O Nanak, this is the way to truly live.

. . . .

If thou wouldst the fruits of salvation cultivate
And let the love of the Lord in thy heart germinate,
Thy body be as the fallow land
Where in thy heart the Farmer sows his seeds
Of righteous action and good deeds,
Then with the name of God, irrigate.

[42] "They [i.e., other religious teachers] perfected forms of dissent rather than planted the germs of nations, and their sects remain to this day as they left them." (Cunningham, *History of the Sikhs*, p. 34.)

what different from that of the Hindus or the Muslims from whom they had sprung. Since Nanak had emphasised the role of truthful companionship (*sat sang*), his disciples naturally interpreted it as being constituted of those who accepted Nanak as their guru. The breakaway from the parent communities started in the guru's lifetime. It began with a different place and mode of worship. The Sikh no longer chanted Sanskrit *ślokas* to stone idols or murmured the Arabic of the Koran while genuflecting towards Mecca; he sang the hymns of Nanak in his own mother-tongue, Punjabi. He ate with his fellow Sikhs at the guru's kitchen, which he helped to organise by collecting rations and in which he took turns to serve as a cook or scrubber of utensils.[43] To greet people he no longer used the Hindu's *namaste* or the Muslim's *salām alāikum* but the guru's *Sat Kartār* (True Creator).[44] All this resulted in building a community of people who had more in common with each other than with the communities to which they had belonged.

As important as the religious and communal aspects of Nanak's preaching were the political. He was the first popular leader of the Punjab in recorded history. And even though the number of his actual disciples was not perhaps very great, the number of those belonging to other communities who paid homage to the ideal of "there is no Hindu; there is no Mussalman," was considerable. It was this ideal which gave birth to Punjabi consciousness and to Punjabi nationalism.

[43] This is expressed in the aphorism:

> *dāṇā pāni guru kā*
> *ṭehal sevā sikhāṇ dī.*

> Food and drink are the gifts of the Guru
> Service and devotion contributed by his servitors.

[44] This greeting changed subsequently to *sat srī akāl*, which means the same thing. *Kartār* means the Creator and *srī akāl* the Timeless One, that is, God.

CHAPTER 3

BUILDING OF THE SIKH CHURCH

Angad (1504-1552)

LEHNA had been a devout Hindu before he met Nanak. At the very first meeting he fell under the spell of the Guru's words and abandoned the worship of his gods and his business, to devote himself to the service of the Sikh community at Kartarpur. Twice Nanak persuaded him to return to his family at Khadur, but both times he came back. His devotion convinced the Guru that Lehna would make a better leader than either of his own sons. An additional factor in preferring Lehna was the fact that he had a sizeable following of his own which he was gradually bringing into the Sikh fold. To forestall subsequent opposition from his sons, Nanak expressed his preference for Lehna in public: "Thou art Angad, a part of my body." Long before his death he had one of his chief disciples, Bhai Buddha, daub Angad's forehead with saffron and proclaim him as the second guru.[1]

Sri Chand was not an ambitious man.[2] Nevertheless, since he was the elder son of the Guru and a man of pious habits, there were many who believed that Nanak's place should go to him. They refused to accept Angad's succession and began to create difficulties. On the advice of Nanak, Angad "left Kartarpur and went and lit the Guru's lamp in Khadur,"[3] where his wife and children were living.

Angad was guru for thirteen years (1539-1552). By his

[1] "Nanak proclaimed the accession of Lehna. . . . He (Lehna) had the same light and the same ways. The Guru merely changed his body." (*Vār. Satta and Balwand.*)

[2] Gurdas and the bards Satta and Balwand hinted that both of the Guru's sons were disobedient.

[3] Gurdas, *Vārāṇ.*

tact and humility[4] he was able to prevent the schism between his Sikhs and Sri Chand's followers, who came to be
known as Udasis.[5] In his own quiet way he filled in the
brickwork of the edifice whose scaffolding had been erected
by Nanak. As the number of disciples increased, the expenses of the *langar* went up. Angad opened more centres
and organised a regular system of collecting offerings to
meet their expenses. He had copies made of Nanak's hymns
and supplied one to each centre. These copies were made
in a script which until then had no precise alphabet of
its own. Angad took the thirty-five letters of the acrostic
composed by Nanak, selected the appropriate letters from

THE GURUS

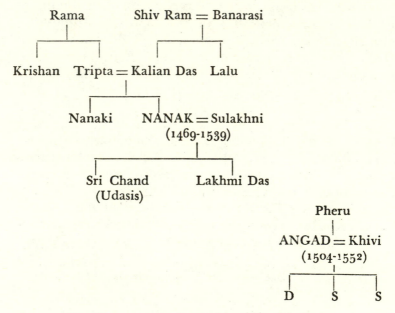

4   Devotion, penance and austerities abide with thee,
O Lehna, great pride with other people."
(*Vār. Satta and Balwand*)

5 From *Udās*, meaning one who has renounced the world, a word which
aptly describes Sri Chand's disposition.

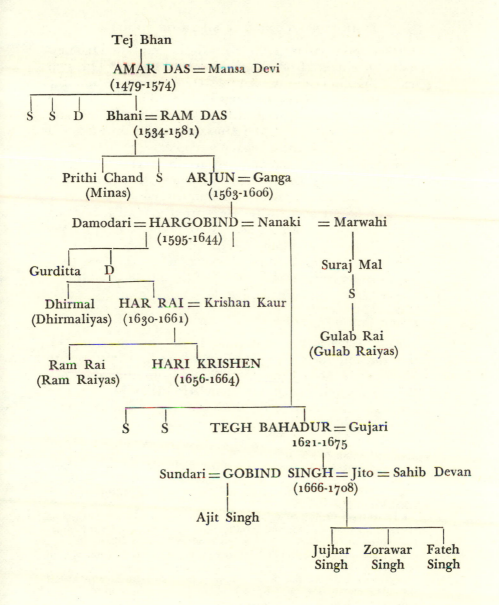

Tej Bhan
|
AMAR DAS = Mansa Devi
(1479-1574)
|
S   S   D   Bhani = RAM DAS
                     (1534-1581)

Prithi Chand   S   ARJUN = Ganga
(Minas)   (1563-1606)

Damodari = HARGOBIND = Nanaki   = Marwahi
              (1595-1644) |
                                     Suraj Mal
Gurditta   D |
   | S
Dhirmal   HAR RAI = Krishan Kaur |
(Dhirmaliyas) (1630-1661)   Gulab Rai
                                    (Gulab Raiyas)

Ram Rai   HARI KRISHEN
(Ram Raiyas)   (1656-1664)

S   S   TEGH BAHADUR = Gujari
                        1621-1675

Sundari = GOBIND SINGH = Jito = Sahib Devan
              (1666-1708)
         |
     Ajit Singh
                        Jujhar   Zorawar   Fateh
                        Singh   Singh   Singh

· 51 ·

other scripts current in Northern India, and called the new script *gurmukhī* (from the mouth of the Guru).[6] This step had far-reaching results. Angad's compilation became the nucleus of the sacred writings of the Sikhs. It gave the Sikhs a written language distinct from the written language of the Hindus or the Mussalmans and thus fostered a sense of their being a separate people.

Angad was very keen on physical fitness. He ordered his followers to take part in drill and competitive games after the morning service. Every community centre had a wrestling arena attached to it. He started a tradition which made it easy for his successors to raise troops of able-bodied men from among the disciples.[7]

Angad had two sons[8] but he chose a seventy-three-year-old disciple, Amar Das, a Khatri of the Bhalla sub-caste to succeed him as the third guru.

Amar Das (1479-1574)

Amar Das had been a devout Hindu enjoying a reputation for kindliness and piety long before his conversion to Sikhism. He showed great devotion in forwarding the work that Nanak and Angad had begun. He made the *langar* an integral institution of the Sikh church by insisting that

[6] There is diversity of opinion about the origin and antiquity of the Punjabi language and the Gurmukhi script. The subject will be dealt with in greater detail in a second volume.

[7] A soldier named Malu Shah sought the Guru's guidance on the morality of using force. The Guru counselled him that if ever the necessity to fight arose, it was the duty of a soldier to give battle regardless of the odds against him.

[8] Amar Das's succession was not recognised by Angad's son Datu, who ejected him from Khadur and installed himself as the third guru. Amar Das moved to Goindwal and from Goindwal to his own village, Basarke. After some time, when Datu's following dwindled, Amar Das was able to return to Goindwal and take up his ministry in earnest.

According to Sikh chronicles, on an occasion when Datu literally kicked Amar Das off his seat, the latter joined the palms of his hands and said humbly: "This must have hurt your foot."

On another occasion Amar Das said, "If anyone ill-treats you, bear it patiently. If you bear it three times, God will himself fight for you the fourth time." (Macauliffe, *The Sikh Religion*, ii, 70.)

anyone who wanted to see him had first to accept his hospitality by eating with the disciples.[9] The number of the
Guru's visitors increased so much that Goindwal, where
he lived, grew from an insignificant hamlet to a sizeable
town. Among the people who visited him was Emperor
Akbar, who was so impressed with the way of life at Goindwal that he assigned the revenues of several villages to the
Guru's daughter, Bhani, as a marriage gift. Royal patronage gave further momentum to Nanak's movement.

Amar Das felt that he alone could not minister to the
needs of the thousands of converts who wanted guidance.
He increased the number of parishes or *mañjīs*[10] to twenty-
two and appointed agents (*masands*) who were fully con-
versant with the doctrines of the faith, to organise worship
and the collection of offerings. He had more copies made
of the hymns of Nanak and Angad and added to them his
own compositions[11] and those of the Hindu Bhaktas whose
teachings were in conformity with those of Nanak. Since
this anthology was in Punjabi, it gained enormous popularity among the masses, who did not understand either
the Sanskrit texts of the Hindus or the Arabic of the Muslims. It reduced the importance of the Brahmin priests,
who had maintained a strict monopoly over the knowledge
of the sacred texts, and that of the mullahs, who alone
could interpret the Koran.[12]

Amar Das introduced many innovations which tended to

[9] The motto was *pehle pangat piche sangat*—"first sit in a row in the
kitchen, then seek the company of the Guru." (*Sūraj Prakāś*, i, 30.)

[10] *Mañjī* literally means a bedstead. It was customary for the gurus to
receive visitors while sitting on their *mañjīs*. Their agents, *masands* (from
the Persian *masnad*, meaning couch) did likewise. A parish under a *masand*
came to be known as a *mañjī*.

[11] 907 hymns of Amar Das are incorporated in the *Adi Granth*. For examples, see Appendix 5.

[12] During one of his journeys Amar Das was asked why he had given
up Sanskrit, which was the language of the gods, and taken to writing in
a rustic tongue like Punjabi. He replied, "It rains on the earth even though
the earth has water in the well," thereby meaning that Sanskrit was like
water in a well which had to be drawn out and could benefit only a few
people, whereas Punjabi was like rain which fell over all the land.

break the close affiliations of the Sikhs with the Hindus. He sanctified a well alongside the temple at Goindwal and fixed the first of the Hindu month of Baisakh, which fell late in spring, as the day for the annual gathering of Sikhs. He also introduced new forms of ceremonial for births and deaths, in which the recitation of hymns of the gurus replaced the chanting of Sanskrit *ślokas*. He tried to do away with the practice of *purdāh* (seclusion of women), advocated monogamy, encouraged inter-caste alliances and remarriage of widows. He strictly forbade the practice of *satī*,[13] the burning of widows on the funeral pyres of their husbands.

These measures aroused the hostility of the Brahmins, who saw the size of their flock and their incomes diminishing. They began to persecute the Sikhs and, when their own resources failed, reported against Amar Das to the Emperor. When Akbar refused to take action against the Guru, they bribed local officials to harass the Sikhs. This was the beginning of the oppression of the Sikhs, which subsequently compelled them to take up arms, and the first break with Hindu social polity.

Amar Das's twenty-two years of ministry were a definite phase in the building of the Sikh church. He was a popular teacher because his sermons were simple and direct. "Do good to others by giving good advice, by setting a good example, and by always having the welfare of mankind in your heart," he said. Amar Das's work is applauded in the *Adi Granth* in the following words:

"He made divine knowledge his steed and
    chastity his saddle.
On the bar of truth he strung the arrow of
    God's praise.
In the age of utter darkness, he rose like the Sun.
He sowed the seed of truth and reaped its fruit."[14]

13 Macauliffe, *The Sikh Religion*, II, 61-62.
14 *Vār. Satta and Balwand.*

Amar Das lived to the age of ninety-five. He did not consider any of his sons fit to succeed him and chose instead his son-in-law, Ram Das, a Khatri of the Sodhi sub-caste who had been living with him for some years.[15]

Ram Das (1534-1581)

Ram Das had spent the better part of his forty years in the service of the community when he was called upon to become its leader. He had looked after the administration of the parishes and had represented Amar Das at the Mughal court. He had a tank dug at the site granted to his wife by Emperor Akbar.[16] When he became Guru, he moved from Goindwal to the neighbourhood of the tank and started building a town around it. The town, which was destined to become the religious capital of the Sikhs, came to be known after him as *Guru kā Cak, Cak Rām Dās*, or *Rām Dās Purā*. He invited tradesmen to set up business in the town, and with the revenues so obtained he was able to expand his activities to distant parts of India. The most distinguished of his missionaries was Bhai Gurdas,[17] who spent some years preaching in Agra.

Like his predecessors, Ram Das composed hymns which were later incorporated in the collection of sacred writings.[18]

Ram Das had three sons, of whom he considered the youngest, Arjun Mal, the most suited to succeed him. This, as was to be expected, aroused the ire of the eldest, Prithi Chand. Nevertheless, when Ram Das felt his end near, he had the ageing Bhai Buddha invest Arjun Mal as the fifth

[15] Ram Das was a man of great humility. The aged Sri Chand, son of Guru Nanak, asked him why he had such a long beard. Ram Das went down on his knees and replied: "To wipe the dust off your feet, O holy one."

[16] "In 1577 he (Ram Das) obtained a grant of the site, together with 500 *bighas* of land, from the Emperor Akbar, on payment of Rs. 700/- to the Zemindars of Tung, who owned the land." (*Amritsar Gazetteer*, 1883-1884.)

[17] See Appendix 3.

[18] His compositions in *Vār Gaurī* refer to many incidents in the life of the third guru.

guru. Ram Das expressed the hope that "As one lamp is lighted from another, so the Guru's spirit will pass into him and will dispel the darkness in the world."

Arjun (1563-1606)

Arjun's path, like that of his three predecessors, was full of pitfalls. As soon as his succession was proclaimed, his elder brother, Prithi Chand, turned violently hostile. Arjun was fortunate in having the loyal support of the venerable Buddha and Bhai Gurdas in thwarting the machinations of Prithi Chand[19] and preventing a schism in the community.

Arjun's first task was to complete the building of a temple in *Cak Rām Dās*. He invited the Muslim divine, Mian Mir of Lahore to lay the foundation stone of the Harimandir, the temple of God. Instead of building the shrine on a high plinth as was the Hindu custom, Arjun had it built on a level lower than the surrounding land, so that the worshippers would have to go down the steps to enter it. And, unlike Hindu temples, which had only one entrance, Arjun had the Harimandir open on all four sides. These architectural features were intended to be symbolic of the new faith, which required the lowest to go even lower and whose doors were ever open to all who wished to enter.[20]

[19] Gurdas gave him the sobriquet *mīnā*, deceitful, by which he is known to this day.

[20] The four doors represented the four castes of Hindus. "The teaching is for all the four castes, the Kshatriya, Brahmin, Shudra, and Vaishya," wrote Arjun (*Sūhī*). The architecture is a happy blend of the Hindu and Muslim styles.

The temple was rebuilt during the period of the Sikh misls. It was destroyed by the Afghans more than once, and was finally built in its present form in marble and gold by Ranjit Singh. The inscription above the entrance of the central shrine states:

"The Great Guru in His wisdom looked upon
Maharajah Ranjit Singh as his chief servitor
And Sikh, and in His benevolence, bestowed
On him the privilege of serving the temple."
(Dated *Sambat*, 1887.)

Arjun had to raise money for the building of the temple. All Sikhs were asked to donate a tenth of their income (*dasvandh*) in the name of the Guru. The *masands* were instructed to come to *Cak Rām Dās* every first of Baisakh to render accounts and bring with them as many Sikhs as could conveniently accompany them. In this way a central finance pool was created for the construction of the temple, as well as for starting other communal projects.[21] The modest town grew into the premier commercial city of the province. After the temple was completed and the tank filled with water, it was given a new name, *Amrit-sar* (the pool of nectar). What Benares was to the Hindus and Mecca to the Muslims, Amritsar became to the Sikhs: their most important place of pilgrimage.

Arjun undertook a tour of the neighbouring country. In A.D. 1590 he had another tank dug at a place about eleven miles south of Amritsar, which he blessed as *taran tāran* (pool of salvation). It soon earned a reputation for having healing properties and Taran Taran became another place of pilgrimage, particularly for those afflicted with leprosy. A large temple and a lepressarium were built near the tank.

From Taran Taran, Arjun went to the Jullundur Doab and raised a third town called Kartarpur.[22] From Kartarpur he went to Lahore and from there to the river Beas, on whose banks he built yet another town which he named after his son, Hargobind, as Sri Hargobindpur. In five years of travelling in Central Punjab, Arjun brought into his fold thousands of Jats of the Majha country, the sturdiest peasants of the Punjab.

Arjun returned to Amritsar in 1595 and discovered that

[21] One commodity in which the Sikhs began to trade extensively was horses. These merchants were the main suppliers to the cavalry, which some years later became the most powerful fighting force in Northern India.

[22] This is distinct from the Kartarpur where the first Guru spent the last years of his life and where he died.

Prithi Chand had not been idle in forwarding his preten-sions. He had begun to compile an anthology of "sacred" writings in which he was inserting compositions of his own. Arjun realised the danger of a spurious scripture gaining currency. He abandoned his other pursuits in order to make an authentic compilation of the writings of his predecessors. He had his father's hymns with him. He persuaded Mohan (son of Guru Amar Das) to give him the collection of the writings of the first three gurus. He sent disciples to scour the country for copies that might have been made. He welcomed contributions from differ-ent sects of Hindus and Muslims for consideration. Then he installed himself by the Ramsar tank, which was well removed from the noise and bustle of the bazaars of Am-ritsar, and devoted himself entirely to the task. The selec-tion was made by the Guru (his own contribution being the largest) and taken down by Bhai Gurdas.

While the Guru was busy with his work, a report was sent to Akbar that Arjun's sacred anthology had passages vilifying Islam. On his way north, the Emperor stopped en route and asked to see the compilation. Bhai Buddha and Gurdas brought a copy of the existent manuscript and read some of the hymns to Akbar. The emperor, his fears dispelled, made an offering of fifty-one gold mohurs to the sacred book and gave robes of honour to the two disciples and sent one for Guru Arjun. At the Guru's request, he also remitted the annual revenue of the district to amelio-rate the condition of the peasants, who had been hard hit by the failure of the monsoon.

In August 1604 the work was completed and the *Granth Sāhib*, the holy volume, was formally installed in the tem-ple at Amritsar. Bhai Buddha was appointed the first reader or *granthī*.

The *Granth* reflected the faith of Nanak in its entirety. Apart from the writings of the gurus, it contained a selec-tion of the compositions of the poet-saints from all parts of Northern India, both Muslim and Hindu of all castes,

including the "untouchables." Its hymns were of a high
poetic order, its language intelligible to the illiterate peasant, its ethics simple and direct. The *Granth* became the
most powerful factor in spreading the teachings of the
gurus among the masses.[23] In the last hymn before writing
the finis, Arjun made the following claim for his anthology:
"In this vessel you will find three things—truth, peace
and contemplation; in this too the nectar that is the Name
of the Master which is the uplifter of all mankind."[24]

Emperor Akbar was impressed by the Guru's work, for
it echoed some of the beliefs he held sacred. On one occasion he stopped at Goindwal for the express purpose
of meeting the Guru. The Emperor's admiration was
an important factor in building Sikh fortunes. During
the seven years between the Emperor's first visit to Goindwal and his death in 1606, the number of Sikhs increased
and trade thrived in the four towns Arjun had built. He
became a leader of national importance, and his church
grew rich and powerful. The Guru began to be addressed
as the *Sacā Pādśāh* (the true Emperor).

The death of Akbar brought a sudden reversal in the
policy of the state towards the Sikhs. The new Emperor,
Jehangir, disapproved of the growing popularity of Guru
Arjun.[25] In his diary he wrote: "At last when Khusrau
[his son] passed along this road this insignificant fellow
[Arjun] proposed to wait upon him. Khusrau happened

[23] For details of the composition of the *Granth* and the controversy
regarding the authentic version, see Appendix 2.

[24] *Mundāvani*.

[25] Shaikh Ahmed Sirhindi (c. A.D. 1546-1624) also known as Mujaddid
Alif Sani, who claimed to be the second prophet of Islam after Mohammed,
felt jealous of Guru Arjun's influence, especially with Muslims, and wrote
in strong terms to Jehangir against the Guru. His letter, given in
Maktubāte Alif Sānī, has not attracted the attention of historians.
Alif Sani was not well disposed towards men like Mian Mir and other
Sufis who preached tolerance of other faiths. By this time some Sufis, particularly of the Naqshbandi order, had begun to advocate the persecution
of infidels. This band of Sufis, though small in numbers, had influence in
the court and with the Muslim aristocracy. With the rise of Banda (see
Part II) the Muslim masses also became somewhat intolerant of other faiths.

to halt at the place where he was, and he came out and did homage to him. He behaved to Khusrau in certain special ways and made on his forehead a finger-mark in saffron, which the Indians call *qaśqā* and is considered to be propitious. So many of the simple-minded Hindus, nay, many foolish Muslims too, had been fascinated by his ways and teachings. He was noised about as a religious and worldly leader. They called him Guru, and from all directions crowds of fools would come to him and express great devotion to him. This busy traffic had been carried on for three or four generations. For years the thought had been presenting itself to my mind that either I should put an end to this false traffic, or he should be brought into the fold of Islam."[26]

Jehangir found an excuse "to put an end to the false traffic" within a few months of his accession. Khusrau rebelled against his father and sought the Guru's assistance and blessing. Arjun received the prince, as indeed he would have even if the visitor had not been of royal blood. He did not give Khusrau any assistance beyond perhaps wishing him well.[27] Nevertheless, after the rebellion had been suppressed and Khusrau apprehended, Jehangir wreaked terrible vengeance on the people he suspected of having helped his son. Arjun was heavily fined and, on his refusal to admit the charge of treason or pay the fine, was arrested and sentenced to death. Jehangir wrote: "I fully knew his heresies, and I ordered that he should be brought into my presence, that his houses and children be made over to Murtaza Khan, that his property be confiscated, and that he should be put to death with torture."[28]

The Guru was taken to Lahore. Among his tormentors was a Hindu banker whose daughter's hand Arjun had refused to accept for his son.[29] Among those who tried in

[26] *Tuzuk-i-Jehāngīrī*, I, 72 (translation by Rogers and Beveridge).
[27] According to the *Dabistān*, II, 272, the Guru prayed for Khusrau's success.
[28] *Tuzuk-i-Jehāngīrī*, I, 72-73.
[29] There is nothing contemporary on record to indicate that the Hindu

vain to intercede on his behalf was the Muslim divine, Mian Mir.[30] Arjun was tortured until he was unable to stand any more. He sent word to his son,[31] Hargobind, who was only eleven years old, to ask Bhai Buddha to instal him as the sixth guru and to assume the ministry of the community.

During one of the intermissions in the torture, Arjun was allowed to wash himself in the Ravi, which ran alongside the prison. On May 30, 1606, the Guru entered the stream. The impact of the cold water proved too much for his fevered body, and the current bore him beyond the reach of his tormentors.

Arjun was an unusually gifted and prolific writer. His lines were resplendent with bejewelled phrases and his hymns full of haunting melody. His most popular composition was the *Sukhmani* (the psalm of peace), in which he wrote: "Of all creeds the sovereign creed is to pray to God and do a goodly deed."[32]

Arjun had become the most quoted poet of the Punjab. His songs were on the people's lips and while they eagerly awaited his voice, Jehangir brutally silenced it for ever.

In the twenty-five years of Arjun's ministry, the seed

---

banker, Chandu Shah, was in any way personally vindictive towards the captive guru. Sikh tradition supported by Mani Singh, however, maintains that he first insulted the Guru by telling the matchmaker who was negotiating the marriage, "You have taken a stone from the upper storey and put it down in the drain." The Guru came to know of this and refused the match—and was consequently persecuted by Chandu Shah (Macauliffe, *The Sikh Religion*, III, 72-75, 89-90).

[30] Macauliffe, *The Sikh Religion*, III, 94.

[31] According to Macauliffe, *The Sikh Religion*, (III, 99) the message Guru Arjun sent to Amritsar was worded as follows: "Let him sit fully armed on his throne and maintain an army to the best of his ability. . . . Let him in all respects, except the wearing of arms hereby enjoined, adopt the practices of the preceding gurus." Macauliffe does not indicate his source, nor has the author been able to locate it. Bhai Gurdas does not mention any farewell message in these words.

[32] *Sarb dharm men srest dharm hari kā nām jap nirmal karm.*

sown by Nanak blossomed into its fullness. Nanak's teaching, which was embodied in the hymns of his successors, had been compiled in the *Granth*. Nanak's way of life had become the way of life of communities of Sikhs scattered all over Northern India. The Sikhs had become conscious of the fact that they were now neither Hindus nor Muslims but formed a third community of their own. This feeling was expressed by Arjun in many of his writings:

> I do not keep the Hindu fast, nor the Muslim
>   Ramadan.
> I serve Him alone who is my refuge.
> I serve the One Master, who is also Allah.
> I have broken with the Hindu and the Muslim,
> I will not worship with the Hindu, nor like the
>   Muslim go to Mecca,
> I shall serve Him and no other.
> I will not pray to idols nor say the Muslim prayer.
> I shall put my heart at the feet of the One
>   Supreme Being,
> For we are neither Hindus nor Mussalmans.[33]
>
> *(Bhairav)*

The death of Arjun was a turning point in the history of the Punjab. He was the embodiment of many things that Nanak had preached and stood for. He had brought the Hindu and Mussalman together in creating a Scripture where both were represented and in raising a temple whose foundation was laid by a Muslim and the superstructure built by Hindus and Sikhs. He was a builder of cities and a merchant-prince who brought prosperity to all communities. Arjun's blood became the seed of the Sikh church as well as of the Punjabi nation.

[33] The distinction was noticed by Muhsin Fani, who lived about this time. "The disciples of Nanak . . . do not read the *mantra* of the Hindus. They do not venerate the idols in their temples nor hold their *avatārs* in esteem. They have no regard for Sanskrit, which according to the Hindu is the language of the gods." (*Dabistān*, 233.)

CHAPTER 4

THE CALL TO ARMS

Hargobind (1595-1644)[1]

THE murder of the saintly Arjun was a profound shock to the people. The Emperor's order to arrest the Guru's family and confiscate his property was not carried out, for the local officials believed that the death of the Guru would keep the Sikhs subdued for a long time. The result was just the opposite. The Sikhs gathered round the eleven-year-old Hargobind and the two veterans, Bhai Buddha and Gurdas, ready to avenge the death of their guru.

The young Hargobind took the seat of his father with two swords girded round his waist: one to symbolise spiritual power, and the other temporal. "My rosary shall be the sword-belt and on my turban I shall wear the emblem of royalty," he said.[2] He made it known to his Sikhs that thereafter he would welcome offerings of arms and horses instead of money. He trained a body of soldiers and spent much time in martial exercise and hunting. He built a small fortress, Lohgarh (the castle of steel) in Amritsar. Across the Harimandir, he built the *Akāl Takht* (the throne of the Timeless God), where, instead of chanting hymns of peace, the congregation heard ballads extolling feats of heroism, and, instead of listening to religious discourses, discussed plans of military conquests.[3] For the

---

[1] The main incidents of Hargobind's life have been taken from contemporary sources. Muhsin Fani's *Dabistān*, which is fairly detailed, is unfortunately wrong about some of the important dates and the sequence of events; Jehangir's memoirs (*Tuzuk-i-Jehāngīrī*) refer to some events, Bhai Gurdas to others. Nevertheless, there is considerable confusion and contradiction on many points.

[2] Macauliffe, *The Sikh Religion*, IV, 2.

[3] The Guru's abode did in fact become like that of the Emperor. He sat on a throne and held court. He went out with a royal umbrella over his head and was always accompanied by armed retainers. He sent envoys to ruling princes and received their agents in durbar, where presents were

first few years little notice was taken of the change in the complexion of the Sikh organisation. But as the number of the Guru's retainers increased, local officials began sending reports to the Emperor. Since the fine imposed on Arjun had not been paid, there was legal justification to proceed against his son. Jehangir ordered the arrest of Hargobind and the disbandment of his private army.[4]

The Guru spent a year or more in imprisonment at Gwalior. He resumed his martial activity as soon as he was released,[5] only a little more discreetly. He was left alone, and was able to raise his private army anew by recruiting Pathan mercenaries and training the sturdier of his own followers.[6] Muhsin Fani writes that: "The Guru had eight hundred horses in his stables, three hundred troopers on horseback, and sixty men with firearms were always in his service."[7]

In the fifteen odd years between his release from Gwa-

---

exchanged. With Arjun the title *Sacā Pādśāh* was only honorific; with Hargobind it became a reality as far as the Sikhs were concerned. He was *mīrī pīrī dā mālik* (the lord of the spiritual and secular domains).

[4] "Hargobind had many difficulties to contend with," writes Muhsin Fani. "One of them was that he adopted the life of a soldier, wore a sword contrary to the custom of his father, maintained a retinue, and began to follow the chase. The Emperor, in order to extort from him the balance of the fine which had been imposed on Arjun Mal, sent him to Gwalior." (Muhsin Fani, *Dabistan*.)

The term of imprisonment is uncertain. Muhsin Fani is obviously wrong in stating that it was twelve years, because most of the Guru's children were born during these years. It is likely that Hargobind was taken in custody some time in 1609 and released by the end of 1611 at the latest.

[5] *Dabistan*, II, 274, states that Sikh disciples used to come to Gwalior to make obeisance before the walls of the fort and that the Emperor was moved out of a sense of pity to release him.

[6] He obviously did not take on a post of any significance under the Mughals, as is maintained by many historians. The *Tuzuk-i-Jehāngīrī*, which has detailed lists of important officers, does not mention Hargobind. The *Tuzuk* also does not support the Sikh view that the Emperor became a personal friend of the Guru. The author of the *Dabistan*, however, maintains that "Hargobind was always attached to the stirrup of the victorious Jehangir . . . and after Jehangir's death Hargobind entered the service of His Majesty Shah Jahan" (*Dabistan*, II, 273-74).

[7] *Dabistan*, II, 277.

lior and Jehangir's death in A.D. 1627, Hargobind consolidated his spiritual and temporal hold on the community. He travelled through the Punjab into Uttar Pradesh as far as Pilibhit. He then went northwards into Kashmir. All along the route of his travels he had temples built and appointed missionaries who could initiate the converts into the pacifist faith of Nanak and the martial mission of Hargobind. On his way back to Amritsar, he accepted from the Raja of Bilaspur a gift of a plot of land lying between the foothills of the Himalayas and the river Sutlej. Here he built himself a retreat which he named Kiratpur (the abode of praise).

With the death of Jehangir and the accession of Shah Jahan in A.D. 1627, the Guru's real troubles began. In 1628 when Shah Jahan happened to be hunting in the neighbourhood of Amritsar, his men clashed with the retainers of the Guru. A bailiff and a posse of constabulary were sent to arrest Hargobind. They found the Guru's household busy preparing for the nuptials of his daughter. They could not find Hargobind, but they plundered his property; all the confectionery prepared for the wedding was eaten by the constables.[8] Hargobind's guards fell on the surfeited Mughals before they had gone very far. Among those killed was the Chief Constable, Mukhlis Khan. Hargobind left Amristar immediately and had his daughter's wedding performed in a nearby village. From the village he went on to Kartarpur in the Jullundur Doab and then to Sri Hargobindpur, the town built by his father. Here too he had to subdue the zamīndārs (landowners) before he was allowed to live in peace.

Two years later he had a second clash with the imperial troops near Lahira. The Mughals were badly mauled by the Sikhs. The Guru feared that a large force would be sent against him and quickly retired to a tract near Bhatinda, where the wild and uncharted nature of the country made pursuit difficult.

[8] Dabistan, II, 275.

After a year in the wilderness, Hargobind returned to Kartarpur. Imperial troops made yet another attempt to capture him. With the Mughals was the renegade Painda Khan, who had been the leader of the Pathan mercenaries in the employ of the Guru. The Guru's forces were encircled at Kartarpur, but were able to turn the tables on the besiegers. Fighting in the van of the Sikh forces were Hargobind's own sons, Gurditta and Tegh Bahadur (who later became the ninth guru).[9] Imperial troops were again routed. Among the slain was Painda Khan.[10]

Hargobind realised that he could not withstand the might of Mughal arms in the plains. Consequently in 1634 he shifted his headquarters to Kiratpur, the haven of refuge in the Himalayan foothills. The remaining years of his life were spent in this sylvan retreat.

The number of Sikhs had been steadily increasing with each guru. The change of emphasis from a peaceful propagation of the faith to the forthright declaration of the right to defend that faith by force of arms proved to be extremely popular. The Punjabis were naturally an assertive and virile race, who only needed a leader to rouse them to action. Hargobind infused in them the confidence that they could challenge the might of the Mughal Emperor. Great numbers of peasants answered the call to arms. The influx of superstition-ridden Hindus placed a heavy burden on the organising abilities of the Guru.[11] He had to set up many more community centres and train more *masands*. In the earlier years, this part of the work had been taken care of by Bhai Buddha and Bhai Gurdas, and, after the death of these men, by the Guru's son, Gurditta. Hargobind entrusted more and more duties to Gurditta, whom, it appears, he was training to be the next guru.

---

[9] Macauliffe, *The Sikh Religion*, IV, 206. [10] *Dabistan*, II, 275.

[11] Muhsin Fani, talking of the Guru's years in Kiratpur, says: "From this time the disciples of the Guru increased considerably, and in this mountainous country, as far as the frontiers of Tibet and Khota, the name of the Mussalman was not heard of." (*Dabistan*, II, 276.)

The last days of Hargobind's life were saddened by a series of domestic tragedies. Within a few years five members of his family, including three of his sons, died one after another. The most grievous of these deaths was that of Gurditta in 1638. To add to his sorrows, Gurditta's son, Dhirmal, turned against his grandfather. For a long time Hargobind could not make up his mind about his successor. He had two sons living: Suraj Mal, who showed little interest in Sikh affairs, and Tegh Bahadur, who was too withdrawn in himself to be entrusted with the leadership of a rapidly growing community. When the time came, Hargobind chose Gurditta's second son, Har Rai, to succeed him as the seventh guru.

Hargobind died peacefully at Kiratpur in March 1644.[12]

Har Rai (1630-1661)

Within one year of his assuming ministry as the seventh guru, Har Rai was compelled to leave Kiratpur with his family and retainers (who are said to have numbered 2,200 men-in-arms), and retire further into the mountains. The Raja of Bilaspur, in whose territory Kiratpur was situated, was having trouble with the government, and Har Rai feared that in the operations against the Raja the Mughal governor might turn on the Sikhs as well. For the next thirteen years, Har Rai lived in comparative seclusion in a small village in Sirmoor State.[13]

The absence of the Guru from the main centres of Sikh activity (Amritsar, Goindwal, Kartarpur, Khadur, and

[12] According to Muhsin Fani, at the cremation of the Guru two of his followers who were crazed with grief threw themselves on the burning pyre. (*Dabistan*, II, 237.)

[13] Cunningham has conjectured that this might be Taksal near Kasauli in Himachal Pradesh.

Muhsin Fani's *Dabistan*, which has nothing more to say on the Sikhs, states: "In *hejirah* 1055 (A.D. 1645), Najabat Khan by the order of Shah Jahan invaded the land of Raja Tara Chand and made him a prisoner. Guru Har Rai betook himself to Thapal [probably Taksal], which town is situated in the territory of Raja Karam Prakash, not far from Sirmoor" (II, 282).

Kiratpur), the hostility of the disappointed claimants to guruship, and the general disintegration of the *masand* organisation, seriously prejudiced the advancement of the community. Har Rai tried to make up for this by undertaking a tour of the centres and by reorganising the missions. During his tenure of guruship some notable conversions were made among the landed families of the Punjab.[14]

At the end of 1658, Har Rai returned to Kiratpur. He became friendly with Shah Jahan's eldest son, Dara Shikoh,[15] who being of Sufi persuasion sought the company of saintly men of all denominations. When the war of succession began between Shah Jahan's sons, the Guru's sympathies were naturally more with the liberal Dara Shikoh than with the bigoted Aurangzeb. Dara Shikoh was defeated and fled northwards to the Punjab. He called on the Guru and asked for assistance. The manner of the assistance given by the Guru to Dara Shikoh is not clear,[16] but it was sufficient to arouse the wrath of Aurangzeb,

[14] The ancestors of the princely families of Patiala, Nabha, and Jind, who had come into contact with Guru Hargobind, became closely associated with the Sikh community. So did the ancestors of two other notable families, Kaithal and Bagarian, whose descendants played a distinguished role in the building of Sikh power.

[15] Sikh records maintain that the Guru cured Dara Shikoh of the effects of poison. When asked why he had saved the life of a son of Shah Jahan, who had tormented his father and grandfather, the Guru replied: "The man breaks flowers with one hand and offers them with the other, but the flowers perfume both hands alike. The axe cuts the sandal tree, yet the sandal perfumes the axe." (*Panth Prakās*, 121-22.)

[16] Some historians believe the Guru joined Dara Shikoh (Trumpp); others, that he covered his retreat by blocking Aurangzeb's troops on the Beas (Sarkar and Cunningham). Sujan Rai, in his *Khulāsat-ut-Tawārikh*, has this to say: "When after his defeat Dara Shikoh came to Lahore, he became very much afraid of his brother and made up his mind to flee to Multan and (then to) Kandahar. Of this he spoke to some of his confidants. Raja Rajrup said that he would go home to make better arrangements for the collection of troops and leaving his son and vakeel at Lahore he went away. And after a few days the vakeel and the son also fled. Guru Har Rai, who had come with a large army, left his camp with the plea that he was going to collect more troops for help."

who, on the conclusion of hostilities, summoned Har Rai to Delhi to explain his conduct. Har Rai sent his elder son, Ram Rai, to represent him. Ram Rai succeeded in winning the confidence of the Emperor.[17] Aurangzeb decided to keep Ram Rai in Delhi in the belief that, with the future incumbent of the guruship in his power, he would become the arbiter of the destinies of the Sikh community. Ram Rai's sycophancy at the Mughal Court turned his father's mind against him, and he announced his intention of passing the guruship to his younger son, Hari Krishen. Ram Rai did his best to re-establish himself with his father and succeeded in winning over a section of the Sikhs to his side. Aurangzeb encouraged him in his pretensions to guruship and gave him land on which to build his community centre.[18] But Har Rai's mind was made up and before he died he proclaimed the succession of his five-year-old son, Hari Krishen.

Har Rai's seventeen years of ministry were not marked by any spectacular events. Although he had inherited a militant tradition and a small army, he was a man of peace. He loved to hunt, but only to bring back wild animals for his private zoo at Kiratpur. He hated to hurt any living thing. "You can repair or rebuild a temple or a mosque but not a broken heart," he said. He adhered strictly to the routine of a life of prayer exhorted by Nanak. One of his disciples asked him whether there was any point in reciting the Guru's hymns without understanding

---

[17] Sikh chronicles narrate an incident which made Ram Rai acceptable to Aurangzeb and discredited him in the eyes of his father and community. He was asked to explain a passage in the *Granth* which was considered offensive to Muslims. It ran: "The dust of a Mussalman's body finds its way in the hands of the potter, who makes pots and bricks out of it. He fires the clay; it cries out as it burns" (*Vār Āsā*, VI, 2). Ram Rai substituted the word *beimān* (faithless) for Mussalman and saved his skin. Ram Rai was only a boy in his early teens when he was presented at court. If the above-mentioned incident took place, it is likely that he was prompted by some elder person accompanying him.

[18] This was in the present-day town of Dehra Dun, where descendants of Ram Rai called *Rām Rāīās* still have a couple of gurdwaras of their own.

them. "Yes," replied Har Rai, "as the grease sticks to the pot when it is emptied, so does the Guru's word stick to the heart. . . . Whether you comprehend it or not, the word bears the seed of salvation. Perfume persists in the broken pieces even after the vase that contained it has been shattered."

Hari Krishen (1656-1664)

The investiture of Hari Krishen did not suit Aurangzeb, who wanted to play a decisive role in the affairs of the Sikhs. He summoned the infant Guru to Delhi with the intention of arbitrating between his claims and those of his elder brother, Ram Rai. It is not very likely that Ram Rai, who was little more than a boy himself, could have pursued the matter of succession on his own initiative. At his back were some masands, who, like the Emperor, wished to have the Guru as a puppet in their hands. After some hesitation Hari Krishen arrived in Delhi and was put up at the house of Mirza Raja Jai Singh in the suburb of Raisina.[19]

Aurangzeb was in no hurry to announce his arbitration (nor indeed would the Sikhs have paid any heed to it). He was content to have both the claimants under his surveillance. Hari Krishen was, however, stricken with smallpox. Before he died, he indicated to the people about him that the next guru was not to be either Ram Rai or Dhirmal, both of whom had been eagerly pressing their claims, but an older man living in the village of Bakala.

Tegh Bahadur (1621-1675)

It was quite clear that by his dying words *"Bābā Bakāle,"* Hari Krishen had meant his grand-uncle, Tegh Bahadur, who had been living in the village ever since the death of his father Hargobind in 1644. Nevertheless, a

19 The temple which stands on the site is consequently named *baṅglā sāhib* (the place of the residence). The village of Raisina was demolished in the building of New Delhi.

whole army of claimants set themselves up at Bakala and sent out *masands* announcing their succession.[20] The chief contenders were Dhirmal and Ram Rai.

Tegh Bahadur was a man of retiring habits who did not wish to fight for his rights. But his very reluctance to press for recognition turned the Sikh masses in his favour. This soured Dhirmal and Ram Rai all the more. Dhirmal tried to have him murdered; fortunately the assassin he had hired failed to execute his mission. Tegh Bahadur left Bakala for Amritsar; there the doors of the Harimandir were slammed in his face by the *masands*. From Amritsar he went to Kiratpur, the town built by his father. The place was full of envious cousins and nephews who gave him no respite. Tegh Bahadur was compelled to retire into the wilderness. He bought a hillock near the village of Makhowal, five miles north of Kiratpur, and built himself a village where he could be away from his contentious relations. Here he expected to find peace and solitude, and hopefully named it *ānandpur* (the haven of bliss). But even in Anandpur his kinsmen did not leave him alone, and he decided to leave the Punjab until the atmosphere became more congenial.

Tegh Bahadur left Anandpur with his wife and mother and travelled eastward towards Uttar Pradesh. Wherever he went, the Sikhs acclaimed him as their guru. When he arrived in the vicinity of Delhi, Ram Rai, who was still in attendance at the Mughal Court, had him arrested as an impostor and a disturber of the peace. After investigation the charge was dropped and the Guru allowed to proceed on his way.[21] He travelled through Agra, Allahabad, Benares, Gaya, and arrived at Patna. His wife, being in an advanced stage of pregnancy, could not go any further.

[20] Until recent years several members of the Sodhi caste claiming descent from the Sodhi Guru were in the habit of styling themselves as gurus and accepting worship and offerings from credulous peasants.

[21] Forster (*Travels*, I, 260) states that Tegh Bahadur was put under restraint and then released at the intervention of the Raja of Jaipur.

The Guru made arrangements for her confinement and left her and his mother in Patna.[22]

Tegh Bahadur crossed the Brahmaputra and visited Sikh centres in Sylhet, Chittagong, and Sondip.[23] He was in Dacca when the news of the birth of his son (on December 26, 1666) in Patna was brought to him. From Bengal the Guru went on to Assam. He spent nearly three years in the province before returning to Patna to join his family.

Tegh Bahadur did not spend much time with his infant son, Gobind Rai. There were urgent messages asking him to return to the Punjab. He left his family in Patna and returned to his homeland. He found the Hindus and Sikhs of the Punjab in a state of nervous agitation. Emperor Aurangzeb had embarked on a policy of religious persecution.[24] There were stories of the demolition of temples and forcible conversions; taxes had been reimposed on Hindus visiting their places of pilgrimage. Tegh Bahadur's rivals had discreetly disappeared from the scene. It was left to him to instill confidence among his own people and the Hindus, who had now begun to look to the Sikhs to protect them from the tyranny of officials.

Tegh Bahadur undertook an extensive tour of the Punjab. Wherever he went he attracted great crowds and was given handsome donations by his admirers. His exhortation to the people to stand firm could not have been

[22] There were Sikh communities in several towns of Bengal and the Guru might have considered it more important to visit them than be with his wife during her confinement. It has also been suggested that he had earlier undertaken to accompany a Rajput general commanding Aurangzeb's army invading Assam and was fulfilling his engagement.

[23] For details of Sikh communities in East Bengal at the time, see the articles "Sikh Relics in East Bengal" by G. B. Singh in *Dacca Review*, Oct./Nov. 1915; Jan./Mar. 1916.

[24] Sir Jadu Nath Sarkar, *History of Aurangzeb*, III, 267ff., gives an account of the repressive measures taken by the state against non-Muslims. He quotes Khafi Khan to the effect that "Aurangzeb ordered the temples and the Sikhs to be destroyed and the Guru's agents [masands], for collecting the tithes and presents of the faithful, to be expelled from the cities."

palatable to the government. He was summoned to Delhi. Mughal officers who carried the summons to Anandpur reported him missing. He was declared an absconder and a warrant was issued for his arrest. He was apprehended, along with a band of devotees, at Agra, brought to Delhi, and arraigned before the Kazi's court.[25]

[25] Sikh and Muslim sources are at variance on the reasons for Tegh Bahadur's arrest and subsequent execution. Cunningham and Trumpp have based their versions on *Siyār-ul-Mutākherīn* written by Ghulam Hussain over one hundred years after the event. They accepted Raymond's translation, which is as follows:

"This man [Tegh Bahadur] finding himself at the head of so many thousands of people, became aspiring; and he united his concerns with one Hafyzadam, a Mahomedan fakir. . . . These two men no sooner saw themselves followed by multitudes, implicitly addicted to their chief's will, then, forsaking every honest calling, they fell to subsisting by plunder and rapine, laying waste the whole province of Pendjab." (Raymond's translation, p. 85.)

Professors Ganda Singh and Teja Singh have rendered the same passage in the following words:

"Tegh Bahadur gathering many disciples became powerful, and thousands of people accompanied him. A contemporary of his, Hafiz Adam, who was a fakir belonging to the order of Shaikh Ahmed Sirhindi, had gathered about him a great multitude of followers. Both of these took to the practice of levying forcible exactions and moved about in the land of the Punjab. Tegh Bahadur took money from Hindus and Hafiz Adam from Mussalmans. The royal newswriters wrote to the Emperor that two fakirs, one Hindu and the other Muslim named so-and-so, had taken to that practice. It would not be strange if, with the increase of their influence, they created trouble." (*A Short History of the Sikhs*, p. 57.)

The latter translation is the more accurate and certainly says nothing of "subsisting by plunder."

Ghulam Hussain is also wrong about the place of execution. Tegh Bahadur was executed in Delhi and not in Gwalior as stated in the *Siyār-ul-Mutākherīn*. This Muslim chronicler's scanty reference to the Sikhs is full of inaccuracies and biased to the extent of being abusive. The Sikh version, though undoubtedly biased in favour of their guru, has the advantage of being based on contemporary sources. According to this, a delegation of Kashmir Brahmins had approached the Guru to help them out of their predicament. (They had been ordered to accept conversion to Islam.) The Guru is alleged to have advised them to tell the Mughal officials that if Tegh Bahadur would accept conversion they would follow suit. The Guru was consequently summoned to Delhi, and on his refusal to renounce his faith was beheaded. This version is supported by Tegh Bahadur's son, who was then old enough to know what was going on. (Macauliffe, *The Sikh Religion*, IV, 371-72.)

Tegh Bahadur was sentenced to death[26] and executed on November 11, 1675.[27] Before his body could be quartered and exposed to public view, it was stolen under cover of darkness by one of his devotees. The Guru's body was cremated a few miles from the place of execution; the head was brought to Anandpur and cremated by Tegh Bahadur's son Gobind.[28]

Guru Gobind wrote of his father's martyrdom in the following words:

> To protect their right to wear their
> caste-marks and sacred threads,
> Did he, in the dark age, perform the supreme
> sacrifice.
> To help the saintly he went to the utmost limit,
> He gave his head but never cried in pain.

[26] Emperor Aurangzeb was not in Delhi at the time. But there is little doubt that the policy of persecution of the non-Muslims had been renewed at his personal command, and the execution of Tegh Bahadur, who was looked upon as the leader of the Hindus, had his tacit approval. Two followers of Tegh Bahadur were also beheaded; the others had escaped.

[27] There are different versions of the manner in which Tegh Bahadur died. Ratan Singh Bhangu in his *Prācīn Panth Prakāś* maintains that on the Guru's refusal to accept Islam the Chief Kazi asked him to exhibit some of the miraculous powers he was supposed to possess. Thereupon the Guru wrote something on a piece of paper and tied it with a string round his neck. This, he said, would prevent the executioner from cutting off his head. When the Guru's head was severed, the piece of paper was opened. It read: *Sīs diyā par sirr nā diyā*—"I gave my head but not my secret."

Some English historians (Cunningham, Malcolm, Gordon) have fabricated yet another version of the execution. According to them, the Guru was accused of looking towards the Emperor's harem. When questioned, he is alleged to have said that it was not the women of the harem he had looked at but towards the east, whence a power was advancing which would destroy the Mughals. The power is understood to have been the British. There is absolutely no basis for this version.

[28] The site of the execution in Chandni Chowk of Delhi is marked by a temple called *Sīs Ganj*. *Rikāb Ganj*, which is next door to Parliament House, marks the site of the cremation of the Guru's body. The place where the head was cremated in Anandpur is also called *Sīs Ganj* (the place of the head).

He suffered martyrdom for the sake of his faith.
He lost his head but revealed not his secret.
He disdained to perform miracles or juggler's
    tricks
For such fill men of God with shame.
He burst the bonds of mortal clay
And went to the abode of God.
No one hath ever performed an act as noble as his.

.   .   .   .

Tegh Bahadur passed, the world was with sorrow
    stricken.
A wail of horror rent the earth,
A victor's welcome given by the hosts of heaven.
(Bicitra Nāṭak)

CHAPTER 5

FROM THE PACIFIST SIKH TO THE MILITANT KHALSA

Gobind Singh (1666-1708)[1]

◆❖◆❖◆ GOBIND RAI was only nine when his father's
❖◆❖◆❖ severed head was brought to Anandpur for
◆❖◆❖◆ cremation. The shock to the child's mind and
to other members of his family need not be exaggerated.
The leaders of the community were concerned about the
safety of Gobind, for the possibility of his being taken to
Delhi as a hostage could not be ruled out. To avoid any
chances, the young Guru and his entourage were shifted
from Anandpur further into the mountains at Paonta.[2]
Gobind spent many years of his childhood in this small
Himalayan town on the banks of the Jumna. He was
taught Sanskrit and Persian (in addition to the Hindi and
Punjabi which he had been learning in Patna). He learned
to ride and shoot, and he spent a great deal of his time
hunting. The classical education and the life in the mountain retreat brought out the poet in Gobind. He began
to compose verses in the four languages he had learned,
sometimes using all four in the same poem. He rewrote
the stories of Hindu mythology in his own words, his

[1] The chief source of information on Guru Gobind Singh's life is his
own *Bicitra Nāṭak*, which he wrote about A.D. 1692. On events preceding
its composition, the *Bicitra Nāṭak* is to be considered authentic. For the
remaining period of the Guru's life we have nothing earlier than the Sikh
chronicles written eighty to a hundred years after the Guru's death. *Gur
Bilās*, by Sukha Singh, was written in 1797. Santokh Singh and Gyan
Singh's works are of even later date. Fortunately these chronicles can be
checked with Mughal records of Aurangzeb's and Bahadur Shah's time. A
careful sifting of the material gives a fairly accurate picture of the Guru's
life and times.

[2] Apparently so named after the Guru's residence at the place from
pāoṅṭā (the footstool). "The true Guru came from Anandpur and rested
his foot. It was consequently named Paonta." (*Sūraj Prakāś*.)

favourite being the exploits of the goddess *Caṇḍī*, the destroyer of demons.[3] He wrote of moonlit nights made heavy with the fragrance of wild jasmine and of lovers' trysts by the Jumna, sparkling like a stream of quicksilver through the black mountains.[4]

Besides schooling, hunting, and the writing of verse, there was also the serious aspect of life—Gobind's responsibilities as the leader of his community. He learned of the peaceful mission of Nanak and his four successors. He was also told of the martyrdom of Arjun and of how Arjun's son, Hargobind, had taken up arms to avenge the killing. As he grew into manhood, he was able to disentangle one strand which ran through the confusion of ideas: that although love and forgiveness are stronger than hate and revenge, once a person was convinced that the adversary meant to destroy him, it was his duty to resist the enemy with all the means at his disposal, for then it was a battle of the survival, not only of life, but of ideals. It became the *dharma yudh* (the battle for the sake of righteousness). His mission in life became clear to him. In his autobiography (*Apnī Kathā*), which forms a part of the *Bicitra Nāṭak*, he wrote: "I came into the world charged with the duty to uphold the right in every place, to destroy sin and evil. O ye holy men, know it well in your hearts that the only reason I took birth was to see that righteousness may flourish: that the good may live and tyrants be torn out by their roots." In an epistle he later addressed to the Mughal Emperor, he justified the method he adopted to fulfil this end. "When all other means have

[3] This, and the fact that the Guru visited the temple of Naina Devi near Anandpur, have led some Hindu writers to conclude that Gobind became a worshipper of *Durgā* (both *Caṇḍī* and *Nainā Devī* being reincarnations of the goddess of destruction). This is wholly inaccurate. In more than one passage Gobind describes himself as "the breaker of idols." There is also an anecdote of his making fun of hill rajas who had protested against one of Gobind's Sikhs cutting off the nose of the Devi.

[4] See Appendix 4, on *Dasam Granth*.

failed," he wrote in the *Zafarnāmā,* "it is permissible to draw the sword."[5]

Gobind Rai drew the sword while he was still at Paonta. Like his grandfather Hargobind, he let it be known that he would welcome offerings in arms and horses; and, more than the offerings, he would welcome able-bodied men willing to join his crusade. Also like his grandfather, he made sure that his crusade would not be wrongly construed as one of Sikhs against Muslims: the nucleus of his private army consisted of five hundred Pathan mercenaries.

The Guru's troubles came from an unexpected quarter. He had been encouraged by the Rajput chiefs of the hills to believe that they would support him against the Mughals. But as soon as he started organising his army, Raja Bhim Chand of Bilaspur, in whose territory Anandpur was located, turned hostile and successfully pressed the chiefs of several neighbouring hill states to try and expel the Guru from their midst. They did not like the growing power of the Guru in their region, nor, what appeared to them as an even greater danger, the increasing insubordination of the lower castes, who had begun to turn to the casteless fraternity of the Sikhs for leadership. When threats failed to dislodge the Guru, the chiefs tried to eject him by force. They bought over Gobind's Pathan mercenaries and then attacked him. Gobind Singh met their combined forces six miles out of Paonta at a place called Bhangani. Despite the desertions and numerical superiority of the Rajputs and Pathans, the Sikhs (most of whom were Hindus of the trading castes) carried the day.

The battle of Bhangani was fought in 1686. It was Gobind's first baptism in steel.[6]

---

5   *Cu kār az hamā hilate dar guzaśt*
          halāl ast būrdan ba śamśīr dast.

When all avenues have been explored, all means tried, it is rightful to draw the sword out of the scabbard and wield it with your hand.

6 Gobind's conception of God had undergone a martial metamorphosis.

The victory at Bhangani gave Gobind Rai confidence to descend from the mountains to his ancestral home in Anandpur. The attitude of the feudal overlord, Bhim Chand of Bilaspur, also changed. He was now looking for someone to organise the hill chiefs to resist the Mughal governor, who was on his way to collect arrears of revenue. Bhim Chand asked the Guru to lead the hill men against the Mughals.

The Guru's second battle was fought at Nadaun[7] in A.D. 1687—a few months after his return to Anandpur. The initial engagement was won by the confederates led by Gobind. Despite the victory, the hill chiefs decided to come to terms with the Mughal commander and thus avoid the likelihood of another force being sent against them. Gobind refused to enter into these discussions. After spending eight days at Nadaun he returned to Anandpur.

The Mughal Emperor did not approve of the settlement which condoned a defiance of his authority, and he sent his own son Moazzam (later Bahadur Shah) and General Mirza Beg to the Punjab. The General proceeded to the hills and quickly reduced the hill chiefs to subservience. It seems that Mirza Beg had secret instructions not to bother the Guru.[8] Gobind was left unmolested for twelve

---

In the prayer he offered before the battle of Bhangani, he addressed God in the following words:

> Eternal God, Thou art our shield,
> The dagger, knife, the sword we wield,
> To us protector there is given
> The timeless, deathless, Lord of Heaven,
> To us all-steel's unvanquished might,
> To us all-time's resistless flight,
> But chiefly Thou, protector brave,
> All steel, wilt Thine own servant save.
>
> (*Akāl Ustat.* Translation by Macauliffe.)

[7] In the *Bicitra Nāṭāk*, the battle is referred to as the *Hussainī Yudh* after the name of the Mughal Commander, Hussain Khan.

[8] The Sikh chronicler of *Gur Bilās* maintains that this was due to the good offices of one Nand Lal "Goya," a Sikh poet of Persian, who had influence over the prince. The prince could not have been indifferent to the policy of gaining supporters for his own cause; his father's advancing

years and was able to turn his unbounded energy to re-organising his community.

The first thing the Guru did was to fortify the centre at Anandpur. He bought the neighbouring land and built a chain of fortresses—Anandgarh, Keshgarh, Loh-garh, and Fatehgarh. Although the foothills between the Sutlej and the Jumna where these fortresses were built lay in the territories of the Rajput Chiefs, the Guru became more powerful than they.

The twelve years at Anandpur were also full of intel-lectual activity. Gobind selected five of the most scholarly of his disciples and sent them to Benares to learn Sanskrit and the Hindu religious texts, to be better able to inter-pret the writings of the gurus, which were full of allusions to Hindu mythology and philosophy. These five began the school of Sikh theologians known as the *nirmalās* (the unsullied).[9]

Poets from many parts of Northern India sought Go-bind's patronage and at one time fifty-two bards[10] were in

---

age must have made him increasingly conscious of this. The consideration paid him dividends, for the Guru was on his side in the war of succession. (*Gur Bilās*, 172.)

[9] The *nirmalās* follow the traditional pattern of life of the Hindu Brahmacharya. They are celibate, wear white garments, and are strict vegetarians. Since they begin their studies with Sanskrit and the Vedas, their interpretations of the writings of the Sikh Gurus have a Brahman-ical bias which is not acceptable to many Sikhs.

The first five *nirmalās* were Karam Singh, Ganda Singh, Vir Singh, Saina Singh, and Ram Singh.

[10] The works of some of the Guru's court-poets have come down to us. The following are the better known:

(a) Saina Pat, author of *Gur Sobha*, which mentions the Guru's bap-tismal ceremony, the traditions of the Khalsa, some of the Guru's battles, and his assassination.

(b) Bhai Nand Lal "Goya," a poet of undoubted ability who wrote in Persian. He wrote many works, including *Tausīf-o-sanā*, *Khātmā*, *Ganj Nāmā*, *Zindgī Nāmā*, *Dīvān Goyā*, *Inshā Dastūr* and *Arzul Alfāz*.

(c) Bhai Mani Singh was an eminent theologian entrusted with the care of the temple at Amritsar after the Guru's death. At the instance of the Guru he prepared the final rescension of the *Adi Granth*. His main work is the *Bhagat Ratnāvalī*. He was executed at Lahore in A.D. 1738.

residence at the Guru's court. Since Gobind was himself a poet of considerable talent, his own preference for heroic poetry set the pattern of the compositions. Every evening the Sikhs heard ballads extolling the deeds of warriors who had defied tyranny by the force of arms. A martial atmosphere came to pervade the Sikh court at Anandpur.

In Anandpur the Guru wrote and reared his family. Four sons, Ajit Singh, Jujhar Singh, Zorawar Singh, and Fateh Singh, were born to his two wives, Sundari and Jito. He spent much time pondering over the disunity and decadence that had come into the movement launched by Nanak. He was able to put his finger on the two causes which had contributed to this state of affairs: the wranglings over the succession to the guruship and the *masands*.

Belief in the spiritual tutelage of the guru was an integral part of Nanak's teachings. But Gobind felt that a living mentor could now be dispensed with, provided he could be replaced by some institution which discharged the same functions. The examples of Prithi Chand, Dhirmal, Mehrban, and Ram Rai, each of whom had disputed the succession in their time and set up as rival gurus, were no doubt the deciding factor in Gobind's mind. Although he had four sons of his own, he felt that it would be better to end the line of personal gurus and invest the guruship in something permanent and inviolable. There was the *Granth Sahib*, by then well established as the book par excellence for people seeking spiritual guidance. On matters other than spiritual, there was the institution of the *pancāyat*, with which all Punjabis were familiar. All that was needed was to adapt the *pancāyat* to the need of the time. Between the two, i.e., the *Granth* and the elected representatives of the community (*panth*), both the spiritual and secular functions of the Guru could be taken care of: the *Granth* could become the spiritual Guru, the *panth* itself the secular Guru, and the combination of the two, the mystic entity, the *guru granth panth*.

Before giving practical shape to these ideas Gobind decided to abolish the institution of *masands* which had become a fertile cause of disruption in the community. Many *masands* had set themselves up as gurus in their own districts and had begun to nominate their own successors. Instead of propagating Sikhism and forwarding the collections they made to the Guru, many of them engaged in money-lending and trading on the "offerings" they extorted from the poor peasants. Gobind realised that the abolition of the *masands* would for some time deprive the central exchequer of its only source of income. Nevertheless, he felt that the risk was worth taking and might in the end prove beneficial. He did not compromise on half measures like trying to reform the *masands* or separating the less corrupt from the thoroughly corrupt, but with one stroke of his pen pronounced an excommunication on the lot of them.

Gobind had to give his people something positive to replace what he had destroyed. He had created a martial atmosphere and an expectancy of military action. His father's murder was still unavenged, and the persecution of religious minorities continued as before.

Gobind had already written about his life's mission. He decided to proclaim it and take practical steps to fulfil it. Early in 1699 he sent messages inviting his followers to make a special effort to come to Anandpur for the festival of the first of Baisakh. He specifically exhorted the Sikhs to come with their hair and beards unshorn.[11]

The crowd that collected at Anandpur is said to have been great. After the morning service the Guru appeared before the congregation, drew his sword out of its scabbard, and demanded five men for sacrifice. After some trepidation one rose to offer himself. He was taken into a

---

[11] The wording of the *Hukamnāmā* according to the author of the *Sūraj Prakāś*, iii, 21, was: "The Sikhs should come to me wearing long hair. Once a man becomes a Sikh, he should never shave himself. He should not touch tobacco, and should receive baptism of the sword." (Teja Singh and Ganda Singh, *A Short History of the Sikhs*, p. 69.)

tent. A little later the Guru reappeared in front of the throng with his sword dripping with blood and asked for another victim. In this manner five men were taken for a "sacrifice" into the tent. Then the Guru came out with the five "victims" (he had slaughtered goats instead) and announced that the *pañj piyāre* (five beloved ones) were to be the nucleus of a new community he would raise which was to be called the K͟hālsā, or the pure.[12]

He baptised the five men[13] in a new manner. He mixed sugar in plain water and churned it with a double-edged dagger, to the recitation of hymns, including some of his own compositions. The five who had until then belonged to different Hindu castes (one was a Brahmin, one a Kshatriya, and the remaining three of lesser castes) were made to drink out of one bowl to signify their initiation into the casteless fraternity of the Khalsa. Their Hindu names were changed and they were given one family name "Singh,"[14] for thenceforth their father was Gobind Singh (so renamed after his own baptism), their mother Sahib Devan,[15] and their place of birth Anandpur. The bap-

[12] The choice of the number five—the same as in the case of the *pañcāyats*—is significant. The following lines are ascribed to the Guru:

> *pañcoṇ meṇ nit bartat maiṇ hūṇ*
> *pañc milan so pīrāṇ pīr*
> Where there are five (elected) there am I
> When the five meet, they are the holiest of the holy.

[13] The names of these men are repeated in the *ardās* at the end of every prayer. They were Daya Ram, Dharam Das, Mohkam Chand, Sahib Chand, and Himmat Rai.

[14] Singh is derived from the Sanskrit *simha*, meaning lion. It was (and is) commonly used as a surname by the Rajputs, Gurkhas, and many others belonging to Hindu martial classes. The distinction between Sikh surnames and those of others is that whereas all Sikhs are Singhs, all Singhs are not Sikhs.

A Sikh woman takes the surname *Kaur* on baptism. Kaur was also a common surname for Rajput women and means both a princess and lioness.

[15] She was the Guru's third wife. Having no children of her own she was honoured by Gobind by being made the mother of the Khalsa. According to Sikh tradition the Guru took her under his protection, but never consummated his relationship with Sahib Devan. Her marriage is described as the *kuvārā ḍolā* (virgin wedlock).

tism symbolised a rebirth, by which the initiated were considered as having renounced their previous occupations (*krit nās*) for that of soldiering; of having severed their family ties (*kul nās*) to become the family of Gobind; of having rejected their earlier creeds (*dharma nās*) for the creed of the Khalsa; of having given up all ritual (*karm nās*) save that sanctioned by the Sikh faith.

Five emblems were prescribed for the Khalsa. They were to wear their hair and beard unshorn (*kes*); they were to carry a comb (*kanghā*) in the hair to keep it tidy; they were always to wear a knee-length pair of breeches (*kach*), worn by soldiers of the times; they were to carry a steel bracelet (*karā*) on their right wrist; and they were to be ever armed with a sabre (*kirpān*).[16] In addition to these five emblems, the converts were to observe four rules of conduct (*rahat*): not to cut any hair on any part of their body (this was a repetition of the oath regarding the *kes*); not to smoke, chew tobacco, or consume alcoholic drinks; not to eat an animal which had been slaughtered by being bled to death, as was customary with the Muslims, but only *jhaṭkā* meat, where the animal had been despatched with one blow; and not to molest the person of Muslim women.[17]

At the end of the oath-taking the Guru hailed the converts with a new form of greeting:

> *Vāh guru jī kā khālsā*
> *Vāh guru jī kī fateh*
> The Khalsa are the chosen of God
> Victory be to our God.

---

16 Since they all begin with the letter "k" they are known as the five *kakās*, the letter in the Gurmukhi alphabet corresponding to k.

The *Rahatnāmās* do not prescribe the five *kakās* or the *rahats* with anything like the precision with which Sikh historians have now begun to list them. These were obviously crystallised into a code at a later date.

17 At the time when the Sikhs were fighting Muslims, the Gurus outlawed retaliation against women. This *rahat* was subsequently widened to forbid carnal knowledge of any woman other than one's wife.

Having initiated the five Sikhs, Gobind asked them to baptise him into the new fraternity. The Guru was no longer their superior; he had merged his entity in the Khalsa.[18]

Gobind Singh is said to have explained these innovations in a lengthy address to the assemblage: "I wish you all to embrace one creed and follow one path, obliterating all differences of religion. Let the four Hindu castes, who have different rules laid down for them in the *śāstras* abandon them altogether and, adopting the way of co-operation, mix freely with one another. Let no one deem himself superior to another. Do not follow the old scriptures. Let none pay heed to the Ganges and other places of pilgrimage which are considered holy in the Hindu religion, or adore the Hindu deities, such as Rama, Krishna, Brahma, and Durga, but all should believe in Guru Nanak and his successors. Let men of the four castes receive baptism, eat out of the same vessel, and feel no disgust or contempt for one another."[19]

The newswriter of the Mughal Court who was present on the occasion wrote in his report that: "When the Guru had thus addressed the crowd several Brahmins and Khatris stood up and said that they accepted the religion of Nanak

[18] *Khālsā mero rūp hai Khās*—the Khalsa is exactly like me. Later on, the convention developed of calling a resolution carried out by the majority of the congregation the *gurmatā* and treating it as the order of the Guru.

[19] The above address is based on the report of a newswriter sent to the Mughal court and is vouched for by the Persian historian, Ghulam Mohiuddin. (Teja Singh and Ganda Singh, *A Short History of the Sikhs*, p. 68; Macauliffe, *The Sikh Religion*, v, 93-94.)
In Gobind's own writings there are passages which give the impression that they might be summaries of the address he delivered on this occasion: "He who keeps alight the unquenchable torch of truth and never swerves from the thought of one God; he who is full of love for God and has confidence in Him; he who never puts his faith in fasting, the worship of graves of Muslim saints or of Hindu sepulchres; he who recognises the one God and believes not in pilgrimages, throwing of money to beggars, preserving all forms of life, doing penances or austerities; and in whose heart the light of the Perfect One shines—he is to be recognised as a pure member of the Khalsa." (*Svaīyās. Dasam Granth.*)

and of the other Gurus. Others, on the contrary, said that they would never accept any religion which was opposed to the teaching of the Vedas and *Śāstras*, and that they would not renounce at the bidding of a boy the ancient faith which had descended to them from their ancestors. Thus, though several refused to accept the Guru's religion, about twenty thousand men stood up and promised to obey him, as they had the fullest faith in his divine mission."

The turbulent period that followed this baptismal ceremony did not give the Guru much time to explain the significance of the symbols[20] he made obligatory for his followers.[21] But they are not very difficult to understand. The chief symbol was the wearing of the hair and beard unshorn. This had been customary among ascetics in India from time immemorial. There is reason to believe that all the gurus after Nanak and many of their disciples had abstained from cutting their hair. (The injunction did not surprise the Sikhs, since it was not really an innovation.) By making it obligatory for his followers, Gobind intended to raise an army of soldier-saints who would wield arms only in a righteous cause, as would saints if they were so compelled. The other emblems were complementary to this one and the profession of soldiering.[22]

[20] They have been dealt with in various *rahatnāmās* (codes of conduct) by writers who were contemporaries of the Guru. The better known *rahatnāmās* are of Nand Lal "Goya," Desa Singh, Chaupa Singh, and Prahlad Singh. These authors are, however, not precise on the subject, nor wholly in agreement with each other. Present-day theologians are also somewhat non-committal in explaining the exact significance of the symbols.

[21] There is little doubt that he did proclaim these rules; only their symbolism was left unexplained. The *Sūraj Prakāś*, which does embody the tradition handed down, supports this view (iii, 21).

[22] The *karā* is the most difficult to explain. It was apparently an adaptation of the Hindu custom of tying charms on the wrists of warriors before they went to battle. (The custom survives to this day, with sisters tying coloured strings on the hands of their brothers on the festival of *rakṣā bandhan*.) The steel bracelet had its practical use in guarding the vulnerable portion of the right hand which wielded the *kirpān*, the left hand being protected by the shield.

A more important question than the significance of the
new forms was: did Gobind mean to change the faith of
Nanak? Yes, and no. In its essential beliefs Gobind introduced no change. His Sikhism was that of Nanak, believing
in the One Supreme Creator who was without form or
substance and beyond human comprehension.[23] He condemned the worship of idols.[24] He gave the institution of
Guruship a permanent and abiding character by vesting
it in the immortality of the Granth and in the continuity
of the _Khālsā Panth_. Being the author of so many traditions, he was particularly conscious of the danger of his
followers imposing divinity on him.

> For though my thoughts were lost in prayer
> At the feet of Almighty God,
> I was ordained to establish a sect and lay
>   down its rules.
> But whosoever regards me as Lord
> Shall be damned and destroyed.
>
> I am—and of this let there be no doubt—
> I am but the slave of God, as other men are,
> A beholder of the wonders of creation.[25]
>   _(Bicitra Nāṭak)_

[23] Gobind used many names for God that emphasised the aspect of
power, e.g. _sarb loh_ (all steel). But his favourite name was _akāl purukh_
(timeless person). He also said that God could not be defined:

> He hath no quoit, nor mark, no colour, caste, nor lineage,
> No form, no complexion, outline, nor garb,
> No one can describe Him in any way.
>   _(Jāp Sāhib)_

[24] I am the destroyer of turbulent hillmen
Since they are idolators and I am the breaker of idols.
>   _(Zafarnāmā)_
> Some worship stones and on their heads they bear them,
> Some the phallus strung in necklaces wear its emblem.
> Some behold their god in the south, some to the west bow their head.
> Some worship images, others busy praying to the dead.
> The world is thus bound in false ritual
> And God's secret is still unread.
>   _(Śvaiye)_

[25] In another passage Gobind refuted the claims of divinity made by
others:

Like Nanak, Gobind Singh believed that the sovereign remedy for the ills of mankind was *nām*—a life of prayer. He did not alter the form of prayer—the *Adi Granth* remained the scripture; his own works were never accorded the same sanctity. He disapproved of asceticism[26] and ridiculed the caste system. His motto was: *mānas kī jāt sab ek hī pahcānbo*—know all mankind as one caste. Like Nanak, he believed that the end of life's journey was the merging of the individual in God:

> As sparks flying out of a flame
> Fall back on the fire from which they rise;
> As dust rising from the earth
> Falls back upon the same earth;
> As waves beating upon the shingle
> Recede and in the ocean mingle
> So from God come all things under the sun
> And to God return when their race is run.
>
> *(Akāl Ustat)*

The only change Gobind brought in religion was to expose the other side of the medal. Whereas Nanak had propagated goodness, Gobind Singh condemned evil. One preached the love of one's neighbour, the other the punishment of transgressors. Nanak's God loved His saints; Gobind's God destroyed His enemies.

> God has no friends nor enemies.
> He heeds no hallelujahs nor cares about curses.
> Being the first and timeless
> How could He manifest Himself through these
> Who are born and die?
>
> *(Jāp Sāhib)*

[26] "If you want to practise asceticism," said Gobind, "do it in this way:

> Let thine own house be the forest
> Thy heart the anchorite.
> Eat little, sleep little,
> Learn to love, be merciful and forbear.
> Be mild, be patient,
> Have no lust, nor wrath,
> Greed nor obstinacy."
>
> *(Sabad Hazāre)*

It would be idle to pretend that this change of emphasis was purely theological. The results were visible within a few months of the famous baptismal ceremony, when a sect of pacifists was suddenly transformed into a militant brotherhood of crusaders. The hills around Anandpur began to echo to the beating of wardrums and military commands. Gobind ordained that the day after the Hindu festival of Holi in spring was to be celebrated with mock battles between parties of Sikhs.[27]

The complexion of the Sikh community also underwent a radical change. Up until that time the leadership had remained in the hands of the non-militant urban Khatris[28] from whom the *masands* had been drawn. They had been quite willing to pay lip service to the ideal of a casteless society preached by Nanak, but they were not willing to soil their lips by drinking *amrit* out of the same bowl, as Gobind wanted them to do. Few of them accepted conversion to the new faith. They remained just Sikhs, better known as *Sahajdhārīs* (those-who-take-time-to-adopt), and separated from the *kesādhārī* (hirsute) Khalsa. The bulk of the converts were Jat peasants of the central districts of the Punjab who were technically low in the caste hierarchy. They took over the leadership from the Khatris. The rise of militant Sikhism became the rise of Jat power in the Punjab.

Sikh chronicles maintain that the baptism of twenty thousand Sikhs at Anandpur was followed by mass baptisms all over Northern India. The Guru had dinned into the timid peasantry of the Punjab that they must "take the broom of divine knowledge and sweep away the filth of timidity." Thus did Gobind "train the sparrow to hunt the hawk and one man to fight a legion." Within a few months a new people were born—bearded, beturbanned,

---

[27] The day after Holi is known as Hola Mohalla. The Nihangs foregather in their thousands at Anandpur to participate in mock battles.
[28] In the Punjab the term is used for both Kshatriyas and Vaishyas.

fully armed, and with a crusader's zeal to build a new commonwealth. They implicitly believed that

> The Khalsa shall rule.
> Their enemies will be scattered.
> Only they that seek refuge will be saved.[29]

The eruption of this large and aggressive community in their midst made the hill chiefs, particularly the Raja of Bilaspur, extremely nervous. They realised that if they did not do something about it, the wrath of the Mughal government would fall on them.

The Raja of Bilaspur consulted his fellow chiefs, and they agreed that the Guru should be ejected from the hills. They first tried to provoke him. Bilaspur asked him to pay rent for the territory he occupied. Gobind replied that the lands had been bought freehold by his father and no rent was due. The hillmen encircled Anandpur and stopped supplies of food-grains. The Sikhs, led by Gobind's eldest son, Ajit Singh, who was only a lad of fourteen, broke through the cordon more than once, but eventually the difficulty of getting supplies regularly could not be overcome and the Guru moved out of Anandpur to a small village called Nirmoh near Kiratpur. The Raja of Bilaspur tried to ambush his forces but was defeated and paid the price of having several of his villages plundered in retaliation.

The hill chiefs realised that the Guru was too strong for them, and they petitioned the Emperor for help. Mughal forces from Sirhind and Lahore joined the hillmen and invested the Guru at Nirmoh. The Khalsa held them at bay and, after twenty-four hours of continuous fighting, broke through the besiegers. They also defeated an attempt by the Mughals to circumvent them. The Guru found

---

[29] The lines *Rāj Kare gā Khālsā* are not found in the *Dasam Granth* but are by tradition ascribed to Guru Gobind Singh. They are repeated every time after the supplicatory prayer, the *ardās*.

refuge in Basali. The Raja of Bilaspur made one more attempt to annihilate his forces but, badly beaten, made terms with the Guru, and the Khalsa returned to Anandpur.

Gobind Singh began to prepare himself for the more serious trouble which he knew lay ahead of him. Until then Anandpur was only a fortress in name with a few turrets on the sides of a steep hill. He had it surrounded by a massive wall and stocked it with weapons of war.

The trouble he had anticipated was not long in coming. The hill rajas again approached the Emperor and warned him of the growing power of the Guru. Aurangzeb ordered the *sūbedārs* (district governors) of Sirhind and Lahore to help the rajas destroy the Khalsa. Anandpur was again besieged by a combination of hillmen and Mughals. The stock of food in Anandpur ran out and the attempts to break out of the town were frustrated. The Sikhs held on doggedly until the besiegers were as wearied of fighting as they. The Mughals offered Gobind safe conduct if he evacuated Anandpur. Gobind then set fire to his stores and evacuated the fort with his family and a small band of soldiers who remained with him. He had not gone very far when, contrary to their most solemn oaths, the imperial forces and the hillmen came in pursuit. Gobind entrusted his mother, wife, and two of the younger sons to a Brahmin servant and proceeded southwards. A band of Sikhs under the command of Udai Singh fell back and held the pursuers until they were killed to a man. The rearguard action gave the Guru time to reach Chamkaur, where he and forty men who were left with him built a stockade and decided to fight to a finish.[30]

The gallant little band kept the enemy at bay. Every few hours some of them would issue forth and fight the besiegers until they were killed. Among those who fell at Chamkaur were Gobind's elder sons, Ajit Singh and Jujhar

[30] *Zafarnāmā.*

Singh. When all seemed lost, a Sikh who resembled Gobind Singh put on the Guru's clothes and, like the rest of the party, went out of the stockade to fight. While the besiegers were celebrating their kill, the Guru himself made his escape.

The Guru's life was saved by two Pathans he had known earlier. At Machiwara, where the imperial troops again closed in on him, the Pathans put Gobind in a curtained palanquin and passed the Mughal sentries with the explanation that they were carrying their *pīr*. That was the end of the pursuit as far as the Guru was concerned. He arrived in the village of Jatpura, weary of limb but still full of faith and courage. "I shall strike fire under the hoofs of your horses," he wrote to Aurangzeb, "and I will not let you drink the water of my Punjab."[31]

At Jatpura he learned of the execution of his two remaining sons, Zorawar Singh, aged nine, and Fateh Singh, aged seven,[32] and the death of his own mother from shock. Gobind took the news with stoic calm.[33] "What use is it to

---

[31] *Zafarnāmā.*

[32] According to Sikh chronicles, the boys were betrayed by their Brahmin servant and executed by the order of Wazir Khan, the governor of Sirhind. There is a difference of opinion about the manner of their execution. The current tradition is that they were walled in alive. *Sūraj Prakāś* and *Gur Bilās* state that they were decapitated.

Wazir Khan and his adviser Sucha Nand (who exhorted him to put an end to the boys' lives because "the young ones of a snake are as poisonous") were held by the Sikhs to be equally responsible for the murders.

A part of the *Zafarnāmā* was apparently written before the news of the murder of these children was conveyed to Gobind, because verses 14 and 15 refer only to the death of two of his sons: "It matters little if a jackal through cunning and treachery succeeds in killing two lion cubs, for the lion himself lives to inflict retribution on you." Subsequently, in verse 98, the *Zafarnāmā* mentions the death of all four children.

[33] It is probable that Gobind composed his famous lines *hāl murīdāṇ dā Kahṇā* in a mood of despondence about this time. The poem is one of the very few he wrote in Punjabi.

> Beloved Friend, beloved God, Thou must hear
> Thy servant's plight when Thou art not near.
> The comfort's cloak is as a pall of pest,
> The home is like a serpent's nest.

put out a few sparks when you raise a mighty flame instead?" he wrote.[34]

The news of the dastardly murders spread all over the countryside and thousands of Sikhs flocked to the Guru's camp at Kot Kapura to help him to avenge the crime. At Kot Kapura, Gobind got news that Wazir Khan's forces were marching against him. The Guru now had enough men with him to make a stand. At the village of Khidrana, he turned on his pursuers and scattered them. The village was renamed Muktsar (the pool of salvation).

The Guru spent almost a year in the country around Muktsar. The stay was most fruitful, for hundreds of thousands of Jats of the Malwa region accepted baptism and joined the Khalsa fraternity; among them were the ancestors of the houses of Patiala, Nabha, and Jind whose families had already become Sikhs. Gobind retired for some time to the village of Talwandi Sabo (now called *dam damā*, "breathing place"), where he busied himself with his disciple Mani Singh, preparing a definitive edition of the *Granth*[35] and collecting his own writings which were

---

The wine chokes like the hangman's noose,
The rim of the goblet is like an assassin's knife,
But with Thee shall I in adversity dwell.
Without Thee life of ease is life in hell.

(*Śabad Hazāre*)

[34] *Zafarnāmā*, verse 99. Sikh chronicles state that Emperor Aurangzeb sent for the Guru in the hope that since he had lost everything he would be willing to submit; and that the Guru sent him a reply—the *Zafarnāmā*, or the epistle of victory. It is further maintained that the contents of the *Zafarnāmā* touched the Emperor's heart so that he ordered free egress to the Guru and invited him to court. This version cannot be correct, as the *Zafarnāmā* is defiantly offensive about the Emperor and could never have softened him towards the Guru. It describes Aurangzeb as a deceitful fox and an irreligious man whose oaths on the Koran were not to be trusted. The epistle that the Guru sent must have been in a different tone, because Aurangzeb was in fact induced by it to invite the Guru to meet him.

[35] It is generally believed that the only version of the *Granth* incorporating his father's writings was dictated by the Guru at Talwandi Sabo. This is not correct, for at least two manuscript copies containing the hymns of the ninth Guru are available, and both were compiled before the Guru's arrival at Talwandi Sabo. See Appendix 4.

subsequently put together by Mani Singh and entitled *Dasven Pādśāh kā Granth* (the *Granth* of the tenth emperor) or the *Dasam Granth,* distinct from the first or the *Adi Granth.*[36] The months of intense literary activity gave Dam Dama the new title *guru kī kāśī* (Benares of the Guru).[37]

From Dam Dama Gobind sent a letter[38] to the Emperor telling him of the perfidy of his officials, particularly of the crime committed by Wazir Khan of Sirhind. Gobind's emissary travelled to the Deccan and succeeded in handing the letter to the Emperor. Aurangzeb was apparently moved by the contents of the letter and issued orders that the Guru was not to be molested any further. But Aurangzeb either did not want to or was unable to punish Wazir Khan. Gobind left Dam Dama to go and see Aurangzeb himself. He got as far as Rajputana when he heard of the death of the Emperor at Ahmednagar on March 2, 1707.

The battle for succession started between Aurangzeb's sons. Bahadur Shah had shown consideration to Gobind in his troubles with the hill chiefs. The Guru felt it was his turn to help the prince and he sent a detachment of Sikh horsemen who fought in the battle of Jajau on June 8, 1707. When Bahadur Shah was firmly in the royal seat, Gobind came to Agra to pay him a formal visit. He was welcomed and given a jewelled scarf and presents worth Rs. 60,000.[39] Gobind stayed in Agra for four months, but the Emperor did not take any action on behalf of the Guru against Wazir Khan, and left for Rajputana. Gobind and his retinue of horsemen accompanied the imperial troops without participating in any of their battles.

[36] See Appendix 4.

[37] It is said that one day the Guru flung a handful of reed pens over the heads of the congregation, saying: "Here we will create a pool of literature. No one of my Sikhs should remain illiterate." The *Rahatnāmā* of Desa Singh states: "Brother, the letters of the Gurmukhi alphabet, let one Sikh learn from another."

[38] This was obviously not the *Zafarnāmā.*

[39] *Bahādur Shāh Nāmā* (August 2, 1707).

Bahadur Shah turned towards the Deccan to suppress the rebellion of his brother Kam Baksh. Gobind and his band also went south. They arrived in Nanded, a small town on the banks of the Godavari, in September 1707, and encamped there.

All along the march the Guru continued instructing his followers and those who cared to come to his prayer meetings.[40] His guards were not allowed to question or stop anyone. One evening two young Pathans entered his tent and, finding the Guru alone, stabbed him in the abdomen. The motive for the murderous assault was never known, since the assassins[41] were slain immediately. The Guru's wounds were stitched and it was hoped that he would recover. But the stitches burst a few days later and Gobind realised that his end was near. He assembled his followers and told them the line of Gurus was to end with him and the Sikhs were thereafter to look upon the *Granth*[42] as the symbol of all the ten Gurus and their constant guide. The Guru died an hour and a half after midnight on October 7, 1708.[43]

Guru Gobind Singh was the *beau ideal* of the Punjabis. He was a handsome man, whose feats as a cavalier, swordsman, and archer were enough to endear him to a people

[40] "At this time the army was marching southwards towards Burhanpur. Guru Gobind Singh, one of the descendants of Nanak, had come into these districts to travel and accompanied the royal camp. He was in the habit of constantly addressing assemblies of worldly persons, religious fanatics, and all other sorts of people." (*Tārīkh-i-Bahādur Shāhī*. Elliot and Dowson, VII, 566.)

[41] There is little doubt that the assassins were hirelings of Wazir Khan, who wanted to prevent the Guru from turning the Emperor against him.

[42] It should be noted that the *Granth* that was installed as the Guru was the *Adi*—the first *Granth*—and not the compilation of his own works.

[43] The account of the Guru's travels from Dam Dama, his note to Aurangzeb, his meeting with Bahadur Shah, and his assassination are based on the account of a contemporary writer, Saina Pat, recorded in his *Gur Sobha*. This is at variance with the current Sikh tradition. See *Last Days of Guru Gobind Singh*, by Ganda Singh, and *A Short Sketch of the Life and Works of Guru Gobind Singh*, by Bhagat Lakshman Singh.

who set store by physical prowess. Stories of his prodigious strength and valour multiplied, and he became a legendary figure in his lifetime. The tips of his arrows were said to be mounted with gold to provide for the family of the foe they transfixed, and he was reputed to be able to send his shafts as far as the eye could see. The Punjabis pictured him leading them to battle on his roan stallion. On one hand fluttered his white hawk; in the other flashed his sabre. Their favourite titles for him were, the rider of the blue horse (*nile ghore dā asvār*), the lord of the white hawks (*citiāṇ bājāṇ vālā*), and the wearer of plumes (*kalgīdhar*). While Gobind's picture was in the minds of the people, his words were on their lips. For the amant, there was the sensuous poetry of the earlier days at Paonta; for the downcast, there was the inspiration and reaffirmation of faith; for the defeated, there was the Epistle of Victory (*Zafarnāmā*), breathing defiance in every line; for the crusader, there were the heroic ballads full of martial cadence in their staccato lines with a beat like that of a wardrum. Above all, in everything he wrote or spoke or did there was a note of buoyant hope (*caṛhdī kalā*) and the conviction that even if he lost his life, his mission was bound to succeed.

> O Lord, these boons of Thee I ask,
> Let me never shun a righteous task,
> Let me be fearless when I go to battle,
> Give me faith that victory will be mine,
> Give me power to sing Thy praise,
> And when comes the time to end my life,
> Let me fall in mighty strife.[44]

The two hundred years between Nanak's proclamation of faith[45] (A.D. 1499) and Gobind's founding of the Khalsa

[44] *Caṇḍī Caritr.*

[45] "The sword which carried the Khalsa's way to glory was undoubtedly forged by Gobind, but the steel had been provided by Nanak, who had obtained it, as it were, by smelting the Hindu ore and burning out the

Panth (A.D. 1699) can be neatly divided into two almost equal parts.[46] In the first hundred years the five gurus pronounced the ideals of a new social order for the Punjab. The religion was to be one acceptable to both the Muslims and Hindus; it was to be monotheistic, non-idolatrous, and free of meaningless form and ritual. The social order was to embrace all the people; no class was to be beyond the pale, and even though the caste system continued to count when it came to making matrimonial alliances,[47] it was abolished in matters of social intercourse. The doors of Sikh temples were thrown open to everyone and in the Guru's *langar* the Brahmin and the untouchable broke their bread as members of the same family. The code of this new order was the non-denominational anthology of hymns, the *Granth*; its symbol, the Harimandir, an edifice whose first stone was laid by a Muslim, the rest being built by Hindus and Sikhs together.

It is not surprising that the Sikhism of the first five gurus and the *Granth* found ready acceptance among the masses. They responded to it because it was eclectic, simple, and propounded by men who were too modest either to claim kinship with God or to clothe their utterances in the garb of prophecy. What they wrote or said had a familiar ring in the people's ears. The Hindus caught the wisdom of the Vedas, of which they knew but little because of the monopoly over Sanskrit learning maintained by the Brahmins. The Muslims were reminded of the exhortations of the Sufis. To both the Hindus and the Muslims, the message of the gurus came in a language they understood. Although

---

dross of indifference and superstition of the masses and the hypocrisy and phariseeism of the priests." (Narang, *Transformation of Sikhism*.)

[46] The three gurus represent, as it were, the three aspects of the Hindu Trinity. Nanak, like Brahma, was the creator of Sikhism; Arjun, like Vishnu, its preserver; and Gobind, like Shiva, the destroyer of its enemies.

[47] Neither the gurus nor any members of their families married outside the Kshatriya castes. As has been noted earlier, Nanak was a Bedi, Angad a Trehan, Amar Das a Bhalla, and the remaining seven were Sodhis belonging to one family.

this fact prejudiced the spreading of Sikhism to those who could not understand Punjabi, within the Punjab its appeal was irresistible. It had all the elements of a national faith and until it crystallised into a distinct sect with a political purpose, it continued to excite the admiration of all Punjabis.

The second period of a hundred years saw the development of traditions which supplemented this social order. The sixth guru was the first to appeal to arms; the tenth put the army on a regular footing. The movement also found its martyrs and heroes: Arjun, Tegh Bahadur, and the sons of Gobind wore the crown of martyrdom; Hargobind and Gobind, the halo of heroism. The movement had its hard inner core consisting of nearly a hundred thousand baptised Khalsa, and a much larger number of close associates among the Sahajdhari Sikhs.

The movement had the active support of the vast majority of Punjabi Hindus who joined it in large numbers and for a time gave it the semblance of Hindu resistance against the onslaught of Islam. This was particularly so in the years following the death of Guru Gobind Singh, when the Muslim ruling class exploited the religious sentiments of the Muslim masses and for a time were able to stem the rising tide of Punjabi nationalism.

PART II
THE AGRARIAN UPRISING

CHAPTER 6

THE RISE AND FALL OF BANDA BAHADUR

The First Round:
Peasant Upsurge in Eastern Punjab

GURU GOBIND SINGH tried for many months to persuade Bahadur Shah to take action against Wazir Khan before he arrived at the conclusion that he would obtain no justice from the Mughals. He continued to negotiate with the Emperor, but decided to send one of his followers back to the Punjab to rouse the peasantry in the event that the negotiations proved fruitless. Although there were many old and trusted disciples with him, the choice fell on a comparative stranger whom the Guru had known for only a few weeks. This was an ascetic named Lachman Das, who had spent the last fifteen years or more of his life in a hermitage on the banks of the river Godavari. Being a northerner, he was well acquainted with the Guru's mission and in full sympathy with it. The Guru caught the fanatic gleam in the hermit's eye and felt that in the spare frame of the ascetic smouldered the Promethean fire which could be fanned into a flame. He summoned Lachman Das and charged him with the duty of punishing the men who had persecuted the Sikhs and murdered his sons. He gave Lachman Das a new name which the latter had himself chosen to describe his relationship to the Guru—*bandā*, or the slave.[1]

[1] Banda was born in 1670 at Rajauri (Poonch) of Rajput parents and named Lachman Das. He joined an order of *bairāgī* (mendicants) at an early age and was given a new name, Madho Das. He went south and spent many years in Hindu monasteries in Central India. He had set up an establishment of his own at Nanded, where he had lived for fifteen years before he met Guru Gobind.

Guru Gobind's choice of Banda in preference to many of his own companions has never been adequately explained. From the chronology of the Guru's travels, it appears that he did not live more than one month in Nanded. It is hardly likely that he would have chosen a complete

Guru Gobind Singh armed Banda with five arrows from his quiver and gave him his own standard and battle drum. He also issued orders (*hukamnāmās*) to the Sikhs, urging them to volunteer for service.

Banda left the Deccan with a small band and came northwards. In the vicinity of Delhi he learned that the Emperor, Bahadur Shah, was still involved fighting his own brother in the Deccan and that the Rajputs were in open revolt. Banda also received information of the murderous assault on Gobind Singh. Before the assassin's dagger could achieve its fatal consummation, he planted the Guru's standard in a village thirty-five miles from the capital and forwarded the Guru's letters ordering the Sikhs to join him.[2]

---

stranger to lead the Sikhs unless he had either known of the man earlier or Banda had already earned the reputation of a leader. Some writers have naïvely accepted a dramatised and obviously imaginary meeting between the Guru and Banda given by Ahmed Shah of Batala in his *Zikr-i-Guruān vā Ibtidā-i-Singhān vā Mazhab-i-Eshān*. Ahmed Shah does not claim to have heard the story from any one who was present. The *Siyār-ul-Mutākherīn*, which is not otherwise very reliable, is much closer to reality in stating that Banda was a Sikh by persuasion, that is, "one of those attached to the tenets of Guru Gobind and who from their birth or from the moment of their admission, never cut or shave either their beard or whiskers, or any hair whatever of their body." (Briggs translation, pp. 72-73.)

At that time the distinction between a formally baptised "Singh" and a Hindu who, while retaining his Hindu name and practices, was in close sympathy with the Khalsa, was not very great.

It is possible that Banda was only one of a number of Sikhs sent by the Guru to foment rebellion in the Punjab but, being the most successful, was able to gain preponderance over all the others and became the leader of the entire community.

For a discussion of whether or not Banda was baptised as a Khalsa, see *Sikh Review*, April 1961.

2 Bahadur Shah did not learn of the activities of Banda nor of Banda's connection with the late Guru Gobind Singh until much later. In the *Bahādur Shāh Nāmā* dated November 17, 1708 there is a report regarding "The disposal of the movable property left by Guru Gobind Nanak. . . . It was considerable and according to rule ought to be confiscated. The Emperor with the remark that he was not in favour of sequestering the goods of a *darveś*, ordered the whole to be relinquished to the heirs. . . . One Ajit Singh, who passed as the Guru's son, was brought to the Em-

Although the Guru had specifically restricted his role
to that of military commander of a punitive expedition,[3]
Banda widened it to embrace a spiritual ministry as well.
Crowds began to flock to his camp; men in arms to join
his colours; women to seek his blessings for their families.[4]
He preached sermons and gave benedictions. Having an
avowed contempt for worldly goods, he gave away the
offerings people placed before him. As stories of his piety
and generosity spread, more men and money began to
pour in. Encouraged by the response, Banda issued a
proclamation offering protection to any one "threatened
by thieves, dacoits or highway robbers, troubled by Mohammedan bigots, or in any way subjected to injustice or
ill-treatment."[5] The proclamation was like a spark in a
highly inflammable situation. The peasants of Malwa rose
against the zamindars and local officials. Banda opened
the flood-gates to a sea of pent-up hatred, and all he could
do was to ride on the crest of the wave of violence that he
had let loose. He could not, nor did he try to, direct its
course, knowing full well that he who rides a tiger cannot
afford to dismount.

Banda left the neighbourhood of Delhi and travelled

---

peror, was invested with a robe of honour, and taken into imperial
service." (This Ajit Singh was an adopted son of Mata Sundari. He was
later executed in Delhi.)

[3] Gyani Gyan Singh in his *Panth Prakāś* has Banda claim the following
mission:

> To wreak vengeance on the Turk hath the
>   Guru sent me who am his slave.
> I will kill and ruin Wazira's household;
>   I will plunder and rob Sirhind.
> I will avenge the murders of the Guru's sons,
>   then destroy the chieftains of the hills.
> When all these I have accomplished, then
>   know me as Banda, the Slave of the Guru.

[4] "Those who asked for sons he blessed with sons; to those who asked
for milk he gave milch cattle. If any one came stricken with pain, he
prayed for him and removed his suffering. . . ." (Ratan Singh Bhangu,
Prācīn Panth Prakāś, p. 94.)

[5] Sohan Singh, *Bandā Singh Bahādur*, p. 39.

northwards along the Grand Trunk Road. He entered
Sonepat, looted the state treasury and the homes of the
rich, and distributed whatever he got among his men. He
sent a column to take Kaithal and led another to Samana.

Kaithal fell without much resistance and was spared.
But a grim fate awaited Samana, a wealthy town with
many palatial buildings and mosques. It was also the home
of the executioners of the ninth guru, Tegh Bahadur, and
Gobind's two sons. The town was stormed on November
26, 1709. The frenzied followers of Banda overcame resistance by sheer weight of numbers. The defenders did
not expect to receive any quarter from the attackers. They
fought on for three days until all that remained was a heap
of smouldering ruins and ten thousand corpses strewn
about the streets.[6] Samana was the first notable victory to
Sikh arms.[7]

The fate of Samana left no doubt in the mind of Wazir
Khan, the subedar of Sirhind, of the real objectives of
Banda. Armed peasants from all over the central districts
of the Punjab were reported to be converging towards
Sirhind. Wazir Khan sent urgent messages for help to
Bahadur Shah and took the only chance he had of holding
out by preventing the Majhail peasants north of the Sutlej
from crossing the river and joining the men of Malwa
under Banda. An army consisting largely of Afghans from
Malerkotla was sent to keep the Majhails on the north
side of the river, while strong detachments were posted on
the fords and all ferries grounded.

[6] Sohan Lal, *Umdāt-ut-Tawārīkh*, I, 78.

[7] "It is unnecessary to state the particulars of this memorable invasion
which, from all accounts, appears to have been one of the severest scourges
with which a country was ever afflicted. Every excess that the most wanton
barbarity could commit, every cruelty that an unappeased appetite of
revenge could suggest, was inflicted upon the miserable inhabitants of the
provinces through which they passed. Life was only granted to those who
conformed to the religion and adopted the habits and dress of the Sikhs."
(Sir J. Malcolm, *Sketch of the Sikhs.*)
The tales of atrocities are supported by Sikh historians, Gyan Singh in
Śamśir Khālsā and Ratan Singh Bhangu in *Prācīn Panth Prakāś.*

Banda proceeded on his triumphant march through the heart of Malwa. He plundered Ghuram, Shahabad, Mustafabad, Kapuri, and Sadhaura and came to Sirhind, detested in the eyes of the Sikhs for the executions of their Guru's sons, and the home of the murderers Wazir Khan and Dewan Sucha Nand.

Banda's progress made the Afghans on the Sutlej anxious for the safety of their rear and they deployed a part of their forces to oppose him. The Majhails utilised the opportunity and crossed the river near Ropar. The Afghans fought a delaying action and then retreated before they could be crushed between the jaws of the Majhail-Malwa nut-cracker. Banda joined the advancing Majhails half-way from Ropar.

The winter months were spent in training and collecting arms. Since Banda promised land to the landless and loot to everyone, there was no dearth of recruits. But he was not able to get guns or many muskets. Nevertheless, by spring he felt strong enough to measure swords with the Mughals, and he led an enormous host against Sirhind.

Wazir Khan had not been idle. He convinced the Muslim landowners that if Banda won, they would be ruined. He also persuaded the mullahs to preach a holy war against the infidel.[8]

Wazir Khan's troops met Banda's peasants ten miles outside the city and immediately ordered his batteries to open fire. The peasants charged the cannons and came to grips with the enemy. The preponderance of numbers gave them an advantage in the hand-to-hand struggle that en-

---

[8] There are many accounts of the battle of Sirhind. The most reliable of them is that of Mohammed Hashim Khafi Khan in the *Muntakhib-ul-Lubāb*. He mentions Wazir Khan's forces as comprising 15,000 men equipped with muskets and cannon. In addition, there were the volunteer *ghāzīs* (crusaders) armed with swords, spears, bows and arrows. Banda's forces must have considerably outnumbered Wazir Khan's. But he had neither cannon nor elephants, only a few horsemen and some musketeers. His army was largely composed of peasants armed with spears, hatchets, and farming implements which could be used as weapons.

sued. Wazir Khan was killed and the morale of his troops collapsed. The battle ended in the complete rout and massacre of the Mughal army and the _ghāzīs_. "Not a man of the army of Islam escaped with more than his life and the clothes he stood in," wrote Khafi Khan. "Horsemen and footmen fell under the swords of the infidels, who pursued them as far as Sirhind."[9]

Two days later Banda stormed Sirhind. He entered the town on May 24, 1710. Wazir Khan was dead, but Sucha Nand, the Dewan who had pressed him to execute Guru Gobind's sons, was taken alive. Besides the odium which attached to the names of these men for their share in the crime, the peasants had their own grievances. "I have heard from reliable people of the neighbourhood," wrote a diarist of the times, "that during the time of the late Khan there was no cruelty that he had not inflicted upon the poor subjects, and that there was no seed of which he now reaped the fruit that he had not sown for himself."[10]

Sirhind was destroyed in detail; only a few mausolea were spared. Wazir Khan's palace and the treasury of Sucha Nand yielded handsome booty to the conquerors.

Banda was now virtual master of the territories between the Jumna and the Sutlej, yielding an annual revenue of thirty-six lacs of rupees. His sun was in the ascendant. Either from conviction or fear or profit (or a combination of the three) a great many Hindu and Muslim peasants accepted conversion to Sikhism.[11] Banda was too shrewd to place much reliance on the loyalties of the new converts and he made the old fort of Mukhlisgarh, in the safety

---

[9] _Muntakhib-ul-Lubāb_ II, 654; _Later Mughuls_, pp. 27-28 (where the atrocities committed by Banda's peasants are mentioned in detail).

[10] Mohammed Qasim, _Ibrat Nāmā_, 20-21.

[11] Names of officers on record bear testimony to quick conversions, e.g. Ali Singh, Mir Nasir Singh, Dindar Singh. This is supported by a contemporary account by Aminuddaulah: "A large number of Mohammedans abandoned Islam and followed the misguided path and took solemn oaths and firm pledges to stand by him." (Ganda Singh, _Bandā Singh Bahādur_, p. 73.)

of the Himalayas, his headquarters. Thus, Banda the *bai-rāgī*—hermit, who as a military commander had become Banda *bahādur*—the brave, assumed his third incarnation as Banda *pādśāh*, the Emperor. He introduced a new calendar dating from his capture of Sirhind. He had new coins struck to mark his reign, bearing the names of Guru Nanak and Gobind. His seal had inscribed on it not only the names of the gurus but also the two things which had contributed most to the popularity and power of the Sikhs and their church—the *degh* or cauldron in the Guru's *langar* and the *tegh*, the sword of the Khalsa.[12]

At Mukhlisgarh, Banda learned that Bahadur Shah, after subduing his brother in the Deccan, was contemplating the subjugation of Rajasthan and not likely to return to Delhi before the monsoons. Banda decided to utilize the opportunity to destroy the remaining vestiges of Mughal rule in Northern India.

In the height of summer, when the river bed was almost dry, Banda crossed the Jumna and invested Saharanpur. His arrival was a signal for Gujjar herdsmen to rise against the Nawabs and zamindars, who had oppressed them for many decades. They declared themselves *Nānakprasth* (fol-

---

[12] The Persian inscription on Banda's coins was as follows:

OBVERSE

Sikkā zad har do ālam tegh-i-Nānak sāhib ast
fateh Gobind Singh śāh-i-śāhān fazl-i-sacā sāhib ast.
Coins struck for the two worlds with the sword of Nanak and the victory granted by the grace of Gobind Singh, King of Kings and the true Emperor.

REVERSE

Zarb ba amān-ud-dahar masavarat śahar zīnat-ul-takht-i-mubarak bakht.
Struck in the haven of refuge, the beautiful city, the ornament of the blessed throne.

The inscription on Banda's seal became a model for future inscriptions on Sikh coins and seals:

degh o tegh o fateh o nusrat-i-bedrang
yaft az Nānak guru Gobind Singh.
Through hospitality and the sword to unending victory granted by Nanak and Guru Gobind Singh.

lowers of Nanak) and joined their fellow peasants from the Punjab. The local *faujdār* (military commander), and those who could get away, fled to Delhi. Of those that remained "many men of noble and respectable families fell fighting bravely and obtained the honour of martyrdom."[13]

Saharanpur was ruthlessly plundered. After Saharanpur, fell the neighbouring towns of Behat and Ambheta. Just as the monsoons broke, Nanauta was captured by the Gujjars and razed to the ground.

Panic spread in the Jumna-Gangetic Doab. The rich fled eastwards to Oudh or northwards into the hills. The sight of one Sikh lancer on horseback was enough to terrorise a whole village.[14]

Banda's progress eastwards was halted by the monsoons and the resistance put up at Jalalabad. He also received appeals from the peasants of the Jullundur Doab to help them against the Mughal *faujdār*. He raised the siege of Jalalabad and recrossed the Jumna before the monsoon made it unfordable.

The news of Banda's return to the Punjab was enough to put heart into the Malwa peasantry. They defeated the Mughal *faujdār* at Rahon (the *faujdār* was the first victim of the tactics for which the Sikhs became famous. This was the *dhāī phuṭ*—hit, run, and turn back to hit again. They seized Jullundur and Hoshiarpur and by the autumn of 1710 liberated the whole of Jullundur Doab.

[13] *Muntakhib-ul-Lubāb*, II, 655.
[14] The revolution that had taken place in one year is well summed up by Irvine in his *Later Mughuls*: "A low scavenger or leather dresser, the lowest of the low in Indian estimation, had only to leave home and join the Guru [referring to Banda], when in a short time he would return to his birth-place as its ruler with his order of appointment in his hand. As soon as he set foot within the boundaries, the well-born and wealthy went out to greet him and escort him home. Arrived there, they stood before him with joined palms, awaiting his orders. . . . Not a soul dared to disobey an order, and men who had often risked themselves in battlefields became so cowed down that they were afraid even to remonstrate. Hindus who had not joined the sect were not exempt from these." (i, 98-99.)

The Second Round:
From the Plains to the Hills

The revolt spread across the Sutlej over the whole of the Majha country. Starting from Amritsar, the peasant armies marched northwards towards the hills, taking Kalanaur, Batala, and Pathankot. Then they overran the tract between the Sutlej and the Ravi. The Punjab became like a surging sea of free peasantry with only two small islands of Mughal authority in its midst—the capital city of Lahore and the Afghan town of Kasur.

Mughal officials tried to suppress the uprising by appealing to the religious sentiments of the Mohammedan peasantry. For some time this policy paid dividends and the newly-recruited *ghāzīs* helped the Mughal militia to keep the Sikhs at bay a few miles from Lahore. Then their sympathies with the peasants overcame the feeling of religious animosity which had been whipped up by the landlords, and they turned back to their homes. The Sikhs advanced, decimated the militiamen near the village of Shilwal, and swarmed over the countryside round Lahore.

From the Jumna to the Ravi and beyond, the only person who mattered was Banda, and the only power that commanded respect was that of the peasant armies. In those fateful days, had Banda shown more enterprise he could have captured Delhi and Lahore and so changed the entire course of Indian history. But the otherwise daring Banda showed a lack of decision which proved fatal to his dreams. Meanwhile, Bahadur Shah abandoned his plans to subdue the Rajputs and without pausing at Delhi hurried north to the Punjab.[15]

[15] Khafi Khan writes: "For eight or nine months, and from two or three days march from Delhi to the environs of Lahore, all the towns and places of note were pillaged by these unclean wretches, and trodden under foot and destroyed. Men in countless numbers were slain, the whole country was wasted, and mosques and tombs were razed. . . . These infidels had set up a new rule, and had forbidden the shaving of the hair of the head

The Emperor ordered a general mobilisation of all his forces in Delhi, Uttar Pradesh, and Oudh, and called for volunteers for a *jihād* (holy war)[16] against the Sikhs. He also persuaded the Bundela Rajputs to join in the campaign. With him were his four sons and the flower of the Mughal army. Firoz Khan was appointed leader of the campaign.

Firoz Khan took the offensive at once and defeated the peasant army at Amingarh. Within a month the imperial armies recovered possession of Thanesar, Karnal, and Shahabad. By December 1710, Mughal rule was re-established in the Malwa plains.

Banda retreated to his fortress in the mountains. The concourse of Mughals, Meos, Pathans, Afghans, and Rajputs went after him. When the fleeing peasants came in sight of the hills, they turned on their pursuers and severely mauled the van of the Mughal army. The name of Banda had become a source of terror. He was reputed to be able to deflect a bullet from its course and work such spells that neither spear nor sword could injure his men.[17]

Imperial armies eventually surrounded the fortress of Mukhlisgarh. But Banda and a small band of picked swordsmen made a sortie one night and hacked their way out of the imperial cordon.

Next morning (December 11, 1710) the Mughals

---

and beard. . . . The revolt and ravages of this perverse sect were brought under the notice of His Majesty, and greatly troubled him" (32-33).

[16] Bahadur Shah rightly suspected that most Hindus were in sympathy with the rebellion and had secretly accepted conversion to the Sikh faith. Early in September 1710 he issued a proclamation to "all Hindus employed in the Imperial offices to shave off their beards." (*Bahādur Shāh Nāmā*.)

Iradat Khan, a courtier in Bahadur Shah's camp, wrote: "Though this insurrection was not of such importance as to disturb the general repose of the Empire, yet His Majesty, Defender of the Faith, hearing that the malice of the rebels was directed against the religion, thought it his duty to engage them in person." (Syed Mohammed Latif, *History of the Punjab*, p. 277.)

[17] Khafi Khan wrote that "the Sikhs in their Fakir dress struck terror in the royal troops." (*Muntakhib-ul-Lubāb*, II, 669-70.)

stormed the fortress and captured the few men who had remained. Among them was one Gulab Singh who resembled and had dressed himself like Banda. The exultation over the capture of the dreaded Banda turned to chagrin when it was discovered that "the hawk had flown and they had trapped an owl instead."

Bahadur Shah spent his wrath on the handful of prisoners who were taken and on the innocent Raja of Nahan, into whose territories Banda had escaped. The Raja and the heroic Gulab Singh were put in iron cages and sent to Delhi. Other prisoners, including thirty retainers who had accompanied the Nahan Raja to plead for their ruler, were handed over to the executioner.

Within fifteen days of his escape from Mukhlisgarh, Banda began to send *hukamnāmās* exhorting the people to liberate the Punjab once more and to join him at Kiratpur in the Shivalik hills. He decided to secure the submountainous hinterland before descending on the plains. His first victim was the tormentor of his guru, Raja Bhim Chand of Bilaspur.

The ageing Bhim Chand did not have the stamina to fight the tireless Banda. Bilaspur capitulated and was sacked. Mandi, Kulu, and Chamba submitted of their own accord.

In the spring of 1711, Banda came down into the plains again. Early in June 1711 an engagement was fought at Bahrampur near Jammu, in which the Mughals were worsted. Banda took Bahrampur and Raipur and then sacked Batala. The Emperor came in hot pursuit and Banda again retreated into the hills. Once again Bahadur Shah (who had begun to show symptoms of a deranged mind) wreaked his vengeance on innocent men and women: an order was issued for the wholesale massacre of Sikhs.[18]

The Emperor reached Lahore in August 1711. For the next five months his courtiers fed him on stories of Mu-

[18] Khushal Chand, *Tārīkh-i-Mohammed Shāhī*, 224-A.

ghal victories over Banda's rabble. But as the days rolled by with Banda still free, still defiant, the Emperor became a depressive melancholic. He died on February 28, 1712.

The battle for succession between the Emperor's sons began immediately. It was too good an opportunity for Banda to miss. He descended on the plains, re-occupied Sadhaura, and once more sent out proclamations.

The Third Round:
Banda's Final Stand at Gurdaspur Nangal,
His Capture and Execution

The battle for succession was eventually won by Jahandar Shah. As soon as he had disposed of his brothers, he turned his attention to the rebellion in the Punjab. Mughal armies again closed in on Sadhaura and Mukhlisgarh. The siege dragged on for eight long months. He had some relief towards the end of 1712, when the attention of the besieging force was diverted by the rebellion of Jahandar's nephew, Farrukh Siyar. But Banda was unable to come down into the plains and as soon as Farrukh Siyar became Emperor, he sent two very energetic officers, Abdus Samad Khan, and his son Zakarya Khan, with specific instructions to destroy Banda.

Abdus Samad Khan's troops drove Banda out of Sadhaura and Mukhlisgarh and compelled him to retreat further into the Himalayan fastnesses. The peasant uprising was considered over. Abdus Samad Khan and his son were recalled to Delhi, where they were loaded with honours. They were ordered to direct their energies to the reconquest of Rajasthan.

Banda disappeared from the Punjab scene for over a year. He found a haven of peace in a small village a few miles above Jammu (since named after him Dera Baba Banda), and lived there with his two wives and children. Peasant leaders were, however, active in the plains and Farrukh Siyar had to send Abdus Samad Khan and his son back to the Punjab to chastise "that sect of mean and detestable Sikhs."[19] An army of seven thousand peasants attacked Ropar and, though the attack was repelled, it was apparent that the people were restive again. In February 1715 Banda came down from his mountain retreat to measure his sword again with the Mughals.

Abdus Samad Khan assembled an army of Mughals, Pathans, Bundela Rajputs, and Rajputs of Katoch and Jasrota and moved northwards to face Banda.

In a village near Batala Banda dug himself in. Before he could complete his defence fortifications, the imperial forces came upon him. Artillery blasted Banda into the open field. Banda stood his ground and, to the amazement of Abdus Samad Khan, almost trounced his vastly superior forces. Even after the Mughals had recovered from the shock of Banda's violent assault and the tide of battle had begun to turn in their favour, they were unable to press the advantage to a successful conclusion. "For although vigorously pursued, he retired from post to post, and like a savage of the wilderness from thicket to thicket, losing an endless number of men and occasioning losses to his pursuers."[20]

Banda fled northwards. But instead of disappearing into the mountains, he stopped a few miles above the present town of Gurdaspur and turned back to face his pursuers. He cut a canal and flooded the surrounding country in the hope that this would prevent the imperial artillery from getting too close to him. The operation proved to be the decisive factor in his defeat, for, although it prevented the besiegers' cannon from being placed within range, it also cut him off from supplies of food. Abdus Samad Khan surrounded Banda's artificial island and waited patiently for his victims to starve themselves into submission.

The siege dragged on interminably. There were occasional sorties by Banda's men to get provisions, and at-

[19] Mohammed Hadi Kamwar Khan, *Tazkira-us-Salātīn Chughtiyā*, 176-B.
[20] *Siyār-ul-Mutākherīn*, 77.

tempts by the Mughals to test the Sikh defences. An eye-witness gives the following account of the siege: "The brave and daring deeds of the infernal Sikhs was wonderful. Twice or thrice every day some forty or fifty of these black-faced infidels came out of their enclosure to gather grass for their cattle, and when the combined forces of the imperialists went to oppose them, they made an end of the Mughals with arrows, muskets, and small swords, and disappeared. Such was the terror of the Sikhs and the fear of the sorceries of the Sikh chief that the Commanders of this army prayed that God might so ordain things that Banda should seek safety in his flight from the fortress."[21]

The cordon round Banda was tightened by large reinforcements sent from Delhi. Abdus Samad Khan raised a wall around the island to make egress impossible. So great was the belief in Banda's magical powers and so acute the anxiety to get him that even dogs and cats that strayed out of his fortress were immediately destroyed (lest Banda may have undergone a feline or canine transformation to make his escape).

Banda's provisions ran out. His men ate their horses, mules, and even the forbidden oxen. Then dysentery broke out in epidemic form. Banda's right-hand man, Binod Singh, suggested making a mass sortie and trusting their fate to the Guru. Banda pleaded with his men to hold out a little longer until the monsoon compelled the Mughals to raise the siege. Disagreement and bickering led to open defiance of Banda's authority. Binod Singh and a small band slipped out under cover of darkness, cut their way through the Mughal guards, and escaped to the hills.

Banda held on doggedly. At the end of eight months not one of the besieged garrison had strength left to wield his sword or spear. They accepted an assurance from Abdus Samad Khan that he would intercede on their behalf with

21 Mohammed Qasim, *Ibrat Nāmā*, 42.

the Emperor, and laid down arms on December 17, 1715.[22]

Abdus Samad Khan showed the manner in which he meant to plead for the lives of the vanquished foe. He ordered the immediate execution of over two hundred of the prisoners and filled "that extensive plain with blood as if it had been a dish."[23] The remainder, including Banda and his family, were put in chains and sent first to Lahore and then to Delhi.

Banda's hands were manacled to two soldiers on either side, his feet bound in fetters, an iron collar put round his neck, and he and his guards locked inside an iron cage. The other prisoners were likewise secured by iron chains around their necks, hands, and feet, and marched between flanks of Mughal soldiers. Zakarya Khan, who escorted the captives to Delhi, rounded up all the Sikhs he could find in the villages along his route until he had seven hundred bullock carts full of severed heads and over seven hundred prisoners. The gory caravan passed through Sirhind and reached Delhi at the end of February 1716. The captives were paraded through the streets. Banda was dressed in gold brocade to mock his pretensions to royalty; other prisoners had fool's caps put on their heads. Flanking the prisoners were soldiers bearing two thousand Sikh heads mounted on spears. The scene is described by an eye-witness in the following words: "Those unfortunate Sikhs, who had been reduced to this last extremity, were quite happy and contented with their fate; not the slightest sign of dejection or humility was to be seen on their

[22] Banda's heroic stand won admiration from his enemies. The contemporary historian Kamwar Khan wrote: "It was by the grace of God and not by wisdom or bravery that this came to happen. It is known to everyone that the late Emperor Bahadur Shah, with four royal princes and numerous generals, had made efforts to repress this rebellion, but it was all fruitless, and now that infidel of the Sikhs and a few thousand of his companions have been starved into surrender." (Mohammed Hadi Kamwar Khan, *Tazkirā-us-Salātin Chughtiyā*, 179.)

[23] *Muntakhib-ul-Lubāb*, viii.

faces. In fact most of them, as they passed along on their camels, seemed happy and cheerful, joyfully singing the sacred hymns of their Scripture. And, if any one from among those in the lanes and bazaars called out to them that their own excesses had reduced them to that condition, they quickly retorted saying that it had been so willed by the Almighty and that their capture and misfortune was in accordance with His will. And, if any one said: 'Now you will be killed,' they shouted: 'Kill us. When were we afraid of death?' "[24]

The executions began on March 5, 1716 and continued for a week. They were watched by thousands of citizens, including two Englishmen who were then in attendance at the Mughal court. In a despatch dated March 10, 1716, they described what they saw:

"The great Rebel Gooroo who has been for these twenty years so troublesome in the *sūbāship* of Lahore is at length taken with all his family and attendants by Abdus Samad Cawn, the *sūbā* of that province. Some days ago they entered the city laden with fetters, his whole attendants which were left alive being about seven hundred and eighty, all severally mounted on camels which were sent out of the city for that purpose, besides about two thousand heads stuck upon poles, being those who died by the sword in battle. He was carried into the presence of the king, and from thence to a close prison. He at present has his life prolonged with most of his *mutsadīs* in hope to get an account of his treasure in the several parts of his kingdom and of those that assisted him, when afterwards he will be executed, for the rest there are a hundred each day beheaded. It is not a little remarkable with what patience they undergo their fate, and to the last it has not been found that one apostatised from this new formed religion."[25]

24 Mirza Mohammed Harisi, *Ibrat Nāmā*.

25 Report by John Surman and Edward Stephenson in J. T. Wheeler, *Early Records of British India*, p. 180.
Even the author of *Siyār-ul-Mutākherīn* admitted reluctantly that "these

For three months Banda was subjected to systematic torture in the hope that he would give some clue to the wealth he was reputed to have accumulated. Eventually, on Sunday, June 19, 1716, he, his four-year-old son, and five of his commanders, along with another batch of Sikh prisoners, were again paraded through the streets of Delhi on their way to the tomb of Bahadur Shah in Mehrauli, eleven miles from the city.

Before execution Banda was offered pardon if he renounced his faith and accepted Islam. On his refusal to do so, his son, Ajai Singh, was hacked to bits before his eyes. A Mughal nobleman said to Banda: "It is surprising that one, who shows so much acuteness in his features and so much of nobility in his conduct, should have been guilty of such horrors." Banda replied: "I will tell you. Whenever men become so corrupt and wicked as to relinquish the path of equity and abandon themselves to all kinds of excesses, then Providence never fails to raise up a scourge like me to chastise a race so depraved; but when the measure of punishment is full then he raises up men like you to bring him to punishment."[26]

Thus died Banda Bahadur—a man who first chose to renounce the world to live in the peaceful seclusion of a sylvan hermitage, then renounced both pacificism and the life of solitude to rouse a downtrodden peasantry to take up arms; a man who shook one of the most powerful empires in the world to its very foundations with such vio-

---

people not only behaved firmly during the execution, but they would dispute and wrangle with each other for priority in execution" (79).

A particularly harrowing tale is told by Khafi Khan in the *Muntakhib-ul-Lubāb*. One of the prisoners was a newly married young boy, the only son of a widow. The mother succeeded in obtaining a pardon from the Emperor. She brought the order of release just in time to save her son. The boy refused to be saved. "My mother is a liar. I devote my heart and soul to my Gurus. Let me join my companions." The boy went back to the executioner and "was enrolled among the truest of the martyrs produced by the Sikh religion." (II, 761; reproduced in *Later Mughuls*.)

[26] *Siyār-ul-Mutākherīn*, 79-80.

lence that it was never again able to re-establish its authority.[27]

Although Banda's success was short-lived, it proved that the peasants were discontented and that the administration had become feeble. In seven stormy years Banda changed the class structure of land holdings in the southern half of the state by liquidating many of the big Muslim zamindar (land-owning) families of Malwa and the Jullundur Doab. Large estates were first broken up into smaller holdings in the hands of Sikh or Hindu peasants. With the rise of Sikh power these holdings were once again grouped together to form large estates, but in the hands of Sikh chieftains.

The movement to infuse the sentiment of Punjabi nationalism in the masses received a setback with Banda. The wanton destruction of life and property of Mughal officials and landowners alienated the sympathies of great numbers of Muslims who began to look upon the Khalsa as the enemies of Islam. Until then only the richer classes of Muslims had been inbred with notions of Islamic revival preached by men like Shaikh Ahmed Sirhindi; Ban-

[27] Muslim historians, who were invariably attached to and dependent on the patronage of the ruling class, have for these obvious reasons interpreted the role of Banda as an enemy of Islam and also exaggerated the tales of atrocities committed by his followers. Syed Mohammed Latif's opinion based on these reports (*History of the Punjab*, p. 280) is as follows:
"Though bravery is a qualification which is highly meritorious, and in all cases one which is handed down to posterity, yet the audacious achievements of this monster are an exception to the rule. His triumphs are not remembered as heroic acts, but as malicious and cold-blooded atrocities. His ruling and insatiable passion was that of pouring out Mohammedan blood. At the present day his name is never mentioned in any part of India unaccompanied with maledictions on his savagery and blood-thirsty propensities. His memory is held in the same detestation by the Sikhs as by the Mohammedans."
As pointed out by Thornton (*History of the Punjab*, p. 176), "a Mohammedan writer is not to be implicitly trusted upon such a point"; nor, it might be added, a Sikh like Gyan Singh, exaggerating the reports in a spirit of anti-Muslim exultation. Banda's followers were undoubtedly guilty of savagery practised by most victorious armies of the time, but the movement was clearly an agrarian revolt and not an anti-Islamic crusade.

da's savagery hardened the hearts of the Muslim peasants and made them as anti-Sikh as their government.

The Muslims looked upon Banda as the author of the *Siyār* described him: "a barbarian, whom nature had formed for a butcher . . . an infernal monster."[28] It was a long time before the Muslim masses were willing to join the Hindus and Sikhs to defend their country against the imperial forces and foreign invaders.

[28] *Siyār-ul-Mutākherīn*, 72, 76.

CHAPTER 7

PERSECUTION OF THE SIKHS AND THE
REORGANISATION OF THE KHALSA ARMY

THE disintegration of the Mughal Empire was caused by many factors, of which the two most important were the rise of the Marathas and the Sikhs.[1] What Sivaji did in Central India, Banda achieved a little later and in a more spectacular manner in the Punjab. Their success encouraged the Rohillas, Rajputs, and Jats. It also encouraged the Satraps in Bengal, Uttar Pradesh, and the Deccan to elevate their status from one of viceroyalty to kingship.

In the Punjab, the governor, Abdus Samad Khan, continued to pay lip service to the Emperor as long as it suited him. But it was both in his interests as well as of the imperial government to put down the Sikhs, who had become the spearhead of the agrarian revolt. Consequently measures against them were intensified. The execution of Banda and seven hundred men in Delhi was followed by a vigorous campaign in the Punjab. A garrison was cantoned in Amritsar and an edict was issued by the Emperor to apprehend the Khalsa wherever found and, if they resisted, to kill them.[2] Since the Khalsa were easily identifiable because of the unshorn hair under their turbans and their flowing beards, the only choice left to them was either to give up the external emblems of their faith or keep out of the way of Mughal soldiers. Many succumbed to the terror which was let loose and became clean-shaven *sahajdhārīs;*[3] others who were determined to remain Khal-

[1] The basic cause of disruption was of course the bigotry and repression of non-Muslims started by Emperor Aurangzeb. He realised the folly of trying to rule by tyranny and prophesied that after him only turmoil would remain—*az mā ast hamā fasād bāqi.* (Edwardes and Garrett, *Mughal Rule in India,* p. 155.)

[2] Forster, *Travels,* I. 271.

[3] The authors of *A Short History of the Sikhs* (p. 110) maintain that the

sa left the care of their lands, their women and children to their kinsmen and retreated to inaccessible hill tracts and jungles. For them, the only way of survival was the way of all outlaws—to plunder state treasuries and the homes of the rich. The most important result of this policy of repression was to uproot a large number of peasants from the land and convert them into professional soldiers. Thus the Sikhs were provided with a standing army with an intimate and continuing connection with the peasantry. It provided an added economic incentive and made the rising of the Sikhs like that of the Jacquerie: the reaction of desperate landless men fortified by religious enthusiasm and a militant creed.

The Sikhs, who were now without a personal leader, started the tradition of deciding matters concerning the community at the biennial meetings which took place at Amritsar on the first of Baisakh and at Divali. These assemblies came to be known as the *Sarbat Khālsā* and a resolution passed by it became a *gurmatā* (decree of the Guru). The Sarbat Khālsā appointed *jathedārs* (group leaders), chose agents, and entrusted them with powers to negotiate on behalf of the Sikhs.

For the first five years after Banda's execution, very little was heard of the Sikhs. The focal point shifted from the Punjab to Delhi, where Guru Gobind Singh's two widows, Mata Sundari and Sahib Devan, were living in retirement. Bhai Mani Singh looked after them and gave advice to parties of Sikhs who came to pay them homage. The *sahajdhārīs* settled down to peaceful trades. The Khalsa, who remained in the plains, were divided between the *bandaī*, who wished to deify Banda and the *tat khālsā*, who, while revering the memory of their leader, disapproved of the attempt to apotheosise him. The differences between the two groups found expression in matters of

---

term *sahajdhārī* came into use at this time; until then, the word for the clean-shaven Sikh was *khulāsā* as distinct from the *khālsā*.

trivial detail,[4] but, as is usual with frustrated people, the trivialities assumed unwarranted importance. This led to squabbling and then to an open fight to gain control over the Harimandir in Amritsar (the government having in the meantime relaxed its measures and allowed Sikhs access to the temple). The position became serious enough for the leading Sikhs to appeal to Mata Sundari for intervention. In A.D. 1721, she sent Bhai Mani Singh to Amritsar to take charge of the Harimandir. The *bandaī* gave up their claim and, after a time, most of them threw in their lot with the *tat khālsā*.

Once the internal squabbles were settled, the Sarbat Khalsa became a real force. Under its instructions *jathedārs* formed small bands of outlaws[5] and began taking villages near their mountain and jungle hideouts under their protection. The combined strength of the *jathās* was enough to persuade Zakarya Khan, who, on the transfer of his father to Multan, had become governor of Lahore, to try to conciliate the Sikhs. His envoy came to the meeting of the Sarbat Khalsa on the first of Baisakh A.D. 1733 and offered Dipalpur, Kanganwal, and Jhabal, which were worth a lac of rupees in revenue as a *jāgir* (estate). The

[4] Banda was a strict vegetarian and had introduced the war cries *"fateh darśan"* or *"fateh dharma"* in preference to the orthodox *"vāh guru jī kī fateh."* He was also said to have baptised people by the ceremony of *caran pahul*, where the initiate drank water touched by Banda's foot instead of the *amrit* stirred by the dagger.

There were many other splinter groups of Sikhs at the time, of which the *Gulāb Rāīās* (followers of Gulab Rai, a cousin of Guru Gobind Singh), *Gangū Śāhīās* (followers of Gangu, a disciple of Guru Amar Das) and the *Handālīās* (followers of Handal, also a disciple of the third guru), later known as *Nirañjanīās*, were notable. In addition, there were also followers of Prithi Chand (*Minās*), Dhirmal (*Dhīrmalīās*) and Ram Rai (*Rām Rāīās*).

[5] A name which became a legend in the countryside was Tara Singh of the village of Van, who looted many district treasuries. His band of desperadoes was liquidated in 1726. By then many more bands of Sikh outlaws were operating in different parts of the province.

offer was accepted with some reluctance and Kapur Singh,[6] of village Fyzullapur, was nominated *jāgirdār* and given the title of Nawab. Nawab Kapur Singh was thus recognised as the leader of the Sikhs, both by the Sarbat Khalsa as well as the provincial governor. Closely associated with Kapur Singh was another remarkable man, Jassa Singh Ahluwalia.[7] These two men became the chief architects of Sikh power in the country.

Kapur Singh and Jassa Singh made full use of the conciliatory attitude of Zakarya Khan. The Khalsa were ordered to come out of their hideouts. At another meeting of the Sarbat Khalsa held at the Akal Takht[8] facing the Harimandir, the *jathās* were reorganised. They were assured complete freedom of action except when the future of the community was in jeopardy; then they had to merge their units in the *Dal Khālsā*, the army of the Khalsa. A central fighting force which was billetted at Amritsar consisted of two divisions, the *Budhā Dal* (veterans), and the *Tarunā Dal*, consisting of more youthful

[6] Kapur Singh, a Virk Jat of the village of Fyzullapur, died in 1753 at Amritsar and was succeeded by his younger brother Hameer Singh. The village of Kapurgarh in Nabha is named after Nawab Kapur Singh.

[7] Jassa Singh Kalal of the village Ahl (hence *Āhlūvāliā*) was born in 1718. He lost his father, Badar Singh, when he was only five years old, and was brought up by Guru Gobind Singh's widow, Mata Sundari, and later by Nawab Kapur Singh. In 1774 he wrested Kapurthala from Rai Ibrahim Bhatti and made it his headquarters. Jassa Singh died in Amritsar in A.D. 1783, and, being issueless, was succeeded by Bhag Singh (d. 1801), whose son Fateh Singh became a close collaborator of Ranjit Singh.

[8] Several writers have given accounts of these meetings. No Sardar was entitled to treat with a foreign emissary on his own. The emissary was brought to the meeting (frequently in the Gurdwara), where all the others had gathered. The proceedings commenced with an *ardās* (prayer), followed by an announcement that a particular emissary had come to treat with the Khalsa. The emissary would then address the congregation or have his message read. A discussion would follow, often leading to clamorous disputation. The real business was done by the leading Sardars. After the meeting had "let off steam," the senior Sardars "talked" the congregation into an agreement. Approval was signified by loud shouts of "*sat srī akāl*" and ratified by another *ardās*.

soldiers. The former was commanded by Nawab Kapur Singh himself. The latter, which was more active and numerous, by a number of *jathedārs* who had separate billets for their men.

The *jāgir* did not prove as much of a sop to the Sikhs as Zakarya Khan had hoped. The Taruna Dal moved across the Bari Doab into Hariana and forcibly collected the revenue which was due the state. The policy of appeasement was given up. The *jāgir* was confiscated and Zakarya Khan's minister, Lakhpat Rai, drove the Budha Dal out of Amritsar into the Bari Doab and then across the Sutlej. Ala Singh of Patiala joined forces with the Budha Dal, and, as soon as Lakhpat Rai turned back to return to Lahore, they occupied a large portion of Malwa. Lakhpat Rai bided his time; when the Budha Dal recrossed the Sutlej he intercepted it on its march towards Amritsar. In the skirmish that followed, many officers of the Lahore army, including Lakhpat Rai's nephew, were slain. Zakarya Khan took the field himself, re-established his authority in the region, and maintained it with an iron hand for almost two years.

In the autumn of A.D. 1738 the aged Mani Singh, who was manager of the Harimandir, applied for permission to hold the Divali fair in Amritsar. He was given a licence on undertaking to pay Rs. 5,000 into the state treasury immediately after the festival. Mani Singh expected to raise this sum from the offerings of pilgrims. A few days before Divali, Zakarya Khan sent a large force towards Amritsar with the ostensible object of maintaining order in the city. This frightened away the pilgrims, and Mani Singh was unable to pay the fee. He was arrested, brought to Lahore, and condemned to death. On his refusal to save his life by accepting conversion to Islam, Mani Singh was tortured and executed.[9]

[9] Sohan Lal states that Mani Singh was tortured to death for his proselytising activities. There is no doubt that the number of Sikhs in-

The killing of the pious and venerable head priest caused deep resentment among the Sikhs. But before they could retaliate, the situation changed with dramatic suddenness with the news of a Persian invasion from the northwest.

The Persian Invasion, 1738-1739

The Persian, Nadir Shah, swept across northern Punjab scattering all opposition. Zakarya Khan made his submission; the Khalsa retreated to the hills. The Persians defeated the imperial army at Karnal and pushed on to Delhi. The capital was plundered and its population massacred. In the summer of 1739 Nadir Shah turned homewards laden with enormous booty, which included the bejewelled peacock throne, the famous Koh-i-noor diamond (the mountain of light), and thousands of slaves. He chose to travel back along the foothills of the Himalayas to avoid the heat of the plains as well as to find new pastures. The Khalsa, who were already there and were well acquainted with the terrain, found Nadir's loot-heavy army an easy prey. They began plundering the invader's baggage train as soon as it entered the Punjab, and continued to do so all the way to the Indus. They never faced Nadir in open combat, but as soon as darkness fell, Sikh bands closed in on the Persian encampments.[10] While passing through Lahore, Nadir Shah is said to have questioned Zakarya Khan about the brigands who had been audacious enough to attack his troops. The governor replied: "They are fakirs who visit their guru's tank twice

---

creased rapidly under his influence and this may have been an additional factor against him. Orthodox Sikhs believe that he had re-arranged the contents of the *Granth* and was the victim of a curse that any one who tampered with the holy book would die a horrible death.

[10] "The Sicque forces appeared in arms at the period of Nadir Shah's return from Delhi, when the Persian army, encumbered with spoil, and regardless of order, was attacked in the rear by detached predatory parties of Sicque cavalry, who occasionally fell upon the baggage guards, and acquired large plunder." (Forster, *Travels*, I, 272.)

a year, and after having bathed in it disappear." "Where do they live?" enquired the Shah. "Their homes are their saddles," replied Zakarya Khan. Nadir is said to have prophesied, "Take care, the day is not far distant when these rebels will take possession of your country."[11]

Interlude between the Invasions, 1739-1747

Nadir Shah's five months' stay in India utterly disrupted the administration of the Punjab. Zakarya Khan could do little more than retain his post by dancing attendance on the Persians. The only people who refused to have any truck with the foreigner were the Sikhs. Their conduct during the occupation, particularly in liberating Indian prisoners, changed their reputation from that of highwaymen to fighters for freedom and did much to restore their prestige among the common people. With the confidence that the peasantry was behind them, the Khalsa returned to the plains, built themselves a mud fort at Dallewal on the banks of the Ravi, and resumed their pilgrimage to Amritsar. According to a contemporary Muslim writer: "Sikh horsemen were seen riding at full gallop towards their favourite shrine of devotion. They were often slain in the attempt and sometimes taken prisoner; but they used on such occasions to seek instead of avoiding, the crown of martyrdom. . . . No instance was known of a Sikh taken on his way to Amritsar consenting to abjure his faith."[12]

Zakarya Khan, who had submitted to the foreigner, showed great alacrity in taking the offensive against the

[11] This dialogue, which is quoted by most historians, is apocryphal. According to Latif, Nadir Shah's last sentence on the subject was: "Surely they ought to be crushed and their country seized." The dialogue is based on Ahmed Shah Batalvi's report in which the last line is: "It seems probable that these rebels will raise their heads." *Tawārīkh-i-Hind*, 859.

Khushwaqt Rai states that Zakarya Khan, while witnessing a farce making fun of the Sikhs' boast that they would become rulers of the Punjab, said, "By God! They live on grass and claim kingship!" *Tawārīkh-i-Punjāb*, 71.)

[12] John Malcolm, *Sketch of the Sikhs*, p. 88, quoting a contemporary Muslim writer.

Sikhs. He had the fortress at Dallewal blown up and ordered village officials to round up Sikhs and hand them
over for execution. He made head-hunting a profitable
business by offering a graded scale of rewards: a blanket
for cutting off a Sikh's hair, ten rupees for information of
the whereabouts of a Sikh, fifty rupees for a Sikh scalp.
Plunder of Sikh homes was made lawful; giving shelter to
Sikhs or withholding information of their movements was
made a capital offence. Zakarya's police scoured the countryside and brought back hundreds of Sikhs in chains.
They were publicly beheaded at the *nakhās*, the horse-
market of Lahore, since then renamed *Śahīdgaṅj* (place of
martyrdom), in memory of the dead.[13] Persecution had the
opposite effect. Since the peasants were in sympathy with
the Khalsa, they thwarted the administration by giving
shelter to the fugitives, and many joined hands with
Khalsa bands to ambush the state constabulary. The only
notable exceptions were the Niranjanias[14] of Jandiala near
Amritsar, who collaborated with the authorities.

The Khalsa suffered terrible hardships during Zakarya
Khan's stern rule.[15] But they remained as defiant as ever

[13] Sikh historians Ratan Singh Bhangu (whose grandfather, Mehtab
Singh of Mirankot, was one of the many thousands of Sikhs to be executed at Lahore) and Gyani Gyan Singh go into great detail on the
tortures and executions carried on at Shahidganj. The names of some of
the martyrs are held in great esteem by the Sikhs, particularly Mehtab
Singh, slayer of the notorious Massa Ranghar, who had desecrated the
Harimandir by using it for drinking and debauchery, and the youthful
Taru Singh, whose only offence was to have supplied rations to Sikh
fugitives.

[14] See footnote 4.

[15] Although Zakarya Khan showed little mercy to the Sikhs (and they
did little to deserve it) he was an able administrator and did much to
relieve the suffering caused by the Persian invasion. He pleaded with Nadir
Shah and had him release many artisans of Delhi who were being taken as
captives. When he died "there was so much grief for him among all
people, especially in the city of Lahore, that for three nights in succession
no lamp was lighted in any house. Thousands and thousands followed his
coffin through the streets, lamenting aloud, beating their breasts, and heap-
ing up flowers on his bier, till at last not a handful of flowers was left
in the city." (Anand Ram Mukhlis, *Tazkira*, 139. Quoted by J. N.
Sarkar, *Fall of the Mughal Empire*, I, 106.)

and developed a spirit of bravado which enabled them to face adversity.[16]

Zakarya Khan[17] died on July 1, 1745. His son Yahya Khan, who was also the son-in-law of the chief wazir at Delhi, had no difficulty in securing an appointment as the governor of Lahore. His ambitious younger brother, Shah Nawaz, was made governor of Multan. As far as the Sikhs were concerned, there was little change in the govern-ment's attitude towards them. They were, however, now more numerous and decided to reorganise their forces.

Up to 1745 bands of a dozen or more horsemen (*dharvi*) under a *jathedār* had operated independently. On the Divali of 1745 (October 14) the Sarbat Khalsa resolved to

[16] To the Sikh desperado of the time, the Punjabi language owes some of its charming vocabulary of braggadocio still used by *Nihaṅgs*. A Sikh describes himself as *savā lakh* (the equal of 125,000) or as an army (*fauj*). When he goes to urinate, he says he is going to "see a cheetah off"; when he defecates he announces that he is going to "conquer the fort of Chittor" or "give rations to a Kazi." Coarse food like gram is "almonds"; onions, "pieces of silver"; a chillie, "a quarrelsome dame." A one-eyed man was, and often is, called *Lakh-netrā Singh*, the lion with a hundred thousand eyes. Death is simply an order to march—and so on.

[17] Zakarya Khan was succeeded by his son Yahya Khan. Within one year Yahya was supplanted by his younger brother, Shah Nawaz Khan, who, in his turn, was ousted by Yahya's wife's brother, Mir Mannu. The rapid change of rulers and the appearance of yet another foreign invader, Ahmed Shah Abdali, who had succeeded to the throne of Kabul on the assassina-tion of Nadir Shah, were decisive factors in the rise of Sikh power.

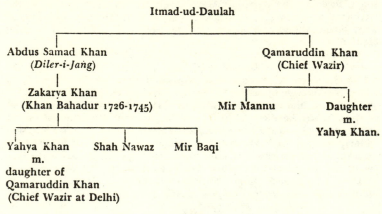

Itmad-ud-Daulah

Abdus Samad Khan (*Diler-i-Jaṅg*) — Qamaruddin Khan (Chief Wazir)

Zakarya Khan (Khan Bahadur 1726-1745) — Mir Mannu — Daughter m. Yahya Khan.

Yahya Khan m. daughter of Qamaruddin Khan (Chief Wazir at Delhi) — Shah Nawaz — Mir Baqi

merge the small *jathās* into twenty-five sizeable regiments of cavalry and confirmed Nawab Kapur Singh as overall commander of the army. The commanders of some of these regiments, namely, Hari Singh Bhangi, Naudh Singh of Sukerchak, Jassa Singh Ahluwalia, and Jai Singh Kanhaya, played a decisive role in liberating the Punjab from the Mughals and foreign invaders.

As soon as the reorganisation had been effected, Sikh leaders incited the peasants to refuse payment of revenue to the government. A fracas between a band of Sikh horsemen and the state constabulary resulted in the death of the brother of Lakhpat Rai. The minister wreaked terrible vengeance for the slaying of his brother.[18] Sikhs living in Lahore were rounded up and beheaded at Shahidganj; those copies of the *Granth* that could be found were burned; the tank surrounding the Harimandir at Amritsar was fouled with rubbish. Then Lakhpat Rai and Yahya Khan went in pursuit of a Sikh concentration on the banks of the Ravi north of Lahore. The Sikhs retreated further northwards, only to find their path blocked by troops of hillmen. Some fought their way through and escaped into the mountains; others turned back and tried to get across the Bari Doab to Sikh columns coming to their help. The governor's troops inflicted heavy punishment on the Sikhs; nearly seven thousand were killed and three thousand prisoners were taken to Lahore and executed at Shahidganj.[19] The disaster of June 1746 is known as the *ghallūghārā* (the holocaust.)[20]

The Sikhs had five months respite after the *ghallūghārā*.

18 Ratan Singh Bhangu relates Lakhpat Rai's oath of vengeance. He is said to have appeared before Yahya Khan, flung his turban on the floor, and sworn that he would go bareheaded until he had destroyed the Sikhs. "I am a Kshatriya, but I shall not call myself by that name until I have erased their [the Khalsa's] name from the page of existence." (*Prācīn Panth Prakāś*, pp. 291-93.) A general massacre of the Sikhs of Lahore took place on March 10, 1746.

19 Ratan Singh Bhangu, *Prācīn Panth Prakāś*, p. 296.

20 The holocaust of June 1746 is known as the *choṭā ghallūghārā*, to distinguish it from the greater disaster, the *vaḍā ghallūghārā* of 1762.

Shah Nawaz revolted against the authority of Yahya and
the civil war went on through the winter months of 1746-
1747. In March 1747 Shah Nawaz forced his way into Lahore, put his brother in jail, and proclaimed himself governor of the Punjab. To win over the Sikhs, he had Lakhpat Rai gaoled and appointed a Sahajdhārī Sikh, Kaura
Mal, as his minister. Another man who came to the fore-
front at this time was Adina Beg Khan, who had earlier
(1739) been appointed governor of the Jullundur Doab
by Zakarya Khan.

Shah Nawaz did not have a long term as governor of
Lahore. Yahya Khan escaped from jail and appealed to
his father-in-law, Wazir Qamaruddin, to help him regain
power in the Punjab. Shah Nawaz, on the advice of Adina
Beg, invited Ahmed Shah Abdali, who had succeeded his
master, Nadir Shah, as ruler of Afghanistan, to invade the
country.

While Zakarya Khan's sons were busy fighting each
other, the Sikhs were quietly recouping their strength.
After the general meeting of the Sarbat Khalsa on the first
of Baisakh, March 30, 1747, they built a mud fortress just
outside Amritsar which they named Ram Rauni in honour of the founder of the city, Guru Ram Das.

CHAPTER 8

AHMED SHAH ABDALI AND THE SIKHS

First Afghan Invasion, A.D. 1747-1748:
Emergence of the Misls

AHMED SHAH ABDALI,[1] the new ruler of Afghanistan, claimed the right to conquer India as successor to the Persian, Nadir Shah, who was murdered in June 1747. Shah Nawaz's invitation assured him of support. In the middle of December 1747 he left Peshawar at the head of a small (18,000 men) but powerful army of Afghan and Pathan tribesmen and in twenty days reached the outskirts of Lahore. Shah Nawaz had in the meantime been chided for his lack of patriotism and had changed his mind. The Afghans took scant notice of his last-minute efforts to stop them and entered Lahore on January 12, 1748. They plundered the suburbs and exacted a heavy tribute for sparing the rest of the city. After a month's sojourn at Lahore, Abdali resumed his march towards Delhi.

Wazir Qamaruddin came out with an army of over 60,000 men to meet the invaders. On March 11, 1748, the two armies clashed at Manupur near Sirhind. Although Wazir Qamaruddin was killed, his son Mir Mannu, who took over the command of the Mughal army, compelled the Afghans to retire.

This was a golden opportunity for the Sikhs. The twenty-five regiments split into more than sixty bands of freebooters, and harried the retreating Afghans all the way up to the river Indus, depriving them of their stores and horses. At the same time, Jassa Singh Ahluwalia moved

[1] Ahmed Shah Abdali was an Afghan of the Saddozai clan. He was Nadir Shah's most trusted general, and on his master's assassination took possession of much of the treasure looted from India, including the famous Koh-i-noor. He became ruler of Afghanistan under the title of *Durrānī* (from *dur-i-daurān*, the best of pearls).

into the vacuum created in the Central Punjab by the Mughal-Afghan conflict. He defeated Adina Beg Khan at Hoshiarpur and arrived in triumph at Amritsar in time to celebrate the Baisakhi fair.

At the meeting of the Sarbat Khalsa it was resolved to merge the independent *jathās* into one army, the Dal Khalsa. Jassa Singh Ahluwalia, who had gradually taken over the leadership from the ageing Kapur Singh and who had come to be addressed as the *pādśāh* (king) of the Sikhs, was made the supreme commander. The Dal was divided into eleven misls.[2]

1. Ahluwalia, under Jassa Singh Ahluwalia, who was also the supreme commander of all the misls.

2. Fyzullapuria or Singhpuria, under Nawab Kapur Singh.

3. Sukerchakia, under Naudh Singh of the village Sukerchak near Gujranwala. (Naudh Singh was the father of Charhat Singh Sukerchakia, whose grandson, Ranjit Singh, became the first Sikh monarch of the Punjab.)

4. Nishanwalia, under Dasaundha Singh, the standard-bearer (*nisānvālā*) of the Dal Khalsa.

5. Bhangi, under Hari Singh of the village Panjwad. The name Bhangi came from the addiction to hashish (*bhang*) of Bhuma Singh, who preceded Hari Singh as leader of the misl.

6. Kanhaya, under Jai Singh of the village Kahna.

7. Nakkai, under Hira Singh of the village Baharwal, situated in a tract near Lahore called Nakka.

8. Dallewalia, under Gulab Singh of the village Dallewal.

9. Shaheed, under Deep Singh. The name *sahīd* (martyr) was taken after the death of the leader.

[2] The Arabic word *misl* means "like." The Sikh misls were "alike" in the sense that they were considered equals. Their fighting strength was, however, far from equal. Some had only a few hundred men; others, like the Bhangis, could put more than ten thousand soldiers in the field.

10. Karora Singhia, under Karora Singh of the village Paijgarh.

11. Ramgarhia under Nand Singh.

Phoolkia, under Ala Singh of Patiala, was the twelfth misl, but it was not a part of the Dal Khalsa, and sometimes acted against the interests of the community.

Every Sikh was free to join any misl he chose, and every misl was free to act in any way it wished in the area under its control. Only in matters affecting the community as a whole were they to take orders from the Supremo, Jassa Singh Ahluwalia. The strength of the misls varied from time to time. It is estimated that the total force which the Dal Khalsa could put in the field at one time was about seventy thousand horse and foot.

The *misldārī* system was ideally suited to the conditions of the time and worked well under leaders like Kapur Singh and Jassa Singh Ahluwalia. It combined freedom of action with the discipline of a unified command; it channelled the energies of the fiercely independent Khalsa soldier in the service of a cause which he held dear—the expulsion of foreigners from the Punjab and the fulfilment of the prophecy of Guru Gobind of the establishment of a Sikh state.

By the time the last of Abdali's men had been cleared from the Punjab, the misls had spread out into the three doabs: between the Chenab and the Ravi, between the Ravi and the Beas, and between the Beas and the Sutlej. They were firmly entrenched in Amritsar with the mud fortress of Ram Rauni guarding the city.

Mir Mannu was confirmed as governor of the Punjab in April 1748. But he was far from being in effective control of the province. The Afghans still held Multan; the Sikhs the three doabs; the Raja of Jammu had cast off the Mughal yoke and declared an independent Dogra state.

Mannu was not strong enough to fight all three at once. His biggest handicap was lack of support from the government at Delhi, where the new Wazir, Safdar Jang, was doing his best to undermine the growing power of the Turanis (Turks) of whom Mir Mannu was the leader.

Mir Mannu instructed Adina Beg Khan to curb the Sikh leaders while Kaura Mal, with a force of Turanis and Sikh mercenaries, ejected the Afghans from Multan.

Adina Beg Khan[3] won over Jassa Singh Ramgarhia and proceeded to Amritsar, where the Sikhs had foregathered to celebrate Divali. Mir Mannu and Kaura Mal came down from Lahore and joined Adina in besieging Ram Rauni.

After two months of desultory fighting, Mir Mannu offered to raise the siege and give the Sikhs a *jāgīr* if they agreed to remain peaceful. Jassa Singh Ahluwalia accepted the offer of one-fourth of the revenue of Patti.

The real reason for Mannu's placating the Sikhs in this

[3] Adina Beg Khan is an excellent example of the amoral Machiavellian "prince" produced by unsettled times. The author of *Siyār-ul-Mutākherīn* describes him as "the very devil under the appearance of a man." He had no loyalty save to himself. He was eminently successful in making use of others by convincing them that the course he advocated was in their interest. And he was a past master at the game of playing his enemies against each other.

He persuaded Shah Nawaz to invite the Afghans and, at the same time, informed the Delhi Wazir of Shah Nawaz's treachery. He proclaimed a holy war against the Sikhs one day, and pledged eternal friendship with them on the next. ("Adina Beg Khan would drive away flies from the face of the Durranis at one time and brush the dust from the beards of the Sikhs at another," *Imādus Saādat*.) He incited the Marathas against the Afghans, and the Afghans and Sikhs against the Marathas, and never did he let his falsehoods catch up with him.

Diwan Bakht Mal writes: "Adina Beg was a greedy man. He did not crush the Sikhs. If he had intended to do so, it was not a difficult task. But he had this idea in his mind that if he quelled the Sikhs some other contractor might be entrusted with the government of the doab for a higher sum and he might be dismissed. He, therefore, treated the Sikhs well and settled terms with them. For this reason the Sikhs grew stronger and they gradually occupied many villages as *jāgīr*." (Folios 58-59, *Khālsā Nāmā*)

manner was the news that Ahmed Shah Abdali had again assembled an army to invade India.

Second Afghan Invasion, 1748-1749: Sikh Collaboration with Kaura Mal

In December 1748, Abdali left Peshawar for the Punjab. Mannu sent frantic appeals to Delhi for help, but Wazir Safdar Jang, who was more anxious to see Mannu out of power than to repel the foreigner, prevaricated and Mannu had to face the Afghans with whatever forces he could muster. Mannu stopped the invading army on the banks of the Chenab four miles east of Wazirabad. Abdali hesitated to open hostilities with the man who had beaten him only nine months earlier. Then he realised that if he let the winter days go by, the summer's heat would turn the odds against his mountaineers. He kept the bulk of his army with him, facing Mir Mannu, while a column under General Jahan Khan bypassed Mannu's forces and made for Lahore. The Sikhs got information that while Mir Mannu was facing Abdali on the Chenab, Mannu's deputy in Lahore had left the city unguarded to check the advance of Jahan Khan. They swooped down on Lahore and for some hours Nawab Kapur Singh had the pleasure of having the capital at his mercy. He evacuated the city when he heard of the return of the governor.[4]

The impasse on the Chenab was resolved by the willingness of both parties to come to terms. Jahan Khan having been unsuccessful at Lahore, the Afghans wanted to return home with whatever they could lay their hands on. Mannu had not received any assistance from Delhi and decided to "shake the chain of friendship and accommodation in Abdali's ears and smother the fire that had not yet broken out into a flame."[5] The Afghan was given all territory west of the Indus (as had been ceded to the Persian Nadir Shah)

---

[4] Khushwaqt Rai, *Kitāb-i-Tawārīkh-i-Punjāb*, 82.
[5] *Siyār-ul-Mutākherīn*, III, 288.

and the revenue of four districts of the Punjab: Sialkot, Aurangabad, Gujarat, and Pasrur, yielding an annual revenue of fourteen lacs of rupees. In short, Mir Mannu became a feudatory of the Afghan king as well as of the Mughal emperor.

Mir Mannu returned to Lahore resolved to teach the Sikhs a lesson for their audacity in entering the capital in his absence. Their *jāgīr* was confiscated, mobile columns armed with long-firing jezails were sent out to shoot down Sikhs.[6]

This campaign did not last very long. Wazir Safdar Jang continued making difficulties for Mir Mannu. In July 1750, he bribed Nasir Khan, who had been a trusted employee of Mir Mannu and was administrator of the four districts assigned to Abdali, to revolt against his master. (The Wazir promised him the *sūbedārī* of Lahore in place of Mannu.) Mannu defeated the ungrateful Nasir Khan at Sialkot and packed him off to Delhi to seek compensation from Safdar Jang. The Wazir had other arrows in his quiver. Soon after the Nasir revolt had miscarried, he announced the appointment of Shah Nawaz Khan as independent governor of Multan. He also gave Shah Nawaz to understand that if he ousted Mir Mannu he could add Lahore to his gubernatorial domain. Shah Nawaz fell into the Wazir's trap and as soon as he was installed at Multan began to make preparations to capture Lahore.

The only man Mir Mannu could rely on was Kaura Mal, and Kaura Mal made no secret of his attachment to the

---

[6] An eyewitness gives the following account of Mannu's campaign. "Muin appointed most of them [*jezailcīs*] to the task of chastising the Sikhs. They ran after these wretches up to 28 kos in a day and slew them wherever they stood up to oppose them. Everyone who brought Sikh heads to Muin received a reward of Rs. 10 per head. Anyone who brought a horse belonging to a Sikh could keep it as his own. Whosoever lost his own horse by chance in the fight with the Sikhs got another in its place from the government stable." (Miskin, *Tazkira-i-Tahmāsp*, folios 68-69. Miskin was a personal servant of Mir Mannu, and after Mannu's death, of his widow, Mughlani Begam.)

faith of Nanak. On the Dewan's advice the mobile columns of *jezailcis* were withdrawn, the Sikhs were allowed to remain in possession of Ram Rauni and were invited to join the campaign against Shah Nawaz.

Kaura Mal led a motley host consisting of Mughals, Punjabi Mussalmans, Afghans, and Sikhs (under Jassa Singh Ahluwalia). He defeated the Multan army, cut off the fallen Shah Nawaz's head and sent it as a trophy to Mir Mannu.

The grateful Mannu gave Kaura Mal the title of *Mahārājāh Bahādur* and made him governor of Multan. The Dewan, who felt that he owed his success to Sikh collaboration, heaped the *misldārs* with favours. He retained many Sikhs in service and assigned the revenue of twelve villages to the Harimandir.

In the years 1749 and 1750 a great many peasants joined the Sikh fold.

Third Afghan Invasion, 1751-1752:
The Punjab under Sikh Protection

By the autumn of 1751 the Punjab was rife with rumours of another Afghan invasion. Mir Mannu had failed to pay the revenue of the four districts ceded to Abdali and, in the middle of November, advance units of the Afghan army under General Jahan Khan crossed the Indus; Abdali followed closely behind.

Mir Mannu tried to buy off the invaders by paying a part of the arrears. The Afghans took the nine lacs offered them and proceeded further into the Punjab. Mannu knew it was useless to rely for help on the government at Delhi. He summoned Kaura Mal from Multan, Adina Beg Khan from Jullundur, and made preparations to fight the Afghans.

Mir Mannu raised a large army of Punjabis, the largest contingent being Sikhs, who numbered over twenty thousand.[7] In December 1751 he crossed the Ravi to check the Afghans led by Jahan Khan. Instead of joining Jahan Khan, Abdali made a detour, and closed in on Lahore from the northeast. Mannu quickly retraced his steps and entrenched himself outside the city walls. This manoeuvre proved to be an expensive mistake. While the Afghans had the entire countryside to feed them, Mannu had nothing more to fall back on than what was usually stocked in the city in times of peace. At the end of six weeks, all the grain and fodder was exhausted and "no lamp was lighted in any house for a distance of three marches."[8] Mannu sought advice from his counsellors. Kaura Mal advised patience. The Afghans, he argued, had also exhausted their provisions and were living on famine rations. Besides, it was already March; in another fortnight it would become too hot for the enemy, who were encamped in the open. Adina Beg was for immediate action. Mannu accepted Adina Beg's advice and opened hostilities on March 5. Kaura Mal fell on the second day of the battle; Adina Beg quietly disappeared from the field. Mir Mannu fought as long as he could and then laid down arms.

The Afghans extracted an indemnity of thirty lacs of rupees in cash from Mannu.[9] By the terms of the treaty

[7] The Sikhs did not do much fighting on this occasion. Mannu did not trust them and promised them a *jāgīr* to keep them quiet while he was preoccupied with the Afghans. The citizens of Lahore were also averse to having them in the city and maltreated a party of Sikh horsemen. Thereafter Sikh forces were withdrawn. Some even went over and joined the Afghans. (Ratan Singh Bhangu, *Prācīn Panth Prakāś.*)

[8] Miskin, 75.

[9] When Mannu was brought before Abdali, the Afghan King asked: "What would you have done if I had fallen in your hands?" "I would have cut off your head and sent it to my master," replied Mannu. "Now that you are at my mercy what do you expect of me?" asked Abdali. "If you are a tradesman, sell me; if you are a tyrant, kill me; but if you are a King, pardon me," replied Mannu. Abdali embraced Mannu and addressed him as his brave son and the champion of India—*Farzand Khān Bahādur, Rustam-i-Hind.*

The dialogue is recorded by most Persian and Punjabi historians. (*Ahmed Shāh Durrānī,* by Ganda Singh, pp. 117-118.)

(ratified by the Mughal Emperor on April 13, 1752), Lahore and Multan were ceded to Abdali. Thus the Punjab passed out of the Mughal orbit into the Afghan. Before leaving India, Abdali also conquered and annexed Kashmir to his kingdom.

ROYAL FAMILY OF THE SADDOZAIS

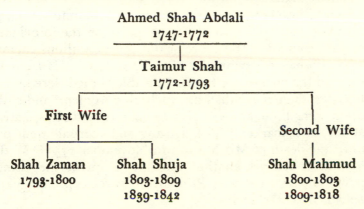

Ahmed Shah Abdali
1747-1772

Taimur Shah
1772-1793

First Wife

Second Wife

Shah Zaman
1793-1800

Shah Shuja
1803-1809
1839-1842

Shah Mahmud
1800-1803
1809-1818

The death of Kaura Mal snapped the only link between Mir Mannu and the Sikh *misldārs*. They had taken advantage of the conflict between the Afghans and the Mughals to spread out in the Bari Doab, Jullundur Doab, and across the Sutlej as far as Jind and Thanesar. They came within fifty miles of Delhi before they were stopped. In the north, the Sukerchakias under Charhat Singh crossed the Jhelum and subdued the Muslim tribes of the region, including the Gakkhars.

Mir Mannu recovered from the Afghan visitation to discover that most of his domains were in the hands of the Sikhs. Adina Beg Khan was even more concerned, for his territory was the one most affected by Sikh incursions. On the festival of Hola Mohalla in March 1753, Adina fell upon Sikh pilgrims at Anandpur and killed a great many. The Sikhs retaliated by plundering villages in the Jullundur and Bari Doabs. Adina was as quick in coming to terms as he was in taking offence. He assigned some of the revenue of his territory to the Sikhs and took many, including Jassa Singh Ramgarhia, in his employ.

It was Mir Mannu's turn to take the field. He marched up to Batala and then invested Ram Rauni at Amritsar. He blew up the fort and slew the entire garrison of nine hundred Sikhs.

Skirmishes between Sikh bands and Mannu's roving columns took place in different parts of the province. Mannu could do little more against an ubiquitous enemy who also had the sympathy of the peasantry. His *jezailcīs* combed the villages for Sikhs. The able-bodied were killed fighting; the non-combatants, including women[10] and children, were brought in chains to Lahore and decapitated at the horse-market.[11] The fighting and reprisals went on until the death of Mir Mannu in November 1753.[12] With Mannu ended yet another attempt to quash the rising power of the Khalsa. A Punjabi doggerel expresses Sikh sentiment at the time:

> Mir Mannu is our sickle,
> We the fodder for him to mow,
> The more he reaps, the more we grow.[13]

[10] It is perhaps not accurate to describe Sikh women as non-combatants, because many fought alongside their menfolk. The English adventurer George Thomas states in his memoirs: "Instances indeed have not infrequently occurred, in which they [Sikh women] have actually taken up arms to defend their habitations from the desultory attacks of the enemy, and throughout the contest behaved themselves with an intrepidity of spirit, highly praiseworthy" (p. 75).

[11] "The persons who brought Sikhs alive, or their heads or their horses, received prizes. Every Mughal who lost his own horse in battle was provided with another of a better quality at the expense of the government. The Sikhs who were captured alive were sent to hell by being beaten with wooden mallets. At times Adina Beg Khan sent 40 or 50 Sikh captives from the Doab district (Jullundur); they were as a rule killed with the strokes of wooden hammers." (Miskin, 84.)

[12] Miskin, who was a personal attendant of Mir Mannu, states that his master died of the effects of poisoning and not in an accidental fall from his horse, as is stated by others, including Khushwaqt Rai and Ratan Singh Bhangu.

[13] Aliuddin, *Ibrat Nāmā*, iii a.

With the passing of Mir Mannu the administration of the Punjab collapsed. A country over which the Mughals and the Afghans had fought each other was now neglected by both. The Mughal emperor first appointed his three-year-old boy to be governor, with Mir Mannu's infant son as his deputy.[14] Mannu's brother, Intizam-ud-daulah, who had become the Wazir in Delhi, became a sort of guardian-governor. Effective power was, however, vested in the local dignitaries, of whom Adina Beg Khan was one. Ahmed Shah Abdali was too busy with his own problems in Afghanistan to pay much attention to the Punjab and confirmed the appointment of Mir Mannu's son. His only interest was to see that the tribute came in regularly.

This ludicrous state of affairs ended six months later with the death of Mir Mannu's son in May 1754. Mir Mannu's widow, Mughlani Begam, refused to submit to the nominee of the new emperor, Alamgir II. But her power was circumscribed to Lahore and its environs. Even in these cities the day-to-day administration was entrusted to the hands of court eunuchs, leaving Mughlani free to while away the tedium of widowhood in the company of her lovers. Turbulent Punjabis could hardly be expected to be ruled by infants, eunuchs, and amorous widows; the Punjab broke up into many fragments. Multan and the four districts ceded to Abdali (Gujarat, Sialkot, Pasrur, and Aurangabad), continued to pay revenue to the Afghans. Jullundur and Sirhind were farmed by Adina Beg Khan. Different tribes set up semi-autonomous principalities with militias and fortresses of their own.

The strongest force in the province was that of the Dal Khalsa with its headquarters at Amritsar. During the

---

[14] Jadu Nath Sarkar (*Fall of the Mughal Empire,* I, 185-86) gives an account of the three-year-old prince toddling up to the *Diwān-i-khās* to make his bow of thanksgiving in full court, and of the baby-clothes made of cloth of gold which he sent to his deputy in Lahore. At the same time the *sūbedārī* of Kashmir was given to the one-year-old Prince Tala Said Shah, and a boy of fifteen was appointed as his deputy.

months of chaos following the death of Mir Mannu, units of the Dal indiscriminately plundered towns and villages and frequently looted the suburbs of Lahore. In the winter of 1754-1755 Sikh horsemen swept through Ambala and Sirhind and later into Hariana and onwards into the territories of the Raja of Jaipur.

Sikh leaders realised that the Punjab had no government, nor the people any security of life or property. They took the first step towards becoming rulers of the country. Instead of simply robbing the people, as they had done in the past, they offered them protection (*rākhī*) on payment of one-fifth of their takings at the end of each harvest. Since the Sikhs were the only power which could fulfil its obligations, most of the Punjab readily accepted the offer of protection and for all practical purposes the country came to be administered by the Sikhs.

The headquarters of the Sikh military administration remained at Amritsar, where the Nishanwalias, Dallewalias, and other unattached units were kept as a sort of reserve force. The misls continued to be autonomous, with liberty to extend the *rākhī* over any area they chose. The Bhangis and Sukerchakias took over the Rechna and Chaj Doabs; the Kanhayas and Ramgarhias, the land between Amritsar and the Himalayas; the Singhpurias and Ahluwalias, territory on both sides of the river Sutlej.

At Lahore the sordid intrigues continued. Several attempts were made to oust Mughlani and her eunuchs, but she proved more than a match for her adversaries and even outwitted the wily Adina Beg Khan by ejecting his deputy with the help of the Afghans. At last, in March 1756, Mughlani was arrested on the orders of the Wazir and removed to Delhi. The district of Lahore was farmed out to Adina Beg Khan.

Although Mughlani Begam was kept in close confinement, she was able to send word to Abdali exhorting him to reconquer India. She promised to help him loot all her rich relations. "I know that goods and cash worth crores of rupees lie buried in the palace of my late father-in-law, besides heaps of gold and silver stored inside the ceilings. . . . If you invade India this time, the Indian Empire with all its riches will fall into your hands," she wrote.[15]

Mughlani was not the only one to invite the Afghans. Independently of each other, the Mughal Emperor, and the Rohilla Chief, Najibuddaulah, also sent letters pressing Abdali to come to India.

Fourth Afghan Invasion, 1756-1757:
Marathas in the Punjab, 1758

In November 1756 Ahmed Shah Abdali crossed the Indus for the fourth time. The Sikhs let the Afghans through and Adina Beg Khan retired to safety to watch which way the wind would blow. "From Lahore to Sirhind not a village was left tenanted: all men high and low having fled away in all directions."[16]

The Afghans spent twelve days in Lahore before resuming their march on Delhi. They entered the imperial capital on January 28, 1757 and without any provocation began to plunder the city. Widow Mughlani kept her word. She led the Afghans from one palace to another and told them what each noble's family was worth in gold and jewels. The author of *Siyār-ul-Mutākherīn* records: "They [the Afghans] dragged away people's wives and daughters with such cruelty that numbers, overcome by the delicacy of their feelings, rather than fall into their abominable hands, made away with themselves."[17] For one month Delhi was ruthlessly pillaged. Then came the turn of Mathura and Brindaban, where the Afghans' love of loot was further whetted by the fact that these towns were held sacred by the infidel Hindus. The orgy came to an end when the heat and a cholera epidemic made life difficult for the mountaineers. Abdali provided himself with a sixteen-

---

[15] Aliuddin, *Ibrat Nāmā*, 114.
[16] *Tārīkh-i-Ālamgīr Sānī*; Sarkar, *Fall of the Mughal Empire*, II, 61-62.
[17] III, 54.

year-old princess, a daughter of the late Emperor, Mohammed Shah; his son, Prince Taimur, took the daughter of
Alamgir II. With them went troupes of concubines and
female slaves. Abdali added Sirhind to his domains, and
appointed Imad-ul-mulk as Wazir and Najibuddaulah as
his personal representative at the Mughal court. Mughlani Begam got nothing for her pains.

The Afghans left Delhi on their homeward journey.
Prince Taimur led the van; his father followed close behind. A contemporary account states that "Abdali's own
goods were loaded on twenty-eight thousand elephants,
camels, mules, bullocks and carts, while two hundred
camel-loads of property were taken by Mohammed Shah's
widows, who accompanied him and these too belonged to
him. Eighty thousand horses and foot followed him, each
man carrying away spoils. His cavalry returned on foot,
loading their booty on their chargers. For securing trans-
port, the Afghan king left no horse or camel in any one's
house, not even a donkey."[18]

The time for action had come. Sikh bands closed in
from both sides. Prince Taimur was relieved of much of
his booty. A Maratha news-letter records: "At the end of
March 1757 when the front division of Abdali's army
under Prince Taimur was transporting the plundered
wealth of Delhi to Lahore, Ala Singh, in concert with
other Sikh robbers, had barred his path at Sanawar (between Ambala and Patiala) and robbed him of half his
treasures, and again attacked and plundered him at Malerkotla. So great had been the success of these brigands
that rumor had magnified it into the prince's captivity
and even death at their hands."[19]

Abdali took further precautions, but even so he was not
allowed to go unscathed. Sikh bands slew his guards and

[18] *Tārīkh-i-Ālamgīr Sānī*, 89-115; J. N. Sarkar, *Fall of the Mughal
Empire*, II, 93; H. R. Gupta, *History of the Sikhs*, I, 98.
[19] H. R. Gupta, *History of the Sikhs*, I, 100. Not accepted by Ganda
Singh, *Ahmed Shāh Durrānī*, p. 188.

pillaged his baggage at many points. When he arrived at Lahore, he was in a black mood. He could not lay his hands on the elusive Sikhs, so he spent his fury on the city of Amritsar. The Harimandir was blown up and the sacred pool filled with the entrails of slaughtered cows.

Abdali assigned the Punjab to his son, Taimur, and left the prince an army of ten thousand men under General Jahan Khan. He also bestowed on Ranjit Dev, the Raja of Jammu, several parganas. By this gift, the Afghan assured himself of the collaboration of a powerful chief in whose territories Sikh bands often sought refuge.

Abdali resumed his journey homewards. Sikh bands led by Charhat Singh Sukerchakia re-appeared on the flanks of his army and continued to harass him up to the river Indus.

A clash between Prince Taimur's Afghans and the Sikhs was inevitable. The destruction of the Harimandir had caused a lot of heartburning among the Sikhs. Deep Singh, the leader of one of the misls entrusted with the care of the temple, felt that it was up to him to atone for the sin of having let foreigners desecrate the shrine. He emerged from scholastic retirement (he had been making copies of the *Granth*) and proclaimed his intention of rebuilding the temple. As he went from one hamlet to another, many villagers joined him. By the time Deep Singh reached Taran Taran, ten miles from Amritsar, he had over five thousand peasants armed with hatchets, swords, and spears, in his train. They had no illusions about the fate that awaited them and dressed themselves in gaudy clothes like bridegrooms going to their nuptials.

Jahan Khan ordered a general mobilisation of all able-bodied men in Lahore[20] and proceeded towards Amritsar. The peasants intercepted his advance at the village of

[20] Miskin, folios 162-165.

Goharwal but were unable to withstand trained Afghan soldiers and fresh reinforcements which Jahan Khan received in the nick of time. Deep Singh was severely wounded in the neck and was barely able to get to the Harimandir to keep his tryst with death.[21] "The victorious army pursued them closely as far as their shrine," writes Miskin, who witnessed the battle. "At its door we saw five Sikhs standing guard. The heroes of our troops rushed up and killed them."[22] The Harimandir was once again desecrated. A little later, the temple at Kartarpur was demolished.

Jassa Singh Ahluwalia called on the misldars to avenge the death of Deep Singh and the desecration of their shrines. They found a valuable ally in Adina Beg Khan, who suspected that the Afghans wanted to lay their hands on him.[23] The Sikhs and Adina Beg's troops met the Afghans at village Mahilpur in the district of Hoshiarpur and utterly defeated them. The Sikhs pushed on to Jullundur, ransacked the town and its neighbouring villages. Adina Beg Khan expressed his gratitude to his benefactors by offering a thousand rupees to the *Granth* and a lac and a quarter as protection money for the Jullundur Doab.[24]

Prince Taimur sent twenty thousand horse and foot from Lahore to retrieve the situation. The Sikhs defeated this force and captured its guns and military equipment. There was panic in the Afghan camp at Lahore. "After this," writes Miskin, "every force in whatever direction it was sent, came back defeated and vanquished. Even the environs of Lahore were not safe. Every night thousands of Sikhs used to fall upon the city and plunder the suburbs

[21] Deep Singh is one of the most revered heroes of Sikh history. Colour prints show him running with his head on his left palm, still wielding his sword with his right.

[22] *Tazkira-i-Tahmāsp*, Miskin, 165.

[23] He had been persuaded to come out of hiding and to take the administration of the Jullundur Doab. Adina Beg accepted the offer but refused to attend court in person as he suspected foul play.

[24] Ganda Singh, *Ahmed Shāh Durrānī*, p. 197.

lying outside the walls of Lahore; but no force was sent to repel them and the city gates were closed one hour after nightfall. It brought extreme disgrace to the government and utter lawlessness prevailed."[25]

Adina Beg Khan found that the Sikhs had become too strong for his liking. He kept up appearances with the misldars and at the same time invited the Marathas, who had taken Delhi, to come to the Punjab. He offered them one lac of rupees a day on march, fifty thousand on others if they helped him to capture Lahore. He also persuaded the Sikhs to help the Marathas against the Afghans.

In March 1758 the Maratha general, Raghu Nath Rao, entered the Punjab with a mighty army (said to number two hundred thousand men). The Ahluwalia, Bhangi, Ramgarhia, and Sukerchakia misls helped the Marathas in taking Sirhind. The town which had always been anathema to the Sikhs was again despoiled by them. The Marathas, who wanted to loot Sirhind, were irritated by the conduct of their Sikh allies.[26] Thereafter, it was agreed that the Sikhs would keep two marches ahead of the Marathas.

As the Sikh and Maratha armies crossed the Sutlej, Jahan Khan, who was in the Jullundur Doab, hastily retired to Lahore. A few days later the entire Afghan army vacated the city and was in full retreat across the Ravi.

Raghu Nath Rao entered Lahore in April 1758. Adina Beg Khan feted him at the Shalamar Gardens and had the city illuminated in his honour. While the festivities were going on in Lahore, Sikh and Maratha cavalry went in pursuit of the Afghan prince and his commander-in-chief. Taimur and Jahan Khan barely escaped with their lives when crossing the Chenab near Wazirabad.

---

[25] *Tazkirā*, 166.

[26] "As the Marathas and the Sikhs knew nothing but plundering, they so thoroughly looted the inhabitants of Sirhind, high and low, that none, either male or female, had a cloth on his or her person left." *Tārīkh-i-Ālamgīr Sānī*; H. R. Gupta, *History of the Sikhs*, I, 115.

Their rearguard and heavy baggage were captured and brought back to Lahore.

The Sikhs took the Afghan prisoners to Amritsar and made them clean up the pool around the Harimandir. The Marathas returned to Delhi the richer by several crores. Adina Beg Khan got what he wanted: the *sūbedārī* of the Punjab at seventy-five lacs of rupees a year to be paid to the Marathas.

On paper the Punjab now had three masters: the Mughals, the Afghans, and the Marathas. In fact, it had only two: Adina Beg Khan and the Sikhs. And of those two each tried to convince the other that he was the overlord and the other the tenant. The Sikhs had some reason to think that way because Adina Beg Khan had, in fact, sought their protection and paid them *rākhī* money. But Adina was unpredictable. He recruited a great many soldiers and hired a thousand woodcutters to hack down the forest in which the Sikhs were wont to seek shelter in times of trouble. Then he besieged the Sikh fort of Ram Rauni (now renamed Ramgarh).

Adina Beg's *volte face* took the Sikhs by surprise. Nevertheless, once they understood his game, they gave him no respite. They first punished the Randhawas and the Niranjanias of Jandiala who had sided with Adina and then turned on the Beg. Before they could teach the mercurial *sūbedār* a lesson, he succumbed to an attack of colic in September 1758.

The Punjab still had its three claimants, but now only one master, the Sikhs.

A month and a half after Adina Beg Khan's death the Sarbat Khalsa reviewed the situation at their annual Divali meeting. The Mughals, Afghans, Marathas, and a nominee of Adina Beg Khan had staked their claims on the Punjab. The two questions before the Khalsa were whether or not they should occupy Lahore; and, if they did, would they be strong enough to repel the Afghans or the

Marathas, or both? A large Maratha army was already on its way up from Delhi; the Afghans had made another attempt to retake the province and were not likely to write off a country they considered a part of their empire. The consensus of opinion was that the possession of Lahore was more symbolic than real proof of possession of the Punjab. They resolved, however, to take as much of the remainder of the country as they could.

In March 1759 the Marathas re-entered the Punjab. Their progress through Malwa was slow and cautious, for they were uncertain of Sikh reactions. The Sikhs did not check them, and let Sabaji Sindhia occupy Lahore. From the north, General Jahan Khan again crossed the Indus into the Punjab. Sabaji turned to the Sikhs for help. The joint forces of the Marathas and Sikhs defeated the Afghans and sent them scurrying back to their own country.[27]

Fifth Afghan Invasion, 1759:
Battle of Panipat, 1761. Sikhs in Lahore

In the autumn of 1759 Ahmed Shah Abdali mustered a large army of sixty thousand Afghans and Pathans to invade India for the fifth time. His specific object on this occasion was to crush Maratha power in Northern India. His nominee, the Rohilla Chief, Najibuddaulah, had been expelled from Delhi. Muslim rulers from different parts of the country had written to him of the danger that the rising tide of militant Hinduism presented to Islam; even the Hindu chiefs of Rajasthan had pleaded with him to save them from the depredations of the Marathas. Although the Sikhs had no love for the Marathas, they looked to them to take the lead in resisting the Afghans. While the Marathas were making their plans, the Sikhs tried to check Abdali's progress by themselves. A Marathi newsletter records: "Abdali has come to Lahore

[27] H. R. Gupta, *History of the Sikhs*, I, 128, quoting *Delhi Chronicle*, p. 165, which recorded news of the victory on September 19, 1759.

and fought a great battle with the Sikhs. Two thousand Abdali troops were slain and Jahan Khan was wounded."[28]

The Maratha General, Sabaji, fled from the Punjab without making any arrangement for its defence: those of his troops who could not get away in time were decimated by the Afghans. The Sikhs gave way and let Abdali proceed towards Delhi. Abdali defeated three isolated attempts by Maratha chiefs to check his progress. When he received intelligence that a large army was coming up from the Deccan he pitched his camp at Aligarh and decided to wait. Muslims of Northern India, Shujauddaulah of Oudh, the Rohillas,[29] and others joined the Afghan standard in their thousands.

While the Afghans and Marathas were preparing for a final showdown, the Sikhs continued to extend and consolidate their hold in the districts of the Punjab. At the meeting on Divali day of 1760 the Sarbat Khalsa decided that the time was opportune to seize the capital. Jassa Singh Ahluwalia led the Sikh armies. With him were leaders of other misls: Hari Singh of the Bhangis, Jai Singh of the Kanhayas, Charhat Singh of the Sukerchakias. The Sikhs occupied the suburbs without much difficulty. The Afghan governor offered to pay them a tribute. Since the Afghan-Maratha conflict, which could determine the ownership of Lahore, was still unsettled, the Sikhs accepted Rs. 30,000 from the Afghans and withdrew.

After a year and a quarter of jockeying for position the Marathas and Afghans clashed on the famous field of Panipat on January 14, 1761. The battle was virtually lost by the Marathas before the actual fighting began. The pusillanimous Sadashiv Rao Bhao entrenched himself in the town, and remained inactive for several months. Abdali

[28] Rajwade i, 146; H. R. Gupta, *History of the Sikhs*, I, 129.

[29] "I am the bridegroom of this battle field," said the Rohilla leader, Najibuddaulah, on the eve of Panipat. "Everything rests on my head: the others are mere guests accompanying the marriage procession. What is done here will be done by me and to me." *Najibuddaulāh*, LXXIX.

cut off the Marathas' supplies and compelled them to fight on empty stomachs.

The engagement took heavy toll of Maratha life and equipment.[30] But the victorious Afghans also suffered considerable losses and, though they were strong enough to inflict severe chastisement on isolated bands of Sikhs (as they did a year later), they were no longer strong enough to question the might of the Dal Khalsa in the plains of the Punjab. It could be said that the battle of Panipat which was fought between the Marathas and the Afghans was really won by the Sikhs.

After their victory, the Afghans turned on Ala Singh of Patiala, who had sold provisions to the Marathas at Panipat. They sacked Barnala, terrified Ala Singh and compelled him to pay tribute. Ala Singh barely saved himself from excommunication by pleading with Jassa Singh Ahluwalia.

In March 1761 Abdali began his homeward march. As soon as he crossed the Sutlej, the Sikhs closed in on him. The booty-laden and battle-weary Afghans could do little against bands of twenty or thirty horsemen who would suddenly appear from nowhere, discharge their muskets, and gallop away into the wilderness. Every night Abdali had to throw up mud embankments and have his camp guarded by chains of sentries. Every night Sikh bands broke through and turned the Afghan's dreams into a nightmare. It continued in this way right up to the banks of the Indus. They lightened Abdali of much of his spoils and liberated over two thousand Hindu women he was taking to stock Afghan harems.[31]

When Abdali had been seen across the Indus, the Sikhs turned back to expel the garrisons he had left behind. The

---

[30] The Marathas are estimated to have lost: 28,000, killed; 22,000, taken prisoner. Among the dead were the commanders Bhao and Vishwas Rao, eldest son of Peshwa Balaji Rao. See H. R. Gupta, *Marathas and Panipat*, Chapter XIX.

[31] H. R. Gupta, *History of the Sikhs*, I, 150; Ganda Singh, *Ahmed Shāh Durrānī*, p. 264.

first encounter was with Mirza Jan (who was killed) and later with Nuruddin Bamezei, who had been deputed by Abdali to help Obed Khan, the governor of the Punjab, in dealing with the Sikhs. The Bamezei could get no further than the Chenab. Charhat Singh Sukerchakia harassed him all along his march and finally drove him to seek shelter in the fort of Sialkot. The Sardar invested Sialkot and only raised the siege when the Afghans agreed to depart in peace.

Charhat Singh Sukerchakia had become one of the leaders of the Sikh offensive against the Afghans. Obed Khan decided to take this thorn out of his side by reducing the Sukerchakia fortress at Gujranwala. No sooner had the Afghans encircled Gujranwala then the misldars led by Jassa Singh Ahluwalia, Hari Singh Bhangi, Jai Singh Kanhaya, and others closed round the Afghans and compelled them to raise the siege. Obed Khan extricated himself with some difficulty, leaving his siege guns and heavy artillery in the hands of the Sikhs.

The road to Lahore was now open.

The Divali of 1761 was celebrated with great jubilation at Amritsar. The Sarbat Khalsa once again resolved to capture Lahore and clear the Punjab of foreigners and treasonous elements.

The gates of Lahore were thrown open to welcome the Sikhs. Jassa Singh Ahluwalia entered the capital at the head of the Dal Khalsa. Although in the Sikh Commonwealth there was no place for monarchs, Jassa Singh the brewer, who had been humourously called *Pādśāh*, now became one in fact and was hailed as the *Sultān-ul-Qaum* (the King of the nation). A new currency was minted to celebrate the capture of Lahore. The coins had the same inscription on them as had been used by the victorious Banda fifty-one years earlier.[32]

[32] There is some confusion on the subject of Sikh coinage. Cunningham believes that the earliest Sikh coin was struck in 1757, Griffin that it was struck in 1762. C. L. Rodgers is of the opinion that these early coins, if

The Sikhs began systematic operations to expel Afghan officials from the Punjab. Within a few weeks they had the entire province from the Sutlcj to the Indus under their control. Only a few pockets remained to be cleared: Obed Khan, who had locked himself up in the fort of Lahore; Raja Ghamand Chand of Katoch, who had undertaken service under Abdali and was now back in the hills; and the Niranjanias of Jandiala, who were traditional allies of the Afghans.

Before any progress could be made, Abdali was reported to be on the march again. This time his sole objective was to destroy the power of the Sikhs.

Sixth Afghan Invasion, 1762:
The Great Holocaust

The fort inside the city of Lahore was in the hands of the Afghans. To avoid being caught between the Afghans in the citadel and the Afghans marching down from the northwest, Jassa Singh Ahluwalia evacuated Lahore and ordered the raising of the siege of Jandiala. He allowed his soldiers to remove their women and children to safety in the Hariana desert and then report for duty.

Abdali re-occupied Lahore. On receiving intelligence that great numbers of Sikhs were moving southwards, he immediately set out in pursuit. He covered a distance of one hundred and fifty miles in two days and caught up with the Sikhs at the village of Kup. It was an unequal fight. Most of the thirty thousand Sikhs were non-combatants: old men, women, and children. Sikh horsemen

---

they ever existed (none have been found), were fakes minted by local Muslims and sent to Abdali to rouse his anger against Jassa Singh, the inscription being: "Struck in the two worlds by the order of the Timeless in the country of Ahmed conquered by Jassa the brewer." According to Rodgers, the first Sikh coin was minted in 1765 and was called *Gobind Śāhī* (not *Nānak Śāhī*, as stated by Griffin: the *Nānak Śāhī* was minted in 1778). The inscription on the obverse of the *Gobind Śāhī* was as stated above (p. 107). On the reverse was: "Struck in the Kingdom of Lahore (Sambat, 1822)." (C. L. Rodgers, *Asiatic Society Journal*, 1881, L (1), 71-93.)

could not indulge in their favourite hit-and-run tactics
and had to engage the Afghans, who outnumbered them,
in a hand-to-hand fight. Sikh soldiers put their women
and children in the centre and moved on like a living
fortress from Kup towards Barnala, where they expected
Ala Singh of Patiala[33] to come to their rescue. The Afghans took a heavy toll of Sikh life and gave up only when
night fell and they had wearied of killing.[34]

The Sikhs' troubles were not over. Those who eluded
the Afghans had to run the gauntlet of the Brar tribes,
who turned against them. According to the Sikh historian
Ratan Singh Bhangu, "Not a single Sikh escaped unhurt;
each bore some wounds on his body."[35]

The holocaust of February 5, 1762 is known to the Sikhs
as the *Vaḍā Ghallūghārā* (the great massacre).[36]

Abdali returned to Lahore with fifty cart-loads of heads
and hundreds of Sikhs in chains. According to Forster,
"Pyramids were erected and covered with the heads of
slaughtered Sikhs: and it is mentioned that Ahmed Shah
caused the walls of those mosques, which the Sikhs had
polluted, to be washed with their blood that contamination might be removed, and the ignominy offered to the
religion of Mahomed be expiated."[37] From Lahore, Abdali went to Amritsar. The Harimandir was again blown

[33] Ala Singh failed to come to the help of his co-religionists. Nevertheless he was taken prisoner by the Afghans, and Barnala, which was in his
territory, was burned down. His life was spared on his protesting his neu-
trality and paying a tribute of five lacs of rupees and another one and a
quarter lacs to appear before the Shah with his long hair and beard unshorn. The Rohilla chief Najibuddaulah interceded on his behalf.

[34] The original of the version of the *Adi Granth* recompiled by Guru
Gobind Singh was lost in this engagement.

[35] H. R. Gupta, *History of the Sikhs*, I, 170.

[36] Estimates of the numbers of Sikhs killed in this engagement vary from
between twelve to thirty thousand mentioned by Muslim and English
historians to between five and seven thousand by Rajwade. Whatever the
number of casualties, there is little doubt that they were mostly non-com-
batant, since the Sikh fighting strength was hardly impaired, as was evi-
dent a few months after the *Ghallūghārā*.

[37] Forster, *Travels*, I, 320.

up with gunpowder and the pool filled with the carcasses of cows.

Abdali spent the rest of the year partly at Lahore and partly in cooler Kalanaur. He held out an olive branch to the Marathas, confirmed Shah Alam as Emperor at Delhi, got the Raja of Jammu to help recapture Kashmir for him, and persuaded the *zamindars* of the Punjab to settle down peacefully on their lands. Only for the Sikhs he had no forgiveness—and they asked for none. The *Ghallūghārā* and the blowing up of Harimandir only strengthened their determination to fight the Afghans. By the month of May, they were up in arms again. When Abdali was in Lahore they defeated the Afghan *faujdār* of Sirhind at Harnaulgarh. Jassa Singh Ahluwalia and Tara Singh Gheba plundered the Jullundur Doab, the Bhangis and Sukerchakias took the doabs between the Ravi and the Jhelum, and bands of Sikh horsemen roving between Panipat and Karnal made communication between Delhi and Lahore impossible.

Despite the *Ghallūghārā* disaster in the preceding spring, by the autumn the Sikhs had regained enough confidence to foregather in large numbers at Amritsar to celebrate Divali. Abdali made a mild effort to win them over and sent an envoy with proposals for a treaty of peace. The Sikhs were in no mood to treat with the Afghan, and heaped insults on the emissary. Abdali did not waste any more time and turned up on the outskirts of Amritsar.

The battle of Amritsar[38] was fought in the grey light of

[38] This battle is not accepted by all historians. Forster in his *Travels* describes the Sikh chronicles of the time as stating: "This event is said to have happened in October 1762, when the collected body of the Sicque nation, amounting to sixty thousand cavalry, had formed a junction at the ruins of Amritsar for the purpose of performing some appointed ceremony, and where they resolved, expecting the attack, to pledge their national existence, in the event of a battle. Ahmed Shah, at that time encamped at Lahore, marched with a strong force to Amritsar, and immediately engaged the Sicques; who roused by the fury of a desperate revenge, in sight also of the ground sacred to the founders of their religion, whose monuments had been destroyed by the enemy they were then to combat,

a sun in total eclipse. It ended when the sunless day was blacked out by a moonless night with the adversaries retiring from the field: the Sikhs to the fastness of the jungles of Lakhi, Abdali behind the walled safety of Lahore.

Disturbances in Afghanistan compelled Abdali to leave the Punjab. After making detailed arrangements for the administration of Northern India, he left Lahore on December 12, 1762. Kabuli Mal was appointed governor of Lahore and other districts were neatly parcelled out between Afghan officers and their Rajput supporters. The pains Abdali took over these appointments only went to show how a man of undoubted military genius could be utterly unrealistic as an administrator. In none of these districts was his writ worth more than the paper on which it was written.

By the spring of 1763, Abdali's nominees were restricted to their encampments. The largest Afghan pocket in the Punjab, Kasur, fell to the Bhangi, Hari Singh, yielding a treasure large enough to finance many expeditions. The Jullundur Doab was retaken by Jassa Singh Ahluwalia. In November 1763 Charhat Singh Sukerchakia and the Bhangis inflicted a defeat on General Jahan Khan at Sialkot. Jassa Singh Ahluwalia defeated Bhikhan Khan of Malerkotla (who was slain) and plundered Morinda. As in the past, the wrath of the Sikhs was vented on Sirhind, which was recaptured in January 1764. At the site of the execution of Guru Gobind's sons, a temple was raised and named Fatehgarh, the fort of Victory.

A few weeks after the fall of Sirhind, the Sikhs invested

---

displayed, during a bloody contest, which lasted from the morning until night, an enthusiastic and fierce courage, which ultimately forced Ahmed Shah to draw off his army and retire with precipitation to Lahore." (Cf. Browne, ii, 25-26; Aliuddin, 125-26.)

Forster doubts the authenticity of the conflict; so do Malcolm, J. N. Sarkar, and N. K. Sinha (*Rise of the Sikh Power*). It is, however, accepted by H. R. Gupta, *History of the Sikhs*, I, 178, and Dr. Ganda Singh, *Ahmed Shāh Durrānī*, p. 286.

Lahore and dictated terms to Kabuli Mal.[39] There was nothing to stop them. The land stretching from the Indus to the Jumna (and often across up to the Ganges), and from the Himalayas down to the junction of the Punjab's five rivers beyond Multan, was under Sikh control. But before the Sikhs could celebrate their reconquest of the Punjab at the Divali festival, Abdali was on the move again.

Seventh Afghan Invasion, 1764: Sikhs Retake Lahore and Extend Operations beyond Delhi

In October 1764[40] an army of eighteen thousand Afghans crossed the Indus and were joined at Eminabad by another twelve thousand Baluch tribesmen under Nasir Khan of Kalat.[41] The forces converged on Lahore, where Kabuli Mal welcomed them.

The Sikhs resumed their usual harrying tactics. Part of the Khalsa army entrenched in the Lakhi jungle began to prey upon the Afghans and Baluchis. "They come stealthily like thieves and attack like wolves," wrote Nur Moham-

[39] Although the Sikhs made their Afghan prisoners clean the Harimandir and retaliated by slaying hogs in mosques, they did not massacre any captives, as the Afghans had done. "The Sikhs," writes Forster, "set a bound to the impulse of revenge, and though the Afghan massacre and persecution must have been deeply imprinted on their minds, they did not, it is said, destroy one prisoner in cold blood" (I, 279).

[40] There is some confusion about this invasion. Hari Ram Gupta and N. K. Sinha ascribe the incidents narrated to a later invasion. Qazi Nur Mohammed, who accompanied Abdali on this expedition, supports the present version. The quotations regarding incidents of this invasion are taken from Dr. Ganda Singh's translation of the *Jaṅg Nāmā* by Qazi Nur Mohammed.

[41] This was a holy war against the infidel Sikh. The Baluch, Nasir Khan, was contemplating a pilgrimage to Mecca when he received Abdali's admonition: "I have heard from Multan and also from the Dera that the accursed dogs and lustful infidels (the Sikhs) have overcome the Muslims. . . . How can you think of going to Mecca while this depraved sect is causing havoc? Come, so that we may destroy this faithless sect and enslave their women and children." The *Ghāzīs*, writes Nur Mohammed, poured in from all sides "hissing like black snakes." (*Jaṅg Nāmā*, pp. 38-44.)

[42] *Jaṅg Nāmā*, p. 77.

med.[42] After a month of shadow-boxing, Abdali marched out towards Amritsar. He was harassed all along the route. (It took the same men who had only two years earlier covered one hundred and fifty miles in two days, four days to cover thirty-five.) The Afghans encircled the city to make sure that no Sikhs escaped. Then some columns advanced gingerly through the tortuous, deserted streets towards the Harimandir. What the Afghans saw at the temple gave them some notion of the sort of people they were up against. Guarding the entrance to the shrine were only thirty Sikhs with "not a grain of fear about them. . . . They were there to sacrifice their lives for the Gurus."[43] The thirty men led by Gurbaksh Singh of the village of Khem Karan fell in the fighting and joined the ranks of the many honoured martyrs of Sikh history.

For the third time the Afghans blew up the Harimandir and filled the pool with dead cows.

Amritsar yielded little loot and no more than thirty Sikh lives. Abdali turned his footsteps towards Batala, ravaging the country in the most savage manner. Nur Mohammed writes: "Whichever way the army turned, the people were massacred in broad daylight. No distinction was made between Sikhs and non-Sikhs. The people ran away and hid themselves wherever they could. . . . No one can count the number of things that fell into the hands of the crusaders. Whether men or beasts, all fed upon nothing but sugar-candy and sugar-cane. The stomachs of all, big and small, slaves and slave-girls, were filled with these four things—beef, sugar-cane, sugar-candy, and sesame."[44]

The visitation of the Afghans and Baluchis is recalled to this day in the saying:

Khādā pītā lāhe dā,
bākī Ahmed Śāhe dā.

[43] *Jaṅg Nāmā,* pp. 97-101.
[44] *Jaṅg Nāmā,* pp. 103-04.

To eat and drink is all we know,
For the rest to Ahmed Shah doth go.

Ahmed Shah Abdali went leisurely across Jullundur Doab, amusing himself hunting deer and tiger and looting the country. He passed along the Himalayan foothills near Pinjaur and arrived at Kunjpura in February 1765.

The warm breeze of spring reminded the Afghans that summer would soon be on them and the blazing inferno of the Punjab plains would then become wholly advantageous to their Sikh adversaries. Nasir Khan Baluch advised Abdali to leave the task of subjugating the Sikhs to his Indian allies: Rohillas, Jats, Marathas, and Ala Singh of Patiala, "for the hare of a country can be best caught by a hound of the same country." Abdali accepted the advice and headed for the territories of Ala Singh. He passed through Sirhind, which had suffered from the hands of the Sikhs a short while ago. "The whole city lay in ruins," wrote Nur Mohammed. "No man, not even a bird, was to be seen there except the owl. . . . When I visited the lofty shrines I felt the breeze of paradise coming from every tomb . . . royal palaces of the city and its gardens, orchards and water tanks were all lying in ruins."[45] Ala Singh cashed in on the Afghan's changed mood and had his fief enlarged. He was invested with the title of Raja and presented with insignias of royalty: a battle drum and a standard. He agreed to pay the Afghans an annual tribute of three and a half lacs of rupees.

Abdali set out on his homeward journey. As soon as he crossed the Sutlej, the Sikhs were on his heels. The Afghan was obviously discomfited. "What, during my reign, my own palanquin trembles for fear of the Sikhs!" roared Abdali. "I will beat these infidels in such a way that the bones within their bodies will be reduced to fluffs of cotton."[46]

[45] *Jang Nāmā*, p. 118.
[46] *Jang Nāmā*, pp. 128-44.

All the misl Sardars, Jassa Singh Ahluwalia, Charhat Singh Sukerchakia, the Bhangis (Hari Singh, Jhanda Singh, Lehna Singh, Gulab Singh and Gujjar Singh), Jai Singh Kanhaya and Jassa Singh Ramgarhia, took part in the running battle. It was not to Abdali's liking, for nowhere would the Sikhs make a stand and fight in the orthodox way. "They came like the lion and fled like the fox," wrote Nur Mohammed.[47] It was the same hit-and-run for full seven days and nights. "If you wish to learn the art of war, come face to face with them in battle. . . . The body of every one of them is like a piece of rock, and in physical grandeur every one of them is equal to more than fifty. . . . If their armies take to flight, do not think they are running away. It is only a war tactic of theirs."[48]

Abdali headed straight for the frontier. He gave his allies much advice on how to deal with the Sikhs and offered them districts as *jāgīrs*. They heard the advice with respect but did not take his grants too seriously, for they knew that the districts of the Punjab were no longer the Shah's to give away.

A few days after Abdali's departure the Sarbat Khalsa met for its annual Baisakhi session (April 10, 1765). The experience of the last Afghan campaign had restored its confidence. The pool of the Harmandir was cleansed and the temple rebuilt at considerable expense. Six of the twelve misls appointed representatives to look after their

---

[47] *Jang Nāmā*, pp. 156-59.

[48] Nur Mohammed is full of vile abuse of the Sikhs. But even he is constrained to pay them tribute as men of character. "In no case would they slay a coward, nor would they put an obstacle in the way of a fugitive. They do not plunder the wealth and ornaments of a woman, be she a well-to-do lady or a maid-servant. There is no adultery among these dogs, nor are these mischievous people given to thieving. Whether a woman is young or old, they call her a *buṛiyā* and ask her to get out of the way. The word *buṛiyā* in the Indian language means 'an old lady.' There is no thief at all among these dogs, nor is there any house-breaker born among these miscreants. They do not make friends with adulterers and house-breakers, though their behaviour on the whole is not commendable." (*Jang Nāmā*, pp. 156-59.)

interests in Amritsar.[49] Religious services and the *guru kā laṅgar* were resumed on a scale larger than ever. The Sarbat Khalsa resolved to take advantage of the absence of Abdali's governor, Kabuli Mal (who was in Jammu recruiting Dogras for his army) to retake Lahore.

On April 16, 1765 the Bhangis, Gujjar Singh and Lehna Singh, forced their way into the capital. They were joined the next day by Sobha Singh Kanhaya. They heeded the words of advice of the leading citizens and forbade all plunder. "This city is called the Guru's cradle," pleaded the citizens (alluding to the fact that Lahore was the birthplace of the fourth guru, Ram Das). "If you look after it, you will prosper. But if you ruin it, you too will derive no profit from it."[50] The city was divided into three. Lehna Singh took over the central part, including the fort; Gujjar Singh,[51] the eastern as far as the Shalamar gardens on the road to Amritsar; and Sobha Singh, the southern extending to Niazbeg. The Sardars issued silver coins in the name of the Founder of their faith and that of their militant fraternity, Guru Gobind Singh.

Lehna Singh, who held the most important part of the city, proved to be an able and enlightened administrator. He had no sectarian prejudices. Since the majority of the citizens were Muslims, he joined them in their festivals and made offerings at their shrines. A few months of Lehna Singh's rule erased anti-Sikh prejudices created by the Afghans and the bigoted mullahs from the minds of the people. The Muslims of Lahore shed their fear of the

[49] H. R. Gupta, *History of the Sikhs*, I, 226.
[50] H. R. Gupta, *History of the Sikhs*, I, 228.
[51] The locality of his fortified city house is still known as Qila Gujjar Singh. Sobha Singh turned the mausoleum of Aurangzeb's daughter, Zebunnissa, into a fortress; the locality bears the name Nawakot (new fort) to this day.

Sohan Lal says that Charhat Singh Sukerchakia demanded a share in the city and was given Abdali's famous cannon, Zam Zama. The Zam Zama later passed from the Sukerchakias through various hands to the Bhangis and was kept at Amritsar. Charhat Singh's grandson, Ranjit Singh, recaptured it.

Khalsa and instead, like their co-religionists in the countryside, began to look upon the Sikhs more as fellow Punjabis than as infidels and to regard the Afghans more as foreigners than as defenders of the faith. This change of heart was the most decisive factor in the success of Ranjit Singh thirty-four years later.

After the monsoon, Sikhs plundered the country north of Delhi and crossed the Jumna into Rohilla territory.[52] They had many skirmishes with Najibuddaulah's troops[53] and when they were hard pressed, recrossed the Jumna. This expedition was more in the nature of a reconnaissance and the misls were back in Amritsar to celebrate Divali. A few days after the celebrations, they were back on the scene of operations and, despite suffering a reverse at the hands of the Rohillas near Karnal, came up to Kharkhauda near Delhi (from whence Banda had first called the Sikhs to arms fifty-seven years earlier). They allied themselves with the Jats of Bharatpur and pillaged Rewari and many villages in the territories of the Raja of Jaipur. In March 1766 a combined army of Sikhs and Jats defeated the Marathas (who were coming up to help the Rajputs) in a battle fought on the banks of the river Chambal. The Jats then occupied Dholpur.

The Sikhs turned back from Madhya Pradesh laden with spoils won during the campaign and money the Jats had

[52] "They (the Sikhs) seized booty beyond count in cash, gold, and jewels, burned the countryside, and carried away many prisoners. Greatly distressed by the news, Najibuddaulah marched at once towards the Sikhs and by rapid marches came upon them. On the arrival of Najibuddaulah, the Sikhs, after plundering the country, recrossed the Jumna and went away in the direction of their own country. Najibuddaulah then returned to the capital." (*Najībuddaulāh*, p. 77.)

[53] "Every day there were skirmishes between them [the Sikhs] and his [Najibuddaulah] troops. The Sikhs continued to burn and plunder the villages and kill people in all directions. They reached the bank of the Jumna and thence they went to the pargana of Shamli. There a stiff battle was fought which lasted till the evening. The Sikh troopers kept moving round the camp of Najibuddaulah." (*Najībuddaulāh*, p. 110.)

given them for their services. News of their approach created panic in Delhi. Najibuddaulah hurried back to the capital and decided to give the Sikhs a taste of their own medicine.[54] The Rohillas caught up with the Sikhs near Panipat, inflicted many casualties, and made them part with the plunder they had amassed.[55]

While some of the Dal's forces were busy on the eastern front, others under the command of the Bhangi Sardars, Jhanda Singh and Ganda Singh, were extending the frontiers of the Sikh state towards the south. In the autumn of 1766 they captured the important town of Pak Pattan and proceeded up to Multan. The operations had to be stopped, for Abdali had entered the Punjab again and all misls were required to muster their full strength to face the Afghans.

Eighth Afghan Invasion, 1766

In November 1766 Abdali came to the Punjab for the eighth time with the avowed object of extirpating "the ill-fated Sikhs."[56] He brushed aside two attempts by them to check him near the river Jhelum and proceeded triumphantly through Gujarat to Sialkot. He ordered the zamindars "to apprehend and despoil with every degree of severity all persons carrying the marks of a Sikh."[57] From

---

[54] Najibuddaulah's biographer, Nuruddin Hussain, gives a detailed account of these operations. "The Sikhs will now receive a good thrashing," he wrote, quoting Najibuddaulah. "They have much booty in their fight with Malhar Rao and have also got large sums from Jawahir Singh, so that they are heavily loaded. We ought to bar their path once more and do a splendid deed." (*Najibuddaulah*, p. 119.)

[55] "The Sikhs were caught helpless and could do nothing. Najibuddaulah thus captured an immense amount of booty, including rows upon rows of camels, horses, and ponies laden with booty. He drove away the Sikhs for five kos up to Kandhala. . . . The Sikhs lost a large number of men. It was after a long time that such an enormous booty was seized from the Sikhs." (*Najibuddaulah*, pp. 119-20.)

[56] Shah Alam II had bemoaned Abdali's failure to "drive to the mansions of perdition this infidel race, the fomentors of all mischief." (C.P.C., ii, 257.)

[57] C.P.C., ii, 16 a; Ganda Singh, *Ahmed Shāh Durrānī*, p. 310.

Sialkot, the Afghans turned to Lahore. The three Sardars who had parcelled the city between themselves left immediately.[58]

Abdali entered the capital on December 22, 1766. The Muslim citizens told the Afghan that they had been well and honourably treated by the Sikhs and persuaded Abali to offer the *subedārī* of Lahore to Lehna Singh. Abdali sent the invitation to the Sardar with trays of the choicest dry fruit of Afghanistan. In return, the Sikh sent a handful of coarse grain with the message that fruit was for royalty; he was a humble peasant who lived on simple food. Lehna Singh politely turned down the offer.[59]

Abdali did not know what to do with a people who would neither fight him in the open nor make friends with him. When he went after them in Sirhind, they fell on his rear and plundered his equipment near Lahore. He had to rush back to save the city.

In January 1767, Abdali's General, Jahan Khan, who had suffered many reverses at the hands of the Sikhs, audaciously marched up to Amritsar. The Sikhs had more than once rebuilt the Harimandir from the debris left by the Afghans and felt they were now strong enough to fight the vandals in the open. The misls gathered in full strength and fell upon Jahan Khan. They killed over five thousand Afghans before Abdali could come to their rescue.[60]

[58] The event is recalled in doggerel with puns on the names of the three Sardars. Sobha (grace), lost his grace; Gujjar (the herdsman), lost his cattle and Lehna (the one who takes), had to give away; all three were thus reduced to penury.

> Sobhā dī sobhā gaī, Gujjar dā giā māl
> Lehne nū denā piyā, tino hoe kaṅgāl.

[59] Ganda Singh, *Ahmed Shāh Durrānī*, p. 312; H. R. Gupta, *History of the Sikhs*, I, 251.

[60] The news of this Sikh victory over the Afghans was received with great relief by the British, who had reason to believe that Abdali's real object in coming to India was to help Mir Qasim against them. A dispatch sent to the Nawab Wazir of Oudh said that Lord Clive "is extremely glad to know that the Shah's progress has been impeded by the Sikhs. If they continue to cut off his supplies and plunder his baggage, he will be

Abdali took Amritsar, but this time spared the Harimandir: perhaps he had been told of the way the Sikhs reacted
to the defilement of their shrines. Instead, he proceeded to
their richest agricultural land in the Jullundur Doab. He
found the entire countryside hostile to the Afghans. A
contemporary news-writer describes the situation: "The
Shah's influence is confined merely to those tracts which
are covered by his army. The Zamindars appear in general
so well affected towards the Sikhs that it is usual with the
latter to repair by night to the villages, where they find
every refreshment. By day they retire from them and again
fall to harassing the Shah's troops. If the Shah remains between the two rivers Beas and Sutlej, the Sikhs will continue to remain in the neighbourhood, but if he passes
over towards Sirhind the Sikhs will then become masters
of the parts he leaves behind him."[61]

Abdali crossed the Sutlej into Malwa, where Najibuddaulah, and Amar Singh of Patiala joined him. He gave
Amar Singh the district of Sirhind and invested him with
insignias of royalty and the title *Rājā-i-Rājgān*.[62] He made
a few desultory attempts to lay his hands on the Sikhs, but
they eluded him every time.[63] At last the wild-goose chase

---

ruined without fighting; and then he will either return to his country or
meet with shame and disgrace. As long as he does not defeat the Sikhs or
come to terms with them, he cannot penetrate into India. And
neither of these events seems probable since the Sikhs have adopted such
effective tactics, and since they hate the Shah on account of his destruction of *Chak*." (C.P.C., ii, 52; H. R. Gupta, *History of the Sikhs*, I, 255.)

[61] C.P.C., ii, 79 and 139; H. R. Gupta, *History of the Sikhs*, I, 256;
Ganda Singh, *Ahmed Shāh Durrānī*, p. 314.

[62] The sycophant Amar Singh expressed his gratitude to his patron
Wazir Shah Vali Khan Bamezei, who had interceded on his behalf, by
adding Bamezei to his own name on the official seal. (Ganda Singh, *Ahmed
Shāh Durrānī*, p. 317.)

[63] Nur Mohammed mentions a victory over the Sikhs in the Mani
Majra hills in March 1767 when the Afghans and Rohillas "brought away
large numbers of captive men and women from the region, but the Sikh
leader escaped. Much plundered property was sold cheap in the Durrani
Camp, to captives also." The expedition was not a great success as the
Shah "was overcome by the jackal tricks of the Sikhs." (J. N. Sarkar, *Fall*

and the insufferable heat wore him out. He gave Najibuddaulah leave to return to his dominions, which were being
ravaged by the Sikhs,[64] and turned his back on the Punjab.
Abdali was barely across the Indus when the three Sardars turned up to reoccupy Lahore. The Afghan governor
could not count on the collaboration of any of the citizens
—not even of the Muslims, in whose interests Abdali had
often professed to act. They petitioned the governor to
hand over the capital to Lehna Singh: "The people are
very glad and satisfied with the rule of the Sikhs. They
might open the city gates in the night or break holes in the
city walls and thus admit them into the town. You will in
that case fall a victim to their wrath. In our opinion, therefore, you should have an interview with them and after
having settled something for yourself by way of allowance
or jagir should entrust the town to them."[65]

By the end of 1767, the Sikhs had retaken the whole of
the Punjab. In the north and northwest Gujjar Singh reduced the Muslim tribes of the Salt range and Pothohar
and established his deputy in Rawalpindi. In the southeast, Sikh horsemen swarmed in the country around Delhi
and spilled over into the Gangetic Doab. Najibuddaulah
defeated their columns more than once. But he too wearied
of ceaseless fighting against a people who increased "like
ants and locusts" and admitted: "The Sikhs have prevailed."[66] Thereafter the people of the Gangetic Doab resigned themselves to the annual incursions of the Sikhs.
"As regularly as the crops were cut, the border chieftains

---

of the Mughal Empire, II, 365-66.) Miskin, however, refers to a battle in
May 1767 in which 9,000 Sikhs were killed. Folio 267-68.

[64] "The Sikhs had taken shelter in places of difficult access, but the
King struck at them wherever he could find them. News was received that
the guru of the Sikhs had concealed himself in the hills of Mani Majra.
There the enemy of Ahmed Shah, accompanied by Afzal Khan, brother of
Najibuddaulah, seized many men and women and made them slaves but
the guru could not be captured." (Najibuddaulāh, p. 121.)

[65] Aliuddin, 130 B; H. R. Gupta, History of the Sikhs, I, 262.

[66] H. R. Gupta, History of the Sikhs, I, 268 and 271.

crossed over and levied blackmail from almost every village, in the most systematic manner. Their requisitions were termed *rākhī*, sometimes euphemistically *kamblī*, i.e. 'blanket money.' Each of them had a certain well-known beat or circle, so well recognised and clearly defined that it is not unusual for the peasantry at the present day to speak of some places being, for instance, in Jodh Singh's *pattī*, others in Diwan Singh's or Himmat Singh's, and so on. The collections, of course, varied with the ability of the people to pay, averaging from two to five rupees a head. Two or three horsemen generally sufficed to collect them, for 2,000 or 3,000 more were never very far off. In case of delay about paying up, a handful of troops, each well-mounted and armed with a spear, sword, and good matchlock, speedily appeared to accelerate the liquidation of the debt. Refusal was fatal."[67]

Ninth Afghan Invasion, 1769

Abdali made his ninth and final attempt to conquer the Punjab in 1769. But he was like a spent bullet and could get no further than the Jhelum.[68] He returned to Kandhar, a sick and broken man, and died on October 23, 1772. The epitaph on his grave stated with pride, ". . . the ears of his enemies were incessantly deafened by the din of his conquests." The Sikhs were certainly his enemies, and they more than any other people heard of his conquests, but all they learned from the din was to turn a deaf ear to it.

Abdali was the bitterest antagonist of the Sikhs and paradoxically their greatest benefactor. His repeated incursions destroyed Mughal administration in the Punjab and at Panipat he dealt a crippling blow to Maratha pretensions in the north. Thus he created a power vacuum in the Punjab which was filled by the Sikhs. Abdali failed to

[67] G. R. C. Williams, *Calcutta Review*, 1875, pp. 28-29.
[68] H. R. Gupta, I, 270, based on C.P.C. ii, 1499. Ganda Singh (*Ahmed Shāh Durrānī*, p. 320) believes Abdali reached the Chenab.

put down the Sikhs because they refused to meet him on his terms. They were everywhere and yet elusive; they displayed temerity in attacking armies much stronger than theirs and alacrity in running away when the tide of battle turned against them. Fighting the Sikhs was like trying to catch the wind in a net. The Sikhs were able to resort to these tactics because the people were behind them. The peasants gave them food, tended the wounded, and gave shelter to fugitives. The Sikhs were also fortunate in having leaders like Jassa Singh Ahluwalia, Hari Singh Bhangi, and Charhat Singh Sukerchakia. By contrast, Abdali's son and generals were men of modest ability. Besides this, Abdali never had time to consolidate his conquests for he had to rush back to his own country to put down some insurrection or the other. Consequently, what he won by his military prowess was lost by the ineptitude of his deputies.

Abdali spilled more Sikh blood than any other; but he also taught them that no people can become a strong and great nation without learning to shed blood.

CHAPTER 9

FROM THE INDUS TO THE GANGES

After the Afghan Invasions

THE death of Ahmed Shah Abdali created a novel situation in the Punjab. Abdali's son and successor, Taimur, could do little more than hold his father's conquests west of the Indus along with Kashmir, Bahawalpur, Multan (which he wrested from the Bhangis in 1780), and Sindh. At the eastern end, the position remained fluid for a long time. The Mughal emperor was living at Allahabad in an undefined subservience to the English, who had already cast their protective mantle over the Nawab Wazir of Oudh. The English were, however, not yet ready to extend their power beyond the Ganges. Delhi was administered by Najibuddaulah[1] on behalf of the absentee emperor. But his writ did not run beyond fifty miles of the city walls because contentious bands of free booters—Sikhs, Rohillas, Jats, Rajputs, and Marathas—roamed the countryside and acknowledged no master save the leader of their own gang. This continued to be the state of affairs for some time until the Marathas seized Delhi. Although they had suffered grievously on the field of Panipat, in eight years they recouped enough strength to be able to contend with their Indian adversaries. In 1769, Peshwa Madhav Rao opened negotiations with the Mughal emperor and his deputy, Najibuddaulah. Three years later (the year Abdali died) Madhaji Sindhia put Shah Alam II back on the throne of his ancestors in the Red Fort and restored a semblance of order in the capital.

With the Afghans quiescent on one side and the Ma-

[1] In 1769 Najibuddaulah was a sick and dying man. A year later, when he had a recurrence of virulent gonorrhea, he invested his son Zabita Khan in his place. He died at Hapur on October 31, 1770 and was buried at Najibabad. (*Najibuddaulāh*.)

· 169 ·

rathas busy consolidating their hold on Delhi on the other, the territory between the Indus and the Jumna was left to the Sikhs. They immediately set about dividing it among themselves. Horsemen galloped madly in different directions claiming village after village by the simple act of leaving a personal token like a turban or a shoe to mark their ownership. Now that there was no danger from abroad and plenty of land to appropriate, the misl organisation began to lack cohesion. The only reason why men continued to owe allegiance to some misl or the other was to safeguard their own possessions or add to them. As soon as they reached the limit prescribed by foreign powers, they had no option but to turn against each other. The Sarbat Khalsa became a snake with many heads. Thus divided, the Sikhs could not contend with the Afghans, the Marathas, or the English.

For the sake of clarity it is better to examine the expansionist and contentious phases of the misls of the Trans-Sutlej zone (Majha and the Jullundur Doab) separately from those of the misls of the Cis-Sutlej (Malwa) zone.

*Expansion of the Misls of the Majha
and the Jullundur Doab*

No sooner had Abdali recrossed the Indus for the last time than the misls proceeded to reoccupy the Punjab. Jassa Singh Ahluwalia extended his hold along the Sutlej and occupied the towns of Sultanpur and Kapurthala. The Ramgarhias and the Kanhayas turned their attention northwards. The Ramgarhias levied tribute on Kangra, Nurpur, Chamba, Basohli, and Mandi. The Kanhayas followed up by capturing the fort of Kangra.[2] The Dogra

---

[2] Forster, who came across bands of Sikh horsemen operating in the hills, gives a vivid account of their doings: "The region lay wholly at the mercy of the Sicques, who are, I think, the plainest dealers in the world. The fort of Sebah, standing pleasantly on the brink of a rivulet, lay on

kingdom of Jammu became a bone of contention among the misls. The Bhangis were the first to levy tribute on the Dogras. The Kanhayas and the Sukerchakias, who followed the Bhangis, fell out among themselves over the plunder of the rich city. The mopping up of Muslim principalities owing loyalty to the Afghans was done by the Nakkais, Sukerchakias, and Bhangis. The Nakkais extended their power along the southern reaches of the Ravi up to Harappa and beyond. The Sukerchakias expanded in all directions around Gujranwala. The misl that rose to supreme preeminence in western Punjab was the Bhangi under Hari Singh (d. 1765), his two sons Jhanda Singh and Ganda Singh, and their numerous kinsmen. The Bhangis had taken the two premier cities of the Punjab: Lahore and Amritsar. They, along with the Ahluwalias, defeated the Pathans of Kasur and made them tributaries. In A.D. 1772 the Bhangis captured Multan and held it for eight years until it was recaptured by the Afghans. Jhanda Singh subdued the Baluch tribes between the Jhelum and the Indus, levied tribute on Mankera, then crossed the Indus and captured Kalabagh. About the same time, Gujjar Singh Bhangi began systematically to reduce the Muslim tribes further north: Gakkhars, Janjuas, Awans, Khattars, and others. His deputy, Milkha Singh, went further; he set up his headquarters at Rawalpindi and later took Pindi Gheb, Fatehjang, and Attock.

Expansion of the Malwa Misls

With the assurance that their hinterland was secure, the Malwais began to expand eastwards and became a source of terror to the people living between the Jumna and the Ganges and beyond the Ganges to the Nawab Wazir of

---

our road, and in passing it, I saw two Sicque cavaliers strike terror into the chief and all his people, though shut up within their fort. They had been sent to collect the tribute which the Sicques have imposed on all the mountain chiefs from the Ganges to the Jumna" (I, 261).

Oudh and his English patrons.[3] These incursions along and across the Jumna brought the Malwais into conflict with the Jats, Rohillas, Mughals, Marathas, Rajputs, and the English.

Across the Jumna

In January 1770 a Sikh force of over twenty thousand horsemen invaded Panipat and after fighting an indecisive engagement with Najibuddaulah's son, Zabita Khan,[4] crossed the river Jumna and camped near Aligarh. It withdrew in the face of a superior force of Jats and Marathas, but later plundered villages around Panipat, Sonepat, and Karnal.

Two years later, the Malwais clashed with the Marathas who had come into Sirhind. They expelled the Marathas from Malwa and followed up their success by again crossing the Jumna. In the winter of 1773-1774 they levied tribute on many towns and villages between the Jumna and the Ganges. Thereafter, their visitations into this doab became a regular post-harvest feature. Their method of operations is described by Francklin: "When determined to invade a neighbouring province, they assemble at first in small numbers on the frontier, when having first demanded the *rākhī* or tribute, if it be complied with, they retire peaceably; but when this is denied, hostilities commence, and the Seiks in their progress are accustomed to lay waste the country on all sides, carrying along with them as many of the inhabitants as they can take prisoners, and all the cattle."[5]

---

[3] Colonel Polier, a Swiss, described the misls as "that formidable aristocratic republic" of Sikh soldiers who are "indefatigable; mounted on the best horses that India can afford. . . . Fifty of them are enough to keep at bay a whole battalion of the King's forces." (*Asiatic Annual Register*, 1800, pp. 34-35.)

[4] A few months before his death, Najibuddaulah had advised his son: "You are free to settle the affairs of the Sikhs either by peace or by war at your discretion." Five years later Zabita thought it discreet to make peace with the Sikhs. (*Najībuddaulāh*, pp. 125-26.)

[5] Francklin, *Shāh Āulum*, pp. 76-77.

Sikh-Rohilla Alliance

In December 1773, Sikhs pillaged the territories of Zabita Khan Rohilla, including the towns of Nanauta and Jalalabad. A month later, Sikh horsemen looted the suburbs of Delhi. The Mughal court was in a dilemma. The ablest man in the capital was Najaf Khan.[6] His plans were, however, often thwarted by an upstart Abdul Ahad Khan, who had the Emperor's ear. Najaf Khan was a Shia from Iran. Abdul Ahad Khan, who was a Sunni from Kashmir, exploited these sectarian and racial differences to his advantage. Najaf Khan wanted to take stern measures against the Sikhs and did his best to win over the Rohillas to his side. Abdul Ahad Khan's chief interest was to prevent the Irani from becoming too strong, and he was not wholly unwilling to see the Sikhs occasionally triumph over Najaf Khan. Because of these divided counsels, the Emperor first tried to buy off the Sikhs by offering them employment. When this failed, he allowed Abdul Ahad Khan to engage the services of Walter Reinhardt, a German paramour of Begam Samru of Sardana. The Malwais made short work of Reinhardt, and returned to pillage the suburbs of Delhi.

The next round against the Sikhs was fought by Najaf Khan. Mullah Rahim Dad Khan, who was the subedar of Panipat, was killed in an engagement against the combined forces of Amar Singh of Patiala and Gajpat Singh of Jind. Later a compromise was brought about by Najaf Khan regarding the territories to be occupied by each, but this was soon ignored by both parties.

The Malwais turned their attention to the Rohillas. In the spring of 1775, Rai Singh Bhangi, Baghel Singh Ka-

[6] Mirza Najaf Khan Zulfiqar-ud-daulah was a member of the Royal Safavid house and was imprisoned by the usurper Nadir Shah. After his release in 1746 he came to India and served with the Nawabs of Oudh and Bengal. In 1765 he joined the service of Shah Alam II and was the Emperor's right-hand man until his death in April 1782. He is buried near the tomb of Safdar Jang in New Delhi. (T. G. P. Spear, *Twilight of the Mughuls*, pp. 19-20.)

rora Singhia, and Tara Singh Gheba crossed the Jumna
with their horsemen and began a systematic conquest of
the territories of Zabita Khan. The Rohilla had no hope
of assistance from the Mughal court which he had offended
nor from his eastern neighbours, the Nawab Wazir of
Oudh and the English. In desperation he offered the Malwais large sums of money and proposed an alliance to
plunder the crown lands. The *misldārs* agreed, and combined bands of Sikhs and Rohillas looted villages around
the present site of New Delhi. In March 1776 the allies
defeated the imperial forces near Muzaffarnagar. The
whole of the Jumna-Gangetic Doab was now at their mercy.
They consolidated their hold on the doab and again appeared at the gates of Delhi. The Emperor was constrained
to receive the rebel Zabita Khan and forgive him his
trespasses.

Sikhs against Najaf Khan. Defeat of the Rohillas

Malwa Sikhs became the most sought-after mercenaries
in India. The Nawab Wazir of Oudh, the Mughals, and
the Rohillas each offered them employment on generous
terms. The Malwais, who had signed a pledge with Zabita
Khan, resisted these tempting counteroffers for some time.
Meanwhile, Najaf Khan turned to the Marathas for assistance and all through 1776 up to the summer of 1777
skirmishes took place between roving bands of Sikhs and
Rohilla horsemen, on the one side, and Mughal and Maratha cavalry, on the other, along the banks of the Jumna.
After the monsoon of 1777, Najaf Khan succeeded in iso-
lating the Rohillas from their Sikh allies and thoroughly
trounced them. Zabita Khan had no alternative but to
throw himself on the mercy of the Sikhs. He is said to have
undergone a nominal conversion to the Sikh faith and
became, as the saying of the times went, "half Sikh and
half Rohilla."[7]

[7]   *Ek guru kā do celā
       Ādhā Sikh ādhā Rohillā.*
He is said to have been baptised with the name Dharam Singh.

Sikh attempts to reinstate Zabita Khan in his possessions were frustrated by the energetic Najaf Khan. But in
the summer of 1778, when Najaf Khan was away in Alwar,
the Sikhs audaciously entered the capital and enjoyed the
hospitality of Abdul Ahad Khan. A few months later, they
crossed the Ganges into the territory of the Nawab Wazir
and were with great difficulty expelled by the English.

Najaf Khan realised that neither he nor the Marathas
were strong enough to deal with the Sikhs. The astute
Irani turned to diplomacy. He appealed to Zabita Khan
to return to the Muslim fold; he flattered the Sikh Sardars as protectors of the empire; and he sowed the seeds
of discord among the Malwais. He succeeded in doing all
three at the same time. Zabita Khan deserted the Sikhs,
went over to the Mughal camp, and cemented his new
alliance by giving his daughter in marriage to Najaf Khan.
The Sikhs spared the imperial domains and instead turned
to plundering each other. Within a few months, the dis-
sensions in the ranks of the Malwais had come to such a
pass that the Mughals felt strong enough to take the offensive against them.

In the autumn of 1779 a large Mughal army under the
command of Prince Farkhunda Bakht and Abdul Ahad
Khan set out from Delhi. Rai Singh of Buria, Bhanga Singh
of Thanesar, Baghel Singh and Bhag Singh of Jind joined
the imperial forces and encircled Patiala. Amar Singh and
Tara Singh Gheba, who had come to his aid, withdrew
their forces behind the city walls and sent an appeal for
help to the Majhails. Jassa Singh Ahluwalia hurried to
their rescue. The news of the progress of the Dal Khalsa
caused large-scale desertions of Sikhs from the imperialist's
army. Panic spread in the ranks of the Mughals and they
decided to return to Delhi. The retreat was, according to
Francklin, "disgraceful and disorderly," and in four days'
march from Patiala to Panipat the Mughal army lost most
of its equipment and a great many men.

The road to Delhi was rolled out for the Sikhs like the
proverbial red carpet. It needed one bold chieftain to lead

his horsemen into the imperial city, take the Emperor under his protection, and with one stroke make the Sikhs the premier power in all Hindustan. But not one of the Malwai Sardars had the sagacity or the courage to take this step. They were little more than brigands to whom the victory at Patiala opened up new pastures to plunder. They bypassed the capital and went across the Jumna to loot the Jumna-Gangetic Doab. Meanwhile Najaf Khan reorganised the Mughal army, chose a trusted relative, Mirza Shafi, to be commander and sent him in pursuit of the Sikhs.

Mirza Shafi's chance came when the Sikhs were returning with the booty they had taken in the territories of the Nawab Wazir. He charged the embittered Zabita Khan, whose estates the Sikhs had despoiled, with the mission of sowing discord among the Sikhs. "Set one party against the other. . . . Put them all to fight among themselves," he counselled. The Rohilla succeeded in his task. The Malwais fell out among themselves. Mirza Shafi captured Gajpat Singh of Jind along with three other Sardars and expelled the others from the Jumna-Gangetic Doab.

Mirza Shafi followed up his success by carrying the war into the Sikh homeland. An army of Mughals and Rohillas proceeded up the Grand Trunk Road and took Buria, Mustafabad, and Sadhaura. The Dal Khalsa under Jassa Singh Ahluwalia again came down from the north to oppose its advance. The two armies avoided fighting a pitched battle; instead, they organised raids behind each other's lines. All that Mirza Shafi achieved in months of desultory skirmishing was to win an engagement at Indri (April 1781) and to keep the Sikhs on the defensive in their own country. He could not prevent them from going behind him and raiding the Gangetic Doab nor, within a few weeks, liberating most of the towns he had captured.

Mirza Shafi's expedition into Malwa was an expensive failure and had to be abandoned by the middle of the year.

Zabita Khan was entrusted by the Mughal government with the task of negotiating with the Sikhs. The *misldārs'* estates were confirmed; their right to levy *rākhī* on lands between Panipat and Delhi and the upper Gangetic Doab was conceded; and they were invited to recruit for service in the imperial army.

In the Suburbs of Delhi

Najaf Khan died in April 1782. The struggle for power that ensued gave the Sikhs another chance to become the sovereign power of Hindustan. And yet again they let the chance slip through their fingers. They reappeared in the neighbourhood of the capital and, instead of capturing it, went over into the doab and crossed the Ganges at several points. "Being at the time in Rohilkhand," wrote Forster, "I witnessed the terror and general alarm which prevailed among the inhabitants who, deserting the open country, had retired into forts and places inaccessible to cavalry."[8] The rulers of Garhwal and Nahan submitted to them. The Shivalik hills, including Dehra Dun, came under their sway.

In March 1783, Baghel Singh established his camp in a suburb of Delhi and started to build temples to commemorate the memory of the gurus who had visited the city. One was erected at the site of execution of the ninth guru, Tegh Bahadur, in the centre of the city's busiest thoroughfare; one to mark the site of the cremation of

---

[8] Forster, I, 326. Forster gives an account of the awe and respect with which the people treated the Sikhs at the time: "I saw two Sicque horsemen, who had been sent from their country to receive the Siringnaghur tribute which is collected from the revenues of certain custom-houses. From the manner in which these men were treated, or rather treated themselves, I frequently wished for the power of migrating into the body of a Sicque for a few weeks—so well did these cavaliers fare. No sooner had they alighted, then beds were prepared for their repose, and their horses were supplied with green barley pulled out of the field. The *Kāfilāh* travellers were contented to lodge on the ground, and expressed their thanks for permission to purchase what they required; such is the difference between those who were in, and those who were out of power."

the guru's body; a third at Guru Hari Krishen's place of residence; and a fourth at the place where the infant guru and the wives of Guru Gobind Singh were cremated.[9]

The English opened diplomatic relations with the Sikhs. Their object was to preserve the territories of their protégé, the Nawab Wazir of Oudh, and they wanted assurances from the Sardars that they would not enter the Nawab's domains. They also posted pickets on all fords on the river Ganges.

In the summer of 1783 Sikh incursions across the Jumna assumed the magnitude of an exodus. After two poor harvests, the monsoon failed completely, and the whole of Southern Punjab up to Delhi was gripped by famine. Sikh horsemen brought their families with them and scoured the impoverished countryside for food. The famine and an epidemic of cholera that followed took a heavy toll of life.

The famine of these years made the Sikh free-booters more ravenous. In January 1784 over thirty thousand horsemen under the leadership of Jassa Singh Ramgarhia and Karam Singh forded the Jumna and began to collect rakhi from the towns and villages between the two rivers. These Sardars, who dared so much in the field of battle, showed surprising timidity in the political field; when sounded by the Emperor they shrank from taking the Imperial city under their protection. In this instance the Emperor turned for help to the English and Marathas. The English in India did not have the confidence that the Directors of the East India Company in London would approve of extending power beyond the Ganges. The best that the governor-general, Warren Hastings, could do was to preserve the status quo and try to keep the Sikhs and Marathas apart without committing his government in any way. He wrote: "It is certainly not for the interest of either

9 The four gurdwaras are (1) Sis Ganj in Chandni Chowk, (2) Rikabganj near Parliament House, (3) Bangla Sahib, and (4) Bala Sahib in New Delhi.

the Company's or the Vizier's Government that the chiefs
of the Seikh tribes should form any friendly connections
with the Mahrattas. On the contrary, a disunion between
them is much to be desired; and if any assurances to the
Seikhs of our determination not to interfere in such disputes could foment or add to them, such assurances ought
to be conveyed."[10]

By the winter of 1784, Shah Alam II concluded that
the English were not willing to take over the administration. He turned to the Marathas, who had earlier brought
him back to the capital. In December, he invested Madhaji
Sindhia with the title of *Vakīl-i-mutlaq* (regent plenipo-
tentiary) and requested him to put in order whatever remained of the Empire.

Baghel Singh and Jassa Singh Ramgarhia again crossed
the Jumna. This incursion was more serious than the previous ones because following in the wake of the Sikhs
were Gujjar herdsmen who took what had escaped the
rapacious Sikhs. After looting the doab the Sikhs cast their
eyes on the land across the Ganges. The Rohillas, led by
Ghulam Qadir, who had succeeded his father Zabita Khan,
the English, and the Nawab Wazir of Oudh lined their
troops along the river to prevent the Sikhs from crossing over.

Madhaji Sindhia ordered his troops to expel the ma-
rauders. After the first skirmish he realised that he would
get better results by talking to the Sikhs than by fighting
them. The Maratha agent in Delhi reported candidly:
"The Emperor rules inside the city, while outside the
Sikhs are supreme." Negotiations were opened by the Marathas with the Sikh chiefs and the terms of a provisional
treaty agreed on in March 1785.

The Sikhs did not trust the Marathas—nor the Marathas the Sikhs. English agents were busy inducing the

[10] SC 20 of 19.4.1785.

Sikhs to break off relations with the Marathas. The Sikh chiefs concluded that the English wanted to treat with them and made proposals for an alliance. We shall not discourage these advances, noted the Governor General, though we shall "not meet them except by general assurances until the real designs of Madhaji Sindhia shall have been ascertained to be of an inimical nature."[11]

The Sikh chiefs lost patience with the English and concluded a treaty with Madhaji Sindhia on May 9, 1785. They agreed to provide the Marathas with a contingent of five thousand horse and give up the right to take *rākhī* in lieu of a jagir of ten lac rupees. The stipulated force of cavalry joined the Maratha camp but were immediately suspected by the Marathas of spying. "The Sikhs are faithless. Having stayed in our camp for two months they have closely studied everything about our troops," said a Maratha dispatch.[12] The atmosphere of suspicion vitiated the treaty and within a few weeks it was forgotten by both sides.

In December 1785 a Maratha force entered Malwa to intercede in a quarrel between the Patiala Raja and the leader of the Singhpurias. While the Marathas were in Patiala, Sikh horsemen were collecting *rākhī* across the Jumna. This was repeated the following year when Bhanga Singh of Thanesar, one of the most ruffianly of the Malwa Sardars, levied tribute on many towns, including Meerut and Hapur. In the monsoon season of 1787, another band of Sikhs under Baghel Singh joined Ghulam Qadir's Rohillas and plundered the imperial domains between Agra and Delhi. With the help of the Sikhs, Ghulam Qadir entered the imperial city and let loose a reign of terror culminating in the blinding of the Emperor, Shah Alam, on August 10, 1788.[13]

---

[11] SC 21 of 19.4.1785.

[12] H. R. Gupta, II, 187.

[13] This dastardly act disgusted the Sikhs, and they broke with Ghulam Qadir, who was captured by the Marathas and executed on March 4, 1789. His family sought asylum with the Sikhs.

The struggle for the possession of the Jumna-Gangetic Doab went on for six years. The Sikhs crossed the Ganges on several occasions and clashed with English pickets. In January 1791, Bhanga Singh of Thanesar captured an English officer, Lieutenant-Colonel Stuart, and extracted a ransom of Rs. 60,000 from his government.[14] With the death of Madhaji Sindhia in February 1794, Sikh incursions became more extensive than ever before.[15]

Sikh expansion towards the east had reached its furthest limits by 1795. Thereafter the Marathas not only stemmed Sikh onslaughts but even pushed them back into their Malwa homeland. General Perron, who commanded Maratha armies in the north, was able to dictate his terms to the Malwais; and the Malwais became so disunited that an English adventurer, George Thomas, who had set up a kingdom at Hansi, was with considerable difficulty ejected from Sikh territory. The success of Perron and George Thomas showed the impotence to which the Cis-Sutlej Sardars had reduced themselves.[16]

[14] The English could do little against Bhanga Singh except pretend that Stuart had been saved by the Sardar from bandits because of his affection for the English. Being unwilling to pay ransom, they kept asking for Stuart's return in the friendliest of terms. Bhanga Singh replied: "I trust that till the time of meeting you will continue to fill the cup of desire with the effusions of your friendly pen." PC 2 of 13.5.1791.

[15] In the autumn of 1794 the Sikhs exploited the situation that had arisen after a quarrel between the ruler of Rampur and the Nawab Wazir of Oudh. Both parties asked for Sikh help; both received promises from rival Sardars. The Rohillas counted on Jassa Singh Ramgarhia; the Nawab Wazir on Rai Singh and Sher Singh of Buria, and Bhanga Singh of Thanesar. Bhanga Singh stated his terms explicitly: "Your Excellency knows the nature of the Sikhs without our describing it: that unless paid they never exert themselves for any one." The Nawab Wazir did not pay; and he got nothing. The Rohillas paid a small sum, and got a small Sikh detachment on their side. The battle was fought on October 26, 1794. The Nawab Wazir's forces defeated the Rohillas. There were no Sikh casualties—nor were any Sikhs taken prisoner.

[16] One of the worst instances of brigandage was in the spring of 1796, when the troops of Sahib Singh of Patiala, Rai Singh, and Sher Singh were involved in a serious riot at Hardwar on the occasion of the Kumbh Mela. They slew over five hundred Gosain and other priests and mulcted the pilgrims.

Break-up of the Misls

In Majha as in Malwa the chief cause of discord between the misls was the relaxation of external pressure and the love of loot.[17]

The mountainous regions in the north had escaped Abdali's attention. Tradesmen had shifted their depots from the plains to the hills and caravans had begun to pass along the foot of the Himalayas. The richest among the hill states was Jammu; it was the riches of Jammu that proved the undoing of the Sikh chiefs of Majha.

In 1774 the Jammu Raja, Ranjit Dev, fell out with his son, Braj Raj Dev. The Sukerchakias and the Kanhayas espoused the cause of the son; the Bhangis, that of the father. In the skirmishes that followed, Charhat Singh Sukerchakia was killed in an accident; Jhanda Singh Bhangi was murdered by an assassin paid by Jai Singh Kanhaya.

In 1775 the Bhangis and the Ramgarhias fought a combination of the Kanhayas, Sukerchakias, and Ahluwalias for ten days without any result. Thereafter the two Jassa Singhs fought each other. At first the Ahluwalia defeated and injured the Ramgarhia. A year later, the Ramgarhia avenged himself by capturing the Ahluwalia and then magnanimously freeing him. The once supreme commander of the Dal Khalsa had to seek the aid of Jai Singh Kanhaya to expel the Ramgarhias from Majha. They moved out to Hissar and immediately plunged into Malwa's equally senseless and violent politics.

In 1782 the Majhails again came to blows over Jammu.

---

[17] "In the country of the Punjab from the Indus to the banks of the Jumna there are thousands of chiefs in the Sikh community. None obeys the other. If a person owns two or three horses he boasts of being a chief, and gets ready to fight against thousands. When a village is besieged by the Sikhs to realise tribute which the zamindars cannot afford, they intrigue with other Sikhs and the Sikhs begin to fight between themselves. Whoever wins receives money according to the capacity of the villagers." (Imamuddin, *Husain Shāhī*, 242-43; H. R. Gupta, II, 19-20.)

Braj Raj Dev, who had succeeded his father, murdered his own brother and nephew. The Kanhayas supported Braj Raj Dev; the Bhangis supported members of the rival faction. The two misls, thereafter, joined hands to plunder Braj Raj Dev. The Jammu Raja turned to Maha Singh Sukerchakia for help. Maha Singh first helped Braj Raj Dev and then himself by looting the town. This angered the Kanhaya, Jai Singh. There was another realignment of misls. The Sukerchakias invited the Ramgarhias back into Majha and the two misls along with the Rajputs of Katoch fought and defeated the Kanhayas.

The sordid game of ganging up sometimes with one, sometimes with the other, went on. Among the most dexterous intriguers was Maha Singh Sukerchakia. With the loot of Jammu he made the family fortune; with his own nimble mind and strong right arm he raised the house of Sukerchakia to the second most powerful among the misls. He was well on the way to reducing the Bhangis when his career of conquest was cut short by his untimely death in 1792.

If a balance-sheet of the century following the promulgation of the Khalsa were drawn up, on the credit side the most significant entry would be the resurrection of the spirit of Punjabi nationalism which had almost been killed by Banda. Men like Nawab Kapur Singh, Jassa Singh Ahluwalia, and the Bhangi Sardars not only built up the Khalsa commonwealth but also won back the confidence of the Muslim peasantry. The credit for this could be equally shared by the Sikh leaders and the Sikh-phobia of the Persian and Afghan conquerors and their Mughal collaborators. In these trying years, the Sikhs led the resistance against the invaders and built up (perhaps unconsciously) the notion that the Punjab would be better off if it were ruled by Punjabis rather than remain a part of the Kingdom of Kabul or the Mughal Empire.

On the debit side of the balance-sheet would be the degradation of the misls from contingents of freedom fighters to bands of robbers and the anarchy they let loose when they turned against each other.

It was quite clear that the misls had seen their day and, if the Punjab was to remain free, it would have to be united under one man who had both the power to abolish the misls and the vision to create a state which all Punjabis, Muslims, Hindus, and Sikhs could call their own. This was the analysis made by the English traveller, Forster, when he wrote in 1783: "We may see some ambitious chief, led on by his genius and success absorbing the power of his associates, display from the ruins of their commonwealth the standard of monarchy." These prophetic words were written when Ranjit Singh of the Sukerchakia misl was only three years old.

PART III
PUNJAB MONARCHY AND IMPERIALISM

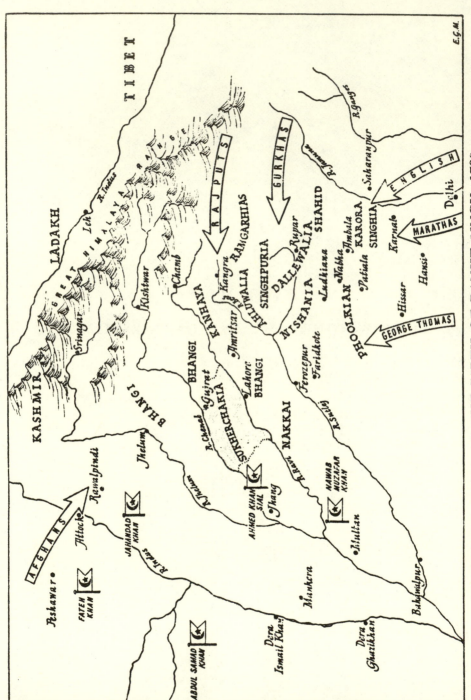

NORTHERN INDIA AT THE BIRTH OF RANJIT SINGH, 1780

E.G.M.

CHAPTER 10

RISE OF THE SUKERCHAKIA MISL

Ranjit Singh's Ancestors

THE man who liquidated the warring misls, nurtured the consciousness of regional nationalism to forge a unified kingdom, and harnessed the restless energy of the Punjabis to conquer neighbouring countries was Ranjit Singh Sukerchakia. He was born on November 13, 1780.

The foundation of the Sukerchakia fortunes was laid by one Budh Singh, who is said to have received baptism from the hands of Guru Gobind. Budh Singh died in 1718, leaving his sons a few villages of their own and many others in the neighbourhood which paid them a fixed sum as protection tax. Naudh Singh fortified his village, Sukerchak (hence Sukerchakias), joined forces with Nawab Kapur Singh and fought several engagements with Abdali. As the Afghans retreated, the Singhpurias and the Sukerchakias occupied the lands between the Ravi and the Jhelum. Naudh Singh was killed in a skirmish in 1752. Charhat Singh, the eldest of Naudh Singh's four sons, shifted his headquarters to Gujranwala, which he fortified and successfully defended against the Afghan governor of Lahore. Abdali razed the fortifications to the ground, but, on the Afghan's retreat, the Sukerchakias rebuilt their fortresses and recaptured their earlier possessions. Charhat Singh's last foray was into the territory of the Raja of Jammu, where he was mortally wounded by the bursting of his matchlock in his hands.

Charhat Singh's son, Maha Singh, inherited his father's daring and ambition. He married a daughter of Gajpat Singh of Jind and thus strengthened his own position among the Sikhs. He captured the territory north and northwest of Gujranwala and levied tribute on the Muslim tribes of

· 187 ·

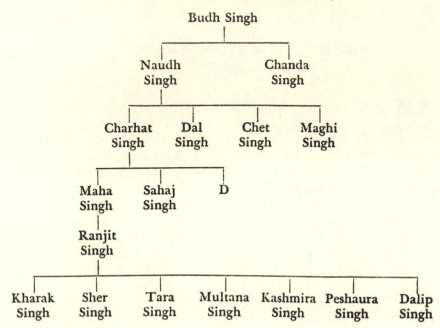

Budh Singh

Naudh Singh — Chanda Singh

Charhat Singh — Dal Singh — Chet Singh — Maghi Singh

Maha Singh — Sahaj Singh — D

Ranjit Singh

Kharak Singh — Sher Singh — Tara Singh — Multana Singh — Kashmira Singh — Peshaura Singh — Dalip Singh

the region. In a short time Maha Singh succeeded in raising his misl from comparative unimportance to one of
the leaders of the confederacy. This aroused the envy of
the misl then most powerful, the Kanhayas. The two
came into conflict over the control of Jammu and in one
of the many skirmishes that took place between them,
Gurbaksh Singh, son of the leader Jai Singh Kanhaya,
was killed. Jai Singh's pride was humbled and he agreed to
the betrothal of his deceased son's only child, Mehtab Kaur,
to Maha Singh's five-year-old son, Ranjit Singh. Jai Singh
died shortly after, leaving the Kanhaya estates to his wid-
owed daughter-in-law, Sada Kaur, the mother of Mehtab
Kaur.

Maha Singh died in 1792. The legacy which Ranjit
Singh inherited from his ancestors consisted of a large
district in the heart of the Punjab and an ambition that
knew no bounds.

Ranjit Singh was twelve years old when his father died. A virulent attack of smallpox had deprived him of vision in his left eye and deeply pitted his face. He did not receive any education save what he learned from life; and life in his early teens meant chase and the companionship of the sons of zamindars. He became an inveterate hunter, and love for horses became an absolute passion. He learned to drink hard and enjoy the good things of life. A sudden change came over him when he reached the age of fifteen, when he assumed control of the Sukerchakia estates and married. The marriage brought him under the influence of his mother-in-law, Sada Kaur, who was the head of the Kanhayas. She more than anyone else directed his unbounded energy towards unifying the Punjab.

The Punjab in 1798

The map of the Punjab in 1798 resembled a jigsaw puzzle consisting of the territories of the misls, the district of Kasur which was ruled by a Pathan family, and Hansi in the southeast where the English adventurer, George Thomas, had set up his kingdom.

The misls through years of internecine quarrels had reduced each other to political impotence. The only exceptions to the general decadence of the misls' organization were the Kanhayas, the Nakkais, the Ahluwalias, and the Bhangis. Ranjit Singh had already married the heiress to the Kanhaya estates. He arranged a second marriage with a Nakkai princess and decided to befriend Fateh Singh Ahluwalia.[1] The Bhangis were the most powerful of the misl fraternity and held Lahore, Amritsar, Gujarat, and a large portion of Western Punjab. Ranjit Singh decided to break the Bhangis and force the other *misldārs* to accept his suzerainty.

[1] Jassa Singh Ahluwalia did not have any issue and was succeeded by Bhag Singh. Fateh Singh was born in 1784 and succeeded to the chieftainship of the Ahluwalia possessions in 1801. He spent his life serving Ranjit Singh and died in 1836.

The chronic factionalism of the misls and the extra-territorial loyalties of the Pathans of Kasur and George Thomas made the Punjab extremely vulnerable—particularly from the north, for the Afghans looked upon most of Northern India as a part of their empire. Abdali's attempts to treat it as such had been frustrated by the Sikhs. His son and successor, Taimur, kept up his father's pretensions, but all he could do was to hold on to Kashmir and eject the Bhangis from Multan. Taimur's sons were not lacking in ambition and as soon as Shah Zaman took his father's place he proclaimed his intention of re-establishing the Afghan empire in India.

Zaman's first attempt to conquer India brought him as far as Hassan Abdal; he had to return to Afghanistan to put down a revolt by his brother, Mahmud. Two years later he was back in the Punjab again and in addition to re-taking Hassan Abdal he captured Rohtas from the Suker-chakias. Ranjit Singh was thus the first Sikh chieftain to suffer at his hands. Once more Zaman had to return home, this time to prevent an invasion of his own country from the west. Ranjit Singh did not have much difficulty in taking back Rohtas. But the Punjab had not yet seen the last of Zaman and his Afghan hordes.

Among the princes upon whom Zaman relied for collaboration was Sansar Chand of Kangra. Sansar Chand had already taken areas adjacent to his domains from the Sikh chiefs and had discovered that their disunity made them an easy prey.

There were three other powers who had their eyes on the Punjab.

The Gurkhas, hitherto known only as a warrior race, had, under Amar Singh Thapa, become a formidable power in the eastern Himalayas. They had begun to move westwards along the mountain ranges until they came to the territory of Sansar Chand of Kangra. The choice for the Gurkhas and Rajputs lay between fighting each other or joining hands to take the Punjab and share the spoils.

The wretched state of the misls made the latter alternative seem more profitable.

The Marathas had recovered from the defeat they had suffered in 1761 on the field of Panipat. They had taken Agra, reduced the Mughal Emperor at Delhi to subservience, and re-entered Southern Punjab. Their troops were trained by Europeans and were better disciplined than the Sikhs. In the north they had French generals—De Boigne, Perron, and Bourquin—to direct their conquests.

The English were less conspicuous but potentially more formidable than the Marathas. Ostensibly their only interest in the region was to protect the Nawab Wazir of Oudh, whose territories extended to the river Ganges. Nevertheless, the conquest of the whole of India had begun to stir the imaginations of most Englishmen in the country, and they seldom missed an opportunity to extend their frontiers. They had agents in all the big cities of India, Persia, and Afghanistan, and were fully informed of what was going on. It was the English, more than anyone else, who realised that Zaman's invasions spelled danger to their own possessions in India, and shrewdly guessed that the people who might be counted on to put up an effective resistance to the Afghans were neither the Marathas, nor the Rajputs, nor the Gurkhas, but the Sikhs. They also knew that the one man who could muster the Sikh forces and unite the Punjab was the young Sukerchakia chieftain, Ranjit Singh.

Shah Zaman Invades the Punjab

In the autumn of 1796 Shah Zaman crossed the Indus for the third time with the intention of proceeding to Delhi. He had a well-equipped army of over thirty thousand men, and was assured of collaboration from many quarters, notably by Nizamuddin Khan of Kasur, who expected to be rewarded with the *sūbedārī* of Lahore, and Sahib Singh of Patiala, who believed in keeping up the family tradition of loyalty to every invader. The Rohillas, the Wazir of Oudh, and even Tippu Sultan of Mysore promised to side with the Afghans if they came to India. Zaman's reply to his Indian Muslim collaborators indicated what he had in mind regarding the Sikhs and Marathas. He wrote: "We shall soon march with our conquering army to wage war with the infidels and polytheists and free those regions from the contamination of those shameless tribes."

As the news of the invasion spread, Sikh chiefs evacuated their families to the hills and foregathered in Amritsar. The two men whose territories lay on the Afghans' route to Lahore were Sahib Singh Bhangi and Ranjit Singh. Sahib Singh made a feeble attempt to halt the invaders, then lost his nerve and fled eastwards. Ranjit Singh, who could barely raise ten thousand undisciplined horsemen, also left his district and repaired post-haste to Amritsar.

The majority of the chieftains who met in Amritsar felt that the best they could do was to retreat to the hills, allow their deserted towns and cities to be plundered, and close in on the Afghans when they tried to take the loot back to their country. Ranjit Singh exhorted them to stay in the plains to defend the people from whom they had taken a protection tax for many years. His boldness turned the scales. Many chiefs agreed to support him. He took command of the Sikh forces, cleared the Afghans from the Lahore countryside, and threw a cordon round the city. Every night he organised raids on different suburbs and kept the Afghans on the defensive.

In January 1797, Zaman received intelligence that his brother, Mahmud, was again trying to usurp his throne. He left his ablest officer, Shahanchi Khan, with twelve thousand Afghan soldiers in the Punjab and took the road back to Kabul. The Sikhs followed on his heels and harassed him all the way up to the Jhelum. Shahanchi Khan, who tried to way-lay the Sikhs at their rear, was thoroughly trounced at Ram Nagar; Ranjit Singh decimated Shahanchi's columns fleeing towards Gujarat, and his prestige rose from that of an obscure Sikh chieftain to that of the hero of the Punjab.

The humiliation of their defeat rankled in Zaman's mind and as soon as he had settled his domestic problems, he turned his footsteps to the Punjab. In command of his troops was the son of Shahanchi Khan, thirsting to avenge the death of his father. In order to induce his countrymen to join his army, Zaman made a proclamation that they would be given permission to plunder Indian homes.[2]

The Sikh chiefs did not show much fight and began to flee to the hills; even in Amritsar, the Harimandir was left with only a handful of guards to protect it. Ranjit Singh and Sahib Singh Bhangi abandoned their possessions and came to Amritsar. In their absence, the Afghans took Gujarat and massacred the inhabitants. Hindus and Sikhs had fled earlier: the victims were Punjabi Mussalmans. Gujranwala was also sacked.

At the meeting at Amritsar, the majority were in favor of fleeing to the hills. But once again Ranjit Singh talked them round and they agreed to stand firm. "Victory is the gift of God," they said. "Let us make one effort to oppose him [the Shah]." Ranjit Singh was again chosen to be the leader.[3]

Shah Zaman sent orders to Sansar Chand and the Raja of Jammu not to afford shelter to Sikh women and children who had been evacuated and sent to the hills,[4] since he intended to extirpate the race. Sikh families found refuge in other hill states. The people who suffered most at the hands of the invaders were the Punjabi Muslims

---

[2] PC 17 of 24.12.1798.

[3] During both these invasions, the person who really persuaded Ranjit Singh to fight the Afghans in the plains was his mother-in-law, Sada Kaur. On the second occasion, Ranjit's uncle, Dal Singh, reassured the Sikhs that the Afghans were overrated as soldiers and that he had looted the Shah's baggage without much difficulty. PC 30 of 11.1.1799.

[4] PC 21 of 24.12.1798.

who, believing that the Afghans would not touch their co-religionists, had remained in their homes. The Afghan army took all the provisions it needed from the Muslim peasantry. Nizamuddin Khan led an assault against the Sikhs across the Ravi at Shahadara. The Pathans were badly mauled and by the time reinforcements were ferried over the river, the Sikhs had vanished. The Pathans and Afghans wreaked vengeance for their dead comrades by falling upon the unarmed local population;[5] Shahadara was almost entirely inhabited by Punjabi Mussalmans.

On November 27, 1798 the Shah entered Lahore. He tried to alienate the Punjab Muslims, Hindus, and Malwais from the Majha Sikhs. Zaman found willing pawns for the game: Nizamuddin Khan of Kasur assured him of the loyalty of the Muslims; Sansar Chand of Kangra guaranteed Hindu collaboration; and Sahib Singh of Patiala promised to bring the Malwais on the Afghan side. The only people to be reckoned with were the Sikhs of Majha led by eighteen-year-old Ranjit Singh.

An Afghan detachment was sent towards Amritsar. Ranjit Singh met it five miles outside the city and after a fierce three-hour encounter compelled the Afghans to retreat. He pursued the Afghans to the walls of Lahore. He ordered that the standing crop in the surrounding countryside be burned and he cut off all food supplies to the city.

As the days went by, Zaman realised that there was no possibility of breaking through the Sikh barricades and proceeding towards Delhi.[6] He gave up talking of a holy

[5] PC 21 of 24.12.1798.

[6] The following news item from Zaman's court reveals the state of affairs in the Afghan camp: "Nizamuddin Khan Kasuria represented that the Sikhs were collecting at Amritsar and that Tara Singh and some other chiefs had crossed the Beas and would soon join them. It would be advisable to send these infidels to hell at once. The King said he would look to it when all collected. . . . Ghazeeuddin approved of the King's plan and advised him further to entertain as many Sikhs as might offer their services. All Muslims in Hindustan would join His Majesty and facilitate his operations. The King ordered Wafadar Khan to contrive to manage the Sikhs for although the Durranis were apparently brave they were at bottom timid." PC 40 of 11.1.1799.

war to exterminate the Sikhs and sent his agent to Amritsar to negotiate with the Sardars. He assured them that their possessions would be guaranteed and asked them the price of their co-operation. He also tried to bring disunity among the chiefs by playing on their jealousies and making offers of cash and *jāgīrs* to buy their support. This manoeuvre was successful. Several chiefs sent their agents to Lahore. They were received with flattering attention by the Shah. "I bestow this country on you free from assessment. Continue to keep and cultivate it in confidence," said Zaman grandly. Ranjit Singh also sent his agent to the Afghan court to negotiate the *subedārī* of Lahore in order to offset the moves of the other Sardars. Sahib Singh Bedi, who by virtue of his descent from Guru Nanak was held in great esteem by the Sikhs, addressed Zaman's envoy on behalf of all the Sardars. "We took the country by the sword and will preserve it by the sword."[7]

Zaman could not proceed beyond Lahore. His brother Mahmud was again stirring up trouble and his soldiers, who had not been paid for many months, clamoured for permission to loot the city or be allowed to return home. The Shah was compelled to give up the projected conquest of Hindustan and to return to Afghanistan.

[7] The newswriter who recorded the negotiations with the Sikhs wrote on the same day: "The Shah's camp is always on the alarm on account of the Sikhs who at night approach Lahore and keep up a fire of musquetry. None go out against them." (PC 18 of 25.1.1799.)

CHAPTER 11

MAHARAJAH OF THE PUNJAB

The Road to Lahore

AS SOON as the news of Shah Zaman's departure for Afghanistan reached the Sikh chiefs at Amritsar, they broke camp and hurried back to reclaim their estates. Ranjit Singh quickly took back Gujranwala and went in pursuit of the Afghans. He kept up a running fight with them right up to the Attock.

The people of India heard of the new star which had risen in the Punjab's firmament. Collins, who was the British Resident at the Mughal court, wrote: "At present this chief is regarded throughout Hindustan as the protector of the Sikh Nation; it being generally believed that were it not for the fortitude and excellent conduct of Ranjit Singh the whole of the Punjab would ere this have become a desert waste since it is the boast of these northern savages [the Afghans] that the grass never grows where their horses have once trodden."[1]

While Ranjit Singh was pursuing the Afghans, Lahore was reoccupied by the three Sardars[1a] who had possessed it before Zaman's invasion. The Sardars were men of loose character who constantly squabbled with each other. "The people of Lahore," wrote Ranjit Singh's official biographer, Sohan Lal, "being extremely oppressed, raised their voices of wailing to the skies." The leading citizens sent a secret invitation to Ranjit Singh to come and take the city.

Ranjit Singh accepted the offer. His forces and those of his mother-in-law, Sada Kaur, encircled Lahore during the night when the citizens were engaged in watching the celebrations of the Shia festival of Muharram. The siege operations began the next morning before the three Sardars could prepare their defences. After the first breach

---

[1] SC 4 of 16.10.1800.
[1a] These were Chet Singh, Sahib Singh, and Mohar Singh.

was made in the wall, the gates of the city were thrown open. Ranjit Singh's first public act on entering the capital was to pay homage at the Badshahi mosque and then at the mosque of Wazir Khan, which was the one most frequented in the city. On July 7, 1799 the massive gates of the fort were opened and its eighteen-year-old conqueror entered the citadel to the boom of guns firing a royal salute.

Shah Zaman, who was still dreaming of an empire in Hindustan, made overtures to Ranjit Singh by sending him presents of horses and expensive dresses. Ranjit Singh took the hand of friendship proffered by the Afghans. Among the gifts he sent in return were some pieces of cannon Zaman had lost in the rivers of the Punjab in his hurry to escape.[2]

The capture of Lahore brought about a combination of Bhangi, Ramgarhia, and other chiefs who envied Ranjit Singh's success and became hostile to him. They met at

[2] There is little doubt that this gift was made after Ranjit Singh had taken Lahore and not before, as has been erroneously stated by most historians: Prinsep, Cunningham, Wade, Griffin, Latif, and Sinha. Two letters from Resident Collins to the Earl of Mornington written in April 1800 (SC 54 and 73) clarify the position; one states: "My private agent at Delhi informs me that Shah Zaman is endeavouring to attach to his interests Ranjit Singh the usurper of Lahore, who has lately received a rich *khilat* from the Durrani Prince. Hence it would appear that the Shah has by no means relinquished his designs on Hindustan." The other letter states: "Advices from Lahore mention that Ranjit Singh has lately delivered to Shah Zaman's Vakeel, 15 pieces of artillery which the Durrani prince lost in his retreat from the Punjab last year by the overflowing of the Chenab."

The affair of the return of the cannons has assumed some importance because of the views expressed by these historians that it was this gesture which led to Zaman granting the *subedārī* of Lahore to Ranjit. It is true that following the return of the cannon Shah Zaman promised to deliver the keys of Lahore to the dependents of Ranjit Singh when next he should visit that city (SC 87 of 30.12.1800) and Ranjit Singh diplomatically kept Shah Zaman informed of his activities at Lahore; but these were more in the nature of moves on the chess-board. The facts are that the cannons were lost by Shah Zaman, recovered by Ranjit (see Ranjit's letter to Collins, SC 95 of 30.12.1800) and presented to Shah Zaman at least six months after Ranjit had made himself master of Lahore; and Shah Zaman was not destined to return to Hindustan as a conqueror.

Amritsar, and, egged on by Nizamuddin Khan, advanced with their armies towards Lahore. Ranjit Singh met them at the village of Bhasin, ten miles east of the capital. The armies faced each other for two months until the leader of the confederate army, Gulab Singh Bhangi, died of the ill effects of liquor; the others quietly returned to their homes.[3]

The "victory" at Bhasin confirmed Ranjit Singh's position as the premier chieftain of the Punjab, and people began to flock to him. He installed himself in the fort and began holding regular court in the Musammam Burj (Octagonal Tower), as had been the practice of the Mughals and their governors. He recruited new talent for the services and reorganised the revenue and judicial administration of the territory under his control. Among the first to take employment with him were three Bokhari brothers of whom the eldest, Azizuddin,[4] became the Maharajah's closest friend and adviser and later Minister of Foreign Affairs. Fateh Singh Ahluwalia, who had hitched his wagon to Ranjit Singh's rising star, became chief adviser on military matters.

After settling the affairs of Lahore, Ranjit Singh led an expedition against the Raja of Jammu, who had promised help to the Afghans. On the way to the hills, he took Vairowal, Narowal, and Jassowal, and with rapid marches came to a halt within four miles of Jammu. The Raja submitted and paid a tribute. After Jammu, Ranjit Singh

[3] Ranjit Singh was, however, in dire financial straits at the end of the Bhasin expedition and was contemplating raising a compulsory loan from the local money-lenders. Fortune favoured him; just about that time a treasure consisting of 20,000 gold *mohurs* was unearthed at Budhu-da-Ava outside the city walls.

[4] Azizuddin, born in 1780, was the son of Hakim Ghulam Mohiuddin. The two brothers in the employ of Ranjit Singh were Imamuddin and Nuruddin. Azizuddin met Ranjit Singh in 1799 when he was summoned to treat the Maharajah for some eye trouble. He served Ranjit Singh for forty years and stayed in court after his death as adviser to Kharak Singh, Nao Nihal Singh, and Sher Singh. He died on December 3, 1845. (*Faqir Azizuddin*, by Lajpat Rai Nair.)

turned his attention to Gujarat. He was constrained to raise the siege on the intervention of Sahib Singh Bedi.[5] But he attached the estate of the chief of Akalgarh, who had gone to the help of the Bhangi chief of Gujarat.

Overtures by Shah Zaman and the British

Ranjit Singh came back to Lahore and found Shah Zaman's messengers waiting for him. He learned that a number of Punjab chiefs, including the Bhangis, who were hostile to him, had entered into correspondence with Zaman and promised him support. Ranjit Singh accepted Zaman's gifts and compliments and dismissed the envoys with even richer gifts and more flattering compliments. The result was exactly as Ranjit Singh had anticipated. The news of his not-too-secret alliance with Zaman caused dismay among his enemies, who had looked forward to the Afghan invasion as a means of getting rid of Ranjit. It caused grave concern even to the British. In April 1800 the governor general decided to counteract the influence of Shah Zaman with Ranjit Singh, and issued instructions that "a native agent appropriately qualified for the occasion should be immediately dispatched to the Court of Ranjit Singh with suitable instructions for impressing that chief with a just sense of the danger to which he would expose his interests and those of his nation by yielding to the insidious proposals of Zaman Shah."[6]

The British sent Mir Yusuf Ali to warn the Sikhs against the Afghans. The Mir met the chiefs of Malwa and then Sada Kaur and Ranjit Singh. Since he had nothing to offer

[5] Sohan Lal gives a graphic description of the scene: "The Exalted One (Ranjit) untied his sword from his waist and placed it on the ground before Baba Sahib Singh (Bedi). All the Sardars, Jodh Singh, Dal Singh, and Sahib Singh did the same. For one hour the swords lay on the ground and the Sardars did not say anything. Afterwards, the said Baba Sahib Singh tied the sword round the waist of the Exalted One and said that within a short time all his opponents would be extirpated and his rule would be established throughout the country." (*Daftar* II, 49)

[6] SC 74 of 24.4.1800.

except gratuitous advice and since Zaman was reported to be mustering a large army for another invasion, the Sikh chiefs treated English overtures with courteous cynicism. Fortunately civil strife in Kabul and the advance of the Persians across Afghanistan's western frontiers prevented Zaman from invading India. The Punjab heaved a sigh of relief and Ranjit Singh decided to make it secure against future invasions.

Maharajah of the Punjab

Ranjit Singh hesitated to assume the formal title of Maharajah, for he wished to avoid doing anything which would give the other chiefs cause to conspire against him. Gradually he came to the conclusion that the advantages of investing an established fact with a legal title would outweigh the danger of arousing the hostility of the feudal aristocracy. The move would undoubtedly be popular with the masses, who had not had a ruler and a government of their own for many centuries. It would induce other Punjabis who were not yet citizens of the new state to recognise the compulsions of language and a common way of life, and throw in their lot with the country. The neighbouring powers which were casting covetous glances on the Punjab would also grow accustomed to the idea that the people of the Punjab were one people and Ranjit Singh was their ruler.[7] On the 1st of Baisakh (April 12) 1801, Sahib Singh Bedi daubed Ranjit Singh's forehead with saffron paste and proclaimed him Maharajah of the Punjab. A royal salute was fired from the fort. In the afternoon the young Maharajah rode on his elephant, showering gold and silver coins on jubilant crowds of his subjects. In the evening, all the homes of the city were illumined.

[7] There was perhaps also a personal reason: the birth of a son to the Nakkain, Rani Raj Kaur, his second and favourite wife. Ranjit's desire to make his son an heir-apparent to a kingdom was perhaps as compelling as any political reasons.

Ranjit Singh's political acumen is well illustrated in the compromise he made between becoming a Maharajah and remaining a peasant leader. Although crowned King of the Punjab, he refused to wear the emblem of royalty in his simple turban. He refused to sit on a throne, and continued as before to hold durbar seated cross-legged in his chair, which looked more like a bathtub than a fauteuil, or, more often, received visitors in the oriental fashion reclining on cushions on a carpet. He ordered new coins to be struck. These did not bear his effigy or his name but that of Guru Nanak, and were named the *Nānak śāhī* coins. The seal of government likewise bore no reference to him. The government was not a personal affair but the *Sarkār Khālsājī* of the people who brought it into being and of those who collaborated with it; the court for the same reason came to be known as the *Darbār Khālsājī*. Despite sonorous titles which the sycophants in the court used for him, the one by which he preferred to be addressed was the plain and simple *Singh Sāhib*. These conventions were a complete departure from the accepted traditions of oriental courts, where protocol was rigidly observed to keep the monarch as far away from the masses as possible. Ranjit Singh did not want to, nor ever did, lose the common touch.

The most important consequence of taking on the title "Maharajah of the Punjab" was that thereby Ranjit Singh assumed rights of sovereignty not only over all Sikhs (the government itself being *Sarkār Khālsājī*) but over all the people who lived within the ill-defined geographical limits of the Punjab. The title also gave Ranjit Singh a legal right to demand that territories which had at any time paid revenue to Lahore—territories such as Jammu, Kashmir, the Rajput hill states, Multan, Bahawalpur, Dera Ismail Khan, Dera Ghazi Khan, Mankera, and others—should pay tribute to him and owe allegiance to the Lahore Durbar.

Ranjit Singh did not derive his title from either the Mughals or the Afghans; it was given to him by that mystic entity, the *Panth Khālsājī*. He acknowledged no earthly superior. He was impelled by the weight of tradition that had grown up over the years, that it was the destiny of the Sikhs to rule (*Rāj Kare gā Khālsā*) and that perhaps he had been chosen by the gurus to be the instrument of their inscrutable design. With this assurance Ranjit Singh was able to harness the dynamic energies of his people and with a clear conscience launched himself on a career of conquest and annexation.

Immediately after his coronation, Ranjit Singh had the city walls and gates, which had suffered many sieges, repaired, and posted pickets at all strategic points to check crime, which had increased enormously under Bhangi misrule. The city was divided into wards under a *caudhrī* (headman), who was responsible for the maintenance of law and order in the district under his jurisdiction and could get police assistance whenever required. He also reorganised the administration of justice in the city. Since the majority of the population were Muslims, he set up separate courts for them under *qādīs* who administered the Shariat Law. But for those Muslims who, like the Hindus and the Sikhs, preferred to be governed by the customary law of their caste or district, there were other courts under judicial officers appointed by the state. Ranjit Singh had a chain of dispensaries opened in different parts of the city where *Yunānī* (Greek) medicine was dispensed free of charge. Hakim Nuruddin, the younger brother of Fakir Azizuddin, was appointed chief medical officer.

Ranjit Singh did not make any changes in the agricultural system or land revenue that had prevailed since Mughal rule. Every village had a revenue collector (*muqaddam*) and a circle of villages (*tappāh* or *tāluqāh*) was in the charge of a *caudhrī*. In addition, there was the keeper of fiscal records, the *qānungo*. The revenue officials were themselves proprietors of land in their respective villages or circle and were compensated by a reduction in revenue.

Revenue was collected directly from the cultivator of the land. The amount and manner of payment varied, but care was taken that all the regular and irregular charges (e.g. supply of grass, timber, fruit, eggs, chicken, etc. to touring officials which went under the title *mulbā*—literally, "rubbish"—or feudal dues in the form of gifts on marriages or festivals to members of the royal family or the local rajas) never amounted to more than half of the gross produce calculated on an estimate of the standing crops or after harvest; if the revenue was paid in cash, the sum was calculated on the value of half the produce. The rate was not considered extortionate and it allowed the agricultural community to thrive.

As important as the right over land which was guaranteed to the actual cultivator was the ownership of wells. As a matter of fact, the most reliable evidence of the ownership of land was the inscription on a well (sometimes placed on the inside to save it from mutilation). The right to dig a well was exclusively that of the cultivator. The proprietor who did not till the land either himself or through hired servants had to be content with a nominal title. The same applied to a *jāgīrdār* whose right to the revenue did not in any way invest him with a title to the land from which it was collected.[8]

The system had worked well for many centuries and Ranjit Singh saw no reason to change it.

Within a short time Ranjit Singh convinced the people of Lahore and the Punjab that he did not intend to set up a Sikh kingdom but a Punjabi state in which Muslims, Hindus, and Sikhs would be equal before the law and have the same rights and duties. He paid assiduous respect to the institutions of other communities and participated in their religious festivities. At Dussehra he went through the

[8] See report prepared by A. Temple on the Jullundur Doab, PC 143 of 29.12.1852; also "Land Revenue Administration under the Sikhs" by S. R. Kohli in the *Journal of the Punjab Historical Society*, 1918.

ritual of the worship of arms as practised by Hindu Rajputs and arranged mock fights between his troops to commemorate the battle of Rama against Ravana. At Divali, all public buildings, including the palace, were illuminated. On Holi, he went among the throngs squirting coloured water and powder and making merry, often in a manner quite unbecoming to a monarch. On Basant he paid homage at the tombs of the Muslim divines, Madho Lal and Hussain. On Amavas and Baisakh he joined his co-religionists in bathing at Amritsar or Taran Taran.

Campaign against the Pathans of Kasur and the Rajputs of Kangra

First priority was given to the reduction of two of the leading collaborators of the Afghans: Nizamuddin Khan and Sansar Chand. Fateh Singh Kalianwala[9] made short work of the Pathan resistance at Kasur. He compelled Nizamuddin Khan to pay a heavy indemnity and recognise Ranjit Singh as his sovereign.

Sansar Chand brought trouble on his own head by seizing some villages in the estates of Sada Kaur. Ranjit Singh proceeded to Batala, took back the occupied villages and also captured a portion of Kangra territory, including two prosperous towns, Nurpur and Naushera.

On his way back to Lahore, Ranjit Singh stopped at Taran Taran, where he and Fateh Singh Ahluwalia exchanged turbans as a gesture of having become brothers in the faith (*dharam bhāī*). They signed a pledge that thereafter their friends and enemies would be common, and in every conquest made by their joint efforts, Ranjit Singh would give over at least one district to be administered by Fateh Singh. The alliance made the two the strongest united force in the Punjab.

[9] Fateh Singh Kalianwala was a Sandhu Jat chieftain who joined Ranjit Singh very early in his career, and was with him in the capture of Lahore. He served his master in many campaigns with great zeal and fell fighting at Naraingarh on October 25, 1807.

The policy adopted towards the chieftains who were dispossessed was humane. Although their forts and cannon were taken away and their militias incorporated in the army of the state, they were given *jāgīrs* for the maintenance of their families, and their sons were offered service in the army. There is little doubt that the motive was to unify the Punjab, not personal enrichment, because the confiscated territories were invariably assigned to some loyal subject who was then obliged to furnish troops to the state; the cost of maintaining such troops seldom made a *jāgīr* a very profitable proposition.

Ranjit Singh and Fateh Singh Ahluwalia proceeded to the northwest and took over Pindi Bhattian, Pothohar, and Chiniot from the Muslim chiefs. In their absence from Lahore, Nizamuddin Khan of Kasur plundered some villages close to the capital. The Maharajah hurried southwards, and without pausing at Lahore appeared at Kasur. The fort of Kasur was bombarded with heavy guns until Nizamuddin laid down arms. He was again pardoned by Ranjit Singh and allowed to hold his fief.

The Maharajah was more considerate in dealing with Muslim chiefs than he was with the Sikh or the Hindu. His treatment of Nizamuddin, whom he defeated more than once, gives ample proof of his generosity. His treatment of the family of the Nawab of Multan was another.

Multan had been a district of the Punjab until it was annexed by Abdali. It had been recaptured by the Bhangis, but their indifference towards the welfare of the people had created a certain amount of animosity towards the Sikhs and a desire to keep aloof from the Punjabi state which was coming into being under Sikh leadership. The Bhangis were ejected by the family of Muzaffar Khan. Despite the recalcitrance of the Multanis and the fact that he was ill-equipped to invest so powerful a fort or face a combination of hostile Muslim tribes in the region, Ranjit Singh proclaimed his intention of bringing Multan back into the Punjab. Ranjit Singh's troops dispersed the peasant mob enlisted by Nawab Muzaffar Khan and took the city, with the exception of the enormous fort which stood in the centre. Muzaffar Khan made his submission by giving an indemnity and agreeing to pay the quota of revenues due to the state of Lahore instead of Kabul.

Capture of Amritsar

After Multan came Amritsar's turn. Amritsar was not the Punjab's largest city but commercially the most important in the province. It was the chief trading centre of Northern India to which caravans brought goods from Central Asia and exchanged them for the products of Hindustan. In its narrow, winding streets were business houses trading in all conceivable kinds of goods: silks, muslins, spices, tea, coffee, hides, matchlocks, and other armaments. Because of the wealthy merchants, subsidiary trades such as those of gold- and silver-smiths had grown up. Apart from its riches, Amritsar had sanctity in the eyes of the Sikhs. Anyone who aspired to be the leader of the Khalsa and Maharajah of the Punjab had to take Amritsar to make good his title.

Amritsar was divided between nearly a dozen families owning different parts of the city. These families had built fortresses in their localities and maintained retinues of armed tax collectors who mulcted the traders and shopkeepers as often as they could. The leading citizens approached Ranjit Singh (who needed little persuasion) to take over the city. The only family of importance which was likely to put up resistance was that of the widow of the Bhangi Sardar who had drunk himself to death at Bhasin three years earlier. The widow, who had the support of the Ramgarhias, occupied the fort of Gobindgarh.

Ranjit Singh took the city piecemeal, overwhelming the Sardars one after another. The Ramgarhias did not come to the help of the Bhangi widow and she surrendered the fort in lieu of a pension for herself and her son.

Gobindgarh was a valuable acquisition. With it Ranjit Singh acquired five big cannon, including the massive Zam Zama.[10] He also took in his employ a remarkable soldier called Phula Singh,[11] who happened to be in Amritsar and had helped him to capture the city.

The Maharajah received a tumultuous welcome in Amritsar. He rode through the streets on his elephant, showering coins on the milling crowds. He bathed in the pool at the Harimandir and made a grant for the temple to be rebuilt in marble and covered with gold leaf.[12]

Modernisation of the Army

The capture of Amritsar brought additional lustre to the Maharajah's name, and men from all over Hindustan began to flock to his standard. Among them were deserters from the regiments of the East India Company. They were paraded before him and he saw, for the first time, soldiers march in step and make battle formations on simple words of command. He recognised that the secret of British success against larger and better equipped armies lay in their superior discipline. He hired their deserters as drill ser-

[10] The Zam Zama was made of copper and brass and was cast by the orders of Ahmed Shah Abdali. It caused havoc in the ranks of the Marathas in the battle of Panipat. It passed from Afghan hands to the Sukerchakias and from the Sukerchakias through various hands to the Bhangis (see Chapter 8, footnote 51) and came to be known as the *Bhangīōn-kī-top*. It saw service in many of Ranjit Singh's campaigns, and after his death faced the English in Anglo-Sikh wars. Thereafter it was pensioned and put on a pedestal in Lahore's main street. It was immortalised by Kipling as Kim's Gun.

[11] Phula Singh was born in the village of Shinh in 1761. He joined an order of *nihaṅgs* at an early age and became the leader of a fanatic band of fighters who formed the suicide squads of the Sikh armies. Ranjit Singh owed many of his victories to the desperate valour of the *nihaṅgs* (also described as Akalis), of whom two, Phula Singh and Sadhu Singh, are most frequently mentioned. They were well known for their devil-may-care attitude and their freedom in speaking their minds even to Ranjit Singh. Akali Phula Singh was killed in the battle of Naushera in March 1823.

[12] The entrance to the central shrine bears an inscription to this effect. (See Chapter 3, footnote 20.)

geants and also picked a batch of young Punjabis to go across the border, enlist in the Company's forces, and learn whatever the English had to teach. Until then the backbone of the Sikh armies had been the cavalier armed with spear, sword, and musket. The Sikhs looked down upon the foot soldier and were contemptuous of drill: they described marching in step as the *ruqs-i-luluān* (the fool's ballet). Ranjit Singh ignored these witticisms and raised infantry battalions of Punjabi Mussalmans, Hindustani deserters, and Gurkhas. After seeing the new foot-soldier in action, the Sikhs overcame their prejudice and began to enlist in the infantry.

The Maharajah also realised the importance of artillery in modern warfare. His batteries were manned by Muslim gunners, of whom Ghaus Mohammed Khan (Mian Ghausa) and later Shaikh Elahi Baksh rose to the highest ranks in this branch of the service. The Sikhs had no inhibitions about joining the artillery and soon learned to cast guns and cannon ball, and to mix gun-powder; they became the most proficient gunners in India.

The Maharajah took keen personal interest in his new recruits and made it a point to spend the better part of the day supervising their drill and gunnery practice. At the end of nine months' rigorous training the new army of the state was ready for action. Its units took part in the Dussehra celebrations of 1803.

After Dussehra the campaigning season began. Emissaries were first sent to the independent principalities in the province to ask them to declare their allegiance to the Durbar. Among those who contemptuously turned down the invitation was Ahmed Khan Sial of Jhang who was also the Punjab's best breeder of horses. The newly trained troops had little difficulty in taking Jhang. Ahmed Khan was reinstated at Jhang as a vassal of Lahore. The Zamindars of Ucch near Jhang followed the Sials in declaring their allegiance to the Lahore Durbar.

The experience of the campaign in the northwest was

reviewed at Amritsar. At a Durbar in Gobindgarh fort the Maharajah announced his decision on the reorganisation of the army. It was divided into three parts. The first, consisting of thirteen thousand men, was placed directly under the Maharajah's command and was always to be ready for action. It had cavalry, infantry, and artillery divisions. The cavalry was almost entirely Sikh and had in it the pick of his generals, such as Hari Singh Nalwa, Hukma Singh Chimni, and Desa Singh Majithia. The infantry was a mixture of Muslims and Hindus with a sprinkling of Sikhs. The heavy artillery, which was still largely Muslim, was put under the command of Mian Ghausa. The second part, consisting of ten thousand men, was made up of the forces of the chiefs liable for military service in lieu of their *jāgīrs*. They were obliged to furnish fully equipped troops at short notice. The third part consisted of the forces of the misls which, like the Kanhayas, the Nakkais, and some others, were allies of the Durbar. The total fighting force which the Durbar could put into the field at this time was about thirty-one thousand men.

The reorganisation gave a clearer picture of the forces available and fixed the responsibility for putting them into the field. Once this had been done, Ranjit Singh prescribed the most exacting standards of efficiency in march, manoeuvre, and marksmanship. He spent three to four hours of his day with the troops, and seldom did a day go by when he did not reward a gunner or a cavalier for good performance. Since he usually accompanied his armies to battle, he was able to encourage individual acts of bravery by rewards of land and pensions.

CHAPTER 12

SUZERAIN OF MALWA

First Treaty with the British, January 1806

◈◈◈◈ IN THE five years following Ranjit Singh's as-
◈◈◈◈ sumption of the title of Maharajah of the
◈◈◈◈ Punjab, the situation on his eastern frontier
changed completely.

In A.D. 1800 the powers to be reckoned with were the
puppet Mughal emperor and, beyond Delhi, the English.
In 1802 Thomas was eliminated by Sindhia's French general, Perron. Perron became the most powerful man in
Eastern Punjab; he began to think in terms of a kingdom
of his own. He exploited the gratitude of the Malwa chiefs
for ridding them of Thomas and had many exchange turbans with him.[1] He made overtures to Ranjit Singh and
did his best to persuade him not to have anything to do
with the British emissaries who were then in the Punjab.[2]

The Frenchman's dreams of a Perronistan in the Punjab
were shattered by the British, who defeated Sindhia's forces

---

[1] He forestalled the English in their designs in this direction by warning
the Sikhs. In a letter to Bhag Singh of Jind (Ranjit's uncle) he wrote:
"It is an invariable custom with the English first to gain a footing by the
excitement of avarice, by the promise of assistance or other flattering terms,
and then by gradual steps to assume the government of the country, viz.
Cheyt Singh, Tippu Sultan, Nawab Cossim Ali Khan, Nawab Asafuddowlah,
Nizam Ally Khan, and others." (SC 51 of 19.3.1801).

[2] In a letter (SC 49 of 16.8.1802) to Collins, Ranjit Singh explained his
position with unusual candour: "Raja Bhag Sing Bahadur (my maternal
uncle), accompanied by Vakeels on the part of General Perron, Raja
Sahib Sing (of Patiala), and Mr. Louis (a subordinate of General Perron)
etc., are arrived here with presents for me. They have proposed to me to
enter into terms of amity and friendship with General Perron. . . . As
Raja Bhag Sing is under many obligations to General Perron, he sought
to gain me by every mode of persuasion, urging at the same time the
great desire of the general to have a meeting with me. In fine, although
my friendship for the Most Honorable the Governor-General and you is
great beyond the possibility of what I can feel towards anyone else, yet I
must preserve appearances on this occasion in consideration of what is due
by me to the will of my uncle."

Guru Nanak and His Companions, Mardana and Bala
Courtesy: M. S. Randhawa

Guru Gobind Singh, last of the Sikh gurus
(an 18th century painting in Mughal style)
Courtesy: M. S. Randhawa

in a series of engagements and became masters of Delhi, Agra, and the Mughal emperor. With the setting of Sindhia's sun, Perron faded out of the Indian scene and the English came a step closer to the Punjab: all that separated them was the remaining Maratha chief, Holkar, and the Sikh chiefs of Malwa.

One year later the English clashed with Holkar and, despite an initial reverse, Lord Lake was able to wrest the initiative from Holkar and his Rohilla ally, Amir Khan. The Marathas and Rohillas made a cowardly dash to safety through Malwa (where they mulcted the Sikh chiefs) and crossed the Sutlej. They also invited the Afghans to re-invade India. Lake halted on the Beas and sent a request to the Durbar to expel Holkar and Amir Khan from the Punjab.

Ranjit Singh was in the neighbourhood of Multan when he heard that the Maratha and Rohilla armies had entered the Punjab. He sent word to his principal Sardars and hurried north to join them at Amritsar.

The Sarbat Khalsa considered both sides of the case. The Marathas and the Rohillas had a large enough army to be a serious menace to the security of the Punjab. Holkar played upon the religious and patriotic sentiments of his hosts. He made a handsome offering at the Harimandir and flattered Ranjit Singh as the only hope of the Hindus of India.[3] (Fortunately Ranjit knew of Holkar's negotiations with the Afghans.) On the other side were the English, who threatened to pursue Holkar if he were not expelled from Amritsar. The position that Lord Lake had taken left no doubt in the mind of anyone that the English demand was no idle threat.[4]

[3] Jaswant Rao Holkar impressed on the Maharajah the need to train his army in the European style, as he (Holkar) had trained his Marathas. The modernisation begun a few years earlier was speeded up.

[4] SC 19 of 9.1.1806. In a despatch Lake wrote: "I resolved to occupy a position on the south bank of the Beas at a distance of about 35 miles from Amritsar, and 45 miles from Ludhiana, which, while it secured my supplies, would be likely to give Ranjit Singh confidence to oppose Jaswant

It appears that Ranjit Singh first convinced himself of British military superiority before coming to the decision that it would not be opportune to join the Marathas to fight the British.[5] He decided to enter into an agreement with the British and become a mediator in the Anglo-Maratha dispute.

On January 1, 1806 Ranjit Singh and Fateh Singh Ahluwalia signed a treaty of friendship and amity with the East India Company, undertaking to "cause Jaswant Rao Holkar to remove with his army to the distance of thirty *coss* from Amritsar immediately." In return, the Company undertook to remove its encampment on the Beas. The Company also gave a solemn undertaking to the effect that "as long as the said chieftains, Ranjit Singh and Fateh Singh, abstain from holding any friendly connection with the enemies of that [i.e. the British] government, or from committing any act of hostility on their own parts against the said government, the British armies shall never enter the territories of the said chieftains nor will the British government form any plans for the seizure or sequestration of their possessions or property."[6]

Meanwhile Lord Wellesley, who had pursued an aggressive policy against the Marathas, was replaced by Lord Cornwallis as governor general. Lord Cornwallis had been given specific instructions not to engage in any more wars nor to make any more annexations.[7] Holkar was consequently allowed to recross the Sutlej and resume his possessions. The British thus became the only real power on the Punjab's eastern frontier, with nothing but the conglomeration of Malwa chiefs between them and the Lahore Durbar.

Rao Holkar or at all events to deter him from embracing the cause of that chief."

[5] Ranjit Singh told several visitors that he had gone to the British camp in disguise and met Lord Lake. Lake makes no mention of this meeting.

[6] Treaty of Lahore, 1806.

[7] On Cornwallis' death, Barlow, who succeeded him temporarily, followed the same policy.

Arbitration in Malwa

Immediately after the danger of an Anglo-Maratha conflict in the Punjab was over, the chiefs of Malwa fell out
with each other and allowed a petty squabble to develop
into a major conflict. The dispute arose over the ownership of the village of Daladi on the Nabha-Patiala border,
a dispute resulting in the death of the Patiala agent. The
chiefs of Thanesar and Kaithal espoused the cause of
Patiala; Bhag Singh of Jind, that of Nabha. In a skirmish
the chief of Thanesar was killed. Patiala avenged the death
of his supporter by inflicting a bloody defeat on Nabha's
forces. The victory was, however, not decisive and it was
feared that the conflagration would spread to the whole of
Malwa. Both factions approached Ranjit Singh to act as
arbitrator.

After the annual muster of forces at Dussehra the Maharajah crossed the Sutlej with an army of twenty thousand
men and marched through the territories of the Singhpurias, the Sodhis of Kartarpur and the Dallewallias, and
through the prosperous towns of Phillaur, Ludhiana, and
Jagraon. Everywhere the chiefs came to him of their own
accord and paid tribute in cash, cannon, horses, and elephants.

The Maharajah arrived at Patiala, where the chiefs of
Malwa waited on him. The only exception was Sahib
Singh of Patiala, who had second thoughts about the wisdom of having invited Ranjit's mediation and, not knowing what to do in the situation, simply locked himself up
in his fort. A few rounds of cannon fire reminded him of
his duties as a host and he too came out to welcome his
guest. Thereafter the Maharajah was entertained lavishly
and given assurances by the Malwa Sardars that they looked
upon him as their sovereign.

Ranjit Singh's verdict on the incident in the village of
Daladi was to exonerate Nabha of responsibility for the
murder and to compensate Patiala for the damage he had

suffered by the grant of a *jāgīr*. Ludhiana was given to Bhag Singh of Jind.

Kangra, Kasur, Multan

On his way back to Lahore, the Maharajah was approached by an emissary of Sansar Chand for help against the Gurkhas, who had occupied the hill tract between the Jumna and the Sutlej and were investing the fort of Kangra. Ranjit Singh had no love for Sansar Chand, but he realised that if the Gurkhas succeeded in taking Kangra, their power in the north would menace the Punjab. He spurned counteroffers made by the Gurkha commander, Amar Singh Thapa, and ordered his army to the relief of Kangra.

The Gurkhas, who had been fighting for many weeks, were suffering from the ill effects of heat and an epidemic of cholera that had broken out in their ranks. Fatigue and disease left them with no stomach to face the Punjab army, and they retired to Mandi, swearing vengeance on Ranjit Singh. Sansar Chand came to Jawalamukhi, where the Maharajah was encamped, and paid tribute in horses and cash.[8]

[8] Ranjit Singh was still in the hills when he received news of the birth of his twin sons to his first wife, Mehtab Kaur, daughter of Sada Kaur. The young princes were given the names of Sher Singh and Tara Singh. Most English and Muslim historians have stated that these children were not borne by Mehtab Kaur but were taken from women of menial classes and, at the instance of her mother, passed off as hers by Ranjit. They also state that Ranjit Singh did not believe the story of the birth of the twins and had very little to do with them. Both these statements are absolutely inaccurate. Court historians have much to say of Ranjit's joy at the birth of his sons and the jubilation in camp. What gave rise to the suggestion of illegitimacy was Ranjit's strained relations with his wife Mehtab Kaur and her mother Sada Kaur. He saw little of the two princes for some years, and the first born, Kharak Singh, remained the favourite. When Sada Kaur fell from power and the princes came to stay with their father, Kharak Singh and his mother were picqued and gave currency to the gossip in order to counteract any possibility of Ranjit Singh's preferring Sher Singh, who was fast becoming the father's favourite, as successor. (Kharak Singh wrote as much in a personal letter he sent to Elphinstone. See Chapter 16, footnote 9.)

On his return home, the Maharajah was apprised of disturbances created by the Pathans of Kasur. Nizamuddin Khan was dead, but his brother, Kutubuddin Khan, who had taken his place, had declared his independence. He had enlisted a large number of *ghāzīs*, fortified his town, and stocked the fort with provisions for a long siege. Muzaffar Khan of Multan encouraged Kutubuddin's recalcitrance and furnished him with some troops. Ranjit Singh sent Fakir Azizuddin to Kasur to bring the Pathans to obedience. Kutubuddin dismissed Azizuddin with the taunt that, since the Fakir ate the salt of the infidel, he was unworthy of attention.

Hostilities commenced early in February 1807 with a clash between the *ghāzīs* and the *nihaṅgs*[9]—Muslim crusaders versus the Sikh. The *nihaṅgs* drove the *ghāzīs* back into the fort. For one month Lahore guns battered its walls without making any impression. Finally a breach was blown by a well-laid mine and the fort carried by assault. Kutubuddin Khan was taken alive and brought into the Maharajah's presence. The Maharajah forgave the Pathan's tirades against the infidel and sent him away with a handsome *jāgīr* across the Sutlej at Mamdot. Kasur, which was close to Lahore, was taken away from the Pathan ruling family and given over to be administered by Nihal Singh Attariwala.

Although the summer was on them, the Maharajah did not want to leave Muzaffar Khan of Multan unpunished for his share in the Kasurians' defiance of authority. Durbar troops took the city and were getting ready to assault the citadel when Muzaffar Khan made terms by paying seventy thousand rupees.

[9] *Nihaṅg*, from Persian meaning "crocodile." *Nihaṅgs* were suicide squads of the Mughal army and wore blue uniforms. The Sikhs took the name and the uniform from the Mughals. The order is said to have been founded by one of the elder sons of Guru Gobind Singh. The *Nihaṅgs* were also known as *akālīs* (servitors of the Timeless God). Members of the present-day Akali party wear blue turbans.

Second Tour of Malwa: Affiliation
of the Hill States

On his return from Multan the Maharajah received a second invitation to visit Patiala. This was from Sahib Singh's wife, As Kaur, asking for his good offices to settle a dispute with her husband regarding the succession of her son. Ranjit Singh arrived in Patiala at the head of a large army. The Cis-Sutlej chiefs once more acknowledged his suzerainty by paying him tributes in money and expensive presents. His verdict was a careful compromise. Sahib Singh was to continue as Maharajah as long as he lived; his son, Karam Singh, was to receive a *jāgīr* of Rs. 50,000 a year. Both parties accepted the judgment and paid the "arbitrator's fee"; the Raja gave Rs. 70,000 in precious stones; the Maharani, a brass cannon.

On his way back from Patiala, Ranjit Singh ordered an assault on Naraingarh, where the Raja of Sirmoor, who had refused to acknowledge the Durbar, was at that time. Naraingarh was taken after a heavy loss of life: among those killed was Fateh Singh Kalianwala.

The Maharajah proceeded on his homeward march through Whadni, Morinda, Zira, and other towns in the district of Ferozepur. On the way he heard of the death of another of his companions, Tara Singh Gheba, head of the Dallewalia misl. He retraced his steps to offer his condolences. He fixed a pension for the widow and the deceased's family, and incorporated the Dallewalia's forces into the state army. The estates, which were worth over seven lacs a year in revenue, extending over the towns of Rahon, Nakodar, and Naushera, were merged with the Durbar. The administration of the Dallewalia estates was entrusted to Dewan Mohkam Chand,[10] who had joined the Durbar's service a few months earlier.

---

[10] Mohkam Chand, the most distinguished of the Durbar's generals, was the son of Wisakhi Mal, a Khatri tradesman of the village Kunjah near Gujarat. Ranjit Singh had seen him in action at Akalgarh three years

Mohkam Chand's first assignment was the reduction of Pathankot, which had one of the strongest forts in the Punjab. Mohkam Chand took Pathankot and then proceeded to Jasrota, Chamba, and Basohli, and compelled the Raja to acknowledge the sovereignty of the Maharajah.

At the end of the campaign in the hills, the Maharajah sent invitations to all the princes and estate holders in the Punjab to attend a Durbar and receive robes of honour from him. When the Durbar was over, the Maharajah took action against two chieftains who failed to attend: Sialkot was taken after a three-day siege; the Bhangi Sardar of Gujarat submitted to a show of force. At the same time the Raja of Akhnur, which was near Sialkot and the Kanhaya chief, whose daughter was engaged to marry Ranjit's eldest son, Kharak Singh, were made to acknowledge the sovereignty of the Durbar by paying tribute. The last conquest of the year was the fort of Sheikhupura only twenty miles from the Lahore capital and one of the most powerful in the Punjab.

In the year 1808, the Durbar acquired the services of two men who subsequently became officers of great distinction. One was the hunchback, Bhawani Das, an accountant in the employ of Shah Zaman. Ranjit Singh's finances had been managed by a banking house in Amritsar. Bhawani Das organised the government's finances by opening a chain of state treasuries in the big cities and introducing a proper system of accounting. He was, how-

---

earlier and again in the fight against the Bhangi Sardar of Gujarat. Mohkam Chand had fallen out with his Bhangi master and had come to Ranjit for employment. Ranjit welcomed him with handsome gifts of an elephant and horses and granted him the Dallewalia possessions as a *jāgīr*. He was made a commander of a cavalry unit with power to recruit 1,500 foot soldiers as well. He died at Phillaur on October 16, 1814. His son (Moti Ram) and grandson (Ram Dyal) also served the state with great distinction.

ever, more able than honest; on several occasions Ranjit Singh had to question his integrity. ("His hunchback was full of mischief"—Sohan Lal.)

The other entrant to the royal service was a young and handsome Brahmin youth from Meerut, Khushal Chand. He enlisted as a common soldier in the Maharajah's personal bodyguard and rose to the rank of Jemadar. His pleasant personality attracted his master and he became a great favourite—particularly after his conversion to the Sikh faith. He was put in charge of the palace, including the private apartments.[11]

[11] The charge of the *deorhi* was of considerable importance since anyone who wanted a personal interview with the Maharajah had first to approach the *deorhidār*. It gave the incumbent political power as well as a handsome income from presents. Jemadar Khushal Singh introduced two relations of his to the court: a nephew, Tej Singh and his younger brother, Ram Chand, renamed Ram Singh after conversion to Sikhism. This family of Brahmins exerted a baleful influence which Ranjit Singh was never able to shake off. It was one of the rare instances of Ranjit's misjudging the quality of the men he employed. Tej Singh played a traitorous role in the Anglo-Sikh wars.

CHAPTER 13

BRITISH ANNEXATION OF MALWA: TREATY OF LAHORE, 1809

IN THE decade that Ranjit Singh had been ruler of Lahore, the northwestern and north-eastern frontiers of the Punjab had ceased to be a source of danger to the Durbar. The Afghans were busy quarrelling among themselves. The Rajputs and the Gurkhas had cancelled each other out and could no longer contemplate descending on the plains. On the east, however, the English, who had eliminated the Marathas, had become masters of almost the whole of India except the Punjab and Sindh. In these years Ranjit Singh had also consolidated his hold on the country north of the river Sutlej. He had annexed Kasur, taken tribute from the Muslim chiefs of Multan and northwestern Punjab, and reduced the misls of the Majha to subservience. All that remained to be done to unify the Punjab was to incorporate the remaining misls holding lands between the Sutlej and the Jumna. Consequently, two of the major problems at the end of the first ten years were the integration of Malwa and the drawing up of the frontier with the English.

Ranjit Singh had twice crossed the Sutlej with his army and been acclaimed as the sovereign of the Punjab: with spontaneous enthusiasm by the populace, with some reluctance by the chiefs. Even the latter had submitted to his orders and paid tribute as they would have done to an overlord. Ranjit Singh's suzerainty over the Cis-Sutlej states was a fact accomplished in all but title. The only thing that remained was for the English on the other side of Malwa to recognise the situation that existed de facto.

The weak point in the Durbar's claim to sovereignty over the Cis-Sutlej chiefs was that, in 1805, when Lord Lake had chased Holkar across the plains of Malwa, Ranjit Singh, fearing that after defeating the Marathas the English commander might annex the whole of the Punjab, had suggested the river Sutlej as the boundary between the two states. Neither Lake nor the governor general had taken any notice of this suggestion. Their sole object was the annihilation of the Marathas; once that was achieved, the Board of Directors of the East India Company (which had been brought to the verge of bankruptcy by the Maratha campaigns) issued instructions to its officers not to involve the Company in any more wars and to consider the river Jumna as the western limit of English possessions in India.

In the three years after the end of the Maratha campaign in 1805 both the Maharajah and the Company changed their attitude to the Cis-Sutlej states. The Maharajah had resumed his claim to being the sovereign of all Sikhs and twice substantiated it with regard to the Malwa chiefs without a word of protest from any one. In these three years the East India Company had been able to refill its coffers and was ready for more adventures.

The Durbar's action in taking over the territories of Tara Singh Gheba in 1807 had caused great consternation among the Cis-Sutlej chiefs. After the attachment of Gheba's estates, Mohkam Chand crossed the Sutlej and, with more zeal than discretion, proceeded to take Anandpur and some other villages across the river. The Malwa chiefs were apprehensive and appealed to the English for protection. The situation took an unexpected turn in their favour. The events that brought this about occurred neither on the banks of the Sutlej nor the Jumna but on the Thames and the Seine. Within a few years Napoleon Bonaparte conquered one European country after another: Austria at Austerlitz, Prussia at Jena, Russia at Friedland. Tsar Alexander and Bonaparte signed a treaty at Tilsit with a not-too-secret understanding that if England continued hostilities against France, Russia would come in on the French side. Britain was supreme on the seas, but the land route through Persia, Afghanistan, Sindh,

the Punjab and into India was open to the Franco-Russian
armies. The British had to revise their policies. Lord Minto, who had taken over as governor general in June 1807,
was instructed to prepare against this danger. British troops
were moved up to Karnal and a military post was set up to
protect Delhi from the north. Hariana was occupied and
Skinner's Horse strengthened to patrol the desert regions.
The grand strategy of erecting a series of dams to prevent
a Franco-Russian invasion was taken in hand. The dams
were to be in Persia, Afghanistan, Sindh, and the Punjab.
Four missions were sent out: Malcolm to Persia, Elphinstone to Kabul, Seton to Sindh, and Metcalfe was chosen
to negotiate with the Lahore Durbar.[1]

The Cis-Sutlej chiefs came to know that the English
were interested in them. They met in the village of Samana to plan a course of action. The feeling which prevailed was that the British, who had already come up to
the Jumna, would inevitably proceed further north; that
they were stronger than the Durbar; that whereas the British would at least guarantee the chiefs their personal privileges and status, the Durbar would abolish their political
power and merge their territories into the Punjab state.
A venerable patriarch summed up their view in the following words: "We do not have a very long life, as both the
British and Ranjit Singh mean to swallow us up. But
whereas the British protection will be like consumption,

---

[1] The idea of sending a British delegation to Lahore was mooted early
in 1808. When intelligence was received that Ranjit Singh might come to
Hardwar to bathe in the Ganges, the Resident at Delhi advised his government to exploit the situation "by acts of kindness and attention to render
the circumstances of Ranjit Singh's visit to the Company's dominions sub-
servient to the plan of pleasing and conciliating him, thereby rendering it
the basis of future intercourse and friendly connection." (Resident Seton to
the governor general, February 18, 1808.) The instructions given to Metcalfe on this occasion also show clearly the British conception of their
northern frontier. He was ordered "to proceed to the banks of the Jumna
and wait for the arrival of Ranjit Singh." (SC 24 of 11.4.1808.) On the
return journey he was to accompany the ruler "up to the British frontier,"
which was again the banks of the Jumna.

which takes a long time to kill, Ranjit Singh's advent will be like a stroke of paralysis which will destroy us within a few hours."[1a]

A delegation consisting of Bhag Singh of Jind, Lal Singh of Kaithal, Bhagwan Singh of Jagadhari, and the Vakils of Patiala and Nabha waited on the Resident at Delhi and presented a lengthy memorandum stating that since the English had replaced the Mughals and the Marathas, the Malwa chiefs now looked upon them as the sovereign power and expected to be protected against Ranjit Singh. The Resident forwarded the memorandum to the governor general without making any commitment. The Company's policy still being "no farther than the Jumna," the governor general decided that the representation should be officially ignored.

The Maharajah summoned the Malwai chiefs to Amritsar. He gave them a solemn assurance that he did not intend to annex their states and invited them to be associated with the Durbar as equals. The chiefs agreed to throw in their lot with their countrymen: "Between the lion and wolf they had to come to terms with one of the lordlier beasts."[2]

At this stage Metcalfe appeared on the Punjab scene.

Although Metcalfe's object was to get Ranjit Singh to line up on the side of the English in the event of a French invasion, there were many factors which led the Durbar to doubt his motives. France was a long way off and there was no real evidence of a French plan to invade India.[3] The

---

[1a] *Umdāt-ut-Tawārīkh*, *Daftar* II, 79.

[2] E. Thompson, *The Life of Charles, Lord Metcalfe*. p. 75.

[3] The official Durbar historian Sohan Lal, who devotes many pages of his *Umdāt-ut-Tawārīkh* to Metcalfe's mission, does not once mention France in his narrative.

V. G. Kiernan in his monograph *Metcalfe's Mission to Lahore* writes: "The negotiations with Ranjit Singh were in fact to turn so little on French affairs, that it might be permissible to suspect Napoleon of being in this case a mere red herring, and the mission of being sent to initiate a penetration of the Punjab" (p. 5).

French government had made no attempt to establish contact with the Durbar nor, to its knowledge, with the Sindhians or the Afghans. On the other hand, the British were sending an envoy to Kabul to make an alliance with the Afghans, who were the traditional enemy of the Punjabis, particularly of the Sikhs. They were also sending an envoy to the Amirs of Sindh when the Durbar was considering expanding its territories in that direction to the sea.

The instructions of the governor general to Metcalfe disclosed that he did not think his government had any rights over the Sikh chiefs of Malwa. He stated categorically that the English would not interfere in the Durbar's plans regarding Malwa "because it would involve the protection of states unconnected with us by the obligation of defensive alliance." Nevertheless, the governor general wanted Metcalfe to use Malwa as a pawn. He instructed Metcalfe "to avoid a declared concurrence in Ranjit's hostile designs against the states in question and until it is known in what degree the security of the British government may require a cordial union of its interests with those of Ranjit Singh, it is not easy to determine what sacrifices it may be expedient to make for the attainment of that object. . . ."[4]

Metcalfe received the Malwa chiefs at Patiala. Sahib Singh made a dramatic gesture by presenting the keys of his citadel to the Englishman, begging him to return them to him to symbolise British protection over Patiala. "The ceremony was quite unnecessary," reported Metcalfe. Nevertheless he "endeavoured to assure him [Sahib Singh] that the British government entertained the most friendly sentiments towards him."[5]

The chiefs began to play off the British and the Durbar against each other. They told Ranjit Singh that the British meant to annex the Durbar's territories. They told Met-

[4] SC 3 of 20.6.1808.
[5] Metcalfe No. 8, 24.8.1808.

calfe that the Durbar was massing troops to fight the British.

The first meeting between the youthful Sikh monarch (27 years) and the even more youthful English ambassador (age 23), took place at Khem Karan near Kasur on September 12, 1808. Some days later the Englishman informed the Durbar that the French, who were trying to establish themselves in Persia, had designs on Kabul and the Punjab, and "the interests of all the states in this quarter required that they should unite in defence of their dominions and for the destruction of the enemy's armies."[6]

The Durbar, while agreeing to the British proposal for a joint defence against the French invasion, suggested that they should go further and "establish the strictest union between the two states and put an end to the reports which were constantly circulated throughout the country, of approaching disputes between the British government and the Rajah." The Maharajah asked specifically that the British government should recognise his sovereignty over the Malwa. Metcalfe was unwilling to discuss the question as it dealt with "a one-sided interest" whereas his mandate was to discuss only questions of mutual interest. Azizuddin corrected him. The settlement of a common frontier, explained the Fakir, was as much a question of mutual interest as that of making an alliance.

Metcalfe prevaricated till the Maharajah's patience was exhausted. He ordered the breaking up of camp and asked the envoy to follow him if he cared to do so. Ranjit Singh crossed the Sutlej and marched to Faridkot. Though nominally under Patiala, Faridkot had revolted and Ranjit Singh was obliged to put down the rebellion as part of his duty as overlord of Patiala.

Faridkot did not offer any resistance. Metcalfe arrived at Faridkot and presented the draft of a treaty. It had three clauses providing for joint action against the French in the

[6] "The information which the Company had collected as to French designs amounted to a handful of mist." E. Thompson, p. 77.

event of an invasion, passage for British troops through the Durbar's territories, and the establishment of a military depot and an intelligence post in the Punjab, if the action were to take place beyond the Indus.

The Durbar presented Metcalfe with a draft of counter-proposals. This too had three clauses: first, that the British and the Durbar should extend most favoured nation treatment to each other; the Afghans were not to be given preference; nor should the British enter into any alliance with the rulers of Bahawalpur and Multan. Second, that Ranjit Singh's suzerainty over the whole of the Sikh nation should be recognised; the British were not to entertain any disaffected Sikh chiefs or meddle with the traditions of the *Khālsājī*; and, third, that the alliance should be in perpetuity.

Metcalfe forwarded the counterproposals to the governor general. After a fortnight in Faridkot, the Maharajah proceeded to Malerkotla, where Metcalfe followed him. The Pathan ruler of Malerkotla submitted to Ranjit Singh. (Metcalfe had to ignore the Nawab's plea to intercede on his behalf and have the levy imposed on him reduced.)[7] From Malerkotla, Ranjit Singh went to Ambala and then to Shahabad.

The Maharajah continued on his triumphant march through the region and was welcomed by the people wherever he went. At Patiala, the petrified Sahib Singh asked to be forgiven. Ranjit Singh overlooked his past conduct, embraced him, and exchanged turbans with him.

---

[7] Metcalfe committed many of his thoughts to paper. It is clear from what he wrote that he had come around to the view that Ranjit's suzerainty over the Cis-Sutlej states was an accomplished fact and, if his government really desired Ranjit's friendship, they should recognise that sovereignty. The only thing that bothered him was the position of the few chiefs of the region who had not yet submitted to Ranjit's overlordship. If his government gave Ranjit unconditional recognition it would be forcing some unwilling people into his arms. If it made recognition conditional on his ability to bring them into his fold, it would be encouraging him to commit aggression. Metcalfe's mind was obsessed with the exact wording of the recognition, not with its substance.

The Maharajah thus gave a clear proof, if proof were needed, that most of the land between the Jumna and the Sutlej was under his control and that almost all the chieftains of the area acknowledged him as suzerain. But the British government had now decided to take the doab between the Jumna and the Sutlej under its protection and began to move its troops northwards. Metcalfe was instructed that, although the alliance with the Durbar was no longed considered necessary, he should "spin things out" until Colonel Ochterlony had assembled his forces and was ready to take the field.

The Maharajah was blissfully unaware of the stab in the back that the governor general, Lord Minto, had planned for him. He returned from the tour of the Malwa to Amritsar, where the populace gave him a hero's welcome, singing songs of joy and showering him with flowers. For several nights the streets and the temple were illuminated. The monarch and his people gave themselves up to merrymaking.

Metcalfe arrived in Amritsar on December 10, 1808, with the governor general's ultimatum. He joined the Maharajah's nautch parties with great enthusiasm.

He had to "spin things out" until Ochterlony was in position, the British agents had had time to renew contacts with the Malwa chiefs, and his colleague Elphinstone had finished his mission in Kabul and had returned (through the Punjab) to British territory.[8]

Metcalfe presented the note containing an "irrevocable demand" that all the territory east of the Sutlej that the Maharajah had taken under his control since the arrival

---

[8] Occasionally Metcalfe's thoughts went back to the initial object of his mission. "I could not forget that I had been sent to establish an alliance and not bring on a war," he wrote in his diary. About the changed attitude of his government, the envoy had no qualms. He was sure that they could find something in the behaviour of Ranjit Singh which would give them the excuse to go to war against him. "His conduct would soon have given an opportunity to get rid of any embarrassment which our engagement with him might have caused."

of the English mission should be restored forthwith. The Maharajah called off his parties and immediately returned to Lahore to consult with his ministers.[9] At Lahore Metcalfe broke the news that a British force was moving up to the Sutlej. The Durbar's counsellors were of two minds. The leader of the fight-the-British group was Mohkam Chand, who pleaded that it was more honourable to die fighting than to capitulate without firing a shot. At his instance orders were issued to the chiefs to bring their forces and stop the British advance on the Sutlej. The forts of Gobindgarh, Phillaur, and Lahore were strengthened. Within a few days nearly a hundred thousand men had answered the call to arms. But even with this vast fighting force, Mohkam Chand could not assure a victory against the Company's better trained and potentially larger army. Fakir Azizuddin was for appeasement and avoiding hostilities as far as possible. The speed with which the British moved induced the Maharajah to accept the Fakir's advice.

On January 2, 1809, Ochterlony had left Delhi for Karnal at the head of three infantry battalions, a regiment of cavalry, and some artillery. His instructions were to compel the Durbar to give up its recent conquests; on the way he was to call upon the Malwa chiefs for assistance. If any of them showed sympathy with Ranjit Singh, they were to

[9] Metcalfe gives another reason for Ranjit Singh's hurried departure from Amritsar. In a letter of December 14, 1808 he writes: "His favourite mistress, Moran, who is of the Moosulman faith, lately converted a Hindoo of the Khutree caste to the Moosulman religion, whether by force or persuasion I do not know. The town of Amritsar has been in a state of ferment, in consequence for many days. . . . The populace on one occasion outrageously plundered the houses of all the Moosulman dancing girls, of whom Moran was formerly one, and forced the Rajah to agree that they should be removed from the town." (SC 100 of 30.1.1809.)

Metcalfe did not do too badly himself. He not only participated in the bacchanalian festivities himself but also took an Indian mistress, who bore him three children. Both Metcalfe and his biographer Kaye (who have much to say of the Orientals' lustful habits) maintain a sanctimonious silence about this liaison. It is mentioned by Edward Thompson, who states that Metcalfe married the woman, who was a Sikh, by "Indian rites." (Edward Thompson, p. 101.)

be told plainly what was in store for them. He was also instructed not to lose the opportunity of making contacts with disaffected elements of the Lahore Durbar.

While Ochterlony was on his way north, Metcalfe began to exhort his government in the event of hostilities to undertake a full-scale war against the Durbar.[10] Fortunately, the necessity for aggression disappeared. Napoleon had attacked Spain and it seemed very unlikely that the French would think of India for some years to come. British policy towards the Durbar underwent a corresponding change. On January 30, 1809 Ochterlony received fresh instructions. In view of the changed situation in Europe, the war with the Durbar, if any, was to be a defensive one and the military post on the Sutlej was only to hold back the Punjabis if they attempted to cross the river.

Ochterlony continued his march. At Patiala, the dim-witted Sahib Singh received him in a state of "childish joy." Nabha was a little less jubilant; he had received many favours from Ranjit. So also had Bhag Singh of Jind, who wanted to exchange the city of Ludhiana, given to him by his nephew but taken over by the British, for Hariana, Karnal, and Panipat. The Malerkotla Nawab was reinstated in his possessions.

On February 9 Ochterlony issued a formal proclamation "to signify the pleasure of the British government" which was motivated solely by the desire "to confirm the friendship with the Maharajah and to prevent any injury to his country," that hereafter "the troops of the Maharajah shall never advance into the country of the chiefs situated on this side of the river." If the Maharajah did not comply, then according to the proclamation "shall it be plain that the Maharajah has no regard for the friendship of the British."[11]

[10] Metcalfe No. 63 of 26.1.1809.

[11] The proclamation was re-issued on May 3, 1809, which states in its preamble: "It is clearer than the sun, and better proved than the existence of yesterday that the marching of a detachment of British troops to this

The Maharajah swallowed his pride and agreed to recognise the Sutlej as the Punjab's eastern boundary. He had earlier returned to Amritsar, where the details of the treaty were to be discussed.

The negotiations of the preceding six months had produced such a state of tension that a small fracas between Phula Singh's *nihaṅgs* and Metcalfe's Muslim escort almost set light to the powder magazine.[12] Fortunately, before news of the incident could reach Calcutta, the governor general had despatched drafts of treaties to be offered to the Durbar. The catastrophe of war was thus averted in the nick of time.

---

side of the river Sutlej was entirely at the application and earnest entreaty of the several chiefs."

Article 1 of this proclamation reads: "The country of the Chiefs of Malwa and Sirhind having entered under the British protection, they shall in future be secured from the authority and influence of Maharajah Ranjit Singh, conformably to the terms of the treaty."

[12] Muharram was on February 25, 1809 and the Shia Muslims in Metcalfe's escort decided to take out a procession in the streets of Amritsar. It also happened to be the day of Holi and a great many Sikhs, particularly Akalis with their celebrated leader Phula Singh, had foregathered in the city to celebrate it. The Shia procession wended its way through the streets of Amritsar, beating their breasts to the chants of "Hassan, Hussain." They came to the opening in front of the Golden Temple, where the Akalis were at prayer. The Akalis remonstrated with the processionists to go elsewhere. Arguments led to a scuffle and the Shia sepoys came to a head-on collision with the Akalis. It is not known who were the aggressors. Even Metcalfe was doubtful and conceded that the first shot had probably been fired by one of his escorts (Metcalfe No. 72, of 7.3.1809). There were more casualties on the side of the Akalis than on that of the Shias. This fact, in view of Metcalfe's own admission that the "matchlocks of our assailants carried further and with surer aim than our musquets," does not lend support to the theory of Akali aggression. Nor does it support the legend created by British historians that, although outnumbered, the sepoys worsted the Akalis and so impressed Ranjit Singh with their superior discipline that he promptly decided to Europeanise his army. His army had been professionally "Europeanised" since 1803. This is stated in detail by Amar Nath in the *Zafar Nāmā-i-Ranjit Singh*. Metcalfe could not utilise the incident as an excuse for war. His report blamed Akali Phula Singh, but not Ranjit, who turned up on the scene immediately and personally helped to quell the riot. He also sent his courtiers to Metcalfe to apologise for the lack of courtesy shown to his guests and promised compensation.

The drafts provided for perpetual friendship and most-favoured-nation treatment for the Durbar, recognition of the Maharajah's sovereignty over territories north of the Sutlej, and a concession to the Durbar in that it would be allowed to keep some troops south of the Sutlej to police its estates on the east of the river. The Durbar troops gave up the territories they had occupied in their last expedition and on the twenty-fifth the treaty was formally signed at Amritsar.[13] It was followed by a week of farewell parties for Metcalfe, and the envoy left the Punjab well pleased with himself.

Despite the treaty and the celebration that followed, ill will continued on both sides for some time. At the Durbar end there were people like Mohkam Chand and Akali Phula Singh of the do-or-die school, who felt that the Maharajah should tear up the treaty and fight. Contacts were made with the Marathas, Rohillas, and Begam Samru, and the air in northern India was thick with rumours of a Sikh-Maratha alliance to expel the English from India. The English were perturbed by these rumours and moved a detachment of troops to Hansi to prevent a junction of the Maharajah's forces with those of Sindhia or Holkar.

The Maharajah kept a cool head. He listened to Mohkam Chand, for whom he had great respect and admiration, but refused to take the Maratha promises of collaboration seriously. "Let the Marathas make the first move and I will join them," he told his courtiers. The Marathas did not make the first move, nor is it likely that they would have moved at all unless the fortunes of war had favoured the Punjabis. As the months went by, the rumours died down, the clouds of suspicion cleared, and the relations between the Durbar and the English became normal and even friendly. By June of that year the governor general was able to write to the Maharajah expressing satisfaction at the relations existing between them. Ranjit Singh an-

[13] See Appendix 6.

swered enthusiastically: "Judge by the state of your own heart, what is the state of mine!"[14]

The treaty of Lahore[15] was a grievous blow to the Punjabi dream of a unified Punjab. Malwa was forever cut off from the rest of the country. Malwai chieftains resumed their favourite pastime of bickering and intrigue; the British government discovered that what they needed more than protection against the Durbar was protection against each other. Consequently on August 22, 1811 another proclamation was made by the British government "for the purpose of ameliorating the condition of the community" which had suffered from the rapacity of the Malwai chiefs; the proclamation authorised interference when the Sardars took the law in their own hands. Thus within two or three years the British enhanced their status from a protecting to a sovereign power. Malwa was virtually annexed and became a part of British India and the Malwais became mere spectators of the military achievements of the independent Punjabi state.

The treaty did at first assure the Durbar of a safe eastern frontier and was a guarantee of non-intervention in the Durbar's plans to extend its territories in other directions, but even that hope proved later to be somewhat illusory. When the British were ready for further conquests they used this very treaty to thwart the Durbar's moves against Sindh, the north, and north-west.

[14] Political Correspondence of Lord Minto, No. 275, Vol. IV, July-December 1809.

[15] There was some heart-searching in London and Calcutta about the ethics of occupation of the Cis-Sutlej states so soon after the passing of the solemn resolution that the Jumna would be the final boundary—and without any provocation from any quarter. The Secret Committee of the Board of Directors in London, when reviewing the Treaty of Lahore, was constrained to remark that there had been a departure from the principles laid down on October 19, 1805 and February 27, 1806 fixing the western limits to the possessions in India. Perhaps it was this sense of guilt which made the English effusive in their protestations of friendship for Ranjit Singh and helped him to overcome the animosity that Metcalfe's visit had aroused.

CHAPTER 14

CONSOLIDATION OF THE PUNJAB

Capture of Kangra and the
Expulsion of the Gurkhas

◈:◈:◈: THE Treaty of Lahore brought little credit
◈:◈:◈: to the Durbar in the eyes of a people well-
◈:◈:◈: known for their pugnacity. Fortunately, an
opportunity to recover face presented itself a few months
after the departure of the English envoy.

Sansar Chand, who was fighting a losing battle against
the Gurkhas, appealed to the Durbar and to the English
for help. To counteract Sansar Chand's move, the Gurkhas
asked the British to join them in taking Kangra and offered tribute to the Maharajah if he stayed his hand. The
British turned down Sansar Chand's appeal and the Gurkha
request on the grounds that they could not interfere in the
affairs of the people living to the west of the Sutlej.[1] The
Durbar decided to help Sansar Chand on the basis that
Kangra was a part of the Punjab; but the offer was on the
condition that Sansar Chand hand over the fort of Kangra.
Sansar Chand accepted these terms and the Durbar's troops
quickly moved into position to cut the Gurkha supply lines
with Nepal. Orders were issued to the chiefs of the Kangra
region to stop selling provisions to the Gurkhas.

The Maharajah arrived in Kangra to take over the fort.
Sansar Chand began to prevaricate. The fort, he promised,
would be handed over as soon as the Gurkhas were expelled. The Maharajah was not taken in by the ruse, and,
since there was little time to argue, Sansar Chand's son,
Anirodh Chand, who was held as hostage by the Durbar,

[1] Sansar Chand later wrote to Minto: "Even imagination itself could
scarcely have found a path through these difficult passes"; the Gurkhas,
however, did so and compelled Sansar Chand to deliver the fort to Ranjit
Singh. "Why was I not given protection by the British?" wailed Sansar
Chand. "What wonder if Kings show favour to the poor!"

was put under arrest. Sansar Chand yielded and on August 24 the Durbar's troops were admitted into the fort.

The Gurkhas held on stubbornly despite their limited rations. When they were physically too weak to fight, the Punjabis took the offensive. The battle was fought along a hillside known as Ganesh Ghati. The siege-weary and famished Gurkhas retreated in disorder and the Nepali menace to the Punjab was ended forever.

The Maharajah held a formal levee in the fort of Kangra. Among those who paid him homage were the chiefs of Kangra, Chamba, Nurpur, Kotla-Shahpur, Jasrota, Basohli, Mankot, Jaswan Mandi, Suket, Kulu, and Datarpur. Desa Singh Majithia[2] was appointed subedar of the hill areas, with Pahar Singh Man[3] governor of Kangra.

The Maharajah could face his people once more. His triumphal journey back was through gaily decorated towns and villages. He reached Amritsar early in January 1810. The guns of the fort of Gobindgarh saluted him on arrival. At night he rode through illuminated streets to the Harimandir, where he offered a prayer of thanksgiving to his gurus. The scenes of jubilation were repeated at the capital. The Rajas of Patiala and Jind sent their envoys to felicitate the Lahore Durbar. The short eclipse of the sun of his fortunes was over.

Unification of the Punjab

After Kangra, the Durbar returned to the task of abolishing the autonomous principalities within the state boundaries.

[2] Desa Singh Majithia was a member of the famous Majithia family, many of whom held high posts in the Lahore Durbar. After administering Kangra, Desa Singh was made Nazim of Amritsar with the administration of the Harimandir as a special assignment. The celebrated Lehna Singh was one of his sons. Desa Singh died in 1832.

[3] Pahar Singh Man was the son of Surja Singh Man of the village of Mughal Chak. His father and grandfather had served the Sukerchakias before him and he, along with three other brothers, was with Ranjit Singh in taking Lahore. He saw action in many of Ranjit Singh's campaigns and held a jagir of Rs. 2 lacs. He died in December 1813.

First came the turn of the Bhangi chief of Gujarat, who had fallen out with his son. The divided Bhangi forces put up a feeble resistance. The old Sardar fled to the hills; the son agreed to become a loyal subject. Fakir Nuruddin took over Gujarat and all the forts of the Bhangis in the name of the Durbar. The Maharajah himself reduced the Baluch tribes occupying the desert areas of Shahpur, Miani, and Bhera. In February 1810 he took Khushab and the fort of Kucch from the Baluch chief, Jafar Khan (who was given a pension for life), and Sahiwal from its chieftain, Fateh Khan.

While Ranjit Singh was occupied with the Baluch tribes, his generals were fanning out in all directions, bringing scattered territories under the authority of the Durbar. Dewan Mohkam Chand took over the estates of Budh Singh, head of the Singhpuria misl. Jullundur, which was his headquarters, and his territory, and yielded an annual revenue of over three lacs, were joined to the Durbar. Earlier, Hukma Singh Chimni, who had incorporated Jammu, joined the Maharajah in reducing Kusk, which controlled the salt mines of Khewra. Desa Singh Majithia, who had been left in charge of Kangra, took the neighbouring states of Mandi and Suket. Nuruddin occupied Wazirabad. Among the important places seized in these whirlwind operations were Daska, Hallowal, and Mangla on the Jhelum, which opened up the northern Himalayan regions. Then came the turn of the Nakkais, who were related to the Maharajah through his second wife and the mother of the heir-apparent. The Nakkai, Kahan Singh, was given a *jāgīr* of Rs. 20,000, and the entire area, which included Chunian, Dipalpur, Sharakpur, and Kamalia, was attached to the state. Sada Kaur's misl, the Kanhayas, also suffered partial eclipse. Her territories were spared, but those of her brother-in-law along the river Beas were seized.

Shah Shuja and Multan

The Maharajah was in the neighbourhood of Khushab when a messenger brought news of the arrival in the Punjab of Shah Shuja. In order to grasp the object of Shuja's mission, it is necessary to understand something of the politics of Afghanistan.

The three grandsons of Ahmed Shah Abdali, who aspired to succeed to the Afghan Empire, were Shah Zaman, Shah Shuja, and Shah Mahmud. The real power had, however, passed out of the hands of the royal family who belonged to the Saddozai clan to the family of the chief minister, Wazir Fateh Khan, who was a Barakzai. The Barakzais favoured Shah Mahmud over the other two brothers. Shah Zaman, who had made four attempts to conquer India, was overthrown by the Barakzais, who installed Mahmud in his place. Mahmud put out Zaman's eyes, hoping thereby to put him permanently out of the picture. Zaman's place was taken by Shuja, who ousted Mahmud from Kabul. When Lord Minto sent his envoys to make alliances against a possible French invasion, Shuja seemed firmly installed. But hardly had Elphinstone turned his back on Kabul when the Barakzais expelled Shuja and put back their nominee, Mahmud, in power. Shuja came to solicit the Durbar's aid to get back his throne.

What transpired at the meeting between the Maharajah and Shah Shuja is not fully known. It appears that Shuja not only expected the Punjabis to help him back on the Kabul throne, but was also anxious to have districts of the Punjab which the Afghans had wrested from the Mughals —particularly Multan. The Maharajah, on the other hand, was equally anxious to get the Afghans to relinquish their title to their early conquests in the Punjab before he would commit the Durbar to an adventure in Afghanistan. It was not surprising, then, that Shuja bid a hurried farewell and retraced his steps towards Peshawar.

The Durbar ordered the army to Multan. Muzaffar Khan sent frantic appeals for help to the English.[4] The English pleaded helplessness because of the Treaty of 1809.

The Durbar troops captured the environs of the city

4 PC 8 of 17.4.1810.

without much trouble. The massive fort, however, defied their guns; even the Zam Zama made little impression on the thick battlements. The short Punjab winter gave way to the heat and to the dust storms for which Multan is famous. The Maharajah's temper became short and in his impatience he took many risks. His officers and men paid dearly with their lives. Among those who fell in this campaign was one of his most loyal officers, Attar Singh Dhari; Nihal Singh Attariwala was seriously injured. Muzaffar Khan discovered that the besiegers were in trouble and took the offensive. The intense heat, however, settled the issue for both parties. Muzaffar Khan agreed to pay a nominal tribute and the siege was raised in April 1810.

Before the end of 1810, the Afghan royal family was back on the Punjab's doorstep. Shah Shuja's success had been short-lived; Wazir Fateh Khan Barakzai again succeeded in putting Mahmud back on the throne. Shuja found his way to Attock, where the governor, Jahan Dad Khan, gave him asylum. Then suspecting Shuja of trying to win over Wazir Fateh Khan, Jahan Dad (who was bitterly opposed to the Wazir) had Shuja put in chains and sent for safe custody to Ata Mohammed, the governor of Kashmir.[5]

The families of Shuja and the blinded Zaman had been given asylum at Rawalpindi and were living on a pension granted by the Durbar. While the Maharajah and his senior officers were occupied in consolidating the Punjab, Zaman started sending out envoys to foreign powers to negotiate for the restoration of the family to the throne of Kabul. The Durbar found this emigré government in its

[5] Sohan Lal's version is slightly different. According to him, Ata Mohammed inveigled Shuja from Jahan Dad, with an invitation, and then imprisoned him. The invitation, according to Sohan Lal, ran: "If you decide to come our way at present, all the objects and ends will be gained and the bride of purpose will come to take the seat in the parlour of happy desire." (*Daftar* II, p. 142.)

territories somewhat embarrassing and persuaded the Afghan household to shift to Lahore.

In November 1811 the one-time conqueror of Lahore returned to the city as a beggar. He was treated with great honour. State troops escorted him to his appointed residence, where the Maharajah personally welcomed him. The only thing that disturbed the peace of the royal refugee was the arrival of an agent of Wazir Fateh Khan and Shah Mahmud, to solicit the help of the Durbar in the conquest of Kashmir, where Shah Shuja was imprisoned.

While the rival Afghan households vied with each other in offering terms to the Durbar, Ranjit Singh devoted himself to the nuptials of his son and heir Kharak Singh.[6]

After the wedding guests had departed, the Afghan invitation to conquer Kashmir was taken up. Wazir Fateh Khan's agent offered half the loot and nine lacs every year if the Punjabis marched alongside the Barakzai Afghans. The refugee family, particularly Shah Shuja's senior wife, Wafa Begam, and her sons, were terrified at the prospect of the Wazir and Mahmud (who had already blinded Zaman) capturing Shuja. They made a counteroffer with the only object of real value which they possessed, the priceless diamond, Koh-i-noor.[7]

[6] Colonel Ochterlony represented the East India Company and came with the Rajas of the Cis-Sutlej states, Patiala, Nabha, Jind, and Kaithal, across the Sutlej. Friend and foe were equally welcome. Sansar Chand of Kangra came himself. The Nawabs of Multan and Bahawalpur sent members of their families to represent them. The cash presented to the bridegroom amounted to over Rs. 2,36,000. Ochterlony gave Rs. 5,000 on behalf of his government.

[7] The *Koh-i-noor* or the "Mountain of Light," perhaps the most brilliant of all the diamonds of the world, was taken from the famous mines of Golconda and came into the hands of the Mughal emperors. The Persian Nadir Shah took it along with the Peacock Throne from the Mughal Mohammed Shah in 1739 when he sacked Delhi and massacred its inhabitants. On Nadir's assassination in 1747, it came into the hands of Ahmed Shah Abdali and after his death into those of his son and successor, Taimur.

Taimur died in 1793. Shah Zaman, one of Taimur's sons, happened to be in the capital at the time and was able to take over the government

THE BARAKZAIS

PAINDAH KHAN

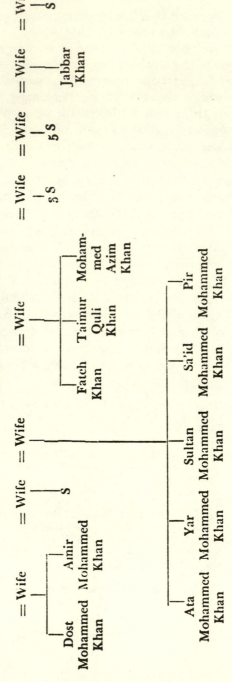

= Wife   = Wife   = Wife   = Wife   = Wife   = Wife   = Wife

Dost Mohammed Khan — Amir Mohammed Khan

S (5 S) (5 S) Jabbar Khan

Fateh Khan — Taimur Quli Khan — Mohammed Azim Khan

Ata Mohammed Khan — Yar Mohammed Khan — Sultan Mohammed Khan — Sa'id Mohammed Khan — Pir Mohammed Khan

In the spring of 1812, Durbar troops under the command of Mohkam Chand were ordered towards Kashmir. Jammu and Akhnur, which had already been incorporated in the Punjab, were properly garrisoned. Bhimbar and Rajauri were taken by sudden assault and their chiefs, Sultan Khan and Agar Khan, were brought in custody to Lahore. By the summer, when a campaign against Kashmir could be mounted, Mohkam Chand had secured the eastern approaches to the valley. The Barakzai envoy was then given leave to return to Kabul.

A few days later Wazir Fateh Khan marched out with his forces and crossed the Attock into the territories of the Durbar. The Maharajah immediately proceeded northwards and encamped at Rohtas. The Afghans could not now bypass the Punjabis and enter Kashmir. Ranjit Singh sent an emissary to Wazir Fateh Khan to enquire of his motives for entering the Punjab.

The Wazir requested a personal meeting with the Maharajah. He came for the interview with his eighteen brothers, fully armed and prepared to assassinate Ranjit Singh if the latter did not agree to a joint invasion of Kashmir.[8] There was no occasion to commit murder, for the Maharajah readily accepted the offer of an equal division of the loot and Rs. 9 lacs per year.[9]

There is little doubt that the Durbar meant to honour its commitment and that the Afghans had no intention of abiding by their word. The Durbar provided an army of twelve thousand men under its ablest generals, Dewan Mohkam Chand and Dal Singh, to accompany the Afghans.

---

and all the royal treasures, including the Koh-i-noor. When he was dispossessed and blinded by his brother, Mahmud, the diamond was taken by Shah Shuja and his wife Wafa Begam.

[8] A. Burnes, *Travels into Bokhara*, III, 237, states that the proposed assassination "did not enter into the policy of Fateh Khan."

[9] The exact terms of the agreement are not known. According to British sources (Metcalfe to governor general, PC 5 of 8.1.1813) Ranjit was to get 11 lacs per year or, failing the fulfilment of this engagement, half of Kashmir.

The two armies left Jhelum on December 1, 1812. The Punjabis proved their good faith by allowing the Afghans to march with them along the Rajauri route, which was through territory already under their control, rather than the one through Muzaffarabad, which was normally under snow at that time of the year.

It did not take long for the shrewd Mohkam Chand to realise that the Afghans meant to trick him, and he warned the Maharajah. Even after receiving information that the Wazir had taken two big forts with their treasuries and had refused to fulfil his part of the agreement, the Maharajah wrote to Mohkam Chand "not to betray the least dissatisfaction or doubt, and to conform himself to the wishes of Fateh Khan, with whom he would settle accounts, should he violate the engagement ratified by oaths."[10] Fateh Khan pressed on through the Durbar's territory at frantic speed and was soon two marches ahead of Mohkam Chand. The Dewan knew that if the Afghans reached their objective first, the fate of Shah Shuja would be sealed. He took a shortcut and surprised the Afghans by arriving ahead of them at the fort of Shergarh, where Shuja was imprisoned. The fortress capitulated without much resistance. While the Afghans were busy looting, the Punjabis searched the dungeons and stole Shah Shuja away to their camp. When Wazir Fateh Khan discovered what had happened, he demanded the custody of the Shah and, on the Dewan's refusal to deliver the royal hostage, attempted to take him by force. The attempt was frustrated; but it gave the Wazir an excuse and he refused to part with the booty they had solemnly undertaken to share. The Afghans also occupied the rest of Kashmir.

The Maharajah opened negotiations with Jahan Dad Khan, the governor of Attock (whose ally, Ata Mohammed, had been ejected from Kashmir and who was inimical to the Barakzais). Jahan Dad Khan accepted the offer

[10] PC 31 of 26.3.1813.

Ranjit Singh, with his favorite Muslim wife, Bibi Gulbahar Begam
Courtesy: M. S. Randhawa

Harimandir, the Golden Temple of the Sikhs at Amritsar
Courtesy: M. S. Randhawa

of a *jāgīr* in Wazirabad and handed over the fort of Attock to the Durbar's envoy, Fakir Azizuddin.

Wazir Fateh Khan discovered to his great chagrin that a fort which was considered the sentinel of India was in the hands of the Punjabis.[11] He was loud in his protestations of a breach of faith. He left his brother, Azim Khan, in charge of Kashmir and returned to Peshawar. From there he wrote offensive letters to the Maharajah to evacuate Attock or take the consequences.

The Koh-i-noor Episode

Shah Shuja was received at Lahore with the pomp and ceremonial that had marked his brother's reception a year earlier. He was delivered to Wafa Begam and she was asked to redeem her promise to hand over the Koh-i-noor. Kashmir had been a costly venture. The Durbar had lost over a thousand men, the Barakzais had taken the province and the loot, and the state treasury was empty.

The Begam evaded the Durbar's request for the diamond. The Maharajah understood her reluctance to part with so rare an object and offered to make a token payment of 3 lacs and assign a *jāgīr* of Rs. 50,000 to the family. Even this did not bring the Begam or her husband around. Ranjit Singh lost patience, made a peremptory demand for the Koh-i-noor, and placed a heavy guard on the Afghan family. After some days on reduced rations, the Afghans handed over the diamond to Ranjit Singh on June 1, 1813.[12]

[11] The British welcomed the passing of the fort from Afghan to Punjabi hands because it made an Afghan (or any other foreign) invasion of India more difficult. According to Sohan Lal, Metcalfe sent a letter of congratulations to Ranjit and advised him never to give up the fort—and even obliquely hinted at the possibility of British help if necessary for the purpose. (*Daftar*, II, 142.)

[12] The Koh-i-noor episode has been distorted by historians inimical to Ranjit Singh. Fortunately Shah Shuja mentions the incident himself in some detail. The narrative after his release from Shergarh runs as follows: "Mohkam Chand, on the part of Runjeet Singh, informed us that his master was anxious that we should proceed to Lahore as soon as at lib-

Shah Shuja was by no means reduced to penury by this loss. He continued to receive an allowance from the Lahore Durbar and still owned, as was subsequently proved, considerable wealth in gold and jewels.

First Punjabi Victory over the Afghans: Battle of Attock, July 1813

Wazir Fateh Khan tried to talk the Durbar into handing over the fort of Attock to him. He professed friendship for the Maharajah, flattered him with presents and words of praise, and promised to capture Multan for the Durbar. The Durbar insisted that Fateh Khan should capture Multan first and then discuss Attock. The Durbar kept up correspondence with the Afghans until a Punjabi force was well on its way to the relief of the fort. To make the possession of Attock more secure, Durbar troops occupied an advance post at Haripur.

Wazir Fateh Khan roused the tribes in the neighbourhood and called for a holy war to expel the "infidels" from

---

erty and visit the residence of our seraglio in that city; he also mentioned that his master's fame would increase by our going." The Shah arrived in Lahore escorted by Mohkam Chand. He continues: "On the morning of the second day, Ram Singh waited on us and demanded the Koh-i-noor for his master. We confessed that it was not in our possession, but after experiencing hospitality and assistance from Runjeet Singh, we should take his wish into consideration. Ram Singh attended the next day and received the same reply. We then experienced privation of the necessaries of life, and sentinels were occasionally placed over our dwelling." Shuja mentions Ranjit Singh's offer to pay forty to fifty thousand rupees and help to recover territory in the north which the Shah expressed willingness to accept. "He then proposed an exchange of turbans, which is among the Seikhs a pledge of eternal friendship and then gave him the Koh-i-noor. Two days after, the interdiction was removed from our visits to the dwelling containing our family." (*Calcutta Monthly Journal*, 1839. Autobiographical sketch by Shah Shuja written by himself in Ludhiana 1826-1827 and translated by Lt. Bennett of the artillery.)

The facts do not reflect any discredit on Ranjit Singh. If he had wanted to rob Wafa Begam, there was nothing to stop him from doing so. He knew that the diamond was with her in February 1810, when Wafa Begam entered his kingdom. In view of the way in which the Koh-i-noor had been taken away from India, even a forcible repossession would have been justified. But the course Ranjit Singh followed was a wholly honourable one.

the frontier. For three months the Afghans and the Punjabis faced each other without any serious action. The winter warmed to spring and the short spring changed to the intense heat of summer. Dewan Mohkam Chand manoeuvred his forces and placed them between the Afghans and the river Attock. He cut off the enemy's supply of drinking water and forced him to take the offensive. The battle, which was fought on the Mansar plain northeast of the fort, took the form of Afghan sallies to break through to the river and Punjabi efforts to keep them away. The Afghans had to fight in the sweltering heat of summer without a drop to slake their thirst. When Mohkam Chand detected Afghan pressure weakening, he ordered his cavalry to charge. The Afghans broke ranks and fled, leaving over two thousand of their comrades dead on the field and all their heavy guns and equipment to the victors.[13]

It was the first victory the Punjabis had ever won over the Afghans and the Pathans. That it should have been on the field of Attock was of even greater significance. Attock had been wrested from Raja Jaipal in A.D. 1002 by Mahmud Ghazni and since then had remained in foreign hands. Its recapture meant the liberation of northern India from the Pathan and Afghan menace. When the news of the victory was received in Lahore, the city went wild with joy. People came out in the streets to sing and dance and shout themselves hoarse. The Maharajah rode out of the palace to join his subjects in their celebrations, and scattered the usual largesse upon the cheering crowds.

While the army was engaged with the Pathans and the Maharajah's attention was completely occupied with the problems of the frontier, a dastardly plot to overthrow the Durbar was set afoot by Shah Shuja. A newsletter of

[13] A different version of the same battle is given by Sir Olaf Caroe, *The Pathans*, p. 289.

June 23, 1813 narrates the incident: "Pir Batish, in charge of the Police Station, came in and stated that the companions of Huzrat Shuja-ul-Mulk had written some letters of their own accord and under their own seal to Sardar Fateh Khan Wazir; that as the messenger carrying those letters had been brought to him as a captive, therefore, he submitted those letters to the Noble Sarkar [Ranjit Singh]. It was written in them that the Noble Sarkar was all alone at that time in Lahore, that he had no troops with him, that if he [the Wazir] would send his troops it would not be difficult to capture Lahore. . . ."

Ranjit Singh was not a man of quick temper but, once his wrath was aroused, his moods could be very black indeed. He asked for an explanation from Shuja and, when he was convinced that the Shah was lying,[14] had the men

[14] Shuja himself wrote to Ochterlony admitting his complicity in the plan to betray his host by inviting his erstwhile enemy Wazir Fateh Khan to invade the Punjab. The letter (PC 12 of 12.11.1813) ran as follows: "Two months ago Mahmud Hussain Khan arrived here from my brother Mahmud with the intention of proceeding to you. When he arrived at Lahore, you will have heard the secrets were discovered by the interception of letters and Mahmud Hussain Khan in consequence put in confinement, where he remained about two months." Mohammed Amir was sent to Ochterlony with a letter which read: "As we worship the same God, it is our duty jointly to extirpate the tribe of infidels who are so many in the garden of Runjeet. As soon as the flame of war shall have been lit and troops under Wazir Fateh Khan put in motion against that quarter, God willing, we shall soon put them in confusion and disorder and then divide the Punjab between us." The plan apparently was that, while the Lahore troops were busy against Wazir Fateh Khan, his brother Azim Khan, the governor of Kashmir, should invade the Punjab and settle the business of infidels in this city.
On her arrival at Ludhiana, Wafa Begam had written several letters to the governor general detailing the circumstances in which she came to Lahore and pleading for intercession for her husband's release. In the first (Vol. 58A, Persian Letters, December 1814) she wrote: "We had no treaty subsisting with Ranjeet Singh but when we took refuge in his domains, he procured the delivery of the King from the sons of Mukhtar-ul-Dowlah [i.e. Wazir Fateh Khan]." Neither in this nor in the second, where she complained of the seizure of her agent Balak Ram and her property, did she make any reference to Ranjit having wrongly taken the Koh-i-noor. And in the third she openly admitted the fact that her husband had been plotting Ranjit's downfall while his guest in Lahore: "His Majesty wished

concerned arrested and the Shah deprived of some more
of the wealth he had with him. Thereafter the guard on
the Afghan family was relaxed and the entourage given
some freedom of movement. This relaxation of surveillance
gave the Begam, and then the Shah himself, the opportunity to escape from Lahore and cross over into British
territory.

---

to meet you and discuss with you what was for the interest of both states.
It was the pleasure of the most High Power that this scheme should be
discovered by Ranjit Singh, who accordingly placed His Majesty under a
guard."

It is clear that Shuja had opened negotiations both with Wazir Fateh
Khan (who had decided to throw over Mahmud and back Shuja instead)
and the English. The Wazir had proposed an invasion of the Punjab from
either end. In his letter, he had waxed poetic:

I am prepared to dive to the bottom of the deep,
Determined to seize the pearl of desire, or perish in the attempt.
My resolution is fixed and I will execute my design.
The crimson tide shall mantle my cheek with joy
Or freeze in my lifeless veins.

CHAPTER 15

EXTINCTION OF AFGHAN POWER
IN NORTHERN INDIA

Second Campaign in Kashmir, 1813-1814

◈◈◈ A MONTH after the victory at Attock, the Durbar resolved to wrest Kashmir from the Afghans. By the time the plans were matured it was autumn and an early fall of snow checked the progress of the troops. All that could be achieved that year was to prepare the ground for a campaign in the following spring.

As the snows thawed, troops were mobilised. Early in June an army of nearly fifty thousand men was encamped at Wazirabad. In the absence of Mohkam Chand, who was taken ill, the Maharajah placed the larger part of the army—thirty thousand men—under the command of the Dewan's twenty-year-old grandson, Ram Dyal. With the youthful commander were a galaxy of famous generals: Hari Singh Nalwa, Meeth Singh Bharania, Jodh Singh Kalsia, and the artillery commander Mian Ghausa. This force proceeded towards Baramulla and Shupaiyan. The remainder of the force under Ranjit Singh's personal command made for Poonch. The pincer movement began in the second week of July. Just then the monsoon broke in the hills.

The Maharajah was held up at Rajauri by torrential rains. The force under Ram Dyal struggled on bravely, took the fortress of Baramgulla (on July 20, 1814) and went through the narrow pass to Adampur, Haripur and on to Shupaiyan. At Shupaiyan, Azim Khan, the governor of Kashmir, and his army of Afghans blocked its passage. The battle commenced in a heavy downpour which gave the entrenched Afghans a decided advantage over the Punjabis. Ram Dyal fought a delaying action to allow a relief column, which was on its way, to join him. But Afghan snipers forced the relief to a standstill a long way away from Shupaiyan.

The Maharajah did not fare any better. The Poonchis burned their standing crops and removed their livestock and chattels. The problem of food supplies became acute and Punjabi morale was further dampened by heavy rain and Poonchi guerrilla bands operating in their rear. Then cholera broke out among the troops. (Among the victims was Mian Ghausa, who died on the way to Lahore.) The Afghans took the offensive and pushed the Maharajah out of the hills.

Ram Dyal stood his ground doggedly not far from Srinagar. Azim Khan did not want to have the Punjabis so close to his capital for longer than he could help, and, having failed to dislodge Ram Dyal, opened negotiations with him. There was an exchange of presents. Azim Khan professed friendship for the Durbar and promised not to side with its enemies. Ram Dyal extricated himself from an awkward position and returned to the Punjab.[1] The campaign had been a dismal failure.

The Durbar did not engage in any major campaign until the autumn of 1815.[2] War had broken out between the Gurkhas and the English and the Durbar wanted to be prepared for any eventuality. An envoy from Nepal came to Lahore and, with the usual flattery about the Maharajah being the defender of the Hindus and the hope of Hindustan, made tempting offers of money. The Durbar turned down the Nepalese approach and instead of-

[1] There seems no evidence for Prinsep's statement that Azim Khan let the Lahore troops go unmolested because of his personal regard for Ram Dyal's grandfather, Dewan Mohkam Chand. Apart from there being no record of any kind to suggest this, it is hardly likely that considerations of this sort would weigh with those who looked upon the Sikhs, who formed the bulk of the Punjab army, as "infidels" and never spared their lives even when they had laid down arms.

[2] In addition to the fiasco in Kashmir, the Durbar lost its great commander, Dewan Mohkam Chand, who died at Phillaur on October 29, 1814.

fered help to the Company. The tide of battle had already
turned in favour of the English. The governor general
expressed his gratitude to the Durbar but did not accept
the offer of assistance.

The Anglo-Gurkha war was watched with keen interest
at Lahore. When the Nepalese were defeated, the Durbar
offered service to the disbanded Gurkhas. (The Kashmir
campaign had proved the need of hill men for mountain
warfare.) Army administration, the purchase of stores and
equipment, and the payment of salaries was at the same
time put on a regular basis by the two Kashmiri Brahmins,
Ganga Ram and Dina Nath.[3]

The new Gurkha platoons were put in action after the
annual muster of forces at Dussehra. The Maharajah personally directed the operations in which Bhimbar, Rajauri, and Kotla were retaken. Later that winter, the Durbar troops reoccupied the hill states of Nurpur and Jaswan, and the Kangra Valley. The operation pointed towards another attempt to capture Kashmir. But when the
snows melted the army was ordered south towards Multan.

Not much excuse was needed to take military action
against the southern Muslim principalities. They did not
send on their revenue in time and always offered the excuse that the Afghans also claimed to be their overlords.
Since Punjabi-Afghan relations had become openly hostile, the Afghans had been talking of reoccupying Multan.

The new commander of the Durbar armies was Misr
Dewan Chand, an officer who had rapidly risen in the
Maharajah's estimation. Dewan Chand's first objective was
Bahawalpur. The Nawab made his submission, paid Rs.
80,000 in cash, and promised to remit Rs. 70,000 annually.
Muzaffar Khan of Multan was, as usual, obstructive. Some
of his forts were occupied and parts of Multan plundered
by Phula Singh's *nihangs* before the Nawab paid up his

---

[3] Dina Nath distinguished himself as one of the Durbar's ablest and
most loyal administrators. He was made Dewan and later invested with
the title of Raja.

arrears. Similar tactics had to be adopted with the chief of Mankera. The Nawab of Jhang, who had been in arrears for three years, was pensioned with a *jāgīr* and his estate, yielding four lacs of rupees a year, was attached to the Durbar. The district of Ucch was likewise taken over. At the same time, on the death of the Ramgarhia *misldār*, the estates of the misl, which were worth four lacs of rupees a year and included important towns like Qadian and Gobindpur and many powerful fortresses, were attached and the Ramgarhia troops were merged with the state army. The Durbar made no distinction between Muslim, Sikh, or Hindu.

The Fall of Multan, June 1818

Multan was an old and prosperous city. It was situated in the centre of an extensive desert between the junction of two important rivers, the Sutlej and the Ravi, which provided water for irrigation and carried flat-bottomed boats laden with merchandise between the Arabian Sea, the cities of Sindh, and the Punjab hinterland. It was the most important trading centre for caravans which came from Central Asia through the Bolan Pass on their way to Delhi. Many conquerors, including Taimur the Lame, took the Multan route to reach the heart of Hindustan.[4]

The Punjabis had made four attempts to take Multan, but had so far only succeeded in capturing the outlying bazaars. The mammoth mud-and-brick fort, which rose like a mountain in the centre of the metropolis, had defeated them every time. Without the fort, possession of the city did not amount to very much: the guns from its high walls could hit the farthest suburb.

The Punjabis had already severed the chain of small states around Multan which were linked together in their allegiance to the Afghans. All that remained was Multan

[4] A Persian couplet lists the four "gifts" of Multan:
  With four things rare Multan abounds,
  Dust, beggars, heat, and burial grounds.

itself. The opportunity came when the Afghans got embroiled with the Persians on their western front. It was rumoured that Fateh Khan Barakzai had been injured in an engagement fought at Khorasan.

A force of twenty thousand men under Misr Dewan Chand immediately set out for Multan. Artillery, which had to play a major role in reducing the fort, was under the command of General Elahi Baksh. The Zam Zama was again ordered south; so also were platoons of *nihangs*.

Preparations were made on an elaborate scale. To ensure a regular supply of provisions to the army, all boats on the Sutlej and Ravi were commandeered. Depots were opened along the route. On his way to Multan, Misr Dewan Chand took the forts of Khangarh and Muzaffargarh.

Nawab Muzaffar Khan was not unaware of these large-scale preparations and guessed that this time he would not be able to buy off the Durbar. Once again he tried to rouse the Muslim peasants with the cry of a holy war against the infidel and he prepared the city and fort for a long siege. He planned to defend himself in three stages: in the countryside, in the city, and in the fort. The first engagement was in the open, where he let his *ghāzīs*, armed only with swords and spears, gain the martyrdom they sought at the hands of well-disciplined troops equipped with cannon and musket. This battle lasted only one day, and Muzaffar Khan withdrew the remnant of his forces behind the city walls. The second round began with the Lahore troops surrounding the city and bombarding its walls. The defenders held them at bay for a few weeks. When the city walls crumbled, the defenders retreated into the fort to fight the third and last round.

The fort was surrounded by a large, deep moat. Although at that time of the year (March) there was no water in the moat, it was broad enough to keep cannon at a safe distance from the battlements; it was also deep enough to make the task of miners very hazardous. For a whole month Elahi Baksh's batteries pounded the massive walls without making any impression. March turned to April and the heat became unbearable. The monsoon was not far off. If the fort was not carried before the moat was filled with water, it would never capitulate.

The Zam Zama arrived in April. This time it proved more effective. With each shot it sent eighty pounds of solid metal hurtling into the wall and tore huge holes in it. While the defenders' energies were concentrated in blocking the damage,[5] a party of *nihangs* stole down the moat under cover of darkness and laid a mine under another portion of the wall. The next morning a huge segment of the battlement was blown sky high.

Muzaffar Khan was willing to lay down arms, but his men forced him to retract the terms of surrender he had accepted. The battle recommenced. The *nihang* leader, Sadhu Singh,[6] led his band in a desperate charge through one of the breaches and closed in on the defenders. Muzaffar Khan, his two sons, and a nephew were killed fighting; two younger sons were taken prisoners.

The fort of Multan capitulated on June 2, 1818. The fort of Shujabad fell soon after. The victor, Misr Dewan Chand, was honoured with the title of *Zafar Jang Bahādur* (the victorious in battle).[7]

The conquest of Multan ended Afghan influence in the Punjab and broke the solid phalanx of the Muslim states

[5] A stirring account of the battle is given by Ghulam Jilani in his *Jang-i-Multān*. Jilani was a spy who mingled with the Durbar troops. He states that a cannon lost one of its wheels and could not be properly fired without support. The Durbar soldiers wrangled among each other to have the honour of supporting the cannon on their shoulders. Many were killed with the recoil of the gun.

[6] Many accounts, including that of Prem Singh, give the credit of the victorious assault to Phula Singh. Sohan Lal correctly states that Phula Singh was in Attock at the time.

[7] Ranjit Singh told the English traveller, William Moorcroft, that the lives of five hundred of Muzaffar Khan's men who surrendered were spared. Griffin (*Ranjit Singh*, p. 187) does not believe this and states (without quoting his source) that the entire garrison was put to the sword. He also states that Multan was plundered and yielded two million sterling, of which five lacs was recovered by the Durbar.

in the south. It subdued the chiefs of Bahawalpur, Dera Ghazi Khan, Dera Ismail Khan, and Mankera. And it opened up the road to Sindh. In addition to all these military and political advantages, Multan was a valuable acquisition. It yielded an annual revenue of nearly Rs. 7 lacs.[8]

An important change in the Durbar which took place in the year 1818 was the appointment of the Dogra Dhian Singh as *deoṛhīdār* (chamberlain) in place of Jemadar Khushal Singh. The new incumbent was soft-spoken and a man of impeccable manners. He introduced two brothers to the court. The elder, Gulab Singh, was an unscrupulous and ambitious man. The younger, Suchet Singh, who was appointed conveyor of petitions, was in addition to his native courtesy, strikingly handsome. So also was Dhian Singh's son, Hira Singh, who soon became a great favourite of the Maharajah. The influence of the Dogras increased steadily until they became the dominant element in the Punjab Durbar.

Across the Indus to Peshawar

In August 1818 Wazir Fateh Khan Barakzai was murdered by Prince Kamran, whose father, Shah Mahmud, had been placed and kept on the throne of Kabul for many years by the Wazir. The Wazir's numerous brothers called for vengeance and Afghanistan was plunged into civil war.

In the heat of the strife both the Barakzai kinsmen of the late Wazir Fateh Khan and Mahmud's branch of the Saddozais left their southeasterly outposts on the Punjab frontier weakly defended. This was a good opportunity to secure Attock, which was like an island in the midst of a

---

[8] According to Sohan Lal, Multan was leased out to one Dewan Sham Singh of Peshawar at Rs. 6 lacs per year, the remaining lac being appropriated towards expenses of administration. The exact figure of income from Multan, according to Sita Ram Kohli, was Rs. 680,975 per annum. (*Maharajah Ranjit Singh*, p. 148.)

sea of hostile tribesmen, by pushing the frontier farther north towards Peshawar, or, if possible, up to the Khyber Pass.

In the middle of October 1818 the Maharajah led his troops towards the northwest. Among the generals with him were two who knew these lands and the people well and whose names were fast becoming a terror among the tribes, Hari Singh Nalwa and the *nihaṅg* Phula Singh.

The army passed through Rohtas, Rawalpindi, Hassan Abdal, and arrived in the plains of Hazara. At Hazara, Khattak tribesmen ambushed a reconnaissance party which had crossed the river Attock and killed every man. The region was a part of the Durbar's territories, and the Khattaks paid tribute to Lahore. The ambush was not an act of war but one of treacherous rebellion.

The news of this incident roused the Maharajah to one of his rare outbursts of passion. He drew his sword and hurled a trayful of gold coins into the Attock as an offering and rode his elephant into the swirling waters.[9] His men followed on horseback or swam across. The tribesmen could not withstand the wrath of the Punjabi troops. Tribal strongholds at Khairabad and Jehangiria were occupied and the soldiers given permission to plunder Khattak villages. Nevertheless, when their chief, Firoz Khan, made his submission, he was forgiven and reinstated.

The Punjabis continued their march to Peshawar. The news of their success against the Khattaks disheartened Yar Mohammed Khan, the Afghan governor of Peshawar, who fled the city, leaving behind fourteen big guns and other war equipment. In November 1819 the Punjabis entered the famous citadel of the Pathans. Contrary to the practice of most Afghans and Pathans who had usually plun-

---

[9] One of the legends which became current in the Punjab and on the northwest frontier was that as soon as Ranjit Singh's elephant stepped into the river, the flood subsided. The legend had enormous psychological value, as it gave currency to a saying among the tribesmen "*Khudā hum Khālsā Śud*"—"God is on the side of the Sikhs."

dered the towns and cities of Northern India, the Maharajah forbade his soldiers to lay their hands on any person or property. The next morning he rode on his elephant through the bazaars. For the first time in eight hundred years the city saw an Indian conqueror ride through its streets.

Jahan Dad Khan (who had five years earlier given the Durbar the fort of Attock) was appointed governor of Peshawar. But no sooner were the Punjabi troops withdrawn, when Dost Mohammed, one of the Barakzai brothers who had become the chief actor on the Afghan stage, expelled Jahan Dad from Peshawar. Dost Mohammed offered to pay revenue of one lac of rupees a year and accept the Maharajah's sovereignty over Peshawar. The Durbar agreed to accept the offer and spare its troops another troublesome campaign.

Capture of Kashmir, July 1819

Azim Khan, the governor of Kashmir, was a brother of Wazir Fateh Khan Barakzai. He had gone to Afghanistan to avenge the murder of the Wazir, leaving his younger brother, Jabbar Khan, with a small force to defend the vale. Jabbar Khan thought the best policy under the circumstances was to rule with an iron hand. His treatment of the non-Muslim Kashmiris was particularly harsh and many Hindus were compelled to leave the valley. Among the refugees was Jabbar Khan's revenue minister, Pandit Birbal Dhar. He came to Lahore to complain of the plight of his countrymen and advised the Durbar that this was the opportune moment to take Kashmir.

The Punjabis had already cut off Kashmir from Afghanistan, and were in possession of the passes leading into the valley of the Jhelum. In April the Punjab army, led in person by the Maharajah, encamped at Wazirabad. Ranjit Singh stayed at the base to organise the supply of rations and war material to the advancing columns. The rest of the army moved up to Rajauri, where it split into two columns:

one under the command of Misr Dewan Chand and the other under Prince Kharak Singh. They were to make a pincer movement towards Shupaiyan, where they expected to meet the Afghans.

Sporadic fighting began at Rajauri, whose raja deserted the Punjabis to go over to the Afghans. The chief of Bhimbar guided the Durbar troops, and Kharak Singh advanced without much opposition through Baramgulla. From the other end, Dewan Chand crossed the Pir Panjal range, and the two columns came in view of each other and of Jabbar Khan with twelve thousand Afghans in battle formation at Shupaiyan. Dewan Chand let his troops rest for a few days. When the men were refreshed, he quietly surrounded the Afghan host.

The battle of Shupaiyan was fought in the early hours of the morning of July 3, 1819. Punjabi superiority in artillery compelled the Afghans to charge and fight at closer quarters. The issue was taken up by the *nihangs*. The Afghans were repulsed and fled into the hills. Jabbar Khan was severely wounded and barely escaped with his life. Kharak Singh and Misr Dewan Chand entered Srinagar the day after the victory of Shupaiyan.

Kashmir was an important acquisition for the Punjab. Apart from the seventy lacs of rupees[10] it fetched every year in revenue, it extended the frontiers of the state to the borders of China and Tibet. Dewan Moti Ram was appointed governor of Kashmir.

Dera Ghazi Khan, Hazara, and Mankera

In February 1820 the Maharajah toured southwestern Punjab. His first long halt was at Multan, where he paid homage at the tomb of his former adversary, Nawab Muzaffar Khan. From Multan, Jemadar Khushal Singh proceeded to Dera Ghazi Khan and expelled the Nawab, who had continued to associate with the Afghans. Dera Ghazi

---

[10] Both Sohan Lal (Daftar, II, 269) and Amar Nath mention the revenue of Kashmir as about 70 lacs of rupees.

Khan was assigned to the Nawab of Bahawalpur at an annual payment of three lacs of rupees a year.

The Maharajah was not able to complete the subjugation of the other southern states because of widespread disturbances in Hazara. The region had been loosely attached to Kashmir, but ever since the valley had been taken over by the Durbar, Hazara tribesmen had been restive. The mopping-up operations took several months, and many lives, including that of Ram Dyal, were lost before peace was restored. Despite the punitive expedition and the chain of forts the Punjabis built, the pacification of the tribes remained a major problem to the Lahore Durbar.

In the autumn of 1821 the Maharajah ordered the sequestration of the estates of his mother-in-law, Sada Kaur. Batala was given as *jāgīr* to Prince Sher Singh (Sada Kaur's grandson through her daughter Mehtab Kaur) and the rest merged with Kangra. Sada Kaur, who was then in her seventies, was apprehended trying to cross over to British territory, and remained in protective custody until she died in December 1832.[11]

The estates of Nawab Hafiz Ahmed Khan of Mankera lay on both sides of the Indus and included important towns like Leiah, Bhakkar, and Dera Ismail Khan. There was considerable commercial traffic on the river and the caravan route from Persia and Baluchistan to India passed

---

[11] Sada Kaur was a "woman of bold and masculine turn of mind" (Ross), who played an important part in making Ranjit Singh the most powerful of all the Sardars of the Punjab. But once he had captured Lahore, she had relied more on his help than he on hers. The failure of her daughter, Mehtab Kaur, to produce an heir-apparent and her inability to get on with her husband had created a rift between Sada Kaur and Ranjit Singh. Sada Kaur had brought her daughter home to live with her and the two had been creating mischief ever since. They had plotted Ranjit Singh's downfall and were ever willing to spread hatred against him. Their role in the negotiations with Metcalfe in 1809 was little short of treason. Ranjit Singh had patiently borne the lash of her tongue and put up with her wayward loyalties because he respected her shrewd intuition and her boldness. But he distrusted her ambition and at the bottom of his heart hated her domineering ways.

through his territory. Despite the barren nature of the land, Mankera was worth ten lacs of rupees a year. It was also politically important. The Nawab, like other Muslim chieftains of the region, had become independent. But when forced by circumstances he, like they, preferred to pay tribute to the ruler of Kabul rather than to Lahore.

In October 1821 the Maharajah crossed the Jhelum into Khushab. Ahmed Yar, chief of the Tiwanas, joined him with his body of horsemen. Misr Dewan Chand and Hari Singh Nalwa followed with their troops.

The fort of Bhakkar capitulated without firing a shot. Ranjit Singh stayed on at Bhakkar and sent out two forces in different directions. One division consisting of fifteen thousand men under the command of Dal Singh Bharania and Jemadar Khushal Singh was ordered to Dera Ismail Khan. The Nawab's officers put up a nominal resistance before surrendering. The other force under Misr Dewan Chand passed through Leiah, and then the three armies converged and marched on to Mankera.

Mankera was in the midst of a sandy desert with no stream or water tank for miles around. The Nawab's only hope was to hold out until the water supply of the besiegers ran out. In three days the Durbar troops dug enough wells to provide themselves with drinking water. The siege lasted only a fortnight. The Nawab accepted the Durbar's offer of a *jāgīr* and safe residence at Dera Ismail Khan, and handed over the fort with its arsenal intact.

With the fall of Mankera, the huge tract of land between the Jhelum and the Indus, the Sind-Sagar Doab, was added to the Punjab.[12]

---

[12] The victories in Kashmir, Peshawar, and Multan were celebrated by naming three new-born princes after them. Princes Kashmira Singh and (later) Peshaura Singh were born to Daya Kaur and Prince Multana Singh to Ratan Kaur. Both women were widows of the Bhangi chief of Gujarat and had been taken into the Maharajah's harem on the death of their husband in 1811.

CHAPTER 16

EUROPEANISATION OF THE ARMY

◈⁝◈⁝◈⁝ IN THE spring of 1822 two officers of Na-
◈⁝◈⁝◈⁝ poleon Bonaparte's disbanded army, Jean
◈⁝◈⁝◈⁝ Baptiste Ventura and Jean François Allard,
arrived at Lahore and sought employment with the Durbar. They were offered generous terms and given new
recruits to train in the methods of warfare practised by the
Grande Armée. This accelerated the Europeanisation of
the Punjab army, which, under the instruction of the
European officers like the two named and many others who
followed them, became one of the most formidable in Asia.[1]

Within a few years there were dozens of Europeans of different nationalities: French, English, Italian, Spanish, Hungarian, Greek, and Eurasian in the employ of the Durbar.
Although they were given higher wages than Indians of
similar rank, special conditions were imposed on them.
They were expected to domesticate themselves in the country and encouraged to marry native women; they were not
allowed to quit service without the formal permission of
the Maharajah; and they undertook to fight any nation
against which the Durbar was at war, even though it was
their own.

The Durbar was only partially successful in persuading
this flotsam and jetsam of Europe to call the Punjab their

[1] Ventura and Allard were not the first European officers in the Punjab
army; the first was an English deserter named Price, who joined service
in 1809. Price was followed by some others, mostly half-castes, who were
the illegitimate offspring of Englishmen through native women. Some were
sons of famous men, e.g. Col. Van Cortlandt, General Sir Robert Dick, and
Jacob Thomas. Ranjit Singh was anxious to keep the number of English
and Eurasians in his service as low as possible, because he was uncertain
of their loyalties in the event of a conflict with the East India Company.
He also had reason to suspect that some of these men had been planted so
that the English might be kept informed of military movements and the
state of preparedness. The only foreigners he could rely on were the
French, or those who at one time or another had fought the English.

homeland. Although they showed no reluctance in conforming to the outward practices of the Khalsa (wearing their hair and beards unshorn, abstaining from eating beef and smoking tobacco) and enthusiastically "domesticated" themselves by taking on harems of Kashmiri women, this conformity did not make them put out roots in the soil or develop loyalty to the state whose salt they ate. When they had made enough money, they left their wives, mistresses, and children frequently unprovided for and returned to their own countries.

The Punjabis looked upon the Europeans as highly paid drill-sergeants. Most of the state's conquests had been made before 1822 by men like Mohkam Chand, Hari Singh Nalwa and Misr Dewan Chand. Even after that date the effective command of the Durbar's campaigns was retained in Punjabi hands. The loyalty of Europeans was always suspect and very rarely were more than two allowed to be in the capital with their troops at the same time.[2]

The names of some European officers deserve notice. The most eminent was the infantryman Ventura, who became a general and then virtually commander-in-chief of the Durbar army. He was later given the title Count of Mandi. Allard, who was a cavalier, did not achieve so much distinction as an officer, but became a great favourite of the Maharajah ("Quite a Suleiman Beg of Ranjit Singh," wrote the French traveller, Jacquemont). Allard brought gifts and a letter of greetings to the Maharajah from Louis Philippe of France. He lived in great style at Lahore[3] and

[2] The distance at which Ranjit Singh kept his Europeans was evidenced by the protocol observed at court. Although some of them attained the rank of general and were made governors of important districts, not one was ever allowed the privilege of a seat at formal functions. Ranjit Singh's attitude to his European officers was consistently distrustful. Once when sacking the German Mevius (self-styled Baron de Mevius) Ranjit Singh exploded: "German, French or English, all these European bastards are alike."

[3] Allard's house still stands like a miniature Versailles in the midst of an Oriental bazaar. On one mound is the dilapidated grave of his daughter,

died a few months before Ranjit Singh. The Italian, Paolo de Avitabile, and the Frenchman, Court, joined service in 1826. Avitabile was appointed governor of Wazirabad and then of Peshawar. His stern rule at Peshawar (for the first few days he hanged fifty brigands every morning before breakfast) taught the tribesmen respect for the law. Court, who trained the artillery and cast guns at the Lahore foundry, was a scholar and a gentleman. He worked in collaboration with the Durbar's best scientific brain, Lehna Singh Majithia. Another favourite of the Maharajah was a Spaniard, Señor Oms (Musa Sahib), who would undoubtedly have risen high if his career had not been cut short by his premature death in a cholera epidemic in 1828. An American quack, Josiah Harlan, was made governor of Nurpur and Jasrota and then of Gujarat. He was ignominiously dismissed for demanding one lac of rupees for medicine from the ailing Maharajah. Harlan was succeeded by the Eurasian, Holmes. Besides these were others like the Hungarian doctor Honigberger, who mixed gunpowder for the artillery and distilled brandy for the Maharajah.

The most important result of the employment of Europeans was a rapid increase in the size of the army, particularly the infantry and the artillery. In one year the infantry was increased from 8,000 to 11,681. (At the time of the death of the Maharajah the infantry numbered over 27,000 men.) In sixteen years the artillery was increased from 22 guns and 190 swivels to 188 guns and 280 swivels; the number of artillerymen in the same period increased sixfold (from 800 to more than 4,500 men). The cavalry was also increased, though not so much, in all its three constituents—the regulars trained in modern style by Allard, the traditional *ghorcarah* (horsemen) composed of the disbanded forces of misls, and the *jāgīrdārī fauj* (the horsemen furnished by holders of *jāgīrs*).

Charlotte. The house is still known as *Kuṛī bāgh* (the daughter's garden). Allard himself lies buried in a cemetery outside the city wall.

Three things should be borne in mind about this enormous increase in the size and efficiency of the army. In the first place, since all the major conquests had already been made, the army had to be maintained out of the revenues, which did not increase. (The expansion on the northwest and beyond Kashmir was not particularly lucrative.) The Maharajah had, as a matter of policy, kept his army in arrears of pay. From 1822 onwards, these arrears increased so much that instead of keeping the incidence of desertion low, as was intended, they became the cause of indiscipline and mutiny.

Secondly, although modern methods of training were introduced, the mode of recruitment remained the same. Men were not recruited individually but in batches from the same village and were frequently members of the same family or clan. Thus the senior member of the family or the tribal elder who had introduced the men to the service joined as officers instead of being promoted by merit. A new kind of army unit consisting of between fifteen to twenty men, usually members of the same family, grew up. These men were banded together into *ḍerās* (camps) and after 1822, the *ḍerās* grouped into divisions (which were under the charge of generals like Lehna Singh Majithia, Misr Dewan Chand, or the Attariwala Sardars). By continuing this method of recruitment in a large army, the Durbar unwittingly sowed the seeds of its own destruction. The real leadership of the men remained in the hands of the leaders of the *ḍerās*. These new *ḍerādārs* began to bargain for better terms for their men and, if salaries remained unpaid for too long, to incite them to rebellion. A spirit of trade unionism began to pervade the army. The generals were gradually reduced to the position of military tacticians and had to lead in the field of battle men they did not know and who owed no personal loyalties to them.

Thirdly, with Europeanisation an anti-English sentiment grew in the Durbar army. Great numbers of the senior foreign officers hated the English. They did little to discourage the notion that the army, which was already too large, was being increased and modernised to become an instrument of Punjabi aggrandisement. As long as there were fields to conquer, all went well. But as soon as the English began to thwart its expansionism, the Durbar army turned violently anti-British.

Battle of Naushera,[4] March 1823:
Death of Phula Singh

The Durbar had an opportunity to see its Europeanised regiments in action on the northwestern frontier in the autumn of 1822. The trouble started with Fakir Azizuddin's visit to Peshawar to collect the dues for the Lahore Durbar. He was well received by Yar Mohammed, who ordered the city to be illuminated in the Fakir's honour. Both Yar Mohammed and his brother, Dost Mohammed, expressed their loyalty to the Maharajah, and Yar Mohammed paid what was due from him in cash and horses. Azizuddin returned to Lahore well satisfied with his mission.

Mohammed Azim taunted Yar Mohammed for paying tribute to infidels, who had already ejected one brother from Kashmir and expelled the Afghans from Multan, Dera Ismail Khan, Dera Ghazi Khan, and Mankera. Mohammed Azim Khan marched out of Kabul and the cry of *jihād* once more echoed in the barren defiles of the Khyber. Within a few days, over twenty-five thousand Khattaks and Yusufzai tribesmen under the leadership of Syed Akbar Shah of Buner volunteered to fight under the green banner of the Prophet and gain either victory or martyrdom. Yar Mohammed abandoned Peshawar and went into hiding in the neighbouring hills. (It was conjectured that he was not altogether unwilling to hand over Peshawar to his brother, since otherwise he might have sought refuge at Lahore.)

[4] The battle is not known after the Naushera cantonment, which did not exist then, but after the old town Naukhar on the left bank of the Landai river. (Olaf Caroe, *The Pathans*, p. 296.)

The Durbar ordered its army northwards. With it went its galaxy of generals: Misr Dewan Chand, Hari Singh Nalwa, Phula Singh, Fateh Singh Ahluwalia, Desa Singh Majithia, and Attar Singh Sandhawalia. So also went Allard, Ventura, and the Gurkha, Balbhadra, with their newly trained battalions.

Prince Sher Singh and Hari Singh Nalwa led the advance columns. They spanned the Attock by means of a pontoon bridge and occupied the fort of Jehangiria. The Maharajah followed in easy stages and arrived on the eastern bank of the river by the end of January. To his dismay he found that the Afghans had destroyed the pontoon bridge and after an early thaw of snow the Attock was in spate. His son was now besieged in the fort with the entire country roundabout thirsting for his blood. The men investing Jehangiria were Azim's brothers, Dost Mohammed (who had more than once paid tribute to Lahore) and Jabbar Khan, the ex-governor of Kashmir.

The Durbar army forded the Attock early one morning, losing much valuable equipment. But the Punjabis caught the enemy unawares and compelled him to retire from Jehangiria.

The Khattak and Yusufzai tribesmen entrenched themselves on an eminence called Pir Sabak or Tibba Tiri on the plain between Jehangiria and Peshawar. The main Afghan force under Azim Khan's brothers was separated from the tribal *ghāzīs* by a small but swift-running stream, the Landai. The Punjabi artillery by-passed the tribesmen, reached the bank of the Landai, and trained its heavy guns on the opposite bank.

When Azim Khan was apprised of the situation, he made a dash from Peshawar and joined his brothers on the bank of the Landai. They could not cross the stream because of the guns on the other side. Before the brothers could find an unguarded ford and go to the help of their tribal allies, the Punjabis launched an attack on Pir Sabak hill.

The tribal *laśkars* (army) fought desperately but were

overcome by the Durbar's Gurkhas and Mussalman Najibs. Then Phula Singh and his *nihangs* moved up to give them the *coup de grâce*. They drove the Khattaks and Yusufzais before them; the heavy artillery on the Landai wheeled round and opened up a barrage to complete the slaughter. Four thousand tribesmen were left dead on the field. Mohammed Azim Khan watched the massacre from the other side of the stream without being able to do anything about it. He was too ashamed to face the people of Peshawar, and he returned to Afghanistan, where he died soon after.[5]

The Punjabis paid a heavy price in men and material for the victory at Pir Sabak. Among the generals who fell were Phula Singh[6] and the Gurkha commander Balbhadra. But it was a crushing defeat for the Afghans, and it convinced the Pathan tribesmen of the superiority of Punjabi arms.

Three days later the Maharajah entered Peshawar at the head of his victorious troops.[7] The citizens welcomed him and paid him homage with *nazarānās* (gifts). The Maharajah's sojourn was, however, not a peaceful one. What the tribesmen could not achieve in open combat, they

[5] For a somewhat different version of the battle see Olaf Caroe, *The Pathans*, pp. 294-97.

[6] Phula Singh's horse was shot under him. He took an elephant and pressed on. The error cost him his life. The *ghāzis* saw the man who had so often humbled them, and trained their muskets on him. Phula Singh was riddled with bullets. He collapsed in his howdah exhorting the *nihangs* with the last breath of his body not to give way. (*Akali Phula Singh*, by Prem Singh.)

[7] The Pathan version of Ranjit Singh's advance is quite different from Sohan Lal's. Olaf Caroe writes: "After the battle Ranjit Singh advanced to Peshawar, slaying and plundering as he went. He battered down the Bala Hissar and sacked the fair palace within. He cut the cypresses and muddied the basins of the garden of Shah Zaman before the fort, and allowed his cavalry to ravage the square miles of delicious orchards, plum, peach, apricot, and pear, the glory of Peshawar. The name of the *Sikhā Sāhī*—the Sikh Rule—is a synonym for misgovernment and oppression in the mouths of teachers and children to this day." (*The Pathans*, pp. 297-98.)

tried to gain by the cold-blooded murder of Punjabi soldiers under cover of darkness.

The Punjabis wearied of the tribesmen's tactics. A few
days later, when both Yar Mohammed and Dost Mohammed presented themselves at court and craved the Maharajah's pardon, he forgave them readily and accepted their
tribute of presents and horses. Yar Mohammed was re-
invested governor of Peshawar on promising an annual
revenue of Rs. 1,10,000 to the Lahore Durbar.

The Punjabi victory over the Pathans and Afghans caused
some apprehension in British circles. The British realised
that the Durbar's conquests had reached the furthest geographical limits of the Punjab in the north and north-west.
Beyond were impassable mountains and inhospitable, un-
profitable regions. If the Punjabi empire was to expand
any further, it could be only across the Sindh desert to
the sea or across the Sutlej to India. The British government felt that it should curb Punjabi aggressiveness before
it got out of hand, and opened negotiations with the Amirs
of Sindh. When news of the Anglo-Sindhian negotiations
reached Lahore, the Punjabis, who were flushed with many
victories, talked loudly of settling the issue with the British
once and for all. Within a few months, India began to
buzz with rumours of troop concentrations on the Sutlej
and the Durbar's plans to extend its arms over the sub-
continent. Before anything could be finalised in Sindh,
war broke out between the British and the Burmese and
made the British particularly nervous about their northwestern frontier. The governor general, however, decided
to trust Ranjit Singh's repeated professions of friendship
and refrained from asking for an explanation of rumours
of warlike preparations in the Punjab.[8]

In July 1825 Misr Dewan Chand died. With the passing
of men like Mohkam Chand, his grandson Ram Dyal,

[8] SC 11 of 22.10.1824.

Phula Singh, and Dewan Chand, the Durbar was left with very few Punjabi generals of any real ability. As a result it had to turn more and more to its European officers, particularly Ventura, to plan its strategy. The nominal command was, as usual, entrusted to one of Ranjit Singh's sons, Kharak Singh or, latterly, to Sher Singh, who was attracting his father's attention as an up-and-coming army commander and who also enjoyed a great measure of popularity with the ranks.

Sher Singh's growing influence over his father gave rise to misgivings in the minds of Kharak Singh and his mother, Raj Kaur. In January 1826, when the Maharajah went on tour, he appointed Sher Singh to deputise for him at Lahore. Kharak Singh's easygoing, indolent, and uncouth ways were his worst enemies. But he was quick to react to the snub his father had administered. Later that year, when Ranjit Singh was taken ill, he opened communication with the British to assure himself of their support for his succession.[9]

The filial situation was still unsettled when Ranjit Singh's old friend and brother-in-arms, Fateh Singh Ahluwalia, suddenly panicked and fled across the Sutlej. His nervousness was not altogether unreasonable. The Maharajah had liquidated all the misls and principalities of the trans-Sutlej region one after another: only the Ahluwalia household remained. People began to say it was just a matter of time until Fateh Singh would go the way of the other Sardars. The chief mischief-makers were Fateh Singh's own agents at Lahore, who exhorted him to escape from the Punjab while he could. Fateh Singh crossed the Sutlej and sought the protection of the English.

[9] It was through these communications that Kharak gave currency to the gossip that neither Sher Singh nor Tara Singh were the real sons of Ranjit Singh but foundlings planted on the Maharajah by Sada Kaur. See Kharak Singh's letter to Elphinstone (PC 18 of 15.6.1827) and Metcalfe to the Governor General (PC 38 of 22.6.1827).

The English were as embarrassed at the arrival of the Sardar as the Maharajah was pained to hear of the suspicions that his closest friend had secretly harboured against him. Fortunately neither party tried to exploit the situation. The Maharajah sent his personal envoys to convince Fateh Singh that his fears had been absolutely imaginary and the British agent persuaded him to go back and make his peace with Ranjit Singh. The crest-fallen Fateh Singh returned to his home in the Punjab. The Maharajah sent his grandson, Nao Nihal Singh, and Dhian Singh (who had only a few days earlier been given the title of raja and made chief of the Council of Ministers) to receive him and escort him to Lahore. The Ahluwalia estates were guaranteed forever, and he was loaded with expensive presents.

CHAPTER 17

DREAMS OF SINDH AND THE SEA

THE activities of British agents in Sindh caused anxiety in Lahore. The Durbar wanted to know how the British construed the Treaty of 1809 by which they had undertaken not to interfere in the affairs of countries west of the Sutlej. There were other minor matters connected with the Durbar's possessions in the Cis-Sutlej area which needed clarification.

The Maharajah despatched Fakir Imamuddin and Dewan Moti Ram to call on Lord Amherst, the governor general at Simla.[1] The envoys took gifts for the governor general and presented a superbly embroidered tent made of the best Kashmir wool for the King of England. They were, however, not able to do more than mention the Durbar's claim to certain towns across the Sutlej and state that since Sindh was on the west of the Sutlej, the British were precluded from meddling in its affairs. Amherst restricted his answer to expressions of good will and enquiries about the Maharajah's health.

The governor general sent a delegation headed by Captain Wade to return the call paid by Fakir Imamuddin and Moti Ram. It was received by the Maharajah at Amritsar in the last week of May 1827. The question of Sindh and the Durbar's title to some towns in Malwa were brought up by the Maharajah's counsellors but the English delegation refrained from making any comment.

There were other things besides the uncertainty of English reactions that made the Durbar hold its hand in Sindh. There was a violent earthquake in Kashmir which took a heavy toll of life and property. It was followed by a failure

---

[1] Ranjit Singh's letter to the governor general (PC 291 of 1.6.1827) read: "God knows how great a desire for a meeting has circumambulated the mansion of my heart!"

of the monsoon, and the valley was gripped by famine. The Durbar could not send much help because Lahore was stricken with an epidemic of cholera. The Maharajah's health broke down and he moved out of the city to Dilku-sha across the Ravi. After the earthquake, famine, and disease came trouble with Anirodh Chand of Kangra, followed by yet another uprising on the northwest frontier.

The trouble with Anirodh Chand (son of Sansar Chand) of Kangra arose out of a domestic misunderstanding. The Dogra brothers had become the most powerful element in the Lahore Durbar. Their father, Mian Singh, had been made a raja and given his home province, Jammu, as a *jāgīr*. Of the sons, the most influential was Dhian Singh, who was both *deorhīdār* and chief of the Council of Ministers. In March 1828 Ranjit Singh formally invested him with the title *Rājā-i-Rājgān* and a few months later also made Dhian Singh's son, Hira Singh, a raja. He was eager to find a suitable bride for Hira Singh. Of the aristocratic families of Rajputs there was none more blue-blooded than that of Sansar Chand of Kangra.

Sansar Chand had died in the winter of 1823, leaving behind a great many children by his wives and concubines. His son, Anirodh Chand, who succeeded him, had two real sisters, both unmarried. Ranjit Singh proposed a marriage between Hira Singh and one of Anirodh Chand's sisters. Anirodh was reluctant to make an alliance between his family, which had a long and proud lineage, and the Dogras, who were upstarts. When the Maharajah expressed his impatience, Anirodh Chand slipped across the frontier and sought the protection of the English. He gave away his two sisters in marriage to the ruler of Nepal.

The Maharajah retaliated by sequestering Kangra and took into his own harem two of Sansar Chand's daughters who were famed for their good looks. A year later he found Hira Singh a bride and arranged the wedding on a lavish scale as though the boy had been a prince of royal blood.

Roads and Judicial Reform

The period of military inactivity was utilised to carry out public works and reorganise the administration of justice. Roads were constructed to link the bigger towns. The one from Lahore to Amritsar was repaired; trees were planted on either side and rest-houses built along the route. Gardens were laid out in Amritsar and Lahore.

The Punjab had no codified law—except to the extent that the Shariat could be described as a code for the Muslims. But all Punjabis (including Muslims) were governed by well-recognised custom. This customary law was administered by a succession of courts, of which the village *pancāyat* was the primary and the most important tribunal. If one of the parties was dissatisfied with the arbitration of the *pancāyat*, it went in appeal to the *kārdār*, or in larger towns to the *nāzim*. In many towns the Durbar appointed officers' *adālatīs* whose sole function was to hear appeals from *pancāyats*. Lahore had an appellate tribunal, the *adālat-i-ālā*, of its own. The Maharajah and his Durbar acted as the Supreme Court where the decisions of the *kārdārs*, *nāzims*, and *adālatīs* could be impugned.

The aforementioned tribunals heard all kinds of cases: civil, revenue, matrimonial, and criminal. Crime was punished by well-understood and generally accepted penalties. There was no capital punishment and except where the *nāzim* enforced martial law (as Avitabile did on the northwest frontier) even murder could be punished only by a fine or mutilation of limbs. Jails were largely maintained for political prisoners. Violence and theft were punished by a fine or corporal punishment, frequently by the cutting of the nose, ears, or hands. Justice was crude, but it was cheap, expeditious, and in conformity with tradition.

The Maharajah began to take more interest in the administration of justice and personally heard complaints of corruption against judicial officers. He was not satisfied with the state of the law, and appointed Bahadur Singh

Hindustani to prepare a civil and criminal code.[2] Prince Sher Singh was given judicial training.

The "Holy" War on the Northwestern Frontier: Fall of Syed Ahmed of Rai Bareli

Within one year of their defeat at Naushera, the tribes of the northwest frontier again challenged the sovereignty of the Durbar. The centre of the insurrection was at Sitana, near which Hari Singh Nalwa had raised a fort named after him as Haripur. Nalwa was reduced to dire straits by the tribesmen until the Maharajah came to his rescue. Yar Mohammed again protested his loyalties and was re-installed at Peshawar. But early in 1827 the whole of the northwest frontier was in ferment. This time they were roused by one Syed Ahmed who had come all the way from India through Sindh to lead a *jihād* against the Sikhs. Before coming to the Pathan country Syed Ahmed and his two lieutenants, Shah Ismail and Maulvi Abdul Haye, had gone on an extensive tour of Hindustan and addressed mammoth gatherings of Indian Muslims, raised corps of volunteers and large sums of money. Among the patrons was the Mughal emperor and many Muslim rulers of Indian states, notably the Nawab of Tonk.

The British government made no attempt to check this crusade against a state with which it had signed a treaty of friendship. Thousands of volunteers were trained and armed in India and then permitted to cross over to Sindh on their way to the northwest frontier of the Punjab. Organisations which collected arms and money for the crusaders were allowed to function without let or hindrance in many big cities of India.[3]

---

[2] Sohan Lal Suri was appointed to assist Bahadur Singh. No record of the written code has, however, been found.

[3] Mirza Hairat Dehlvi writes in the *Hayāt-i-Taiyaba* that, in consultation with Maulana Shah Mohammed Ismail, Syed Ahmed Shah informed the lieutenant governor of the northwest frontier province through Shaikh Ghulam Ali Reis of Allahabad that he was preparing for a *jihād* against the Sikhs and hoped that the British government had no objection to it.

The Indian crusaders were joined by the Pathan tribesmen, mainly the Yusufzais, who were always on the lookout for an excuse to loot the Punjab. Syed Akbar Shah of Buner (a Yusufzai *pīr*) gave his blessings to the venture. Yar Mohammed, true to his fickle nature, decided to throw in his lot with what he believed would be the winning side, and evacuated Peshawar.

The Durbar sent Budh Singh Sandhawalia ("one of the ablest and most intelligent commanders in the Raja's service")[4] along with Ventura and Allard to retake Peshawar. Syed Ahmed met Sandhawalia's forces at Shaidu[5] near Attock. Religious fervour proved a poor match for discipline; the crusaders were pushed aside and Peshawar reoccupied. Yar Mohammed was on his knees again, craving pardon. He sent his brother as hostage to the Durbar and promised to be faithful. Once again he was pardoned by the Maharajah.

The crusaders explained away the defeat as a reverse for Yar Mohammed, whom they branded as a collaborator. Syed Ahmed started harassing stray columns of Punjabi troops. These skirmishes were magnified into victories and the whole of Muslim India was kept in a state of jubilation.[6]

The lieutenant governor wrote back to him in reply that as long as the peace of their territories was not disturbed, they had nothing to say, nor had they any objection to such preparation. (Ganda Singh, *Private Correspondence relating to the Anglo-Sikh Wars*, p. 30.)

[4] Wade to Metcalfe, PC 5 of 20.4.1827.

[5] Budh Singh Sandhawalia was killed in the battle.

[6] Metcalfe reported the repercussions in India to the governor general in the following words: "Syed Ahmed, Maulvi Ismail, and their colleagues have established a very extensive, if not universal, influence over the minds of our Mohammedan subjects. During the period of their recent attack on Ranjit Singh's territories, the most fervent anxiety for their success pervaded the Mohammedan population of Delhi. Numbers quitted their homes and marched to join them, including some who resigned their employments in the Company's service, both the military and the civil branches, for that purpose. It is said that the King of Delhi encouraged this spirit." (PC 38 of 22.6.1827.)

Syed Ahmed's tactics soon put the Punjabis on the defensive. The crusaders swarmed all over the country around Peshawar. In the summer of 1829, Prince Sher Singh took the initiative and inflicted a severe defeat on them. But even this reverse did not hold them back. A few months later they killed Yar Mohammed in a skirmish and would have slain his brother, Sultan Mohammed[7], if he had not been saved by Ventura. Syed Ahmed[8] got bolder and attacked a force under Hari Singh Nalwa and Allard in the Hazara hills and kept the Punjabis on the defensive while he went forward and recaptured Peshawar. He was proclaimed caliph and coins were struck in his name with the inscription "Ahmed the Just: the glitter of whose scimitar scatters destruction among the infidels." Success went to Syed's head. As Muslims from all over India, Sindh, and Kashmir flocked to his banner, he began to assume the airs of a monarch. Pathan tribesmen became restive at the influx of foreigners on their soil and the demands they made for food and women, particularly women. Durbar agents exploited the growing feeling of resentment and bribed some tribal leaders to turn against Syed Ahmed and murder the Hindustanis. Syed Ahmed was compelled to retire from Peshawar. The city was reoccupied by Prince Sher Singh and given to Sultan Mohammed Khan.

Syed Ahmed found himself sandwiched between the Punjabis and hostile tribesmen. He was at Balakot at the bottom of the Kaghan Valley when Prince Sher Singh caught up with him. In a short, sharp engagement, he completely decimated the small band of *ghāzīs*, including the Syed.[9]

[7] Sultan Mohammed presented Ranjit Singh "Leili," the most famous horse in the royal stables. PC 19 of 23.10.1829.

[8] A slightly different version of the conflict with Syed Ahmed is given in *The Pathans*, by Olaf Caroe, pp. 301-5.

[9] The Punjabis did not display any fanaticism in their behaviour towards the man who had roused a million people against them and vilified their faith with contemptuous abuse. The Prince himself draped the body of the Syed with an expensive shawl before it was buried with the honours

The *jihād* was fitfully carried on by one of Syed Ahmed's disciples, Nasiruddin, and met with little success. But soon after the death of the Syed, the Barakzai chief, Dost Mohammed, who was in power at Kabul, took up the cry. He, like other members of his family, was adept in double-dealing: sometimes he acknowledged Ranjit Singh as his master "almost like a father"; at other times he condemned him as an infidel who should be slain.

Sindh and the Punjab's Field of Cloth of Gold

While the Punjabis were occupied with the *jihād* on their northwestern frontier, the British made their next move in Sindh and foreclosed any attempt by the Punjabis to expand in that direction.

The possibility of opening up the Indus to English shipping was mooted in 1829 when Alexander Burnes attempted a reconnaissance of the river and the riparian states. His interest in the matter was, as he said, "stimulated" by the commander-in-chief, Sir Thomas Bradford. Burnes' first expedition had to be postponed because of the suspicions of the Amirs. It was decided to send him out again under a guise which would facilitate his passage. The King of England had sent five massive dray horses to be presented to Ranjit Singh. The governor general agreed to a suggestion made by Colonel Pottinger, the agent in Sindh, that he (the governor general) should add a gift of his own. This was a large-sized coach, which, in the absence of proper roads, could be transported only by boat. The Amirs, it was felt, would not dare to obstruct the passage of these presents for fear of offending Ranjit Singh. After a few mishaps, the convoy of boats began its journey up the Indus in the month of March 1831. The boats were equipped with instruments to record data for future navi-

---

due to a brave adversary. (*Umdāt-ut-Tawārikh*, *Daftar* III, p. 35.) When the news of the Prince's homage to the dead crusader reached the Maharajah, he fully approved of it. Syed Ahmed was a good, if misguided, man.

gation. Burnes was also instructed to investigate the affairs of Sindh, its politics, the military strength of the Amirs, their views on opening up the river to English boats, and so on.[10]

The Durbar sent Lehna Singh Majithia,[11] the only Sardar with a scientific bent of mind, to receive Burnes when he entered the Punjab.

Burnes arrived at Lahore in the latter part of July 1831. The Maharajah had a heart-to-heart talk with him. He told the Englishman how the Durbar had stood by the English and asked bluntly what the British government's attitude was regarding the Durbar's aims in Sindh. Burnes avoided giving a direct reply and said he would convey the Maharajah's views to the governor general.

Burnes met the governor general, Lord William Bentinck, at Simla and reported that the Indus route was full of possibilities; that the Amirs of Sindh were terrified of the Punjabis and would be willing to allow English shipping right of passage if they were guaranteed security from their Punjabi neighbours. The problem before the governor general was how to persuade the Durbar to give up its designs on Sindh, and allow English vessels to navigate all six rivers of the Punjab. Lord William Bentinck got his agent in Ludhiana, Wade, to persuade the Maharajah to

[10] An official minute SC 4 of 14.10.1830 records "The measure proposed from England of sending two dray horses by the Indus to Runjeet Sing is quite feasible as a pretext for examining the Indus to a certain extent, but it would perhaps be still better to send, as Lt. Col. Pottinger proposes, a large carriage which, from the size of the package, could obviously not be conveyed by land." (Letter from the chief secretary, Bombay government.)

In another note to the governor general (SC 14 of 25.11.1831) Trevelyan wrote from Delhi: "In 1809 the rising power of the Sikhs was considered so formidable that it was deemed necessary to place a check upon its further progress. . . . If therefore we open to the Sikhs the door to . . . Sindh their power must rise to an inconvenient height."

[11] Burnes, who had a very poor opinion of Orientals on scientific matters, was impressed with Lehna Singh's knowledge of mathematics, the movement of the stars, and his insatiable curiosity about the working of scientific instruments. He presented the Sardar with a thermometer.

invite him to the Punjab. It was agreed that the meeting would take place at Ropar on October 25, 1831.

Many eye-witnesses have described the gathering at Ropar as the Punjab's field of cloth of gold. There were parades, receptions, dancing, and drinking. While the Durbar's courtiers were trying to impress their visitors with their gold and diamonds, the Englishmen impressed on them the benefits of navigation on the Punjab rivers. The Maharajah asked them plainly whether they meant to extend their dominion over Sindh. "No," replied Bentinck, the object of the negotiations was purely commercial. And what was to happen about the Punjab's dispute with Bahawalpur (who accepted Ranjit Singh's suzerainty) and the Durbar's plans to extend its dominion over Sindh? Bentinck did not say so in so many words, but he indicated that the Durbar was to consider its southern boundary finally drawn. All that the Maharajah got out of the week's extravagance at Ropar was an assurance of perpetual friendship.

The Maharajah's carousal with Bentinck was by no means looked upon with favour by his people. Many courtiers doubted the wisdom of making an agreement with the English and the *nihaṅgs* were outspokenly hostile.[12] After some time the Maharajah himself came around to the view that Ropar had been a waste of time and expense. In a meeting with Dr. Joseph Wolff, a Jew turned evangelist, who visited him a few months later, the Maharajah asked: "You say, you travel about for the sake of religion: why, then, do you not preach to the English in Hindoostan who have no religion at all?"[13]

Dr. Wolff tried to divert the conversation to religious matters and asked: "How may one come nigh unto God?"

[12] A *nihaṅg* actually attempted to assault the Maharajah. Sohan Lal writes: "Out of the adversity of his days and his evil character, one Akali (*nihaṅg*) drew his sword out of its sheath and rushed towards the Maharajah. The orderlies and state servants gathered together on the spot, held that Akali in the clutches of interference and restraint, and brought him before the Maharajah." (*Daftar* III, 93.)

The Maharajah replied with biting sarcasm: "One can come nigh unto God by making an alliance with the British government, as I lately did with the Laard Nawab Sahib at Roopar."

Some months after the Ropar meeting, Burnes was sent to complete his investigation of the lands about the Indus. This time his mission was to cover the tribal areas of Afghanistan. In order to allay suspicion, Burnes divested himself of his official status and gave out that he was taking the overland route to return home to England. He therefore took the liberty of asking the Maharajah "as an old friend" for permission to travel through the Punjab. The permission was readily granted.

The subject of the opening up of the Indus was again mentioned. The Maharajah conceded that, although some benefits might accrue to the Punjab, "he did not relish the idea of vessels navigating all parts of his territories." He feared collision with the British government.[14]

While Burnes went northwest to prepare the ground in Afghanistan, Wade visited Lahore to "persuade" the Maharajah to put his signature to the commercial treaty. The Amirs of Hyderabad and Khairpur signed in April: there was not much the Durbar could now do. On December 26, 1832, the Maharajah affixed his seal to the treaty and so renounced the Punjab's ambition to extend its empire to the sea.

13 Wolff's biographer goes on to relate that when Wolff conveyed this to Lord William Bentinck in Simla, the governor general replied: "This is, alas! the opinion of all the natives all over India."

14 Burnes, *Travels into Bokhara*, II, 28.

CHAPTER 18

ACROSS THE HIMALAYAS TO TIBET

Tension with the British

◆:◆:◆: ON THE surface, the relations between the Durbar and the English continued to be friendly. But an undercurrent of hostility had begun to run down the Hooghly and the Ravi. In Calcutta, the feeling had come to prevail that the Punjab would have to be annexed sooner or later and the Punjabis should therefore not be allowed to become inconveniently strong. The Amirs of Sindh had been talked (and some of them coerced) into signing treaties: now the Afghans were approached with similar proposals. An appearance of friendship with the Maharajah was to be kept up, but the Punjab was to be hemmed in from all sides and, when feasible, strangled in the embrace of friendship.

Ranjit Singh was too shrewd to be taken in by empty gestures of good will, and Punjabi expansionism was still explosive enough to react violently to external restrictions. The Durbar's counter-moves were to encourage the Amirs in their resistance to British demands. If the Punjabis had been reticent, their diplomacy might have been more successful. But the Maharajah continued to talk aggressively about taking Shikarpur, which was like the thin end of a wedge piercing the heart of Sindh. The Sindhians naturally mistrusted the Punjabis and were only too willing to play them off against the British. On the Afghan front, the Durbar encouraged Shah Shuja to make another attempt to recover his throne and eject the Barakzais with whom the English were negotiating commercial treaties. The Durbar received emissaries from the court of Herat and conveyed to the British that the Russians were anxious to treat with the Punjabis. Emissaries from Nepal were received with marked favour at Lahore, and there was an exchange of courtesies with the Maratha chiefs and the Nizam of Hyderabad.[1]

The British government entered into discussions on the Durbar's claims over territory across the Sutlej. These were examined and conceded in the case of towns which were strategically unimportant: Anandpur, Chamkaur, Kiratpur, and Machiwara; but the most important, Ferozepur, was rejected.[2] Ferozepur was only forty miles from Lahore and close to the most important ford over the Sutlej. This step was taken on the advice of the British army commanders, who felt that Ludhiana was too far from Lahore to be an effective base of operations against the Punjab. British troops were moved to Ferozepur and the town was fortified.

The Maharajah sensed the approaching danger. *"Pās āgeyā"* (they have come closer), he remarked. The Durbar countered the move by garrisoning Kasur, which faced Ferozepur on the other side of the river.

The Conquest of Ladakh

While the British were menacing them in the east and blocking them in the south, the Punjabis burst out in a direction which the English could scarcely believe possible: northwards over Kashmir's Himalayan ranges into Ladakh. General Zorawar Singh, who was posted at Kishtwar, exploited a domestic quarrel in the ruling family and moved into the state. He put one of the aspirants in possession on his undertaking to pay Rs. 30,000 per annum to the Lahore Durbar, and occupied some of the strategically placed forts. In the winter of 1836, Zorawar Singh presented the Maharajah with the *nazarānā* he had brought

[1] The Nizam sent Ranjit Singh a bejewelled canopy which he presented to the Golden Temple, where it is to this day.

[2] The excuse to do so was provided by the death in September 1835 of the widow, Lachman Kaur, who had been in possession of the town. The Ludhiana Agent, who had in the past held the Maharajah to be Lachman Kaur's overlord, now announced that her estates lapsed to the English and not to the Durbar.

from Ladakh and asked for permission to advance further westwards to Iskardu to make a common frontier with China. The Maharajah advised him to hold his hand for the time being.

The British Agent at Ludhiana was indignant over the extension of the Punjab frontier and lent a sympathetic ear to the complaints of the members of the dispossessed family. The Durbar reminded him that the territory in question was on its side of Sutlej. The Agent ignored the argument and wrote to his government of the danger of allowing the Punjabis to have a common frontier with the Chinese and continued to express sympathy for the Ladakhi exiles.

The Western Frontier

While Zorawar Singh was carrying the Punjab's standard northwards, the Maharajah was extending its frontiers at the expense of the Afghans. The Durbar had offered to put Shuja back on the throne but on terms that no self-respecting Afghan could have accepted. He was asked to renounce forever his title to Multan, Dera Ghazi Khan, Dera Ismail Khan, Mankera, and Peshawar (which were in Punjabi hands and which Shuja was willing to concede), and also to agree to send gifts of horses, fruit, etc., in the nature of tribute. In addition there were clauses demanding a ban on the slaughter of kine, and the surrender of the sandalwood portals of the temple of Somnath which the iconoclast Mahmud had taken to Ghazni eight hundred years before. Shuja did not turn down these conditions but decided to make another attempt to gain power by himself.

Shuja received some support from the Amirs of Sindh and was assured that there would be a general rising of the tribes in his favour as soon as he entered Afghanistan. When he crossed the Indus many tribal Sardars reiterated their promise to join him but did not budge out of their fortresses: they wanted to be sure of the winning side before committing themselves. In a brief encounter at

Kandhar, Shuja's troops were routed by Dost Mohammed and his brothers. Shuja retraced his steps through Sindh and rejoined his six hundred wives at Ludhiana.

While Shuja and Dost Mohammed Khan were disputing the throne of Kabul, the Durbar removed Sultan Moham-med Khan (who had been appointed governor at the death of Yar Mohammed) from Peshawar and garrisoned the city with Punjabi troops. Hari Singh Nalwa, who was known as a ruthless administrator, was sent to consolidate the frontier.

The Pathans, who looked down with contempt on the plainsmen, had continued to ambush and snipe at the Punjabis until Nalwa took savage reprisals by destroying villages in whose jurisdiction crimes were committed. Within a few months a petrified peace descended on the tribal land and the name of Nalwa became a terror among the Pathans. To prevent rebellion, Nalwa had been build-ing a chain of forts, each within sight of the other. The first two to be completed were near the Khyber Pass: Shab-kadar was garrisoned with one thousand nine hundred men under Lehna Singh Sandhawalia; Jamrud with six hundred men under Maha Singh.

The Durbar's occupation of Peshawar and Nalwa's forts on the Khyber Pass offended Dost Mohammed, and he addressed several rude notes to the Maharajah demanding the evacuation of the Khyber region.[8] He had himself invested with the title of *Amir-ul-mu'mnin* (leader of the faithful) and roused the tribes to fight yet another holy war against the Sikhs.

The Durbar sent Fakir Azizuddin and the American,

[8] Dost Mohammed wrote: "If out of haughtiness the Maharajah does not pay heed to my request, I will gird up my loins for battle and become a thorn in the courtyard of his rose-garden. I will muster an army of crusaders who know nothing except fighting unto death. I will create tu-mult on all sides and a scene of chaos everywhere." Ranjit Singh replied: "We have broken the heads of refractory chiefs and put our foes in irons. If Dost out of avarice and greed desires to give battle with the small force he has, let him come." (*Lahore Durbar*, pp. 178-79.)

Josiah Harlan, who had served with the Afghans, to negotiate with Dost Mohammed. Harlan reported his mission
in the following words: "I divided his [i.e. Dost Mohammed's] brothers against him, exciting their jealousy of his
growing prosperity. I induced his brother Sultan Mohammed Khan, the lately deposed chief of Peshawar, to withdraw suddenly from his camp about nightfall with ten
thousand retainers. The chief accompanied me towards the
Sikh camp, whilst his followers fled to their mountain
fastnesses."[4] Dost Mohammed, continues Harlan, went back
to Kabul and in "bitterness of spirit declaiming against
the eruptions of military renown, plunged himself in the
study of the Koran."

Dost Mohammed's disillusionment with worldly ambitions reduced the tension on the northwest frontier for
some time. It gave the Durbar time to turn to its southern
frontier. The Amirs, who had been reluctant to enter into
commercial relations with the English, were being coerced
into accepting political domination. They took the only
chance they had of avoiding annexation by inciting the
Mazaris, a tribe inhabiting the doab between the junction
of the Indus and the Sutlej, to attack Punjabi outposts
south of Multan, thus inviting the Durbar's interference in
Sindhian affairs. Prince Kharak Singh and Sawan Mal were
ordered to punish the Mazaris and those who had provoked
them.

In the summer of 1836, Durbar troops occupied Mithankot and Rojhan and were on the threshold of Sindh with
the gates wide open. Kharak Singh asked for permission to
proceed to Shikarpur. Although the Durbar had made no

---

[4] *European Adventurers of Northern India*, p. 257. Harlan forgot to mention that Dost Mohammed violated all laws of international usage by im-
prisoning him and the Fakir and turning them over to his brother, Sultan
Mohammed, who, he was sure, would never make terms with people who
had ejected him from Peshawar. Sultan Mohammed was more willing to
trust Ranjit Singh than his own brother. He accepted Ranjit's promise to
give him a *jāgīr* in the Punjab, released the two envoys, and withdrew
with his army. (Ranjit Singh kept his word.)

secret of its claims to Shikarpur (and had a good excuse to take it since Nasiruddin, a disciple of the fanatic Syed Ahmed, had been active in the town), it hesitated to take a step which might involve it in a conflict with the English. The hesitation proved fatal to the Punjab's ambitions in the south.

The English made capital of the Durbar's nervousness. The secretary to the governor general wrote: "The government of India is bound by the strongest consideration of political interest to prevent the extension of the Sikh power along the whole course of the Indus."[5] Wade was sent to Lahore to persuade the Durbar to give up its campaign in Sindh. He was instructed to use every means in his power "short of actual menace to keep His Highness at Lahore and to prevent the further advance of his army."[6] If the Durbar claimed that the expedition was punitive, it was to be told that the Amirs had formally placed themselves under British protection.

The Durbar tried to outmanoeuvre the English. It entered into an agreement with Shah Shuja, undertaking to help him in yet another bid to recover his kingdom in return for the renunciation of his claim on Peshawar (which was already in Punjabi hands) and Shikarpur (which was not). The Durbar faced the English with a threefold argument. It had to punish the people who had instigated the Mazaris; Shuja, who had a valid title to Shikarpur, had passed it on to the Durbar; and by the treaty of 1809 the British had solemnly sworn not to interfere in the affairs of territories west of the Sutlej. The English agreed that the Punjabis had been wronged by the Mazaris, but refused to recognise their right to take Shikarpur, either as a prize or by virtue of an agreement with Shah Shuja. And as for the treaty of 1809, they replied ingeniously that the territories in question were not west of

[5] *The Lahore Durbar*, p. 141.
[6] *The Lahore Durbar*, p. 140.

the Sutlej, but west of the Sutlej *and* the Indus, which was not the same thing.

The Durbar was indignant. The ministers exhorted the Maharajah to make a firm stand, and if necessary go to war. They argued that a nation which had so often violated its solemn promises and which had made systematic expansion a matter of policy would sooner or later find an excuse to annex the Punjab. The Maharajah was extremely angry with the English, but as in the past he did not allow his passion to cloud his judgment. "What happened to the Maratha army of two hundred thousand which fought the English?" he asked his ministers. He tried through Fakir Azizuddin to persuade the English to declare Sindh *mulk-i-mahfūzā* (neutral territory)—which the Amirs would have liked—and to obtain an assurance that a similar policy would not be followed in Afghanistan. Wade refused to consider these propositions and insisted on the Durbar giving a promise not to interfere in Sindh. The Maharajah asked the Englishman what the words "welfare and prosperity" and "respect and consideration" meant; these being phrases that the governor general had used in his letter to Ranjit Singh. Wade ignored the sarcasm and proceeded to explain the meaning of the words at some length. "His Highness betrayed some impatience; he grasped the hand of the Fakir and struck two palms repeatedly," wrote Wade to the governor general.[7] The Durbar gave in and agreed not to go farther for the time being, *bil-fel-o-bil-hāl*. The debate on Sindh was closed, but the Durbar refused to sign a treaty on the subject. It also refused to give up the advance post at Rojhan.

Battle of Jamrud, April 1837: Death of Hari Singh Nalwa

The Durbar had barely finished with Sindh when trouble flared up on the northwest frontier. Nalwa's energetic measures, particularly the chain of forts that he was mak-

[7] SC 17 of 6.3.1837.

ing, gave the Afghans reason to believe that he was contemplating an invasion of their country. Dost Mohammed abandoned the study of the Koran and turned his attention to practical matters. An opportunity for action came sooner than he had expected. Prince Nao Nihal Singh, who had been with Nalwa, returned to Lahore to get married; the Durbar was busy with the arrangements for the wedding; and Nalwa was reported to be ill in bed. Dost Mohammed felt it was the right time to unsheath the sword and hurl the *ghāzīs* against the infidel.

Dost Mahommed's strategy was to isolate the Punjabi garrisons at Shabkadar, Jamrud, and Peshawar, and reduce each in turn. The first on the list was Jamrud, which was the most advanced outpost and the weakest link in the Punjabi chain of fortresses. One detachment was sent to Shabkadar to prevent Lehna Singh Sandhawalia from leaving the fort. Nalwa's illness immobilised the garrison at Peshawar. Jamrud was invested by twenty-five thousand Afghans and Pathans equipped with eighteen heavy guns.

Maha Singh had only six hundred men and a few light guns in the fort. Within a few hours the besiegers' artillery reduced the walls of Jamrud to rubble. Maha Singh's men dug themselves into trenches and for four days kept the Afghans and Pathans at bay. Maha Singh sent a desperate appeal for help to Peshawar.[8] Nalwa rose from his sick bed and made his way to Jamrud.

On Nalwa's approach the enemy raised the siege of Jamrud and took up positions in the valley of the Khyber which would ensure escape in the event of defeat. Nalwa drew up his troops in battle formation and waited for the enemy, who outnumbered him three to one, to attack. For seven days the armies faced each other. When Nalwa realised that the Afghans and the Pathans had no desire for battle, he ordered the Punjabis to advance. The engagement took place on April 30, 1837. The Punjabis drove

[8] A Sikh woman disguised as an Afghan stole through the enemy's ranks at night to carry the message to Peshawar.

the enemy before them. Dost Mohammed's son, Mohammed Akbar Khan, who was watching the Afghan debacle
from an escarpment, espied Nalwa well ahead of the bulk
of his army. Akbar Khan swooped down on the advance
column and poured lead into Nalwa's howdah.

Nalwa was mortally wounded. He ordered his officers to
keep his death a secret until the enemy had been driven
beyond the mouth of the Khyber. For the Afghans the
killing of Hari Singh Nalwa turned the defeat at Jamrud
into a victory.[9]

Much as Dost Mohammed tried to claim the battle of
Jamrud as an Afghan victory (he heaped public honours
upon his son), nothing could stop the stench of eleven
thousand Afghan and Pathan corpses strewn about the
Khyber from reaching the nostrils of the tribesmen in the
neighbouring hills and valleys. The Punjab's standards
still fluttered on Bala Hissar, Shabkadar, and the battered
walls of Jamrud. And now the ghost of the valiant Nalwa
haunted the rocky defiles, spreading terror among the
people.

It was necessary for Dost Mohammed to recover his lost
prestige. He is reported to have written to the Maharajah:
"I have always regarded myself as established by your authority . . . I was your servant." If the Durbar could give

[9] An account of the battle was sent by an Englishman, Dr. Wood, from
Rohtas to the governor general (PC 59 of 29.5.1837). He wrote that in the
great slaughter of the Afghans Mohammed Afzal, the eldest son of Dost
Mohammed, had been killed. According to Punjabi accounts they lost 6,000
men; the Afghans, who outnumbered them, left about 11,000 men dead
on the field. Of the death of Nalwa, Dr. Wood wrote: "He received four
wounds, two sabre cuts across his breast; one arrow was fixed in his breast,
which he deliberately pulled out himself, and continued to issue his orders
as before until he received a gunshot wound in the side, from which he
gradually sank and was carried off the field to the fort, where he expired,
requesting that his death should not be made known until the arrival of
the Maharajah's reliefs."

It is significant that in this sanguinary battle, the Pathan and Afghan
ghāzīs were largely defeated by Sikh *nihaṅgs* and Punjabi Mussalmans
fighting shoulder to shoulder.

him Peshawar, there would be no trouble on the frontier. But if the request were turned down, he would be compelled by circumstances to fight—*tang āmad bajang āmad* (when one is forced one goes to battle).[10]

The Durbar rejected the Afghans' demand for Peshawar and sent a word of warning: the maintenance of peace was not the sole monopoly of the Afghans. If the Afghans could force war on the Punjabis, the Punjabis could force war on the Afghans.

The English tried to make capital out of the tension between the Punjabis and the Afghans. The Russians were pushing eastwards and had won the Persians over to their side. Their agents were reported to be active in Kabul. The governor general sent Alexander Burnes to Afghanistan to try and draw Dost Mohammed into the British camp.[11]

Dost Mohammed made the recovery of Peshawar a condition precedent for his joining the English. The governor general, Lord Auckland, now had to choose between Dost Mohammed and Ranjit Singh. He chose Ranjit Singh and, with the Durbar's help, elected to remove Dost Mohammed from Afghanistan and put Shah Shuja on the throne. The Durbar was divided in its reactions. The chief minister, Dhian Singh, and the majority of ministers were for rejecting the British proposal. Fakir Azizuddin was for co-operation with the English. After some hesitation, the Maharajah agreed with the Fakir and persuaded the Durbar to support the British expedition. A British delegation consisting of Macnaghten and Wade, among others, came to the Punjab and settled the terms of the Tripartite Treaty between the Durbar, the English, and Shah Shuja. The formal ratification was to take place at Ferozepur in

10 PC 28 of 11.9.1837.
11 Burnes' mission to Kabul was also to counteract Russian attempts to win over Dost Mohammed. The Russians had gained influence in Persia and at their instance Mohammed Ali had invested Herat. The British sent Pottinger to help in the defence of Herat and Burnes to Dost Mohammed.

the last week of November 1838 when the Durbar and British contingents, which were to form the "Grand Army of the Indus," as it came to be called, would be reviewed by the Maharajah and the governor general.

Grand Army of the Indus

A month before the Ferozepur meeting, the ostensible reason for the campaign ceased to exist. On October 22, 1838, the Persians raised the siege of Herat and the danger of Perso-Russian infiltration into Afghanistan was removed. The English nevertheless went ahead with their plans to take Afghanistan. If the country had to be saved from the Russians, why could it not be saved for the British from the rest of the world? The reason why the Maharajah, despite advice to the contrary, continued to support the scheme, after it had become abundantly clear that the expedition was to be the British conquest of Afghanistan, will never be known.

The army of the Indus was to invade Afghanistan from two directions. The Punjab army under the command of Colonel Shaikh Bassawan was to force the Khyber Pass and approach Kabul from the east. Prince Taimur's levies and Captain Wade, who was appointed chief liaison officer, were to accompany the Punjabis. A British army (including Pathan and Afghan levies) under the command of Sir John Keane was to go through Sindh to Kandhar, Ghazni, and join the Punjabis at Kabul. Shah Shuja was to accompany the British contingent. Since the terms of the treaty[12] had already been settled, there was little to do at Ferozepur except exchange presents and compliments, inspect parades, and entertain each other with drink and nautch parties.[13]

[12] The British government's attitude to an independent Indian state can be gauged from the fact that it proposed that an English resident be posted at Lahore. The Durbar categorically rejected this suggestion.

[13] There was a happy prelude to the event: the Maharajah's youngest wife, the comely Jindan, bore him a son—his seventh—who was named Dalip Singh.

The End

During the course of the festivities, Ranjit Singh's already impaired health broke down. On December 24, 1838 he was stricken with paralysis and could neither rise from his bed nor speak to bid his guests farewell. For six months he struggled valiantly for life but by the middle of June 1839 all hope of recovery was abandoned. Kharak Singh was invested with the title of Maharajah of the Punjab, with Raja Dhian Singh as his chief minister. At last on the evening of June 27, exactly forty years after he had entered Lahore as a conqueror,[14] death came to Ranjit Singh, Maharajah of the Punjab.

The Maharajah's body was cremated the next day. The newswriter described the scene in the following words: "Having arrived at the funeral pile made of sandalwood, the corpse was placed upon it. Rani Guddun[15] sat down by its side and placed the head of the deceased on her lap; while the other ranis with seven slave girls seated themselves around, with every mark of satisfaction on their countenances."[16] Dr. Honigberger takes up the tale: "The Brahmins performed their prayers from the Shaster . . . the priests of the Sikhs did the same from their holy scripture called *Granth Saheb*, and the Mussalmen accompanied them with their 'Ya Allah! Ya Allah!' "[17] The prayers lasted nearly an hour. The newswriter resumes: "At 10 o'clock, nearly the time fixed by the Brahmins, Koonwar Khurruck Singh set fire to the pile and the ruler of the Punjab with four ranees and seven slave girls was reduced to ashes. . . .[18] A small cloud appeared in the sky over the

14 Reckoned by the Bikrami calendar used by the Lahore Dubar.
15 Daughter of Sansar Chand of Kangra.
16 *Lahore Akhbar*, June 1839.
17 Honigberger, "Thirty-Five Years in the East," p. 102.
18 During the rise of the misls great numbers of Hindus accepted conversion to Sikhism (which they regarded as another branch of Hinduism). The Hindus brought customs and prejudices with them and considerably altered the faith of Nanak and the gurus. The Brahmins again gained influence and re-introduced caste prejudices and cow-worship. The Sikh

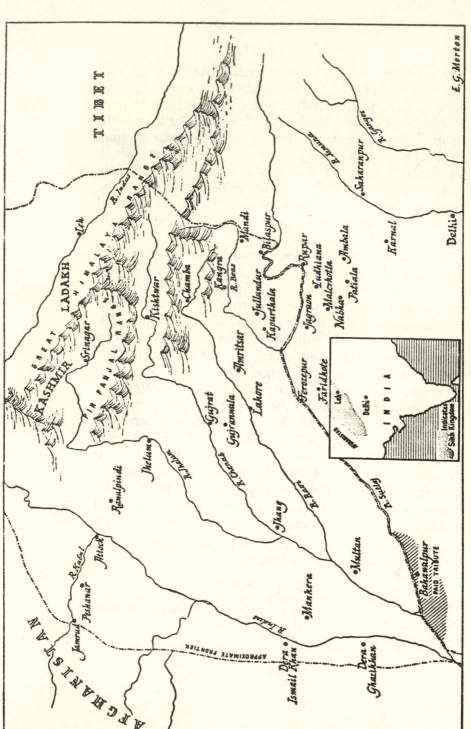

NORTHERN INDIA AT THE DEATH OF RANJIT SINGH, 1839

E. G. Morton

burning pile and, having shed a few drops, cleared away. No one saw hope of relief but in resignation. . . . The heart is rent in attempting a description of the distress and lamentations in the palace among the ranees and among the citizens of every age, sex, and religion."[19]

In the history of the Punjab, no man has excited the imagination of the people as much as Ranjit Singh. His looks contributed little to his popularity. He was of medium stature and dark-brown complexion; he wore a long grey beard on a face pitted with small-pox; his blind left eye was like a gaping wound. He was "exactly like a mouse with grey whiskers and one eye," wrote Emily Eden. Despite his unprepossessing appearance, his face was animated and full of expression. Many people who met him commented on his penetrating look and the restlessness of his fiery eye. Fakir Azizuddin, who led a Punjabi delegation to Lord William Bentinck at Simla in 1831, was asked by an officer of the governor general in which eye Ranjit Singh was blind. "The splendour of his face is such," replied the Fakir, "that I have never been able to look close enough to discover."

Despite his slight stature and spare frame, Ranjit Singh was wiry, as if made of whipcord. He was a superb horseman and, since horses were the ruling passion of his life, he often spent as much as ten hours of the day in the saddle. Although of excellent constitution, he was a hypochondriac. He consulted physicians every other day and insisted on their prescribing drugs (in later years, laudanum) for his imaginary ailments. But this obsession with illness did not produce a fear of death. He was a man of courage who led his men in battle and faced danger without concern for his own life. This quality earned for him the title, "Lion of the Punjab."

---

aristocracy, which was largely Jat, began to look upon itself as the Kshatriya and to imitate the customs of the Kshatriya.

[19] *Lahore Akhbar*, June 1839.

Although ugly himself, Ranjit Singh was a lover of beautiful things. He surrounded himself with handsome men and beautiful women. He wore the plainest of clothes (saffron-coloured cashmere in winter and plain white muslin in summer) but he insisted that courtiers and visitors wear their regalia and jewellery in the Durbar. He maintained a bevy of Kashmiri girls who dressed as soldiers and rode out with him on ceremonial occasions. His appreciation of beauty was not confined to human beings. He loved the open country and spent his morning hours riding out to the river or to some garden. Whenever dark monsoon clouds appeared in the sky or it started to rain he stopped work and gave himself up to merrymaking. The sight of the new moon moved him to rapturous delight and he would order a gun salute to honour its appearance. The Mughal garden at Shalamar (which he renamed *Sālābāgh*, the lover's garden) was his favourite haunt, where he relaxed amid the playing fountains, drank goblets of heady wine, and listened to his favourite flautist, Attar Khan, or watched the nautch. Ranjit Singh was a *bon vivant* who did not find it difficult to combine the lust for living with the lust for power. It would seem that Kipling wrote the following lines for Ranjit Singh:

> Four things greater than all things are
> Women and Horses and Power and War.

An anecdote told in Punjabi circles to this day relates a dialogue between Ranjit Singh and his Muslim wife, Mohran. She commented on the Maharajah's ugliness and asked: "Where were you when God was distributing good looks?"

"When you were occupied with your looks, I was busy seeking power," answered the monarch.

Ranjit Singh did not receive any education, and remained unlettered to the last. But he respected men of learning and, like the illiterate Akbar, made up the deficiency by seeking the company of scholars and satisfied his craving for knowledge by badgering them with questions. "His conversation is like a nightmare," wrote the Frenchman, Jacquemont. "He is almost the first inquisitive Indian I have seen; and his curiosity balances the apathy of the whole of his nation. He has asked me a hundred thousand questions about India, the British, Europe, Bonaparte, this world in general and the next, hell, paradise, the soul, God, the devil and a myriad of others of the same kind."[20] In this way Ranjit Singh became acquainted with the affairs of the world, and acquired a speaking knowledge of Persian, in which language Durbar records were kept.

He had the same capacity for work as he had for enjoying life. When the feasts were over and the dancers' bells silent, he retired to his bedchamber and spent many hours dictating his correspondence to relays of scribes who were always in attendance.[21]

Ranjit Singh had the virtues and vices of Punjabi character. He was simple in his habits, utterly outspoken and warm and generous towards people he liked. Although he became a king, he did not lose the common touch or sympathy with the peasant folk from whom he had sprung.[22] He also had the peasant's shrewdness and cunning, and once his suspicion was aroused he considered no trick unfair to outwit an adversary. But he never held a grudge for very long. He forgave people who had wronged him and rehabilitated enemies he had vanquished. He hated inflicting punishment: never in his entire life did he sentence a man to death—not even an Akali fanatic who tried to assassinate him.

[20] Jacquemont, *Travels*, II, 22.
[21] Shahamat Ali, *Sikhs and Afghans*, p. 15.
[22] Ranjit Singh's concern for the welfare of the peasantry was always a very personal one. In a message to Lehna Singh Majithia on the latter's assignment to collect the revenue, the Maharajah wrote: "Take care that all residents of the country are happy and in the cradle of comfort and ease. . . . See that all the zamindars have prosperous houses and households. . . . Realise the revenue with a sweet tongue."

The factor which contributed most to Ranjit Singh's success was his respect for other faiths.[23] He was a devout Sikh and spent an hour or more every afternoon listening to the reading of the *Adi Granth*. But his devotion to Sikhism did not prevent him from being full of Brahmanical superstition, from worshipping at Hindu temples and surrounding himself with soothsayers, astrologers, and other charlatans of the same ilk which were forbidden by the Sikh gurus. He equally respected the Islamic faith and strongly resented the anti-Muslim prejudices of the Akalis. It is said that a calligraphist who had spent the best part of his life preparing a copy of the Koran came to Lahore after having failed to sell his work to the Muslim chiefs of India. Ranjit Singh paid a fabulous price for the work. When Fakir Azizuddin praised him for his broadmindedness, the Maharajah replied: "God wanted me to look upon all religions with one eye, that is why he took away the light from the other."

Ranjit Singh's court reflected the secular pattern of his state. His prime minister, Dhian Singh, was a Dogra; his foreign minister, Azizuddin, was a Muslim; his finance minister, Dina Nath, was a Brahmin. Mingling with the Sikh Sardars and Hindus, who predominated, were influential Muslims like Azizuddin's brothers, Nuruddin and Imamuddin; artillery commanders, Mian Ghausa (whom the Maharajah honoured with the title "commander and faithful friend"), his son Sultan Mahommed, General Elahi Baksh, and others; the two sons of the late Nawab of Multan—Sarfaraz Khan and Zulfiqar—and the Tiwana chief, Khuda Yar. There were no forced conversions in Ranjit Singh's time. The Muslim women he married, Bibi

23 In February 1835 Karamat Ali Shah, who had been appointed newswriter by the English in Afghanistan, passed through Lahore on his way to Calcutta. He refused to accept presents from Ranjit Singh because the Maharajah was an "infidel." Ranjit Singh's letter to Sardar Gujar Singh (PC 95 of 5.2.1835) refers to the Maharajah's surprise that Karamat Ali "in conversation intruded his religion in a manner that no one has hitherto been known to do in my Durbar."

Mohran, Gulbahar Begam, and others, retained their faith;
Mohran even caused a riot by converting a Hindu servant
to Islam. He spent great sums in the repair of mosques.
His Hindu wives likewise continued to worship their
own gods.[24] This attitude won the loyalty of all his subjects and helped to forge the resurgent feeling of nationalism into a powerful weapon of Punjabi imperialism which,
within a short time after Ranjit Singh's death, struck
across the mountain frontiers. The colours of the Punjab
Durbar were carried by Colonel Shaikh Bassawan's Muslim troops in the victory parade at Kabul. A year later the
Dogra, Zorawar Singh, recommenced his conquests across
the Himalayas. Thus a small principality around Gujranwala was enlarged to a state of over 200,000 square miles
yielding an annual revenue of over three crore rupees,[25]
and possessed one of the most powerful and disciplined
armies in the whole of Asia.[26]

Ranjit Singh summed up his own achievements in the
following words: "My kingdom is a great kingdom: it was

[24] Ranjit Singh married 22 wives through whom he had 7 sons.

[25] The figure given by Shahamat Ali (*The Sikhs and Afghans*, p. 23) is
Rs. 3,00,27,762. Dr. Sita Ram Kohli (*Ranjit Singh*, p. 205) estimates the
income of the state as follows:

1.	Revenue from the provinces of Lahore, Multan, Kashmir, and Peshawar	1,75,57,741
2.	*Nazarānās*	6,03,657
3.	Customs and Excise	15,31,634
4.	*Jāgīrs*	91,96,000
	TOTAL	2,88,89,032

The figure of three crore rupees sounds extremely modest today. It
should, however, be borne in mind that at the time the price of the staple
food—wheat—was fourteen annas per maund. In 1961 it fluctuated between Rs. 18 and Rs. 20 per maund, i.e. more than twenty times as much.

[26] Shahamat Ali's estimate (pp. 23-25) of the Durbar army (exclusive of
garrison troops) in 1839 was 31 regiments of infantry, 9 regiments of cavalry, 288 pieces of artillery of various calibre, 11,800 irregular sowars. The
cost of maintaining this army was, according to Shahamat Ali, Rs.
1,27,96,482 (i.e. more than one third of the state's income). Besides this,
the *jāgīrdārs* furnished 9 regiments of infantry, 5 regiments of cavalry,
87 pieces of artillery, and 6,460 irregular horsemen.

small, it is now large; it was scattered, broken, and divided; it is now consolidated: it must increase in prosperity, and descend undivided to my posterity. The maxims of Taimur have guided me; what he professed and ordered I have done. By counsel and providence, combined with valour, I have conquered; and by generosity, discipline, and policy, I have regulated and consolidated my government. I have rewarded the bold, and encouraged merit wherever it was to be found: on the field of battle, I exalted the valiant; with my troops I have shared all dangers, all fatigues. Both on the field and in the cabinet I shut partiality from my soul, and closed my eyes to personal comfort; with the robe of empire, I put on the mantle of care; I fed faqirs and holy men, and gained their prayers; the guilty as the innocent I spared; and those whose hands were raised against myself have met my clemency; *Srī Purakhjī* [God] has therefore been merciful to his servant, and increased his power, so that his territory now extends to the borders of China and the limits of the Afghans, with all Multan, and the rich possessions beyond the Sutlej."[27]

[27] Major H. M. L. Lawrence, *Adventures of an Officer in the Punjaub* I, 64-65.

APPENDICES

APPENDIX 1

JANAMSAKHIS AND OTHER SOURCES OF INFORMATION ON THE LIFE OF GURU NANAK

THE material on which the present-day biographies of Guru Nanak are based is most inadequate from a historian's point of view. The first attempt to write a biography was made more than fifty years after Nanak's death and, although many people who had known the Guru personally were alive at the time, little attempt was made to record their impressions. Thereafter many other biographies, or *janamsākhīs* (literally, birth stories) as they are known, were written. We do not know who wrote the first one, nor on what material it was based. But once one was written, many others followed, taking material from the others and adding or deleting details as it suited the author. The styles of these janamsakhis (with the exception of the biography of Mani Singh) show clearly that they were written by semi-literate scribes for the benefit of an wholly illiterate people. They abound with stories of miracles performed by the Guru; they contradict each other on material points; and some were obviously touched up to advance the claims of one or the other branches of the Guru's family which had been overlooked in the succession to the guru-ship. Their contents are further vitiated by the Guru's own compositions in the *Adi Granth* and by the *Vārs* of Bhai Gurdas. Nevertheless, the janamsakhis cannot be wholly discarded because they were based on legend and tradition which had grown around the Guru in the years following his demise, and furnish useful material to augment the bare but proved facts of his life.

The sources on which the chapter on Guru Nanak in the present work is based are the following:

I. *Janamsākhīs*

There are many janamsakhis (the word will be in roman, without accents, throughout the rest of the appendix) in existence.

1. *Janamsakhi by Bhāī Bālā*. This work claims to be a contemporary account written by one Bala Sandhu at the instance

of the second guru, Angad. According to the author, he was a close companion of Guru Nanak and accompanied him on many of his travels. There are good reasons to doubt this contention:

(a) Guru Angad, who is said to have commissioned the work and was also a close companion of the Guru in his later years, was, according to Bala's own admission, ignorant of the existence of Bala.

(b) Gurdas, who has listed all Guru Nanak's prominent disciples whose names were handed down, does not mention the name of Bala Sandhu. (This may be an oversight, for he does not mention Rai Bular either.)

(c) The language used in this janamsakhi was not spoken at the time of Guru Nanak or Guru Angad, but was developed at least a hundred years later.

(d) Some of the hymns ascribed to Nanak are not his but those of the second and fifth gurus.

(e) At several places expressions which gained currency only during the lifetime of the last guru, Gobind Singh (1666-1708), are used e.g. *Vāh Guru jī kī Fateh.* Bala's janamsakhi is certainly not a contemporary account; at best it was written in the early part of the 18th century.

2. *Vilāyat Vāli Janamsakhi.* In the year 1883 a copy of a janamsakhi was dispatched by the India Office Library in London for the use of Dr. Trumpp and the Sikh scholars assisting him. (It had been given to the Library by an Englishman called Colebrook; it came to be known as the *Vilāyat Vāli* or the foreign janamsakhi.) This janamsakhi was the basis of the accounts written by Trumpp, Macauliffe, and most Sikh scholars. It is said to have been written in A.D. 1588 by one Sewa Das.

3. *Hāfizābād Vāli Janamsakhi.* A renowned Sikh scholar, Gurmukh Singh of the Oriental College, Lahore, found another janamsakhi at Hafizabad which was very similar to that found by Mr. Colebrook. Gurmukh Singh, who was collaborating with Mr. Macauliffe in his research on Sikh religion, made it available to the Englishman, who had it published in November 1885. This biography agrees entirely with the India Office janamsakhi.

4. *Other janamsakhis*. Many other janamsakhis have since been discovered. They follow the last two mentioned in all material points. The famous historian, Karam Singh, mentions half-a-dozen he came across in his travels.

The only conclusion that can be drawn is that although none of these janamsakhis are contemporary, they are certainly based on some biography which was written earlier but is now untraceable. A historian can neither discard nor accept the janamsakhis in their entirety. Everything they state must be tested against other available material.

II. *Ādi Granth*

Guru Nanak's compositions in the *Adi Granth* have a few references to contemporary events, the most important being his presence at Saidpur when it was sacked by Babar in A.D. 1521. This fact upsets the sequence of events narrated by the janamsakhis. Besides, as stated earlier, the janamsakhis ascribe some hymns to Nanak (e.g. the *Prān Sanglī*), which Guru Arjun, the compiler of the *Adi Granth*, did not consider authentic and, despite the trouble he had taken in getting hold of them, did not incorporate in his anthology.

III. *Vārs of Bhāī Gurdās*

In his thirty-nine *Vārs* Bhai Gurdas only briefly mentions some of the events in Guru Nanak's life: the rest is simply in the nature of an eulogy. These *Vārs* were composed between fifty to seventy years after the death of Nanak and in the lifetime of many people who knew the Guru, particularly Bhai Buddha, who was personally known to the author. Bhai Gurdas unfortunately did not use the available knowledge to produce a biography; but whatever reference he makes in the *Vārs* must be considered authentic.

IV. *Bhagat Ratnāvalī by Māni Singh*

This work was written in the 18th century and is only an exposition of Gurdas's first canto; it does not pretend to add to the information on Guru Nanak. It is significant that in the *Bhagat Ratnāvalī*, which contains a list of Guru Nanak's companions and disciples, there is no mention of Bala Sandhu.

V. *Mahimā Prakāś by Sarūp Dās*
(compiled in 1776)

VI. *Nānak Prakāś by Santokh Singh*

This work was written in A.D. 1823, is based on the janamsakhi ascribed to Bala Sandhu, and suffers from the same dis-
qualifications.

VII. *Dabistān by Muhsin Fānī*

The author was a contemporary of the 6th Guru, Hargobind.
The work contains very scanty references to Guru Nanak
and even these are more in the nature of praise than a narra-
tion of facts. It is not known who Muhsin Fani was.

VIII. *Relics*

From two far separated corners of the earth, tablets have
been unearthed which confirm Sikh tradition of Guru Nanak's
travels. In 1915, a Sikh scholar, Gurbaksh Singh, discovered
traces of old Sikh temples in Dacca (now capital of East Pakistan) and Chittagong, where tablets mentioned the stay of the
first and ninth Gurus. (See *Dacca Review*, pp. 224-32 of October and November 1915; pp. 316-22 of January 1916, and pp.
375-78 of February and March 1916.) In 1916, Sikh soldiers discovered a tablet in Baghdad commemorating Nanak's stay
in the city. The former conclusively proves Nanak's stay in the
city. The latter goes further and fixes the dates of his western
pilgrimage.

Conclusion

It would appear that the gurus succeeding Nanak were more
concerned with preserving his hymns and those of their other
predecessors than with recording the events of the founder's
life. Bhai Gurdas also did not pay much attention to actual
incidents and concerned himself with the exposition of the
hymns of his gurus. But soon after the deaths of Guru Arjun,
Bhai Gurdas, and Bhai Buddha, people less qualified than they
proceeded to write the life of Nanak. They took whatever information was readily available and, for the rest, created situations out of their imagination to give an appropriate setting
to some of the hymns of the Guru, which had already been

compiled in the *Adi Granth* (e.g. the acrostic was thus used to create a story that the Guru was sent to school and at the tender age of seven was able to confound his teacher with his learned answers). Nevertheless, when we put together all the material listed above, check one with another, discard the miraculous, delete the accretions of the credulous, we are still left with enough to recreate a life story with a fair degree of authenticity.

APPENDIX 2

ADI GRANTH OR THE GRANTH SAHIB

THE *Adi Granth* or *Granth Sahib*, as it is popularly known, was compiled by the fifth guru, Arjun, at Amritsar. His immediate problem was to get hold of the genuine compositions of his predecessors and to weed out the spurious writing which had been introduced by some of the unsuccessful aspirants to guruship and their followers. Arjun expanded this task to preparing a sacred book for the community. He sent out scouts to locate and collect all the available texts and went personally to Mohan, the son of the third guru, Amar Das, and persuaded him to hand over the writings of the first three gurus which were in his possession. (This process of collecting the writings of the preceding guru had been started by the second guru and was followed by the third and fourth.) Arjun also invited followers of other religious denominations and contemporary writers of religious verse to send in contributions for consideration. When all this material had been collected, the Guru selected a spot south of the city called Ramsar and began to dictate the text to Bhai Gurdas. They finished their great task in August 1604. The *Granth* was then formally installed in the Harimandir with Bhai Buddha (1518-1631) as the head Granthi.

Since communities of disciples were scattered all over Northern India, it became necessary to have copies of the *Granth* made available to them. In the very first transcription, minor changes were made by the copyists. Editions based on the transcription are consequently not the same as the original dictated by Arjun. Exactly a hundred years later, the last guru, Gobind Singh, took upon himself to compile a final and revised version of the *Adi Granth* with the compositions of his father, the ninth guru, Tegh Bahadur, inserted at the appropriate places. This compilation was lost in the *Vaḍā Ghallūghārā* of 1762. Fortunately, many copies of Guru Gobind's compilation had been made before the disaster. These are somewhat different from the two earlier editions. There are therefore three main versions (*bīrs*) of the *Adi Granth*.

1. *Kartārpur Vālī Bīṛ*, dictated by Guru Arjun to Bhai Gurdas. The compilation was made at Amritsar and later removed to Kartarpur, where it has remained ever since. The opening lines of this volume are in the hand of Arjun himself. It also bears the signature of his son, the sixth guru, Hargobind,[1] at the end. It has several blank pages in it. According to tradition, these were left by Arjun for the compositions of his successors. The location of the blank pages does not lend support to the traditional view.

2. *Bhāī Banno Vālī Bīṛ*. Soon after completing the writing, Guru Arjun asked one of his followers, Bhai Banno, to take the manuscript to Lahore to have it bound. In the course of the journey to and from Lahore, and while it was being bound, Bhai Banno had a copy made for his own use. In this edition he inserted a few extraneous hymns. Bhai Banno's copy is still with his descendants. Some transcriptions based on Bhai Banno's *bīṛ* are available.

3. *Dam Damā Vālī Bīṛ*. The two earlier editions had only the hymns of the first five gurus and the works of some saint-poets. The sixth, seventh, and eighth gurus did not write, but the ninth guru, Tegh Bahadur, and his son, the tenth guru, Gobind Singh, were prolific writers of religious verses. Blank pages in the first editions dictated by Guru Arjun did not provide enough space to take this additional writing; nor indeed did the placing of these blank pages indicate that the fifth guru necessarily intended the additions to be inserted in the same volume. Guru Gobind Singh did not insert his own compositions in the *Adi Granth*. (His disciple, Mani Singh, collected them in a separate volume called the *Dasveṇ Pādśāh kā Granth*.) Gobind did, however, wish to find a place for his father's compositions in it. It appears that he inserted them at Anandpur and, after the destruction of the town, redictated them to Mani Singh at Dam Dama in the few months of respite from battle in 1704. The editions of the *Adi Granth* currently in use in Sikh Gurdwaras are based on the copies of Bhai Mani Singh's *bīṛ* written at Dam Dama.

[1] Rev. C. H. Loehlin, who examined this volume, doubts the authenticity of the writing by the fifth guru and the signature. (*The Sikhs and Their Book.*) Later publications by this author do not say anything on the subject.

Contributors

The *Adi Granth* which is now recognised as authentic and used for worship in Gurdwaras is an enormous volume consisting of nearly 6,000 hymns. Its contributors can be divided into four categories:

(a) *Sikh Gurus.* These include the first five gurus and the ninth guru, Tegh Bahadur. The largest number (2,218) are from the pen of Guru Arjun, followed by Guru Nanak (974), Amar Das (907), Ram Das (679), Tegh Bahadur (115), and Angad (62).

(b) *Hindu Bhaktas and Muslim Sūfīs.* Hymns of sixteen Bhaktas and Sūfīs are in the *Granth.* In chronological order they are Jai Dev of Bengal; Farid of the Punjab; Nam Dev, Trilochan and Parmanand of Maharashtra, Sadhna the Sindhi; Beni and Ramananda of Uttar Pradesh; Dhanna of Rajasthan; Pipa, Sain, Kabir, and Ravidas of Uttar Pradesh; Mira Bai of Rajasthan; Bhikhan of Uttar Pradesh; and Sur Das, the blind poet of Oudh. Of these the greatest number are those of the Muslim weaver of Benares, Kabir, and Farid, the Sufi mystic of Pak Pattan. The hymns of the Bhaktas and Sufis in the *Granth Sahib* represent four centuries of Indian religious thought. They do not, however, correspond strictly to the versions now current in Hindi, Marathi, or the other languages in which they are said to have been originally written. Apparently, by the time they came to be known in the Punjab, they had undergone certain linguistic alterations. But once they had been incorporated in the *Granth,* no further changes were introduced in the text. It is more than likely that the only genuine compositions of the Bhaktas and Sufis that exist are those found in the *Granth*: others now ascribed to them have been touched up by their followers.

(c) *Bhatts or Bards.* There were several bards in the courts of the gurus. Their compositions were largely panegyrics in praise of their masters. It is not easy to determine the exact number of the Bhatts, since most of them used poetic names which merged in the hymn as if they were an integral part and not mere pseudonyms.

The Bhaktas, Sufis, and Bhatts between them account for 937 hymns.

(d) *Other Contributors.* The compositions of men like Mardana, the Muslim companion and disciple of Guru Nanak, Sundar, who is the author of an elegy, the *Rām Kalī Sad* and the eulogistic ballad (*vār*) of Satta and Balwand, do not fall within the three categories listed above.

Arrangement

The hymns of the *Granth* are not arranged by authors or subject matter but divided into 31 *rāgas* or musical modes in which they are meant to be sung. What the Sikh gurus wished to emphasize more than the way of good deeds (*karmamārga*), knowledge (*gyānamārga*), or devotion (*bhaktimārga*) was the path of worship of the name (*nāmamārga*). They considered divine worship through music the best means of attaining that state of bliss—*vismād*—which resulted in communion with God. The selection of *rāgas* was carefully made. Those that aroused passions of any kind were omitted. *Megh* and *Hindol* were not used because of their jubilant tone; *Jog* and *Dīpak* were likewise rejected for their melancholy. The instructions to singers were to avoid indulging in exposition of the intricacies of the *rāgas*, but to sing them in such a way that the meaning of the words was easily and gently conveyed to the listeners.

Within the *rāgas*, the compositions of the gurus intermingle and are followed by those of the Bhaktas.

Sanctity

The compositions of the gurus were always considered sacred by their followers. Guru Nanak said that in his hymns "the true Guru manifested Himself, because they were composed at His orders and heard by Him" (*Vār Āsā*). The fourth guru, Ram Das, said: "Look upon the words of the True Guru as the supreme truth, for God and the Creator hath made him utter the words" (*Vār Gauṛī*). When Arjun formally installed the *Granth* in the Harimandir, he ordered his followers to treat it with the same reverence as they treated their gurus. By the time of Guru Gobind Singh, copies of the *Granth* had been installed in most Gurdwaras. Quite naturally, when he declared the line of succession of gurus ended, he asked his followers to turn to the *Granth* for guidance and look upon it as the symbolic representation of the ten gurus.

The *Granth Sahib* is the central object of worship in all Gurdwaras. It is usually draped in silks and placed on a cot. It has an awning over it and, while it is being read, one of the congregation stands behind and waves a fly whisk made of Yak's hair. Worshippers go down on their knees to make obeisance and place offerings of cash or kind before it as they would before a king: for the *Granth* is to them what the gurus were to their ancestors—the *Sacā Pādśāh* (the true Emperor).

With the influx of Hindus into the Sikh fold, a number of ceremonies associated with the worship of idols have grown around the *Granth*. In the morning, it is opened with elaborate ritual, which is repeated in the evening, when it is wrapped up and put away for the night. On special occasions, there is a non-stop reading of the hymns (*akhaṇḍ pāṭh*) by a relay of readers. This takes two days and nights. A seven-day reading is known as the *saptāh pāṭh*. Another variation is to read a favourite hymn after each one in the *Granth*. A non-stop reading of this kind (*sampaṭ pāṭh*) can take fifteen days. None of these forms of ceremonial recitation have the sanction of the gurus and apparently came into vogue in the latter part of the 19th century. (There is no mention of ceremonies of these sorts in the diaries of Ranjit Singh's court.)

On the birthdays of some of the gurus, the martyrdom of the fifth and ninth gurus and those of the two younger sons of Guru Gobind Singh, the *Granth* is taken out in a procession in the bigger cities.

Despite these customs, the *Granth* is even today not like the idol in a Hindu temple nor the statue of the Virgin in a Catholic cathedral. It is the means and not the object of worship.

Language and Literary Quality

The *Granth* contains the writings of poets of many parts of India speaking different languages. The earliest contributor, Jai Dev, lived in the 12th century; the last guru, Tegh Bahadur, in the 17th. Despite a span of five centuries between the earliest and latest compositions and the distant regions from which they were gathered, there is a certain unity of theme and language in them. Guru Arjun chose only those hymns which echoed sentiments he wanted to inculcate in his own community. He did not have much difficulty with the language, since most saint-poets of Northern India wrote in the *Sant Bhāśā*, which was a sort of esperanto composed of a vocabulary common to Northern Indian languages and used extensively for writing religious verse. In addition, as already stated, whether the poems were from Bengal, Uttar Pradesh, or Maharashtra, the version which was accepted by Guru Arjun was obviously one which the Punjabis could understand. Although the language is now somewhat obsolete, it is easily intelligible to anyone with a knowledge of Hindi and a background of Hinduism. The main appeal of the *Granth* as a scripture is its non-esoteric character and its utter simplicity.

The *Adi Granth* has some of the greatest writing in the Punjabi language. Its two chief contributors, Nanak and Arjun, have been the inspiration of many later poets.

APPENDIX 3

BHAI GURDAS

GURDAS, the amanuensis who wrote the *Adi Granth* at the dictation of Guru Arjun, was also the author of 39 *vārs* (ballads in the heroic metre) in Punjabi and 556 *kabits* (couplets) in Braj, of which the former are of some historical and theological importance. They are the only really authentic references to the period of the 3rd, 4th, 5th, and 6th gurus by a Sikh. His commentary on Sikh practices are valuable indications of the state of things at the time and are therefore regarded as the "key" to an understanding of the Sikh scriptures.

There is some uncertainty about the year of Gurdas' birth. Most historians have placed it in the time of the second guru, Angad. Others believe that he was born after Amar Das' succession as the third guru. They contend that the name Gurdas was given by the third guru and, since the naming ceremony is performed soon after birth, the event could not have taken place very much earlier. He was therefore born sometime between 1540 and 1560.

Gurdas was the son of Datar Chand, the younger brother of the third guru, who took the child's education into his own hands. He was quick to learn and soon became one of the chief exponents of the teachings of the gurus. On the death of Amar Das, the fourth guru, Ram Das, formally initiated Gurdas into the faith and sent him to Agra as a missionary. On the death of Ram Das, Gurdas returned to Amritsar and presented himself before Ram Das' successor, Guru Arjun. He was first engaged in trying to appease Prithi Chand, the Guru's elder brother, who had set himself up as a rival guru and had launched a campaign of vilification against Arjun. Gurdas failed in his mission. His *vār* (36) on Prithi Chand's attitude is full of vituperation. He came back to his master and turned his attention to purely academic pursuits. In 1603, when the Guru started the great task of compiling the *Adi Granth*, he chose Gurdas as the scribe. The volume was completed in the summer of 1604 and installed in the Harimandir.

Emperor Akbar, while passing through the Punjab, desired to scrutinise the sacred volume and see for himself whether there was any truth in the allegation that it contained references derogatory to Islam and the Prophet. Gurdas was entrusted with the mission of taking the *Granth* to the Emperor. The volume was opened at random three times, but none of the passages had anything offensive to Muslim susceptibilities; on the contrary, at least two echoed sentiments complimentary to the Islamic faith. Akbar made an offering of 51 gold *mohurs* to the holy book and presented a pair of expensive Kashmere shawls to Gurdas.

After the execution of the fifth guru and during the years when Guru Hargobind was in prison in Gwalior, the affairs of the Sikh community were left in the hands of trusted followers, among whom were Bhai Buddha and Bhai Gurdas.

On the Guru's release, Gurdas was sent on a mission to purchase horses from Kabul (the Guru having decided to arm his followers and train them as soldiers). Before he could complete the deal, the money was stolen from him and the crestfallen Gurdas, being unable to face his master, fled to Benares. He was apprehended and brought to Amritsar. The Guru forgave him, and he again resumed his duties as the chief organiser of the scattered community. At this time, the Guru's militant ways and his close association with Muslims who had tormented his father caused a certain amount of unrest in the Sikh community. Gurdas rose to his master's defence. To him the Guru was "the destroyer of enemy hordes, the hero of battles, the great Warrior" as well as the "great benefactor."

Gurdas remained celibate and died at Goindwal in 1629. His funeral rites were performed by Guru Hargobind himself.

Historical Importance of Gurdas' Work

Bhai Gurdas did not set out to write a work of history, but there are several references (mostly in *vār* 11) to persons and events which are of some importance to the historian of today. There are 85 passages scattered in the 39 *vārs* which deserve attention, viz. *vār* 1 *pauṛī* 17-48, *vār* 11, *vār* 21 *pauṛī* 13-31, *vār* 24 *pauṛī* 1-25, *vār* 26 *pauṛī* 31 and 34, *vār* 39 *pauṛī* 2 and 3, *vār* 3 *pauṛī* 12, *vār* 20 *pauṛī* 1 and *vār* 38 *pauṛī* 20.

There are several very notable and inexplicable omissions in Gurdas' writings. He has, for instance, produced a list of the important disciples of the earlier gurus. In the list of adherents of Guru Nanak the name of Rai Bular, the landlord of Talwandi, who was among Guru Nanak's earliest and most important disciples, is missing. (And for a better reason, that of Bala Sandhu.) Gurdas has also nothing to say about the compilation of the *Adi Granth* and its scrutiny by Emperor Akbar. The reference to the execution of the fifth guru is in the vaguest terms:

> The Guru hath taken his abode in the river
> among the fish,
> As moths that see the flame fall upon it and
> merge their light with His light,
> As deer hear the sound of a distant drum and
> run to it without a care of doom,
> As butterflies settle on the lotus and die
> on it during the night.
> The Guru's teachings we forget not,
> and like the monsoon birds are ever calling.
> The good have peace, the nectar of love,
> and the company of the gentle.
> Thus is my life a sacrifice to Guru Arjun.

The only possible explanation of these oversights is that Gurdas' primary object was to expound certain points from the Scriptures and to propagate the ideals of the Sikh way of life, not to write a book of history.

Gurdas' Compositions

Gurdas' *vārs* are of a very uneven quality and have a baffling variety of diction. Some run very smoothly and are well ordered; the vocabulary of others is both antiquated and not infrequently violates elementary rules of grammar.

In the copies of Gurdas' *vārs* which are current today, there is a 40th *vār* written by a Sindhi poet of Shikarpur of the same name. The Sindhi Gurdas lived in the time of Banda (1670-1716). His composition, though in the same metre as that used by the elder Gurdas, is of higher poetic quality and is frequently quoted in describing the mission of Guru Gobind Singh.

APPENDIX 4

DASAM GRANTH

THE collection of writings attributed to Guru Gobind Singh is known as the *Dasam Granth* or *Dasven Pādśāh Kā Granth*. It consists of the following eighteen works: *Jāp Sāhib, Akāl Ustat, Bicitra Nāṭak, Caṇḍī Caritr* I, *Caṇḍī Caritr* II, *Caṇḍī dī Vār, Gyān Prabodh, Caubīs Avatār, Mehdī Mīr Budh, Brahmā Avatār, Rudra Avatār, Śabad Hazāre, Sri Mukh bāk Savaiye, Khālse dī Mehimā, Śastra Nām Mālā, Pakhyāṇ Caritr, Zafarnāmā,* and the *Hikāyats*. These works are written in four different languages: Braj (frequently highly sanskritized), Hindi, Persian, and Punjabi.

The compilation can be conveniently divided into four parts: mythological, philosophical, autobiographical, and erotic. The largest portion is mythological and is devoted to retelling well-known tales of Hindu mythology. The *Caṇḍī Caritr* and *Caṇḍī dī Vār* recount the battles of the Hindu Goddess of destruction. The *Caubīs Avatār* and *Mehdī Mīr Budh, Brahmā Avatār* and *Rudra Avatār* are similarly tales of the reincarnations of the different aspects of the Hindu trinity.

The *Jāp Sāhib* (distinct from Guru Nanak's *Japjī*) the *Akāl Ustat, Gyān Prabodh, Śabad Hazāre,* and some hymns are philosophical and devotional and have been used in Sikh ritual and prayer since the time of the Guru.

Most of the works mention the date and place of composition and help to fix the movements of the Guru. *Bicitra Nāṭak* is specifically devoted to recounting the mission of the Guru and is autobiographical. In the same category, though in a different context, is the *Zafarnāmā* (epistle of victory), which the Guru, after having suffered military reverses and having lost all his four sons, addressed to Emperor Aurangzeb in reply to the latter's advice to surrender.

The *Pakhyāṇ Caritr* and the *Hikāyats* are fables of the wiles of women in a corrupt and decadent society. The stories are not original and abound with erotic passages.

Date of Compilation

Most of the *Dasam Granth* was compiled in Anandpur, where the Guru came as a child of eight in 1674 and which he had to abandon thirty years later. After his escape from the besieged fort of Anandpur in 1704 he made his way to the village of Dam Dama, where in comparative safety he devoted his time to recompiling the writings of his predecessors as well as reproducing some portions of the *Dasam Granth*. Because of this literary activity Dam Dama came to be known as the Kashi or Benares of the Sikhs. It must, however, be borne in mind that the Guru did not stay at Dam Dama for more than a few months.

Present Versions of the Dasam Granth

The task of reproducing the works of Guru Gobind was undertaken after his death by his companion and disciple, Bhai Mani Singh, who spent nine years at the task. He was able to get some copies from other disciples and filled in the gaps from memory.

There are many compilations in existence today and more are being discovered. Three are better known than the others: that said to have been written by Mani Singh in his own hand (in the possession of Gulab Singh Sethi of New Delhi), and the volumes at the Gurdwaras at Patna and Sangrur. The version "authorised" by the Singh Sabha and generally available in print closely follows the version ascribed to Mani Singh.

Authenticity of the Writings in the Dasam Granth

Scholars are divided in their views on the subject. In 1896 a panel of theologians was constituted by the Singh Sabha to examine different texts and compile an "authentic" version. They consulted as many as 32 editions before preparing the version of the *Dasam Granth* which is in general circulation today. They were of the view that all the writing ascribed to Guru Gobind was in fact the Guru's work. This view has the support of the majority of scholars, including Dr. D. P. Ashta, Dr. Trilochan Singh, and Dr. Mohan Singh (who had at first expressed dissent).

Messrs. Macauliffe, Cunningham, Narang, and Bannerjee do not believe that all the writing in the *Dasam Granth* is that of Guru Gobind. The author is inclined to agree with this view for the following reasons:

1. The time at the Guru's disposal does not warrant a work of this size. The vocabulary, knowledge of the classics and languages, and the style of writing indicate a maturity of mind and, however precocious a child the Guru might have been, he could not have done much of this sort of writing before he was 18 (1684), nor could have continued it after 1699, when he launched his mission to exterminate Mughal tyranny. Apart from his domestic obligations as a husband and father of four sons, these years were crowded with intense activity in conducting the affairs of a rapidly growing community and in giving spiritual guidance. He was also busy recruiting and training an army, building forts and fighting battles. It is most unlikely that he could devote much time to composing verse. The only portions which could be definitely ascribed to him are those which by his sanction became a part of the Sikh ritual and prayer, and his autobiography. Such are the *Jāp Sāhib, Akāl Ustat, Gyān Prabodh, Sabad Hazāre*, the *Caupayīs*, the *Bicitra Nāṭak* and the *Zafarnāmā*. The scribes in his court must have copied these compositions soon after the Guru composed them at Anandpur. They were then distributed to Sikh communities so that they could be incorporated in daily prayers and religious functions.

2. It is likely that Guru Gobind Singh composed some of the other verses in the *Dasam Granth* as well but since they were from their very nature not intended to be scriptural, it is difficult to distinguish them from the works of the 52 bards whom he patronised. The most disputed of these writings are the erotic portions in the *Pakhyān Caritr*. There is enough evidence in the text itself to prove that these portions were not written by Guru Gobind Singh.

The strongest evidence adduced by scholars who believe that the entire work known as the *Dasam Granth* is the work of Guru Gobind, are the words of a letter from Mani Singh to the Guru's widow, Mata Sundari, in April 1716, which reads: "Among the books I have sent there is the Master's 303 *Triya Caritr Upākhyān*." Both Dr. Ashta and Dr. Trilochan Singh have translated *Sāhib de 303 Caritr Upākhyān* as "written" by the Master, which the original does not warrant. The word "*de*" does not necessarily mean "written by"; it can mean "of" or "belonging to" and probably referred to a volume which

belonged to the Guru. Besides, in the *Triya Caritr Upākhyān*
as it exists in the *Dasam Granth* today, the number of tales
is not 303 but 404. What Mani Singh had sent with the letter
was certainly not the tales that are incorporated in the *Dasam
Granth* of today.

3. The *Dasam Granth* ascribed to Mani Singh also states
that over 125,000 verses were composed in the court of Guru
Gobind Singh. On page 615 of the manuscript in the possession of Gulab Singh Sethi there is a categorical assertion that
the total number of verses composed amounted to 125,000. It
would therefore seem that the *Granth* in question forms only
one tenth of the total and the word *Dasam* refers to one tenth
and not to the tenth guru. The lines run as follows:

> *Savā lākh chaṅd āge soī*
> *Is meṇ ek ghat nahiṇ hoī*

> (A lac and a quarter verses
> existed before and not one
> less than that number.)

4. A large part of the mythological writings in the *Dasam
Granth* follow a conventional pattern very common at the
time. It was an age of plagiarism, and much of the imagery
used in describing scenes was current in Braj and Hindi writing. This would strongly indicate that the 52 bards—not many
of whom could be men of creative poetic genius—brought with
them chunks of memorised verse which found its way into this
work. The martial pieces in the form of *Sirkhaṅḍi Chaṅd* are
an exception to this pattern of plagiarism and were probably
composed at Anandpur. Even the Persian tales, *Hikāyats*, are
reproductions of stories from well-known Persian classics.

5. It is most unlikely that the Guru as the spiritual leader
of his people would have ever allowed his name to be associated with a composition of the type of *Pakhyāṇ Caritr*. His
lofty character and the value he set on Spartan living do not
go with prurience of the kind found in some of the passages
of the *Dasam Granth*.

The only conclusion possible is that much of the writing
in the *Dasam Granth* is from the pen of poets other than that
of Guru Gobind Singh. The only portions that can with some

certainty be ascribed to him are those which he, during his own lifetime, exhorted his followers to recite as parts of their prayer or read in the performance of ritual such as baptism. He may have had a hand in the composition of some of the others, but any categorical assertion on the subject would be hazardous.

Language and Literary Quality

The language of most of the *Dasam Granth* is largely Braj veering towards Sanskrit at one extreme and simple colloquial Hindi at the other. The *Zafarnāmā* and *Hikāyats* are in Persian and several passages in other works are in Punjabi. The authors not only used this melange of languages but also coined words half Arabic half Sanskrit (and sometimes words without any meaning just to create a musical effect). Some of this kind of writing has great power and beauty.

The following lines from *Rāma Avatār* describing the comely Sita are a fair indication of the mixture of languages:

> *Zulphen anūp Jānkī*
> *Nāgin Syāh bānkī*
> *Adbhut adāin tānkī*
> *Aiso ḍholan kahān hai?*

The descriptions of scenes of battle are couched in extremely vigorous staccato rhyme often reduced to lines of one word each. The battles waged by *Caṅḍī* and the Guru's encounters with the hill chiefs at Bhangani and Nadaun are among the most stirring that exist.

The scenes of nature and love, particularly in the *Kriśna Avatār*, are haunting in their loveliness:

> Beside the sparkling waters of the river,
> On the bank in silver moonlight bathed
> Were strewn jasmine petals as if to make a bed
> And blossoms twined overhead to make a bower.
> Krishna took Radha by the hand,
>   tilted up her face
> And gazed upon her beauty. Then clasped
> The damsel fair in his dark arms
> As a black shade eclipses the moon.

Spake Krishna: "Maiden fair, I sent not
        for thee.
I am as a deer wounded by the hunter's dart.
Thy love-lorn eyes have pierced my heart.
Beloved mine! thy wrath's burning fire
Hath singed my limbs but I wished not to
        depart.
I came not at thy command, but to soothe
My burns before the warmth of thy love.

APPENDIX 5

HYMNS FROM
THE ADI GRANTH

FARID

THERE is still some doubt regarding the identity of Farid, 134 of whose hymns are incorporated in the *Adi Granth*. Many Sikh scholars ascribe them to Farid Shakarganj (1173-1265), a disciple of the Sufi saint, Qutbuddin Bakhtiyar Kaki, who lived in Mehrauli near Delhi. This Farid lived in Pak Pattan. The tenth in succession to his post was Shaikh Ibrahim, also known as Farid Sani or Farid the 2nd, who was a contemporary of Guru Nanak. Macauliffe (*The Sikh Religion*, VI, 357) states that the hymns in the *Adi Granth* are the works of the later Farid. Authors of the *Sacred Writings of the Sikhs* (p. 219) ascribe them to Farid Shakarganj. There are others who believe that the hymns were composed by different Sufis of the Pak Pattan Centre, all using the poetic name Farid. (S. S. Amol, *Sāde Purāne Kavī*, p. 33.)

beṛā bandh nā sakio bandhan kī velā

When it was time to build your bark
You did not try.
When you see the ocean angry and the waves lash,
For help you cry.

Touch not the *kusum* flower, Beloved,
It will burn your fingers.
You are tender
And the Master's words are harsh.

As milk taken returns not to the udder,
So a wasted life is without meeting with the Master.
Says Farid: Sisters, when our Husband sends
        for us, go we must.
Our souls like swans fly away, our bodies
        come to dust.

                    (*Sūhī*)

bolai śai<u>kh</u> Farīd pyāre alloh lage

Listen to the words of Shaikh Farid
O dear ones, come to Allah.
This body will be reduced to dust
When it makes the grave its home.
O Shaikh Farid, if you could but stay
The ceaseless swan-flights of your mind
You would meet the Lord this very day.

If I knew that I would die
Never to return again
I would not follow the false ways of the world
Nor let my life be spent in vain.

In your speech be true, in your actions be right,
And spread no falsehood.
O Farid, tread the path the Guru shows.
What takes six months to quicken with life
Dies an instant death.
It is swift as the flight of swans in the spring
And the stampede of beasts in a forest fire.
It is a flash of lightning amid the rains
And transitory as the winter hours
When maidens are in love's embrace.
All that is must cease: on this ponder.

Farid, the earth questioned the sky:
Where are the mighty captains gone?
"In their graves they rot," was the reply
"And are rebuked for tasks not done."
                              (*Āsā*)

Farīdā galīai cikkaṛ dūr ghar

O Farid, the lane is slushy with mud
The house of the one thou lovest is far away.
If thou goest, it will soak thy cloak,
If thou stayest, it will sunder thy love.

I'll let my cloak be soaked.
'Tis Allah who makes the rain come down in torrents.

I will go forth to seek my beloved
The bonds of our love will not sever.

(Ślok)

Farīdā mai jāṇiā dukh mujh ko

Farid believed he alone was stricken with sorrow
But sorrow is spread over the entire world;
I climbed my roof and whichever way I turned
I saw that every home in sorrow burned.

(Ślok)

NAM DEV (1270-1350)

Nam Dev was a tailor of Maharashtra who earned a great reputation as poet and saint. There are 60 hymns of Nam Dev in the *Adi Granth*, but they do not correspond to his hymns in the Marathi language.

malai nā lāchai pārmalo

Pure and splendrous He came
As a waft of fragrance.
No one saw Him come,
No one saw Him go.
How can one describe Him,
How claim to know the nature
Of Him who has no lineage?

The flight of birds in the sky,
The way of fish in the water,
Leave no trace for the eye.
The heat from the heavens creates a mirage—
A vision of water for the thirsty deer.
These are all illusions
As is knowledge of the Lord of Namdev.

(Gujrī)

KABIR (1440-1518)

Kabir, the most celebrated of Bhakta saints, was born in Benares of Muslim parents. He was a weaver by profession but became a disciple of Ramananda and acquired great eminence as a poet. There are 541 hymns of Kabir in the *Adi Granth*.

· 321 ·

oe jo diseh ambar tāre

Those stars in the sky
Who has designed them and put them there?
O learned Pandit, know you what holds the heavens?
Only the fortunate ones know the secret.
He has given light to the Sun and Moon
In everything shines the spirit of the Creator.
Says Kabir, only he will know
Who has God in his heart and His name on his lips.

(Gaurī)

teh pāvas sindhu dhūp nahi chāyā

Neither rain nor sea
Neither sun nor shade
Neither birth nor death
Neither joy nor sorrow—
Beyond all these
Is single-minded meditation
Called *Sahaj.*
It cannot be told nor explained
It cannot be weighed nor spent.
It is neither heavy nor light
Neither high nor low.
Day and night have no power over it
Water cannot drown nor fire burn it
Such has the True Guru made it
Inaccessible and inapprehensible.
It is achieved only by the grace of the
        Guru who abides in every heart.
Says Kabir, let my life be a sacrifice to my guru
And may I live in the company of godly men.

(Gaurī Bairāgan)

bātī sūkī tel nikhūṭā

The wick is dry, the oil runs out,
The drum is silent, the dancer sleeps,
The fire burnt out, no smoke ensues.
He is immortal, no other the vigil keeps.

The string has snapped, the lute is mute,
The player plays not, his art is gone.
It is all sermons, speeches, talk and idle gossip.
When knowledge comes, he forgets his song.
O Kabir, he who has conquered the five sins,
(Lust, anger, greed, attachment and the ego)
To reach the highest seat, he has not far to go.

(Āsā)

ham ghar sūt taneh nit tānā kaṇṭh janeū tumāre

Know you who wears the sacred thread
That its yarn is spun in my house?
You but recite the Vedas and the *Gāitrī*,
While in my heart is His prayer said.

On my lips is the name of God
In my eyes shines His light
In my heart He has His abode.
What about you, O Brahmin,
When death comes what will be your plight?

We are as a herd of cattle
And you our Shepherd from age to age
If you lead us not to pastures new
What sort of husbandman are you?

You are a Brahmin and a humble weaver I
Yet how did I this wisdom find?
You seek favours of the princes
On the Lord have I fixed my mind.

(Āsā)

Kabīr mukt dvārā saṅkṛā

Kabir, the door of salvation is strait
Narrower than the tenth of the mustard seed.
A man's ego is the size of an elephant
How can he pass through the gate?
If he meet a teacher true
And the teacher on him grace bestow
The gates of salvation will be opened wide
At his pleasure he can come and go.

Nanak: the door of salvation is strait
   Only the little can enter.
Thoughts of Self have inflated the ego
How can he pass through the gate?

When he meets the teacher true
The self goeth, within him doth the light shine.
Mortal life gains eternal peace
And mingles with the light divine.

(Gujrī)

NANAK (1469-1539)

There are 974 hymns of Nanak in the *Adi Granth*.

Japji—The Morning Prayer.

There is One God.
He is the supreme truth.
He, the Creator,
Is without fear and without hate.
He, the Omnipresent,
Pervades the universe.
He is not born,
Nor does He die to be born again.
By His grace shalt thou worship Him.

Before time itself
There was truth.
When time began to run its course
He was the truth.
Even now, He is the truth
And evermore shall truth prevail.

1.

Not by thought alone
Can He be known,
Though one think
A hundred thousand times;
Not in solemn silence
Nor in deep meditation.

Though fasting yields an abundance of virtue
It cannot appease the hunger for truth.
No, by none of these,
Nor by a hundred thousand other devices,
Can God be reached.
How then shall the Truth be known?
How the veil of false illusion torn?
O Nanak, thus runneth the writ divine,
The righteous path—let it be thine.

2.

By Him are all forms created,
By Him infused with life and blessed,
By Him are some to excellence elated,
Others born lowly and depressed.
By His writ some have pleasure, others pain;
By His grace some are saved,
Others doomed to die, re-live, and die again.
His will encompasseth all, there be none beside.
O Nanak, he who knows, hath no ego and no pride.

3.

Who has the power to praise His might?
Who has the measure of His bounty?
Of His portents who has the sight?
Who can value His virtue, His deeds, His charity?
Who has the knowledge of His wisdom,
Of His deep, impenetrable thought?

How worship Him who creates life,
Then destroys,
And having destroyed doth re-create?
How worship Him who appeareth far
Yet is ever present and proximate?

There is no end to His description,
Though the speakers and their speeches be legion.

He the Giver ever giveth,
We who receive grow weary,

On His bounty humanity liveth
From primal age to posterity.

4.

God is the Master, God is Truth,
His name spelleth love divine,
His Creatures ever cry: "O give, O give,"
He the bounteous doth never decline.
What then in offering shall we bring
That we may see His court above?
What then shall we say in speech
That hearing may evoke His love?
In the ambrosial hours of fragrant dawn
On truth and greatness ponder in meditation,
Though action determine how thou be born,
Through grace alone cometh salvation.

O Nanak, this need we know alone,
That God and Truth are two in one.

5.

He cannot be proved, for He is uncreated;
He is without matter, self-existent.
They that serve shall honoured be,
O Nanak, the Lord is most excellent.

Praise the Lord, hear them that do Him praise,
In your hearts His name be graven,
Sorrows from your soul erase
And make your hearts a joyous haven.

The Guru's word has the sage's wisdom,
The Guru's word is full of learning,
For though it be the Guru's word
God Himself speaks therein.

Thus run the words of the Guru:
"God is the destroyer, preserver and creator,
God is the Goddess too.
Words to describe are hard to find,
I would venture if I knew."

This alone my teacher taught,
There is but one Lord of all creation,
Forget Him not.

6.

If it please the Lord
In holy waters would I bathe,
If it pleases Him not,
Worthless is that pilgrimage.

This is the law of all creation,
That nothing's gained save by action.
Thy mind, wherein buried lie
Precious stones, jewels, gems,
Shall opened be if thou but try
And hearken to the Guru's word.

This the Guru my teacher taught,
There is but one Lord of all creation,
Forget Him not.

7.

Were life's span extended to the four ages
And ten times more,
Were one known over the nine continents
Ever in humanity's fore,
Were one to achieve greatness
With a name noised over the earth,
If one found not favour with the Lord
What would it all be worth?
Among the worms be as vermin,
By sinners be accused of sin.

O Nanak, the Lord fills the vicious with virtue,
The virtuous maketh more true.
Knowest thou of any other
Who in turn could the Lord thus favour?

8.

By hearing the word
   Men achieve wisdom, saintliness, courage, and
   contentment.

By hearing the word
  Men learn of the earth, the power that
    supports it, and the firmament.

By hearing the word
  Men learn of the upper and nether
    regions, of islands and continents.

By hearing the word
  Men conquer fear of death and the elements.

O Nanak, the word hath such magic for the worshippers,
  Those that hear, death do not fear,
  Their sorrows end and sins disappear.

9.

By hearing the word
  Mortals are to godliness raised.
By hearing the word
  The foul-mouthed are filled with pious praise.
By hearing the word
  Are revealed the secrets of the body and of nature.
By hearing the word
  Is acquired the wisdom of all the scriptures.

O Nanak, the word hath such magic for the worshippers,
  Those that hear, death do not fear,
  Their sorrows end and sins disappear.

10.

By hearing the word
  One learns of truth, contentment, and is wise.
By hearing the word
  The need for pilgrimages does not arise.
By hearing the word
  The student achieves scholastic distinction.
By hearing the word
  The mind is easily led to meditation.

O Nanak, the word hath such magic for the worshippers,
  Those that hear, death do not fear,
  Their sorrows end and sins disappear.

11.

By hearing the word
  One sounds the depths of virtue's sea.
By hearing the word
  One acquires learning, holiness, and royalty.
By hearing the word
  The blind see and their paths are visible.
By hearing the word
  The fathomless becomes fordable.

O Nanak, the word hath such magic for the worshippers,
  Those that hear, death do not fear,
  Their sorrows end and sins disappear.

12.

The believer's bliss one cannot describe,
He who endeavours regrets in the end,
There is no paper, pen, nor any scribe
Who can the believer's state comprehend.

The name of the Lord is immaculate.
He who would know must have faith.

13.

The believer hath wisdom and understanding;
The believer hath knowledge of all the spheres;
The believer shall not stumble in ignorance,
Nor of death have any fears.

The name of the Lord is immaculate,
He who would know must have faith.

14.

The believer's way is of obstructions free;
The believer is honoured in the presence sublime;
The believer's path is not lost in futility,
For faith hath taught him law divine.

The name of the Lord is immaculate,
He who would know must have faith.

15.

The believer reaches the gate of salvation;
His kith and kin he also saves.
The believer beckons the congregation,
Their souls are saved from transmigration.

The name of the Lord is immaculate,
He who would know must have faith.

16.

Thus are chosen the leaders of men,
Thus honoured in God's estimation;
Though they grace the courts of kings,
Their minds are fixed in holy meditation.
Their words are weighed with reason,
They know that God's works are legion.

Law which like the fabled bull supports the earth
Is of compassion born;
Though it bind the world in harmony,
Its strands are thin and worn.
He who the truth would learn
Must know of the bull and the load it bore,
For there are worlds besides our own
And beyond them many more.
Who is it that bears these burdens?
What power bears him that beareth them?

Of creatures of diverse kinds and colours
The ever-flowing pen hath made record.
Can anyone write what it hath writ
Or say how great a task was it?
How describe His beauty and His might?
His bounty how estimate?
How speak of Him who with one word
Did the whole universe create,
And made a thousand rivers flow therein?

What might have I to praise Thy might?
I have not power to give it praise.
Whatever be Thy wish, I say Amen.
Mayst Thou endure, O Formless One.

17.

There is no count of those who pray,
Nor of those who Thee adore;
There is no count of those who worship,
Nor of those who by penance set store.
There is no count of those who read the holy books aloud
Nor of those who think of the world's sorrows
                    and lament.
There is no count of sages immersed in thought
                    and reason,
Nor of those who love humanity and are benevolent.
There is no count of warriors who match their
                    strength with steel,
Nor of those who contemplate in peace and are silent.

What might have I to praise Thy might?
I have not power to give it praise.
Whatever be Thy wish, I say Amen.
Mayst Thou endure, O Formless One.

18.

There is no count of fools who will not see,
Nor of thieves who live by fraud,
There is no count of despots practising tyranny,
Nor of those whose hands are soiled with blood.
There is no count of those who sin and go free,
Nor of liars caught in the web of falsehood,
There is no count of the polluted who live on filth,
Nor of the evil-tongued weighed down with calumny.
Of such degradation, O Nanak, also think.

What might have I to praise Thy might?
I have not power to give it praise.
Whatever be Thy wish, I say Amen.
Mayst Thou endure, O Formless One.

19.

Though there is no count of Thy names and habitations,
Nor of Thy regions uncomprehended,
Yet many there have been with reason perverted
Who to Thy knowledge have pretended.

Though by words alone we give Thee name and praise,
And by words, reason, worship, and Thy virtue compute;
Though by words alone we write and speak
And by words our ties with Thee constitute;
The word does not its Creator bind,
What Thou ordainest we receive,
Thy creations magnify Thee,
Thy name in all places find.

What might have I to praise Thy might?
I have not power to give it praise.
Whatever be Thy wish, I say Amen.
Mayst Thou endure, O Formless One.

20.

As hands or feet besmirched with slime,
Water washes white;
As garments dark with grime
Rinsed with soap are made light;
So when sin soils the soul
Prayer alone shall make it whole.

Words do not the saint or sinner make,
Action alone is written in the book of fate,
What we sow that alone we take;
O Nanak, be saved or forever transmigrate.

21.

Pilgrimage, austerity, mercy, almsgiving, and charity
Bring merit, be it as little as the mustard seed;
But he who hears, believes, and cherishes the word,
An inner pilgrimage and cleansing is his meed.

All virtue is Thine, for I have none,
Virtue follows a good act done.
Blessed Thou the Creator, the Prayer, the Primal
Truth and beauty and longing eternal.
What was the time, what day of the week,

What the month, what season of the year,
When Thou didst create the earthly sphere?
The Pandit knows it not, nor is it writ in his Puran;
The Qadi knows it not, though he read and copy the
    Koran.
The Yogi knows not the date nor the day of the week,
He knows not the month or even the season.
Only Thou who made it all can speak,
For knowledge is Thine alone.

How then shall I know Thee, how describe, praise, and
    name?
O Nanak, many there be who pretend to know, each
    bolder in his claim.
All I say is: "Great is the Lord, great His name;
What He ordains comes to be,"
O Nanak, he who sayeth more shall hereafter regret
    his stupidity.

22.

Numerous worlds there be in regions beyond the skies
    and below,
But the research-weary scholars say, we do not know.
The Hindu and the Muslim books are full of theories;
    the answer is but one.
If it could be writ, it would have been, but the writer
    thereof be none.
O Nanak, say but this, the Lord is great, in His knowledge
    He is alone.

23.

Worshippers who praise the Lord know not His greatness,
As rivers and rivulets that flow into the sea know not its
    vastness.

Mighty kings with domains vaster than the ocean,
With wealth piled high in a mountainous heap
Are less than the little ant
That the Lord's name in its heart doth keep.

24.

Infinite His goodness, and the ways of exaltation;
Infinite His creation and His benefaction;
Infinite the sights and sounds, infinite His great design;
Infinite its execution, infinite without confine.
Many there be that cried in pain to seek the end
    of all ending,
Their cries were all in vain, for the
    end is past understanding.
It is the end of which no one knoweth,
The more one says the more it groweth.
The Lord is of great eminence, exalted is His name.
He who would know His height, must in stature be
    the same.

He alone can His own greatness measure.
O Nanak, what He gives we must treasure.

25.

Of His bounty one cannot write too much,
He the great Giver desires not even a mustard seed;
Even the mighty beg at His door, and others such
Whose numbers can never be conceived.
There be those who receive but are self-indulgent,
Others who get but have no gratitude.
There be the foolish whose bellies are never filled,
Others whom hunger's pain doth ever torment.
All this comes to pass as Thou hast willed.
Thy will alone breaks mortal bonds,
No one else hath influence.
The fool who argues otherwise
Shall be smitten into silence.
The Lord knows our needs, and gives,
Few there be that count their blessings,
He who is granted gratitude and power to praise,
O Nanak, is the king of kings.

26.

His goodness cannot be priced or traded,
Nor His worshippers valued, nor their store;

Priceless too are dealers in the market sacred
With love and peace evermore.
Perfect His law and administration,
Precise His weights and measures;
Boundless His bounty and His omens,
Infinite mercy in His orders.
How priceless Thou art one cannot state,
Those who spoke are mute in adoration,
The readers of the scriptures expatiate,
Having read, are lost in learned conversation.
The great gods Brahma and Indra do Thee proclaim,
So do Krishna and his maidens fair;
Siva and the Saivites do Thee name.
The Buddhas Thou made, Thy name bear.
The demons and the demi-gods,
Men, brave men, seers, and the sainted,
Having discoursed and discussed
Have spoken and departed.
If Thou didst many more create
Not one could any more state,
For Thou art as great as is Thy pleasure.
O Nanak, Thou alone knowest Thy measure.
He who claims to know blasphemeth
And is the worst among the stupidest.

27.

Sodar—(Te Deum)

Where is the gate, where the mansion,
From whence Thou watchest all creation,
Where sounds of musical melodies,
Of instruments playing, minstrels singing,
Are joined in divine harmony?
There the breezes blow, the waters run and the fires
    burn,
There Dharamraj, the King of death, sits in state;
There the recording angels Chitra and Gupta write
For Dharamraj to read and adjudicate.
There are the gods Isvara and Brahma,

The goddess Devi of divine grace;
There Indra sits on his celestial throne
And lesser gods, each in his place.
There ascetics in deep meditation,
Holy men in contemplation,
The pure of heart, the continent,
Men of peace and contentment,
Doughty warriors never yielding,
Thy praises are ever singing.
From age to age, the pandit and the sage
Do Thee exalt in their study and their writing.
There maidens fair, heart bewitching,
Who inhabit the earth, the upper and the lower regions,
Thy praises chant in their singing.
By the gems that Thou didst create,
In the sixty-eight places of pilgrimage,
Is Thy name exalted.
By warriors strong and brave in strife,
By the sources four from whence came life,
Of egg or womb, of sweet or seed,
Is Thy name magnified.
The regions of the earth, the heavens and the universe
That Thou didst make and dost sustain,
Sing to Thee and praise Thy name.
Only those Thou lovest and with whom Thou art pleased
Can give Thee praise and in Thy love be steeped.
Others too there must be who Thee acclaim,
I have no memory of knowing them
Nor of knowledge, O Nanak, make a claim.
He alone is the Master True, Lord of the word,
    ever the same,
He Who made creation is, shall be and shall ever remain;
He Who made things of diverse species, shapes, and hues,
Beholds that His handiwork His greatness proves.
What He wills He ordains,
To Him no one can an order give,
For He, O Nanak, is the King of Kings,
As He wills so we must live.

28.

As a beggar goes a-begging,
Bowl in one hand, staff in the other,
Rings in his ears, in ashes smothered,
So go thou forth in life.
With ear-rings made of contentment,
With modesty thy begging bowl,
Meditation the fabric of thy garment,
Knowledge of death thy cowl,
Let thy mind be chaste, virginal clean,
Faith the staff on which to lean.
Thou shalt then thy fancy humiliate,
With mind subdued, the world subjugate.

Hail! and to Thee be salutation.
Thou art primal, Thou art pure,
Without beginning, without termination,
In single form, forever endure.

29.

From the store-house of compassion
Seek knowledge for thy food.
Let thy heart-beat be the call of the conch-shell
Blown in gratitude.

He is the Lord, His is the will, His the creation,
He is the Master of destiny, of union and separation.

Hail! and to Thee be salutation.
Thou art primal, Thou art pure,
Without beginning, without termination,
In single form, forever endure.

30.

Māyā, mythical goddess in wedlock divine,
Bore three gods accepted by all,
The creator of the world, the one who preserves,
And the one who adjudges its fall.

But it is God alone Whose will prevails
Others but their obedience render.
He sees and directs, but is by them unseen,
That of all is the greatest wonder.

Hail! and to Thee be salutation.
Thou art primal, Thou art pure,
Without beginning, without termination,
In single form, forever endure.

31.

He hath His prayer-mat in every region,
In every realm His store.
To human beings He doth apportion
Their share for once and evermore.
The Maker having made doth His own creation view.
O Nanak, He made truth itself, for He Himself is true.

Hail! and to Thee be salutation.
Thou art primal, Thou art pure,
Without beginning, without termination,
In single form, forever endure.

32.

Were I given a hundred thousand tongues instead of one
And the hundred thousand multiplied twenty-fold,
A hundred thousand times would I say, and say again,
The Lord of all the worlds is One.
That is the path that leads
These the steps that mount,
Ascend thus to the Lord's mansion
And with Him be joined in unison.
The sound of the songs of Heaven thrills
The like of us who crawl, but desire to fly.
O Nanak, His grace alone it is that fulfills,
The rest mere prattle, and a lie.

33.

Ye have no power to speak or in silence listen,
To grant or give away.

Ye have no power to live or die.
Ye have no power to acquire wealth and dominion,
To compel the mind to thought or reason,
To escape the world and fly.

He who hath the pride of power, let him try and see.
O Nanak, before the Lord there is no low or high degree.

34.

He Who made the night and day,
The days of the week and the seasons,
He Who made the breezes blow, the waters run
The fires and the lower regions,
Made the earth—the temple of Law.

He Who made creatures of diverse kinds
With a multitude of names,
Made this the Law—
By thought and deed be judged forsooth,
For God is true and dispenseth truth.
There the elect His court adorn,
And God Himself their actions honours;
There are sorted deeds that were done and bore fruit
From those that to action could never ripen.
This, O Nanak, shall hereafter happen.

35.

In the realm of justice there is law;
In the realm of knowledge there is reason.
Wherefore are the breezes, the waters and fire,
Gods that preserve and destroy, Krishnas and Sivas?
Wherefore are created forms, colours, attire,
Gods that create, the many Brahmas?

Here one strives to comprehend
The golden mount of knowledge ascend,
And learn as did the sage Dhruva.

Wherefore are the thunders and lightning,
The moons and suns,
The world and its regions?

Wherefore are the sages, seers, wise men,
Goddesses, false prophets, demons and demi-gods,
Wherefore are there jewels in the ocean?
How many forms of life there be,
How many tongues,
How many kings of proud ancestry?

Of these things many strive to know,
Many the slaves of reason.
Many there are, O Nanak, their numbers are legion.

36.

As in the realm of knowledge reason is triumphant,
And yields a myriad joys,
So in the realm of bliss is beauty resplendent.
There are fashioned forms of great loveliness;
Of them it is best to remain silent
Than hazard guesses and then repent.
There too are fashioned consciousness, understanding,
    mind, and reason,
The genius of the sage and seer, the power of
    men superhuman.

37.

In the realm of action, effort is supreme,
Nothing else prevails.
There dwell doughty warriors brave and strong,
With hearts full of godliness,
And celestial maidens of great loveliness
Who sing their praise.
They cannot die nor be beguiled
For God Himself in their hearts resides.
There too are congregations of holy men
Who rejoice, for the Lord in their midst presides.

In the realm of truth is the Formless One
Who, having created, watches His creation
And graces us with the blessed vision.
There are the lands, the earths and the spheres
Of whose description there is no limit;

There by a myriad forms are a myriad purposes fulfilled,
What He ordains is in them instilled.
What He beholds, thinks and contemplates,
O Nanak, is too hard to state.

38.

If thou must make a gold coin true
Let thy mint these rules pursue.

In the forge of continence
Let the goldsmith be a man of patience,
His tools be made of knowledge,
His anvil made of reason;
With the fear of God the bellows blow,
With prayer and austerity make the fire glow,
Pour the liquid in the mould of love,
Print the name of the Lord thereon,
And cool it in the holy waters.

For thus in the mint of Truth the word is coined,
Thus those who are graced are to work enjoined.
O Nanak, by His blessing have joy everlasting.

Slok—(Epilogue)

Air, water, and earth,
Of these are we made.
Air like the Guru's word gives the breath of life
To the babe born to the great mother earth
Sired by the waters.
The day and night our nurses be
That watch us in our infancy.
In their laps we play,
The world is our playground.
Our acts right and wrong at Thy court
      shall come to judgment;
Some be seated near Thy seat, some ever kept
      distant.
The toils have ended of those that have
      worshipped Thee,

O Nanak, their faces are lit with joyful
    radiance—many others they set free.

*　*　*

nīcāṇ aṅdar nīc jāt nīcī hū at nīc

Among the low, let my caste be the meanest,
Of the lowly, let me the lowliest be.
O Nanak, let such be the men I know
With such men let me keep company.
Why should I try to emulate the great?
Where the fallen have protected been
Is Your Grace and Your Goodness seen.

(Srī)

bharmai bhāh nā vijhvai je bhave disaṅtar des

The fire of pride is not extinguished
By wandering over distant lands.
The dirt in the mind is not cleansed
By wearing clean garments.
Fie, the life of falsehood; fie, the mask of divinity!

Nothing will make you a Bhakta true
Save the teaching of the True Guru.
O mind, if you seek good and annihilate pride
Let the Guru's word find a place in your heart
And the craving of the ego will be destroyed.

The mind is a priceless pearl
With it you can acquire an honoured place beside the Master.
In the company of the pious seek the Lord
For the Lord loves those on whose lips is His name.
Your pride shall vanish, and yours be the bliss
Of a wave mingling back with the waters.
Those that have not brought the thought of Hari
    to their minds
Shall be caught in the cycle of birth and death.

· 342 ·

Those that come not to the True One, the Supreme Being,
Shall be ruined and like flotsam drift
On the turbulent waters of life.
Human life which is priceless beyond compare
Is thus bartered away for a worthless shell.

Those to whom the True Guru tells the secret,
Acquire complete wisdom.
The Guru takes them across the waters
And they are received with honour.
O Nanak, their faces are radiant
And in their hearts is joy,
Born of the music of His word.

(Srī)

achal chalāi nā chalai

He deprives of delusion
The things that delude;
He blunts the edge of the dagger
And it does not wound.
Man's mind wavers for it is full of craving;
He is safe only in the Lord's keeping.

How then light the lamp when there is no oil?

Let your body be the lamp,
From the holy books take wisdom
And use it as oil.
Let knowledge of His presence be the wick
And with the tinder of truth
Light the spark.
Thus light you the oil-lamp
And in its light meet your Lord.

When the recording Angel claims your body
And catalogues your deeds,
Your good acts will save you from the cycle of birth
and death.
If in life you have served others

Your reward shall be a place in His Court.
Says Nanak: You will raise your arms in joy.

(Srī)

gur dātā gur hivai, gur dīpak teh loe

The Guru is the giver:
The Guru is the haven of peace,
The peace that reigns on snow-clad mountains.
The Guru is the lamp that lights the three worlds.
O Nanak, when He vouchsafes you the divine gift of faith,
Then alone there is peace.

Such is life steeped in ignorance.
First the child's craving for the mother's breast;
Then his awareness of his father and mother,
Of his sister and brother and brother's wife.
He now takes to games and sport
And relishes food and drink
And wallows in lust and passion
That know no caste.
Hoarding wealth he builds a home.
Then choler afflicts his system,
His hair turns grey, his breath is wheezy
Until the flames consume and his body is ashes.
His friends lament and depart.
The swan has flown, who knows where.
He came and he went and his name is forgotten.
After him the obsequies: the eating off leaf-plates
And the feeding of crows.
O Nanak, this is the way of those who grope in the dark,
Without the Guru the world remains sunk in ignorance.

(*Mājh Vār*)

je rat lagai Nānakā, jāmā hoe palīt

If blood falling on garments
Can soil them
How can the mind of those who live on human blood
Be clean?

Says Nanak: First cleanse your hearts, then utter
    the name of God.
With falsehood in your heart, all your acts remain false.
(Mājh Vār)

mehar masīt sidak musallā

If you would be a Muslim true
Let your life these rules pursue.
Let your mosque be the abode of kindness
In it spread your prayer-mat of faith,
And as you read the Koran think of righteous acts.
Let modesty be your circumcision—your troth with God.
And gentle acts the fasts you keep.
Let the reward of good deeds be your kaaba
And truth your preceptor.
Let the *Kalima* be your acts of mercy.
And as you tell the beads of the rosary
Dwell upon the Lord's commandments.
Says Nanak: The Lord will preserve your honour.
(Mājh Vār)

hak parāyā Nānakā us sūar us gāe

O Nanak, to usurp another's right is forbidden
As is the flesh of swine to the Muslim
Or the flesh of the cow to the Hindu.
Your Guru the mentor will stand by you
If you covet not another's goods
But reject it as carrion.
The idle prattler goes not to paradise
Only righteous activity releases one from life's bondage.
Forbidden food remains forbidden even when flavoured
                      with spices.
O Nanak, that which is false is forever false.
(Mājh Vār)

paṅj nivājāṇ vakht paṅj

There are five prayers
Each with a time and a name of its own.
First, truthfulness.

Second, to take only what is your due.
Third, goodwill towards all.
Fourth, pure intentions;
And praise of God, the fifth.
Let good acts be your creed: persevere with them;
Then proclaim you are a Muslim.
O Nanak, the more false the man
The more evil his power.

(*Mājh Vār*)

Musalmān kahāvan muskal

To be a Mussulman is not easy
Only he who is one should make the claim.
He should first follow in the footsteps of the holy
And accept their bitter words as sweet.
Rid himself of worldly goods
As sandpaper rids iron of rust.

A Muslim's faith is to follow his leader
Caring neither for life nor death;
To believe that there is a God above
Whose will is Law,
And abandon all thoughts of self.
O Nanak, if the Creator is merciful
Will you become a true Mussulman

(*Mājh Vār*)

paun pāṇi kā mel

Air, water and fire
Of these elements is our body made
Within it is the restless agitation of the mind.
It has nine doorways
The tenth is the one through which one goes to meet God.
O learned one, have you thought of this?

Every one can discourse, speak, and listen.
Only he who knows himself understands the nature of
the soul
And is a learned divine.

The body is made of clay
The sounds that emerge are of substance airy.
Know you, O learned one
What dies when a man dies?

Consciousness dies
Then dies the Ego
But the soul dies not.

What seek you in pilgrimage to sacred rivers?
The priceless jewel is within your breast.
The learned Pandit reads much, declaims much
But knows not the treasure within himself.

It is not I who die
But the demon of ignorance who is destroyed;
The soul that sustains dies not.
Says Nanak, this is what the Lord the Creator has shown me
Now I know there is no birth nor death.

(Gauṛī)

jāto jāe kahāṇ te āvai

Know you whence comes life?
How we are born? Where go we when we die?
Why some are caught in the cycle of birth and rebirth
While others are freed to merge in the Deathless One?

Those who have Him in their hearts
And have His Name ever on their lips;
Those who worship Him but seek no gain
To them come birth and death peacefully.
Thoughts rise in the mind, in the mind do they subside.
Only the Guru's word gives us freedom
Contemplating upon it we achieve liberation.

Like birds at dusk settling on trees
To roost for the night
Some joyous, some sorrowing; all lost in themselves.
When dawns the day and gone is the night
They look up at the sky and resume their flight.

So does man fulfil his destiny.

Those who through Your Name have knowledge
Know that the world is but a temporary shepherd's hut
In a pasture land.
Man is a pitcher overflowing with lust and anger.
Without stores the shop looks desolate
And so does the home
So also the human frame without the treasury of the Name.
The Guru throws wide open the portals of wisdom.

By virtue of your past deeds you meet the Guru.
Truth smiles on godly men.
Those that gently give up their bodies and souls to
                                            the Lord
At their feet will Nanak fall.

                                            (*Gauṛī*)

suṇ nāh prabhu jī ekalṛī ban māhi

All alone am I in the wilderness
O Lord, my Husband, listen to me!
How can a wife be free of care
Unless she finds You who are free of all care?

She cannot live without her Husband
Her nights are long and hard to endure
For sleep comes not to her.
O Lord of Love, listen to my prayer!

Only my Love cares for me, none else gives a thought
Alone am I in my lamentation.
O Nanak, the fortunate woman has her tryst with her Lord
And becomes one with Him.
Without Him her life is one of sorrow.

                                            (*Gauṛī*)

vidyā vīcārī tāṇ parupkārī

When one's acts are righteous
Learning and knowledge follow.
When the five senses are mastered
Life becomes a pilgrimage.
When the heart is in tune

Then tinkle the dancer's ankle-bells.
What can Yama do
When I am in unison with You?
He who abandons desires,
He is the real *sanyāsī*.
He who has mastered passions
Has become a true yogi.
He who has compassion
Is the true monk,
For he has killed his self without killing himself.
O Nanak, he who knows God's sportive ways
Knows God is One but has many disguises.

(*Āsā*)

simal rukh sarāyā at dīragh at mac

The *simal* tree stands tall and straight
But if one comes to it with hope of gain
What will he get and whither turn?
Its fruit is tasteless
Its flowers have no fragrance
Its leaves are of no use.
O Nanak, it is the lowly that have goodness and true worth.
He that bows before all, before him all will bow.
It is the heavier in the balance that does lower go.
The wicked man bends double as does
The slayer of deer when shooting his dart.
What use is bending or bowing of head
When you bow not the heart?

(*Āsā*)

dīvā balai andherā jāe

When a lamp is lit, darkness is dispelled
Where scriptures are read, evil thoughts expelled.
When the Sun rises, the Moon is not seen
When knowledge comes, ignorance is repelled.
The reading of the Vedas is now a worldly trade
O Pandit you read much, but without thought,
Without understanding this reading is a loss.
Says Nanak, only those the Guru loves will go across.

(*Sūhī*)

man mandar tan ves kalandar

My mind I have made my temple
My body I have dressed in a pilgrim's garb
In my heart are the holy waters in which I bathe.
His word to me is the breath of life
I'll be born no more, I've ended my strife.

My mind is engrossed in the Merciful Lord, O Mother.
Who can know of my heart's sorrow
Except my Lord, I think of no other.

You Who are beyond reach, beyond description, beyond
                                        knowledge.

You Who are limitless
Think of us!

You are spread over the waters
And across the land.
In the spaces between the heavens and the earth
Are You.
In every heart burns Your light.

All teaching, all understanding, all comprehension
All this is as You ordain.
You are the Shade in which we rest
And the mansions we raise.
None other besides You will I ever know, O Master,
For ever shall I sing in praise of You.

Man and beast, all Your shelter seek
You have to look after everyone.
This is Nanak's one prayer and only request
That he look upon Your will as for the best.
                                        (*Bilāval*)

rain gavāī soe ke divas gavāyā khāe

The nights are spent in sleep
The days in seeking food
The priceless gem that is human life

Is bartered away for a worthless shell.
You knew not the name of Rama
This you will regret and life be hell.

You bury your treasure underground
But seek not Him whose treasury is boundless.
Those that spend their days in amassing wealth
Go from the world without it.

If one could get rich by just wanting to be rich
Then everyone would be wealthy.
But fate is settled by divine decree
And that is what we all seek.

O Nanak, those who have toiled
Theirs is the reward.
If one knows not this as the decree of the Master
How can one then hope for His favour?

(Gauṛī Bairāgaṇ)

Bārā Māhā or the Twelve Months

1. <i>cet basant bhalā bhavar suhāvṛe</i>

It is the month of Chet,
It is spring. All is seemly—
The humming bumble bee
And the woodland in flower—
But there is a sorrow in my soul.

The Lord, my Master is away.
If the Husband comes not home, how can a wife
Find peace of mind?

Sorrows of separation waste away the body.
The <i>Koil</i> calls in the mango grove,
Its notes are full of joy.
Why then the sorrow in my soul?

The bumble bee hovers about the blossoming bough,
O mother of mine, it is like death to me,
For there is a sorrow in my soul.

Nanak says: When the Lord her Master comes home to her,
    Blessed is then the month of Chet.

2. *vaisākh bhalā sākhā ves kare*

In beauteous Vaisakh the bough adorns itself anew,
The wife awaits the coming of her Lord,
Her eyes fixed on the door.
"My Love, You alone can help me across
The turbulent waters of life. Come home.
Without You I am worthless as a broken shell.
When You look upon me with favour, Love,
And our eyes mingle;
Then shall I become priceless beyond compare."

Nanak says: "Where seek you the Lord?
Whom are you awaiting?
You have not far to go to find Him.
He is within you, you are His mansion.
If your body and soul yearn for the Lord,
The Lord shall love you and Vaisakh be beautiful."

3. *māh jeṭh bhalā prītam kiuṇ bisrai*

Why forget the Beloved in the month of Jeth
When the land shimmers in the summer's heat?
Grant me the Virtues, O Lord,
As win favour in Your eyes.
You are free from all attachment
And live in Truth.
And I am lowly, humble, helpless.
How shall I approach You?
How find the haven of peace?

Says Nanak: She who knows the Lord
Becomes like the Lord.
She knows Him
By treading the path of virtue.

4. *asāḍ bhalā sūraj gagan tape*

In Asad the Sun scorches.
The sky is hot

The earth burns like an oven,
Waters give up their vapours.
It burns and scorches relentlessly in the month of Asad.

The Sun's chariot passes the noon's sky
The wife watches the shadow creep across the courtyard.
And the cicada calls from the glades.
The beloved seeks the cool of the evening.
If the comfort she seeks be in falsehood,
There will be sorrow in store for her.
If it be in truth,
Hers will be a life of joy.

Says Nanak: Life and life's end are at the will of
                            the Lord
            To Him have I surrendered my soul.

5. *sāvan sars manā ghan varsai*

The season of rain has come.
My heart is full of joy,
My body and soul yearn for the Master.
But He is away in foreign lands
If He return not, I shall die pining for Him.

The lightning strikes terror in my heart.
I am alone in my courtyard
In solitude and sorrow.

O Mother of mine, I stand on the brink of death,
Without the Lord I have no hunger nor sleep
I cannot suffer the clothes on my body.

Nanak says: She alone is blest
                Who becomes One with the Lord.

6. *bhādoṇ bharm bhūlī bhar joban pachtānī*

Lost in the maze of falsehood
I waste my full-bloom youth.
River and land are one expanse of water
For it is the glad season of the rains.

It rains.
The nights are dark.
There is no peace for me.
Frogs croak in contentment.
Peacocks cry with joy.
The *papeeha* calls peeooh, peeooh.
The fangs of serpents that crawl,
The bite of mosquitoes that fly,
Are full of venom.

The seas have burst their bounds in the ecstasy
       of fulfilment.
I alone am bereft of joy,
Whither shall I go?
How shall I find Him?

Nanak says: Ask of the Guru the way
     He knows the path which leads to the Lord.

7. *asun āu pirā sādhan jhūr muī*

O Master come to me,
I waste and will die.
If the Master wills,
I shall meet Him.
If He wills not,
I am lost utterly.
I took the path of falsehood,
And the Master forsook me,
Age has greyed my locks
I have lived many winters
The fires of hell still lie ahead,
And I am afraid.

The bough remains ever green
For the sap that moves within
Night and day, renews life.

If the Name of the Lord courses in your veins,
Life and hope will for ever be green.
Meditate calmly on the Name.
That which ripens slowly ripens best.

Nanak says: Come now, my Love,
Even the Guru pleads for me.

8. *katak kirat paiyā jo prabh bhāe*

What pleases the Lord
Is all I merit.
The lamp of wisdom burns steadily
If the oil that feeds it
Be reality.
If the oil that feeds the lamp be Love
The beloved will meet the Lord and find fulfilment.

Full of faults, she is caught
In the cycle of birth and death
And finds no favour with the Lord.
Good deeds alone will end her sorrow.

Those who are granted the worship of Your Name
Hope to meet You in Your mansion.

Nanak says: O Lord till You grant us Your vision
And break the bonds of superstition,
One watch of day will drag like half a year.

9. *maghar māh bhalā harigun ank smāvai*

The month of Maghar is bliss
To her who is lost in the Lord
For she is the virtuous one
And loves the Lord Eternal.

He Who is eternal, omniscient, wise is also
the Master of destiny.
The world is in turmoil without faith.
She who has knowledge and contemplates on Him
Loses herself in Him.
By His grace she loves the Lord.

Proclaim the name of Rama in song and dance and verse,
And sorrow will flee away.

Nanak says: Only she is loved
               Who prays to her Lord
               With her heart.

10. *pokh tukhār paṛe vaṇ triṇ ras sokhai*

As the winter snow
Freezes the sap in tree and bush,
The absence of the Lord
Blights the body and the soul.
O Lord why do You not come?

He who gives life to the world
Him do I praise through the Guru's word.
His light is in all life born
Of the egg or womb or sweat or seed.
O Merciful Master, O Bounteous You
Grant me Your vision
That I may find salvation.

Nanak says: She who is in love with the Lord
               Is infused with grace.

11. *māgh punīt bhai tīrath aṅtar jāṇiā*

The Lord has entered my being.
I make pilgrimage within myself and am purified.
I met Him.
He found me good
And let me lose myself in Him.

"Beloved! If you find me fair
My pilgrimage is made,
I am cleansed.
More than the sacred waters of Ganga, Yamuna and
               Tribeni mingled at the Sangam;
More than the seven seas,
More than charity, almsgiving and prayer
Is the knowledge of Eternity that is the Lord."

Nanak says: He who has worshipped the Great Giver of life
               Has earned more merit than those who bathe
               at the sixty and eight places of pilgrimage.

12. *phalgun man rehsī prem subhāe*

She whose heart is full of love
Is ever in full bloom.
Joy is hers for she has no love of self.
Only those who love You
Conquer love of self.
Come, Lord, and abide in me.

Many a garment did I wear,
The Master willed not and
His palace was barred to me.
When He wanted me, I went
With garlands and strings of jewels and raiment of
        finery.

Nanak says: A bride welcomed in the Master's mansion
        Has found her true Love.

(Tukhārī)

ANGAD DEV (1504-1552)

There are sixty-two hymns of Angad's in the *Adi Granth*.

akhiṇ bājhoṇ vekhṇā bin kanā suṇanā

To see without eyes,
Without ears, hear,
To walk without feet,
Without hands, work,
To speak without a tongue—
Thus living, yet detached from life.

O Nanak, if you follow the word of your Master
You shall surely meet Him.

AMAR DAS (1479-1574)

There are 907 hymns by Amar Das in the *Adi Granth*.

manmukh lok samjhāyīai kadoṇ samjhāyā jāe

If you preach to the wicked
Can you turn them from their wicked ways?
They will not mingle with the good however much you try
But will tread their own wayward paths
For such is their desert.

There are two ways:
Love of the Lord and love of gold.
By His ordinance alone one finds the right path.
The good conquer their sinfulness
And the touchstone of the Guru's word
Declares them pure.

It is with the mind we must battle,
With the mind we must come to terms
And with the mind make peace.
The mind gets what it wills
By the power of Truth and love of the word.

Drink deep of the nectar that is the Name
And let your deeds be righteous.
If your battles are not with your own mind
But with others
You will have wasted your life.

The wicked surrender to their wilful minds
Their ways are false, their reward evil.
The good win their battles over their minds
For they have their thoughts fixed on God.

Nanak says: The good through Truth attain salvation
The wicked escape not the cycle of birth
and death.

(*Srī*)

māyā kis no ākhīai, kyā māyā karm kamāe?

What is *māyā*? What acts spring from it?
The snare of joy and sorrow in which our lives are caught,

The thought of self that moves us to action.
Without the word there is no wisdom,
Nothing to tear apart *māyā's* veil of illusion,
Nothing to exorcise the ego.
Without love you cannot be a devotee,
Without the word, you will find no rest.
It is the word alone that conquers self
And destroys illusion.
The pious receive the gift of the Name
By gentle ways and good conduct.

Without the Guru one cannot tell
The good from the bad.
Without goodness, prayer has no meaning.
If God is in the heart
He can be met face to face.
He comes as gently as comes sleep.

O Nanak, raise your voice in praise of the Guru
By His grace you shall attain salvation.

(Srī)

kajal phūl tambol ras

She put black in her eyes, flowers in her hair,
With betel leaves sweetened her breath and her lips stained;
But the Lord came not to her bed
All her adornments were in vain.

Woman and man who just live together, speak not of
                  them as truly wed,
When in two bodies a single light burns, then are
                  man and woman truly wed.

Without the fear of the Lord
One cannot be a true devotee
For one has no love of the Name.
Love is born on meeting the true Guru.
Fear and love together give the proper hue
They kill the hunger of the ego
And with His Name, body and soul imbue.
Body and Soul thus cleansed, made of beauty rare
Give to the Lord, the Destroyer of Evil.

Both fear and love to him the Lord does give
Who in this world do truthfully live.

(Sūhī)

RAM DAS (1534-1581)

There are 679 hymns by this guru in the *Adi Granth*.

gur satgur kā jo sikh akhāe

He who would call himself the disciple of the Guru, the
              True Guru,
Should rise early and meditate on Hari who is God.
He should bathe in the "nectar-pool"
And labour during the day.
He should hear the words of the Guru his teacher
And repeat the names of Hari
For then will his sins be forgiven him and his
              suffering cease.
As the day advances, let him sing the hymns of the Guru
And keep the Lord in his mind in all he does.
He that repeats the name of Hari with every breath
And with every morsel that he eats
He is the real Sikh, him the Guru loves.
He to whom the Lord is gracious
Listens to the Guru's teaching and becomes his disciple.
Nanak, your servant begs for the dust of the feet of Sikhs
Who worship and lead others to the path of worship.

(Gauṛi Vār)

mero sundar kaho milai kit galī?

What shall I do to meet my Love?
O you who worship Him show the way
Let me follow in your footsteps.
The path that leads to Him is of obedience to Love's
              commandments,
Of treasuring them in the heart.
They matter not: your untidy scattered locks,
Your short stature, your bent and ugly body.

· 360 ·

If you find favour in His eyes
You shall be beautiful and sit beside Him.

Our Lord is the One Lord
And we his consorts.
She who His beloved is
Is the best of wives.

O Nanak, why need you bother yourself
If the Lord wills, He will show the way.
(Dev Gaṅdhārī)

ARJUN DEV (1563-1606)

The Guru's 2,218 hymns form the largest single contribution in the *Adi Granth*.

prīt lagī tis sac sioṇ marai nā āvai jāe

I love Him who is the Truth.
He dies not; nor is reborn to die again.
I flee from Him but He does not forsake me,
He is in all our hearts.

He knows the sorrows of the poor,
He destroys their pain and suffering,
He upholds those who serve Him.

This wondrous form is the Formless One
The Guru took me to meet Him, O Mother.

Listen, my brothers, befriend Him
Shun the love that is *māyā's* snare
For none that love *māyā* are happy.

He knows all
He is the Great Giver
He is serene
He is charitable
He is the true friend and helper
He is very great
He towers above all
And is limitless.

He has no childhood, no old age
His Court and His Commandments are Eternal.
What we beg, He grants.
He is the hope of those without hope.

One vision of Him destroys all sin
And our soul and body find tranquility.
With single-mindedness meditate on the One
And the mind's illusions will be dispelled.

He is the treasury of goodness
Ever youthful He is
And full of charity.
Worship Him all the time
Forget Him not night or day.

Those who are His chosen
Are befriended by Him.
I dedicate my body, soul, and my possessions,
And sacrifice my life to Him.

He sees and hears all
He dwells in the recesses of our hearts.
Even the ones who show Him no gratitude
Are helped by Him.
Nanak's God is ever forgiving.

(Srī)

jā ko muskal at banai dhoī koi nā deī

When troubles come and you have no one to turn to
When enemies are at your heels and your kinsmen desert you
When hope is fled, all hope shattered
Let your thoughts turn to Him who is your Maker
And no ill wind will harm you.

The Master is the strength of the feeble.
He does not come and go, He is forever where He is.
The Guru's words shall reveal the truth to you.

When you are weak and frail,
Without clothes, without food,

When no one drops a coin in your apron
Nor gives you comfort.
When no one helps you and you succeed not in your actions
Let your thoughts turn to Him who is your Maker
And your affairs will forever go well.

When cares crowd upon you
When your body is foul with disease
When you are obsessed with thoughts of your wife and
    your kinsmen
Are sometimes happy and sometimes sad,
When restless and agitated you wander in all directions
Without a moment's rest, without a moment's sleep
Let your thoughts turn to Him who is your Maker,
And your body and mind will forever be whole.

When lust, anger, and attachment have you captive
And full of greed you are ever wanting, covetous,
When you have committed the four sins
(Drunk wine, thieved, fornicated, and killed)
And in the company of devils have become a devil,
When neither books of wisdom nor songs nor hymns of praise
Fall upon your ears
Let your thoughts turn to Him who is your Maker
And in the twinkling of an eye will you be saved.

Books of wisdom you might know by heart, and recite
Prayers and practise the penances of the Yogis, all
    pilgrimages undertake
And twice perform the six good acts
(Learn and impart learning to others,
Sacrifice and make others give in sacrifice
Give alms and accept charity),
Bathe in holy water and do worship.
If you love not the Lord with all your being,
It is all in vain and for you there is nothing but hell.

Empires, kingdoms, and baronies may be yours
And the wherewithal of power and pleasure.
You may own orchards, beautiful and bountiful,
And have power over others without any limit

And indulge in sports and pastimes to keep yourself amused.
If your thoughts turn not to Him who is your Maker
Yours will be the rebirth as a serpent.

You may have much wealth,
Live well and have gentle ways
Love deep your mother and father, sons, brothers and friends,
Own armies of footmen and archers, and many to bow to
    you in salutation,
Many to shout "Long may you live."
If your thoughts turn not to Him who is your Maker
You shall surely be dragged down to hell.

Your body may be free of fever and without sores,
Your mind free of cares and affliction.
Without ever the thought of death
Night and day you may enjoy yourself
And take everything as your own
Without any reserve or hesitation.
If your thoughts turn not to Him who is your Maker
For you will be the servitude of hell's demons.

Those to whom the Creator is merciful
Are given the company of holy men,
The more they are with such companions
The more they love Him.
He is the Lord of good and evil
There is none other than Him.

O Nanak, only by His Grace will you find Him,
The True Guru, whose Name is Truth.

(Srī)

    tūn peṛ sākh terī phūlī

       You are the tree,
       And the world its branches.
       You were unknown
       And You made Yourself manifest.
       You are the ocean,
       You the bubbles, You the foam;
       There is nothing that is without You.

You are the string,
You the beads strung on it;
You the knot and the central bead of the rosary.
The beginning and the end and the middle
Are You; none else is there beside You.

You are *nirgun*, transcending all attributes,
You are *sargun*, teeming with attributes,
You are the Giver of all joy,
You are without desire
Yet the passionate colouring in all desire
You symbolize.
You alone know Your ways
You alone comprehend Yourself.

You are the Lord
You His servitor
You the secret, You its revelation.
Nanak, your servant, shall ever sing of You
If You grant him a little grace.
                                                    (*Mājh*)

tūn merā pitā, tūn hain merā mātā.

You are my Father
You my Mother
You are my Kinsman
And my Brother.
Everywhere You are my Protector
What reason have I to harbour fear?

By Your grace I recognise You.
You are my Support
You are my Pride
I know of no other beside You.
The world is but an arena for Your sport.

You are the Creator of life and matter
The Dispenser of all destiny.
All that comes to pass is by Your decree;
We have no hand in the performance.

Those that have pondered on Your nature
Have found great bliss.
By singing Your praise
My heart has found peace and comfort.
O Nanak, the Almighty Guru Himself rejoices,
Since you have won the great battle.

(Mājh)

kin bidh kusal hot mere bhāi

Tell me brother, how does one find peace?
How to find the God, Rama, who is our help?
Māyā has spread its net everywhere to catch us.
There is no happiness in the home of the humble
Nor in the lofty mansions of the rich.
In false pursuits we waste our lives
We joy in the possession of horses and elephants
In armies and ministers and retinues of servants,
Thus do we put the halter round our necks
And fasten the noose of the "I am."
We wander in all directions seeking power
We sport in the company of damsels
And being beggars
Dream ourselves to be kings.
One truth has the True Guru told me
What the Lord does His followers should accept as the best.

Nanak, the servant, says: By killing thoughts of self and
merging in Him
Is found peace, O brother of mine.
Only thus we find God who is Rama.

(Gauṛī Guāreṛī)

anik jatan nahi hot chuṭkārā

It is not through trickery that one gets release
However many the tricks one tries.
Much learning only increases the load of sorrows.
It is only service and the love of God
That takes one with honour to His Court.
O Soul of mine! if you make the name of the Lord
your shelter
No ill-wind shall harm you.

As the sight of a boat on stormy seas
As the light of a lamp in the dark
As the warmth of fire in winter's cold
Does prayer bring solace to the soul.

The thirst of your soul will be quenched
Your hopes fulfilled
Your mind will cease to wander
For nectar is the name of the Lord
And the friendship of godly men.
The healing balm of prayer is given only to him
To whom the Lord is gracious and grants the boon.
Those whose hearts echo the name of the Lord Hari
Their sorrow and pain, O Nanak, are banished.

(Gauṛī Guāreṛī)

bhuj bal bīr brahma sukh sāgar

O Lord of Mighty Arms,
Creator of all things,
O Ocean of peace!
Take me by my hand and raise me
Who am fallen in a pit.

My ears hear not
My eyes have lost their light
I am crippled, afflicted
Like a leper I come stumbling to Your door
And cry for help.

You are the Lord of the fallen
Above You there is no Lord
O Compassionate One,
You are my Companion, Friend, Father and Mother.
Let Nanak bear the imprint of Your feet in his heart.
Let Your saints ferry me across the fearful ocean of
    life. (Gauṛī)

jeh man mai karat gumānā

When man has pride in his heart
He wanders around like one possessed.

When he is like dust under the feet of others
He then knows that God is in every heart.
The reward of humility is knowledge of the gentle path
It is the gift the True Guru gave me.

When a man looks down upon others as lowly
He becomes full of fraud and deceit,
When he has no care of "mine" and "thine"
Then none bears him ill-will.

When he claims "this is mine" and "this too is mine,"
His troubles weigh heavy on him,
When he recognizes Him Who is his Creator
Then he is not burnt with envy.

When he is bound by bonds of desire
He comes and goes and is under the eyes of Yama,
When he has shaken off all delusion
God holds back no secrets from him.

If he keeps secrets from the Lord
Then for him is pain, suffering and punishment,
When he recognises Him as One, the Only One
He comprehends all he needs to know.

When he madly seeks wealth
He is neither satisfied nor is his craving lessened,
When he frees himself of such desires
Then Lakshmi, the lotus goddess of wealth, walks in
　　his train.

If by His Grace he meets the True Guru
In the temple of his heart the lamp is lit,
When he is indifferent to victory and defeat
Then alone he knows the Truth.

He alone is the Doer, He alone makes us do
He has wisdom, thought and discretion
He is not far, He is not near
Yet He is with everyone.
Says Nanak, worship the Truth with all your heart.
                                    (*Gauṛī Guāreṛī*)

prithmai tyāgi haumai rīt

I discarded the love of self
And the ways of the world,
I gave up distinction between friend and foe
And was blessed with knowledge to recognise the godly.
In the cave of *sahaj* I sat in meditation
Saw the light, heard divine music
And pondered over the word in utter bliss.
I was the blessed bride taken by the Lord.
Nanak, your servant who has thought much about this, says:
He who listens and then acts
Lands safely on the other shore.
For him there is no more birth and death, no more coming and
    going.
With the Hari he is one forever.

(Āsā)

guṇ avguṇ mero kachu nā bicārio

My merits and demerits You did not reckon
Nor looked upon my face, complexion or adornment.
I knew no winsome ways nor manner of deportment
But You took me by the hand and drew me to Your bed.
Listen my friends—My Groom has become my Master
He puts his hand upon my forehead and calls me His own.
What know the foolish men of the world?
Now has my union been consummated
My Groom knows my sorrows and has dispelled them.
The moonlight shines in my courtyard
Night and day I live in ecstasy with my Love.
My raiments are redder than the rose
I glitter with jewels and garlands of flowers.
My Love looks at me and I have the wealth of the world.
I have no fear of the wicked demons.
I am eternally happy and full of joy—
I have found Truth in my home.
Says Nanak: She who has adorned herself for the Lord
Hers is the true consummation.

(Āsā)

jaise kirsān bovai kirsānī

As a farmer sows his field
And mows it at his will
Be it green or ripe,
So does the Lord take at His will
All that is born
And dies.
Only the worshipper of Govind is immortal.
The day is followed by the night
The night passes and comes the dawn,
But the wretched sleep in *māyā's* delusion,
Only the rare ones are roused
By the Grace of the Guru.
O Nanak, forever sing praise of the Lord
It cleanses the heart and illumines the face.

(Āsā)

jan tūn sāhib tān bhau kehā

What fear have I when You are my Master,
Who else shall I worship?
If I have You I have everything,
I look to no other.
Lord, much venom have I seen in the world,
You are my Shepherd, my Protector,
Your Name is my comfort
You know the anguish in my heart
To whom shall I tell my sorrow?
Without Your Name the world is in turmoil,
Only those who take Your Name find peace.
What shall I say? Who will listen to me?
The Lord alone can speak.

You are the Maker.
Forever and ever You are my hope,
In making me great, You magnify Your greatness,
Now and always it is You I will worship.

Nanak's Lord is the constant Giver of Joy.
His Name is my only strength.

(Āsā)

Śubh ciṅtan gobiṅd ramaṇ, nirmal sādhū saṅg

O Lord, grant me these: purity of thought,
Will to worship, company of godly men,
And the power never to forget You for even a moment.

The night is damp with drops of dew
Stars twinkle in the sky,
Those beloved of the Lord are risen
For those the Lord loves are ever awake.
Night and day His Name is on their lips
In their hearts rest His lotus feet
Their thoughts never stray from Him.

Abandon pride and lust, they silt the mind
And smother it in the smoke of sorrow.
Nanak says, Those that love the Lord are ever awake.

(*Āsā*)

merī sejaṛye aḍambar baṇiyā

Upon my bed I awaited His coming,
My heart leaped with joy when I heard His footsteps.
He came to me, He Who is my Lord and Master.
My desires were fulfilled, I was with joy replete.
He took me in His arms, limb to limb we lay
And my anguish was gone.
My life, my soul, my body were all refreshed.
My wishes were granted; I worshipped Him.
Blessed was the hour I met Him.
Says Nanak: I have met the Lord of Lakshmi
          And joy all is mine.

My companions ask me, by what signs did I know He was
          my Master?
Filled with ecstasy, I could not utter a word in reply.
His goodness is profound and hidden.
Even books of wisdom know not His dimensions.
With love worship Him and meditate on His Name
And ever let your voice be raised in His praise.
Our Lord is with virtues replete, His knowledge is
          supreme and complete.

Says Nanak, she who is filled with His love
Goes gently to His bed to rest.

(Āsā)

nadi tarandṛi maiṇdā khoj nā khumbe

Deep the waters of the stream,
I cannot swim, my feet no foothold find.
I shall ferry across for I am full of love
On the Lord's feet is fixed my mind.
O Nanak, My love is the Boatman.

Only them will I call my friends
At whose sight evil thoughts disappear;
I have sought them over all the world,
O Nanak, such men are very rare.

Let the Master be in your thoughts,
His worshippers have seen Him.
Keep the company of godly men
Then shall your sorrows end, your heart be clean.

The saintly break the fetters
At their sight devils scatter and hide,
They make us fall in love with Him
By Whose Will we all abide.

High is His seat, the highest of all;
It is beyond reach, there is nothing beyond it.
Day and night your hands in prayer join
With every breath bring the Lord to mind.
If He be gracious, He shall grant us the company of the godly.

(Gujrī)

bār vidānṛe humas dhumas

Dense and terrifying is the forest,
Petrifying the stillness before the storm,
Screams of terror assail the wayfarers' ears.
You are our Leader; I hold tight the rope and follow
And thus, O Nanak, traverse the wild woodland.

· 372 ·

Those in whose company our voices rise in prayer
Are verily our true companions.
O Nanak, shun the friendship of those
Who think of nothing but themselves.

That time is auspicious when we enter the presence
      of the True Guru
When we befriend the godly and sorrows do not assail us
When we find blessed rest and escape the cycle of birth
      and death;
For then we see the One Creator wherever we turn our gaze
We know the supreme wisdom of turning our thoughts on God
We know that the best speech is the words of prayer
We know His commandments and find joy in submission.
Such the Lord treasures, for such are of the true mint.

(Gujrī)

bājīgar jaise bājī pāe

As a performing juggler
Acts many parts, wears many disguises
And takes off his mask when the show is done
So is our Creator one, the only One.

What forms he brings into being
And then does banish?
From whence do they come
Where do they vanish?
Countless waves rise from the waters
Many an ornament is made from gold,
Whenever a seed is sown,
It ripens into many fruits, though the seed is one.

The same Light of Heaven is reflected in water
In a hundred pitchers contained,
The pitchers may burst
But the light remains.

Māyā deludes, it creates greed and desire,
When freed of delusion we see
The Creator is One.

· 373 ·

He is immortal, He does not die
He did not come, He will not go.
I have met the Guru
He cleansed my mind of the ego.
Says Nanak: So was I saved
              Thus did I achieve supreme salvation.
                      (*Sūhī*)

umkio hīo milan prabh tāīṇ

My heart leaped up to behold the Lord
I heard of His coming, in my heart made His cot,
I went out to meet my Beloved
I wandered everywhere but saw Him not.

O poor heart, how wilt thou get peace of mind?
I will give my life if the Lord I find.

One couch is spread for the Lord and wife.
She slumbers, Her Lord awaits ever awake
But like one drunk she sleeps.
If the Lord embrace her, she too will wake.

I am without hope, many days have passed
In many lands and continents did I seek Him.
I cannot live if I clasp not His blessed feet
If He be kind, my fortune will turn and we shall meet.

He was good and gave me the company of the true
And my restless wanderings did then cease.
In my house I found my Lord
All my adornments do Him please.

Says Nanak: The Guru has lifted illusion's veil.
Whichever way I turn, O brother, I see my Lord
The doors of ignorance are thrown asunder
The restless mind has ceased to wander.
                      (*Sūhī*)

ghar meh ṭhākar nadar nā āvai

The Master is in the home, but we do not see Him
His image in stone round our necks we wear
Deluded by *māyā* everywhere we wander
Churn water in hope of butter, kill ourselves with care.

The stone that we the Master call
That stone itself will be our fall.

Sinners we are, to our Master's salt untrue
We cannot cross in a boat that of stone is made.
Nanak met the Guru and then knew his Master
He pervades the earth, the sky and water.

(Sūhī)

ek rūp saglo pāsārā

He is One but does in all things pervade
He is the merchandise, His is the trade.
This truth only the rare ones learn
He is present whichever way we turn.

He has many hues, yet He is of one colour
He is the water and the wave
He is the temple and is the God therein
He is the priest, He is the prayer
He is the yogi, He is the Yoga.
The Lord of Nanak in all things you see
Yet the Lord is from all things free.

(Bilāval)

mrit maṇḍal jag sājiyā

The world He created as a house of slaughter
Like castles of sand children make, it lasts not long
It rots as paper under the drip-drop of water.

See for yourself, in your mind weigh:
Yogis, men of action, and householders,
Have left their homes and belongings and gone their way.

As a dream at night, the world is such
And all you see must perish.
O Fool, why love you this world so much?

Open wide your eyes, see and learn:
Your friends and brothers in the shade are gone,
Some have left, others await their turn.

Only those who have served the Lord absolute
Find their places at Hari's gates
They stand firm (and will not be turned away).

Nanak is the servant of the Lord
O destroyer of Evil, protect him.

(*Bilāval*)

prabh ji tūṇ mere prāṇ adhāre

O Lord, You are the hope of my life,
You I greet, before You I prostrate myself
To You I offer salutations, to You I make sacrifice.

Seated or standing, in sleep or in waking
My thoughts ever turn to You.
My sorrows and joys, all that passes in my heart
I bring to You.

You are my support, my strength, my knowledge,
My wealth are You and all the kinsmen I have.
Says Nanak: What You do is for the best
He finds peace at the sight of Your feet.

(*Bilāval*)

hamro subhāo sadā sad bhūlan

It is in our nature ever to sin,
And in Yours to redeem us.

(*Bilāval*)

TEGH BAHADUR (1621-1675)

115 hymns of the Guru were incorporated in the *Adi Granth*
by his son and the last guru, Gobind Singh.

birthā kahoṇ kaun sioṇ man kī

Whom shall I tell of the anguish of my heart?
Greed has me in its hold.
I rush madly in the ten directions
Seeking gold.

I suffer much wanting life of ease
And serve all kinds of people,
And like a dog go from door to door
But I have no thought of prayer.
I waste my human existence,
I have no shame when people laugh at me.
O Nanak, why sing you not in praise of the Lord
And rid your mind and body of impure thoughts?

(*Āsā*)

jo nar dukh mai dukh nahī mānai

He who in adversity grieves not
He who is without fear
He who falls not in the snare of sensuality
Who has no greed for gold knowing it is like dust.
He who does not slander people when their backs are turned
Nor flatters them to their faces.
He who has neither gluttony in his heart
Nor vanity nor attachment with worldly things.
He whom nothing moves,
Neither good fortune nor ill,
Who cares not for the world's applause,
Nor its censure,
Who ignores every wishful fantasy
And accepts what comes his way as it comes.
He whom lust cannot lure
Nor anger command,
In such a one lives God Himself.
On such a man does the Guru's Grace descend,
For he knows the righteous path.
O Nanak, his soul mingles with the Lord
As water mingles with water.

(*Soraṭh*)

APPENDIX 6

TREATY OF LAHORE, 1809, BETWEEN THE BRITISH GOVERNMENT AND THE RAJAH OF LAHORE

WHEREAS certain differences which had arisen between the British Government and the Rajah of Lahore have been happily and amicably adjusted, and both parties being anxious to maintain the relations of perfect amity and concord, the following Articles of Treaty, which shall be binding on the heirs and successors of the two parties, have been concluded by Rajah Runjeet Singh, on his own part, and by the agency of Charles Theophilus Metcalfe, Esquire, on the part of the British Government.

ARTICLE 1. Perpetual friendship shall subsist between the British Government and the State of Lahore. The latter shall be considered, with respect to the former, to be on the footing of the most favored powers; and the British Government will have no concern with the territories and subjects of the Rajah to the northward of the River Sutlej.

ARTICLE 2. The Rajah will never maintain in the territory occupied by him and his dependents, on the left bank of the River Sutlej, more troops than are necessary for the internal duties of that territory, nor commit or suffer any encroachments on the possessions or rights of the Chiefs in its vicinity.

ARTICLE 3. In the event of a violation of any of the preceding Articles, or of a departure from the rules of friendship on the part of either State, this Treaty shall be considered to be null and void.

ARTICLE 4. This Treaty, consisting of four Articles, having been settled and concluded at Umritsur, on the 25th day of April 1809, Mr. Charles Theophilus Metcalfe has delivered to the Rajah of Lahore a copy of the same in English and Persian, under his seal and signature, and the said Rajah has delivered another copy of the same, under his seal and signature; and Mr. Charles Theophilus Metcalfe engages to procure, within the space of two months, a copy of the same duly ratified by the Right Honourable the Governor-General in Council, on the receipt of which by the Rajah, the present Treaty shall be deemed complete and binding on both parties, and the copy of it now delivered to the Rajah shall be returned.

SEAL AND SIGNATURE OF   SIGNATURE AND SEAL OF
C. T. METCALFE.   RAJAH RUNJEET SINGH.
COMPANY'S SEAL   (SIGNED) MINTO.

Ratified by the Governor-General in Council on the 30th May 1809.

APPENDIX 7

TRIPARTITE TREATY OF 1838

WHEREAS a Treaty was formerly concluded between Maharajah Runjeet Singh and Shah Shooja-ool-Moolk, consisting of fourteen Articles, exclusive of the preamble and the conclusion, and whereas the execution of the provisions of the said Treaty was suspended for certain reasons, and whereas at this time Mr. W. H. Macnaghten having been deputed by the Right Honourable George Lord Auckland, G.C.B., Governor-General of India, to the presence of Maharajah Runjeet Singh, and vested with full powers to form a Treaty in a manner consistent with the friendly engagements subsisting between the two States, the Treaty aforesaid is revived and concluded with certain modifications, and four new Articles have been added thereto, with the approbation of, and in concert with, the British Government, the provisions whereof, as contained in the following eighteen Articles, will be duly and faithfully observed.

ARTICLE 1st. Shah Shooja-ool-Moolk disclaims all title on the part of himself, his heirs, successors and all the Suddozais to all the territories lying on either bank of the River Indus, that may be possessed by the Maharajah, viz., Cashmere, including its limits E.W.N.S., together with the Fort of Attok, Chuch, Hazara, Khebel, Amb, with its dependencies on the left bank of the aforesaid river, and on the right bank Peshawur, with the Eusufzai Territory, Kheteks, Hisht Nagar, Meehnee, Kohat, Hungoo, and all places dependent in Peshawur, as far as the Khyber Pass, Banno, the Viziri Territory, Dowr Tank, Gorang, Kalabagh, and Khushalgher, with their dependent districts, Derah Ismail Khan and its dependency, together with Derah Ghazee Khan, Kot Mithan, Omarkote, and their dependent territory, Singher, Heren, Dajel, Hajeepore, Rajenpore, and the three Ketches, as well as Mankera with its district, and the Province of Multan situated on the left bank. These countries and places are considered to be the property and to form the estate of the Maharajah—the Shah neither has nor will have any concern with them. They belong to the Maharajah and his posterity from generation to generation.

ARTICLE 2nd. The people of the country on the other side of Khyber will not be suffered to commit robberies or aggressions, or any disturbances on this side. If any defaulter of either State, who has embezzled the Revenue, take refuge in the territory of the other, each party engages to surrender him, and no person shall obstruct the passage of the stream which issues out of the Khyber defile, and supplies the Fort of Futtehgurh with water, according to ancient usage.

ARTICLE 3rd. As agreeably to the Treaty established between the British Government and the Maharajah, no one can cross from the left to the right bank of the Sutlej without a passport from the Maharajah, the same rule shall be observed regarding the passage of the Indus, whose waters join the Sutlej, and no one shall be allowed to cross the Indus without the Maharajah's permission.

ARTICLE 4th. Regarding Shikarpore and the Territory of Sinde on the right bank of the Indus, the Shah will agree to abide by whatever may be settled as right and proper in conformity with the happy relations of friendship subsisting between the British Government and the Maharajah through Captain Wade.

ARTICLE 5th. When the Shah shall have established his authority in Cabool and Candahar, he will annually send the Maharajah the following articles, viz. fifty-five high-bred Horses of approved color and pleasant paces, eleven Persian Scimitars, seven Persian Poignards, twenty-five good Mules, Fruits of various kinds, both dry and fresh, and Sirdas or Musk Melons, of a sweet and delicate flavour (to be sent throughout the year), by the way of Cabool River to Peshawur, Grapes, Pomegranates, Apples, Quinces, Almonds, Raisins, Pistahs or Chestnuts, an abundant supply of each, as well as pieces of Satin of every color, Choghas of fur, Kinkhabs wrought with gold and silver, and Persian Carpets, altogether to the number of one hundred and one pieces. All these articles the Shah will continue to send every year to the Maharajah.

ARTICLE 6th. Each party shall address the other on terms of equality.

ARTICLE 7th. Merchants of Affghanistan who will be desirous of trading to Lahore, Amritsur, or any other part of the Maharajah's possessions, shall not be stopped or molested on their way; on the contrary, strict orders shall be issued to facilitate their intercourse, and the Maharajah engages to observe the same line of conduct on his part, in respect to traders who may wish to proceed to Affghanistan.

ARTICLE 8th. The Maharajah will yearly send to the Shah the following articles in the way of friendship, fifty-five pieces of Shawls, twenty-five pieces of Muslin, eleven Dopattahs, five pieces of Kinkhab, five Scarves, five Turbans, fifty-five loads of Bareh Rice (peculiar to Peshawur).

ARTICLE 9th. Any of the Maharajah's Officers who may be deputed to Affghanistan to purchase horses or on any other business, as well as those who may be sent by the Shah into the Punjaub for the purpose of purchasing Piece Goods or Shawls, etc. to the amount of eleven thousand rupees, will be treated by both sides with due attention, and every facility will be afforded to them in the execution of these commissions.

ARTICLE 10th. Whenever the armies of the two States may happen to be assembled at the same place, on no account shall the slaughter of kine be permitted to take place.

ARTICLE 11th. In the event of the Shah taking an auxiliary force from the Maharajah, whatever booty may be acquired from the Barakzais, in jewels, horses, arms, great and small, shall be equally divided between the two contracting parties. If the Shah should succeed in obtaining possession of their property without the assistance of the Maharajah's troops, the Shah agrees to send a portion of it by his own agent to the Maharajah in the way of friendship.

ARTICLE 12th. An exchange of missions charged with letters and presents shall constantly take place between the two parties.

ARTICLE 13th. Should the Maharajah require the aid of any of the Shah's troops "in furtherance of the objects contemplated by this Treaty," the Shah engages to send a force commanded by one of his principal officers; in like manner the Maharajah will furnish the Shah, when required, with an auxiliary force composed of Mahomedans, and commanded by one of his principal officers, as far as Cabool, in furtherance of the objects contemplated by this Treaty. When the Maharajah may go to Peshawur, the Shah will depute a Shahzadah to visit him, on which occasions the Maharajah will receive and dismiss him with the honor and consideration due to his rank and dignity.

ARTICLE 14th. The friends and enemies of each of the three high powers, that is to say, the British and Sikh Governments and Shah Shooja-ool-Moolk, shall be the friends and enemies of all.

ARTICLE 15th. Shah Shooja-ool-Moolk engages, after the attainment of his object, to pay without fail to the Maharajah the sum of two lakhs of Rupees of the Nanukshahie or Kuldar currency, calculating from the date on which the Sikh troops may be despatched for the purpose of reinstating His Majesty in Cabool, in consideration of the Maharajah's stationing a force of not less than five thousand men, Cavalry and Infantry, of the Mahomedan persuasion, within the limits of the Peshawur Territory, for the support of the Shah, and to be sent to the aid of His Majesty, whenever the British Government, in concert and counsel with the Maharajah, shall deem their aid necessary; and when any matter of great importance may arise to the westward, such measures will be adopted with regard to it as may seem expedient and proper at the time to the British and Sikh Governments. In the event of the Maharajah requiring the aid of any of the Shah's troops, a deduction will be made from the Subsidy proportioned to the period for which such aid may be afforded, and the British Government holds itself responsible for the punctual payment of the above sum annually to the Maharajah so long as the provisions of this Treaty are duly observed.

ARTICLE 16th. Shah Shooja-ool-Moolk agrees to relinquish for himself, his heirs, and successors, all claims of supremacy and arrears of tribute over the country now held by the Ameers of Sinde (and which will continue to belong to the Ameers and their successors in perpetuity), on condition of the payment to him by the Ameers of such a sum as may be determined under the mediation of the British Government, fifteen lakhs of such payment being made over by him to Maharajah Runjeet Singh. On these payments being completed, Article 4 of the Treaty of the 12th of March, 1833, will be considered cancelled, and the customary interchange of letters and suitable presents between the Maharajah and the Ameers of Sinde shall be maintained as heretofore.

ARTICLE 17th. When Shah Shooja-ool-Moolk shall have succeeded in establishing his authority in Affghanistan, he shall not attack or molest his nephew, the ruler of Herat, in the possession of the territories now subject to his Government.

ARTICLE 18th. Shah Shooja-ool-Moolk binds himself, his heirs, and successors to refrain from entering into negotiations with any Foreign State, without the knowledge and consent of the British and Sikh Governments, and to oppose any power having the design to invade the British or Sikh Territories by force of arms to the utmost of his ability.

The three Powers, parties to this Treaty, viz. the British Government, Maharajah Runjeet Singh and Shah Shooja-ool-Moolk, cordially agree to the foregoing Articles. There shall be no deviation from them, and in that case the present Treaty shall be considered binding for ever, and this Treaty shall come into operation from and after the date on which the seals and signatures of the three contracting parties shall have been affixed thereto.

Done at Lahore, this 26th day of June, in the year of Our Lord 1838, corresponding with the 15th of the month of Asark, 1895—Era of Bikarmajit.

Signed and sealed this 25th day of July, in the year A.D. 1838, at Simla.

(SIGNED) AUCKLAND.

SEAL OF THE GOVERNOR GENERAL	SEAL AND SIGNATURE OF RUNJEET SINGH	SEAL AND SIGNATURE OF SHAH SHOOJA-OOL-MOOLK.

BIBLIOGRAPHY

GURMUKHI

Amol, S. S. *Sāde Purāne Kavi*
Arjun, Guru, *Ādi Granth*, 1604 (See Appendix 2)

Gaṇḍā Singh, *Mahārājāh Kauṛa Mall Bahādur*, Amritsar 1941
  Sikh Itihās Bāre, Amritsar 1942
  Sikh Itihās Val, Lahore 1945
  Panjāb diāṇ Vārāṇ, Lahore 1946
Gobind Singh, Guru, *Dasam Granth* or *Dasveṇ Pādśāh kā
  Granth* (See Appendix 4)
Gur Bilās Chevīṇ Pādśāhī (Biography of Guru Hargobind)
Gurdās Bhallā, Bhāī, *Vārāṇ*, c. 1600 (see Appendix 3)
Gurdit Singh, Gyānī, *Jīvan Sandeś*, May 1951
Gyān Singh, Gyānī, *Panth Prakāś*, Amritsar 1880
  Tawārīkh Guru Khālsā, Amritsar
  Nirmal Panth Pradīpkā, Sialkot 1892

Harinder Singh Roop, *Bhāī Gurdās*
Harnām Singh Ballabh, Gyānī, *Śri Daśmeś Kāvya Pradīp*

Janamsākhī (See Appendix 1)
Jodh Singh, Bhāī, *Prācīn Biṛaṇ Bāre*

Kāhan Singh, *Gur-Śabd Ratnākar Mahāṇ-koś*: Encyclopaedia
  of Sikh Literature, 4 vols., Patiala 1931
  Gurumat Prabhākar
  Gurumat Sudhākar
Karam Singh, *Mahārājāh Ālā Singh*, Taran Taran 1918
  Bandā Bahādur, Amritsar 1907
  Mahārājāh Raṇjīt Singh
  Kattak ke Baisākh, 1912
  Pahlā Ghallūghārā
  Gurpurb Nirnai
Kesar Singh Chibbar, *Bansāvalīnāmā Dasāṇ Pādśāhīāṇ dā*,
  1780
Kohli, Sītā Rām, *Mahārājāh Raṇjīt Singh*, Delhi, 1953

· 385 ·

Manī Singh, *Bhagat Ratnāvalī*

Pothi Itihās, MSS 1779
Prem Singh, *Mahārājāh Raṇjīt Singh*
  Navāb Kapūr Singh
  Bābā Phūlā Singh Akālī
  Sardār Harī Singh Nalvā, 1937
  Khālsā Rāj de Usāriye

Rahatnāmās, by Chaupā Singh, Nand Lāl "Goyā," Desā
  Singh, Prahlād Singh, Sumer Singh, and others.
Rām Sukh Rāo, *Jassā Singh Binod*, Kapurthala MSS
Raṅdhāwā, M. S., *Punjāb* (Bhāśā Vibhāg), Patiala 1961
Ratan Singh Bhaṅgū, *Prācīn Panth Prakāś*, Amritsar 1914

Sainā Pat, *Srī Gur Sobhā*, Amritsar 1925
Santokh Singh, *Srī Gurpratāp Sūraj Granth*, otherwise known
  as *Sūraj Prakāś*, ed. by Bhāī Vīr Singh, Amritsar 1934
  Nānak Prakāś, 1823
Sarūp Dās, *Mahimā Prakāś*, MSS 1773
Singh, G. B., *Srī Guru Granth Sāhib dīāṇ Prācīn Biṛaṇ*,
  Lahore
Sohan Singh, *Bandā Singh Bahādur*
Sukhā Singh, *Gur Bilās Dasvīṇ Pādśāhī*, Lahore
Sumer Singh, *Pothī Gur Bilās kī*, Lahore 1882
Sūraj Singh, Gyānī, *Vaḍā Khālsā Sidq*, Amritsar
Sūraj Singh and Darbārā Singh, *Itihās-i-Rāmgaṛhīāṇ*, Lahore
  1915

PERSIAN

Abdul Karīm Kashmīrī, *Ibrat Miqāl*, MSS 1816 (Punjab Pub-
  lic Library, Lahore)
Ahmed Shāh Batālīā, *Tawārīkh-i-Hind*, MSS 1818
  Zikr-i-Guruāṇ vā Ibtidā-i-Singhāṇ vā Mazhab-i-Eshāṇ
Ahvāl-i-Salātīn Hind, MSS 1822 (Khuda Baksh Library, Patna)
Aliuddīn, *Ibrat Nāmā*, MSS 1854 (India Office Library, Lon-
  don)
Amar Nāth, Divān, *Zafar Nāmā-i-Raṇjīt Singh*, Lahore 1928
Amīnuddaulāh, *Ruqqāt-i-Amīn-ud-Daulāh*, MSS 1712-1718
Ānand Rām Mukhlis, *Tazkirā-i-Ānandrām*, MSS 1748

Bābar, *Bābar Nāmā* or *Tuzuk-i-Bābarī* (Translated by Leyden & Erskine), Oxford 1821

Bahādur Shāh Nāmā, MSS (Translated by Elliot and Dowson in *History of India*)

Ba<u>kh</u>t Mall, *<u>Kh</u>ālsā Nāmā*, MSS 1814 (Punjab University Library, Lahore)

Ba<u>kh</u>tāvar <u>Kh</u>ān, *Ibrat Maqāl, Tawārī<u>kh</u>-i-Muhammad Muazzam Bahādur Shāh <u>Gh</u>āzī*, MSS 1717 (Punjab Public Library, Lahore)

Beale, T. W. and Munshī Dānīshvar, *Miftah-ut-Tawārī<u>kh</u>*, Cawnpore, 1867-1868

Behārī Lāl-bin-Badrī Dās, *Ahvāl-i-Najīb-ud-Daulāh-va-Alī Muhammad <u>Kh</u>ān-va-Ḍonḍe <u>Kh</u>ān*, MSS 1787 (Khalsa College, Amritsar)

Budh Singh, *Risālah-i-Nānak Śāh*, MSS 1785 (Bodleian, Oxford)

Bute Shāh, *Tawārī<u>kh</u>-i-Punjāb*, MSS 1848 (Punjab Public Library, Lahore)

Daulat Rāi, *Mīrāt-i-Daulat-i-Abbāsī*, MSS 1846 (J. N. Sarkar Collection)

Delhi Chronicle, *Vāqa-i-Shāh Ālam Sānī*, MSS 1738-1798

Ganeś Dās Vadherā, *Risālah-i-Sāhib Numā* or *Cahār Gulśan-i-Punjāb*, MSS 1855 (Khalsa College, Amritsar)

Ghulām Alī <u>Kh</u>ān, *Imādus-Saādat*, Cawnpore 1864

Ghulām Hussain <u>Kh</u>ān, *Siyār-ul-Mutā<u>kh</u>erīn*, Calcutta 1836

Ghulām Hussain Samīn, *Halāt-i-Andān-i-Ahmed Shāh Durrānī dar Hindustān*, MSS (Khalsa College, Amritsar) (Part Translation in *Indian Antiquary of 1907* by W. Irvine)

Ghulām Jilānī, *Jang-i-Multān*

Ghulām Muhiuddīn, *Zafar Nāmā-i-Muīn-ul-Mulk*, MSS 1749 (Khalsa College, Amritsar)

Hairat Dehlvī, Mirzā, *Hayāt-i-Taiyabā*

Imāmuddīn, *Husain Shāhī*

Irādat <u>Kh</u>ān, *Tazkirā-i-Irādat <u>Kh</u>ān*, MSS 1716 (Punjab Public Library, Lahore) (English Translation in S. Scott, *History of the Deccan*)

Jehāngīr, *Tuzuk-i-Jehāngīrī* (Translated by Rogers & Beveridge)

Kāmvar Khān, Mohammed Hādī, *Tazkirā-us-Salātīn Chughtiyā*, MSS 1724 (Khuda Baksh Library, Patna)

Kanhayā Lāl, *Zafar Nāmā-i-Raṇjīt Singh*, Mustafi Press, Lahore 1876

Khāfī Khān, Mohammed Hashim, *Muntakhib-ul-Lubāb*, Calcutta 1874

Khushāl Chand, *Tawārīkh-i-Mohammed Shāhī* or *Tawārīkh-i-Bahādur Shāhī*

Khushvaqt Rāi, Kitāb-i-Tawārīkh-i-Punjāb, MSS 1812 (Punjab Public Library, Lahore)

Mohammed Ahsān Ijād, *Farrukh Siyār Nāmā*, MSS (British Museum, London)

Mohammed Harīsī, Mirzā, *Ibrat Nāmā*, MSS 1719 (Khuda Baksh Library, Patna)

Mohammed Qāsim, *Ibrat Nāmā*, MSS 1720 (Punjab Public Library, Lahore)

Muhsin Fānī, *Dabistān-ul-Mazāhib*, Calcutta 1809 (Translated by Dr. Ganda Singh as well as D. Shea and A. Troyer)

Murasalāt-i-Ahmad Shāh Durrānī, 1762 (Khalsa College, Amritsar)

Qāzi Nūr Mohammed, *Jang Nāmā*, 1765 (Translated by Dr. Ganda Singh)

Shāh Navāz Khān, *Maāsir-ul-Umarā*, Asiatic Society, Calcutta 1889

Sohan Lāl Sūrī, *Umdāt-ut-Tawārīkh*, 5 Vols., Lahore 1889 (Translated in part by V. S. Suri, S. Chand & Co., Delhi, 1961)

Sujān Rāi Bhaṇḍārī, *Khulāsat-ut-Tawārīkh*, Delhi 1918

Tahmāsp Khān Miskīn, *Tazkirā-i-Tahmāsp*, MSS 1779 (Khalsa College, Amritsar)

Tawārīkh-i-Ahmad Shāhī, MSS 1754 (Translated by J. N. Sarkar)

Tawārīkh-i-Ālamgīr Sānī, MSS 1759 (Khalsa College, Amritsar) (Translated by J. N. Sarkar)

Tawārikh-i-Khāndān-i-Mahārājāh Karam Singh-va-Khāndān-i-Phulkīān, MSS (Punjab Archives)
Totā Rām, *Gulgaśt-i-Punjāb*, MSS 1864 (Punjab Archives)

Yār Mohammed Qalandar, *Dastūr-ul-Inshā*, MSS 1710 (Khuda Baksh Library, Patna)

ENGLISH

Aitchison, C. U., *Collection of Treaties and Engagements and Sanads Relating to India and Neighbouring Countries*, Calcutta 1892-1893
Akbar, Muhammad, *The Punjab under the Mughals*, Ripon Press, Lahore 1948
Ali, Abdul, *Notes on the Life and Times of Ranjit Singh*, London Historical Records Commission
Ali, Shahamat, *History of Bahawalpur*, John Murray 1848
Sikhs and Afghans, John Murray, 1847
Amar Singh Vasu, *Life of Guru Angad*, 1927
Andrew, W. P., *The Indus and Its Provinces: Their Political and Commercial Importance*
Archer, J. C., *The Sikhs in Relation to Hindus, Muslims, Christians and Ahmadiyyas: a Study in Comparative Religion*, Princeton 1946
Archer, Major, *Tours in Upper India and in Parts of the Himalayan Mountains*, London 1833
Ashta, D. P., *Poetry of the Dasam Granth*. Arun Prakashan, Delhi 1959
Asiatic Annual Register
Atkinson, James, *The Expedition into Afghanistan*, Allen & Co. 1842
Attar Singh, *Sakhee Book*, Benares 1873
Travels of Guru Tegh Bahadur & Guru Gobind Singh (Translated from Ghulam Hussain Khan), Allahabad 1876
Auckland, Lord, *Private Letters. 1836-1842*, MSS British Museum, London
Autar Singh Sandhu, *General Hari Singh Nalwa*, Lahore 1936

Bamber, C. J., *Plants of the Punjab*, Govt. Printing Press, Lahore 1916

Banerjee, I. B., *Evolution of the Khalsa*, 2 vols., Mukerjee & Co., Calcutta 1947

Bannerji, S. N., *Ranjit Singh*, Lahore 1931

Baqir, Muhammad, *Lahore Past and Present*, Punjab University Press, Lahore 1952

Barr, Wm., *Journal of a March from Delhi to Peshawar and from thence to Kabul including Travels in the Punjab*, James Madden 1844

Basham, A. L., *The Wonder that was India*, Grove Press 1954

Bentinck's Papers, Lord William

Bingley, Capt. A. H., *Sikhs*, Govt. Printing Press, Calcutta 1918

Boolchand, Dr. N. W., *Question of Indian History, 1798-1830*

Boulger, D. C., *Lord William Bentinck*, Clarendon Press, Oxford 1897

Browne, Major James, *History of the Origin and Progress of the Sikhs*, London 1788

Burnes, Alexander, *Travels into Bokhara*, 3 vols., Murray 1834
Sindh and Afghanistan, Calcutta 1839
Correspondence (privately printed)
Reports and Papers: Political, Geographical and Commercial, Calcutta 1839
On the Political Power of the Sikhs beyond the Indus, Calcutta 1839

Bute, Marchioness of (ed.), *Private Journal of the Marquess of Hastings*, 2 vols., 1858

Calendar of Persian Correspondence, Vols. I-X, National Archives of India

Caroe, Olaf, *The Pathans*, Macmillan, London 1958

Chatterjee, G. C., *The Punjab Past and Present*, 1939

Chhabra, Dr. G. S., *Advanced Study in the History of the Punjab*, 2 vols., Sharanjit, Ludhiana 1961

Chhajju Singh, *The Ten Gurus and Their Teachings*, Lahore 1903

Chopra, Gulshan Lall, *Punjab as a Sovereign State, 1799-1839*, Lahore 1928

Commonwealth Relations Office (late India Office) unpublished records: Bengal judicial, political, public, and secret consultations and records; Home miscellaneous series

Compton, H., *A Particular Account of the European Military Adventurers of Hindustan from 1784-1803*, Fisher Unwin 1892

Connolly, A., *Journey to the North of India*, 2 vols.

Correspondence of Sir George Russel Clerk, 1831-1843, Historical Interpretation, P.G.R.O.

Cotton, J. J., *Life of General Avitabile*, Calcutta 1906

Court, Henry, *History of the Sikhs*, Lahore 1888

Cunningham, J. D., *History of the Sikhs*, First edition, 1849; Second edition 1853

Dardi, Dr. Gopal Singh, *Translation of the Adi Granth*, 4 vols., Gur Das Kapur 1960

Douie, Sir James, *The Punjab, North West Frontier Province and Kashmir*, Cambridge 1916

Dowson, J., *Classical Dictionary of Hindu Mythology and Religion*, Kegan Paul 1928

Dunbar, Janet, *Golden Interlude*, John Murray, London 1955

Eden, Emily, *Up the Country*, 2 vols., Richard Bentley, London 1866
  Miss Eden's Letters edited by her great niece Violet Dickinson, London 1919

Edwardes and Garrett, *Mughal Rule in India*, 1930

Elliot, H. M. and Dowson, J., *History of India as told by its own Historians*, 8 vols., 1867-1877

Elphinstone, Mountstuart, *An Account of the Kingdom of Cabul*, 2 vols., 1839

Falcon, F. W., *Handbook on the Sikhs*

Fane, H. E., *Five Years in India*, 2 vols., London 1842

Farooqi, B. A., *British Relations with the Cis-Sutlej States 1809-1823*, P.G.R.O. 1941

Field, Dorothy, *Religion of the Sikhs*, London 1914

Fleury, C., *Notices Historiques sur le General Allard et sur le Royaume de Lahore*, Paris 1836

Forster, G., *A Journey from Bengal to England through North India, Kashmir, Afghanistan and Persia into Russia, 1783-1784*, 2 vols., London 1798

Forster, Wm., *Early Travels in India, 1583-1619*, Oxford 1921

Francklin, W., *History of the Reign of Shah Aulum*, Cooper and Graham 1798
  Military Memoirs of George Thomas, Calcutta 1803

Fraser, J. Baillie, *The Military Memoirs of Lt.-Col. James Skinner*, 2 vols., Smith Elder & Co., London 1851

Fraser-Tytler, Sir Kerr, *Afghanistan: A Study in Political Developments in Central Asia*, Oxford 1953

French, Charles J., *Journal of a Tour in Upper Hindustan Prepared During the Years 1838 and 1839*, 1854

Ganda Singh, *Ahmed Shah Durrani*
  Banda Singh Bahadur, Amritsar 1935
  Ranjit Singh, death centenary volume edited by Ganda Singh, Amritsar 1839

Gardner, A., *Memoirs of Alexander Gardner*, London (re-edited 1898)

Garrett, H. L. O. and G. L. Chopra, *Events at the Court of Ranjit Singh*, P.G.R.O. 1935

Gazetteers of India, Imperial, Oxford 1908

Geographical, Statistical, and Historical Account of the Country between the Sutlej and Jumna, Oriental Press, Calcutta 1839

Geographical Memoir, Territories ceded by Shuja to Ranjit, 1839

Gordon, J. H., *The Sikhs*, Blackwood, London 1904

Greenlees, Duncan, *Gospel of the Guru Granth Sahib*, Madras 1952

Grey, C. and Garrett, H. L. O., *European Adventurers of Northern India 1785-1849*, Punjab Govt. 1929

Griffin, Lepel H., *Ranjit Singh*, Oxford 1905
  Rajas of the Punjab, Lahore 1870

Griffin and Massey, *Chiefs & Families of Note in the Punjab*, 2 vols. and appendix, 1909

Gupta, Hari Ram, *Studies in Later Mughal History of the Punjab*, Lahore 1944
  History of the Sikhs, Vol. I, 1739-1768, Calcutta 1939
  Cis-Sutlej Sikhs, Vol. II, 1769-1799, Minerva, Lahore 1944
  Trans-Sutlej Sikhs, Vol. III, 1769-1799, Minerva, Lahore 1944
  Marathas and Panipat, Punjab University 1961

Harlan, J., *Memoir of India and Afghanistan*, Philadelphia, 1842
  Central Asia, 1823-1841, London 1939

Havelock, H., *Narrative of the War in Afghanistan in 1838-1839*, London 1840

Holman D., *Sikander Sahib*, Heinemann 1960

Honigberger, J. M., *Thirty-Five years in the East*, H. Bailliere, London 1852

Hough, Major Wm., *Political and Military Events in British India in 1756-1849*, 2 vols., 1853

Hügel, Baron Charles, *Travels in Kashmir and the Punjab*, John Petheram, 1845

Hutchison and Vogel, *History of the Punjab Hill States*, 2 vols., Govt. Printing Press, Lahore, 1933

Ibbetson, D. C., *Punjab Castes*, Govt. Printing Press, Lahore 1916
The Religion of the Punjab, Calcutta 1883

Ikram, S. M. and Percival Spear, *The Cultural Heritage of Pakistan*, Oxford 1955

Indian Historical Records Commission

Irvine, W., *The Later Mughuls*, Calcutta 1922

Jacquemont, Victor, *Letters from India describing a Journey in the British Dominions of India, Tibet, Lahore and Cashmeer*, 2 vols., Edward Churton, London 1835

Kacker, Hansraj, *The Punjab 1792-1849*, Moon Press, Agra 1916

Kartar Singh, *Life of Guru Nanak*, Amritsar 1937
Life of Guru Gobind Singh, Amritsar, 1933

Kaye, J. W., *The Life & Correspondence of Charles Lord Metcalfe*, 2 vols., Smith Elder & Co., 1858
History of the War in Afghanistan, 3 vols., R. Bentley, London

Khazan Singh, *History and Philosophy of the Sikh Religion*, 2 vols., Lahore 1914

Khushwant Singh, *The Sikhs*, Allen & Unwin, London 1953
Japji: Sikh Morning Prayer, Probsthain, London

Kiernan, V. G., *Metcalfe's Mission to Lahore 1808-1809*, Lahore 1943

Kirpal Singh, *Maharajah Ala Singh*, Khalsa College, Amritsar

Kohli, Sita Ram, *Catalogue of Khalsa Durbar Records*, 2 vols., Govt. Press 1927

Lakshman Singh, Bhagat, *A Short Sketch of the Life and Work of Guru Gobind Singh*, Lahore 1909
Sikh Martyrs, Madras 1928

Latif, Syed Mohammed, *History of the Punjab*, Central Press, Calcutta 1891
 Lahore—Its History, Architectural Remains & Antiquities, Lahore 1892
 Early History of Multan, Lahore 1891
Lawrence, Major H. M. L., *Adventures of an Officer in the Punjaub*, 2 vols., H. Colburn, London 1846
Lockhart, Dr. L., *Nadir Shah*, London 1938
Loehlin, Rev. C. H., *The Sikhs and their Book*, Lucknow Publishing House 1946

Macauliffe, M. A., *The Sikh Religion*, 6 vols., Oxford 1909
MacNicol, N., *Indian Theism from the Vedic to the Mohamadan period*
Malcolm, Sir John, *A Sketch of the Sikhs*, London 1812
Masson, Charles, *Narrative of Various Journeys in Baluchistan, Afghanistan and the Punjab*, 3 vols., R. Bentley 1842
Medlicott, H. B., *Sketch of the Geology of the Punjab*, Calcutta 1888
M'Gregor, W. L., *History of the Sikhs*, 2 vols., James Madden, London 1846
Minto, Countess of, *Lord Minto in India, 1807-1814*, 1880
 Life and Letters of the First Earl of Minto, 1807-1814, Longmans Green 1880
Mohan Lal, *Life of Amir Dost Mohammed Khan of Kabul*, London 1846
 Journal of a Tour through the Punjab, Afghanistan, Turkestan etc., Longman Green 1834
Mohan Singh, *History of Punjabi Literature*
 Guru Gobind Singh as a Poet
Moorcroft and Trebeck, *Travels in the Himalayan Provinces of Hindustan and the Punjab, in Ladakh and Kashmir, in Peshawar, Kabul, Kunduz and Bokhara*, 2 vols., John Murray 1837
Murray, Wm., *History of the Punjab*, 2 vols., William Allen 1846

Nair, Lajpat Rai, *Fakir Azizuddin*, Ilmi Markaz, Lahore
 Sir Wm. Macnaghten's Correspondence relating to the Tripartite Treaty, 1942

Narang, Sir Gokul Chand, *Transformation of Sikhism* (5th edition), New Book Society 1960

National Archives of India (late Imperial Record Dept.) Unpublished Records: Foreign Dept., Secret & Political Consultations

Nizami, Khaliq Ahmed, *The Life and Times of Farid-ud-Din Ganj-i-Shakar*, Muslim University, Aligarh 1958

Orlich, Leopold Von, *Travels in India including Sind and the Punjab*, 2 vols., Longmans 1845

Osborne, W. G., *Court and Camp of Ranjit Singh*, London 1840

Panikkar, K. M., *The Founding of the Kashmir State*, Allen & Unwin, London 1953

Payne, C. H., *A Short History of the Sikhs*, Nelson & Sons, London

Press list of Old Records in the Punjab Civil Secretariat, 9 vols., Lahore 1915

Prinsep, H. T., *The Origin of the Sikh Power in the Punjab*, Calcutta 1834

Punjab and N. W. Frontier of India by an old Punjaubee, London 1878

Punjab Government Records, Vol. I (Delhi Residency & Agency 1807-1857), Lahore 1911

Punjab Government Records, Vol. II (Ludhiana Agency 1808-1815), Lahore 1911

Qanungo, K. R., *History of the Jats*, Calcutta 1925

Radhakrishnan, Sir S., *The Hindu View of Life*, Allen & Unwin, London
Indian Philosophy, 2 vols., Allen & Unwin, London 1923

Ramakrishna, L., *Les Sikhs*, Paris 1933
Punjabi Sufi Poets, Oxford, 1938

Ram Dyal, *Life of Bhai Nand Lal*, 1923

Rashid, Abdur, *Najibuddaulah* (translation of an Account by Sayyad Nuruddin Husain), Cosmopolitan, Aligarh 1952

Ritchie, A. T. and R. Evans, *Lord Amherst*, Clarendon Press 1894

Ross, David, *Land of the Five Rivers*, London 1893

Sarkar, J. N., *Fall of the Mughal Empire*, 4 vols., Calcutta 1949-1950
History of Aurangzeb, 5 vols.
Scott, G. B., *Religion and Short History of the Sikhs*, London 1930
Seagrim, D., *Notes on Hindus and Sikhs*
Sethi, R. R., *Lahore Durbar, 1823-1840*, P.G.R.O. 1950
Sewa Ram Singh, *A Critical Study of the Life and Teachings of Guru Nanak*, Rawalpindi 1904
The Divine Master, Lahore 1930
Shastri, Prakash, *Organisation Militaire des Sikhs*, Librairie Russe, Paris 1932
Sher Singh, *Philosophy of Sikhism*, Sikh University Press, Lahore 1944
Thoughts on Symbols in Sikhism, Lahore 1927
Shungloo, K., *Metcalfe Mission* (unpublished thesis, Punjab University)
Sinha, N. K., *Rise of the Sikh Power*, Calcutta 1946
Ranjit Singh, University of Calcutta 1933
Smyth, Major Carmichael, *History of the Reigning Family of Lahore*, Calcutta 1847
Sohan Singh, *The Seekers Path*, Orient Longmans 1959
Spear, Percival, *Twilight of the Mughuls*, Cambridge 1951
Steinbach, Lt.-Col., *The Punjaub: being a brief account of the country of the Sikhs*, Smith & Elder, London 1845
Stulpnagel, C. R., *The Sikhs*, Lahore 1870
Suri, V. S., *Some Original Sources of Punjab History*
Swynnerton, The Rev. Charles, *Romantic Tales from the Punjab*, Archibald Constable & Co., 1903

Tara Chand, *Influence of Islam on Indian Culture*, Allahabad 1954
Teja Singh (and Ganda Singh), *Short History of the Sikhs*, Orient Longmans, India 1950
Teja Singh, *Sikhism: Its Ideals and Institutions*, Bombay 1938
Essays in Sikhism, Lahore 1945
The Growth of Responsibility in Sikhism, Amritsar 1928
The Psalm of Peace, Oxford 1938
Temple, R. C., *The Legends of the Punjab*, 3 vols., Bombay Education Society

Thompson, Edward, *Life of Charles, Lord Metcalfe*, London 1937

Thorn, Major Wm., *Memoirs of the War in India conducted by General Lord Lake, Major General Sir Arthur Wellesley, Duke of Wellington*, T. Egerton, Military Library, Whitehall 1818

Thornton, T. H., *History of the Punjab*, 2 vols., London 1846

Trevaskis, H. K., *The Land of the Five Rivers*, Oxford 1928

Trotter, L. J., *Earl of Auckland*, Oxford 1893

Trumpp, Ernest, *The Adi Granth*, London 1871

Unesco, *Sacred writings of the Sikhs*. Anthology of Translation. Allen & Unwin, London, 1960

Vigne, G. T., *Travels in Kashmir, Ladakh, Iskardo etc.*, London 1844
A Personal Narrative of a Visit to Ghazni, London 1840

Wade C., *Report on the Punjab and Adjacent Provinces forming the territories of Maharajah Ranjit Singh together with a historical sketch of that Chief*. MSS.

Warren Hastings Correspondence, MSS British Museum

Wheeler, J. T., *Early Records of British India*, Saunders, Otley & Co., London 1878

Wheeler, Sir R. E. Mortimer, *The Indus Civilisation*. *Five Thousand Years of Pakistan*

Wolff, Rev. Joseph, *Travels & Adventures*, 2 vols., Saunders, Otley & Co., London 1860-1861

INDEX

Abdul Ahad Khan, 173, 175
Abdul Haye, Maulvi, 271
Abdus Samad Khan, 112-16, 120, 128n
Adi Granth, Granth Sahib or Granth, vi, 23n, 53n, 54, 62, 88, 94, 97, 125n, 129, 145, 146, 289, 294, 302, 312; resemblance to the Old Testament, 34n; Arjun compiles anthology, 58; seen by Akbar, 58, 311; description, 59; Ram Rai asked to explain a passage, 69n; Mani Singh prepares final recension, 80n, 93; guruship invested in the Granth by Gobind Singh, 81, 87, 95; Gobind Singh's version lost in Vada Ghalughara, 154n; contradicts janamsakhis, 299; Nanak's compositions, 6, 7, 29, 38, 40, 42-44, 45n, 47n, 301, 324-57; composition of, 304-9; Gurdas the amanuensis, 310; controversy regarding Farid's hymns, 319-21; Japji, 324-41; Bara Maha, 351-57; hymns of Nam Dev, 321; of Kabir, 321-24; Angad, 357; Amar Das, 358-60; Ram Das, 360-61; Arjun, 59, 62, 361-76; Tegh Bahadur, 376-77
Adina Beg Khan, 137, 143; governor Jullundur Doab, 130; defeated at Hoshiarpur, 132; besieges Ram Rauni, 134; character, 134n; advises action against the Afghans, 138; slays Sikh pilgrims, 139; assigns revenue to the Sikhs, 140; position in the Punjab, 141; outwitted by Mughlani, 142; allies himself with the Sikhs, 146; invites the Marathas, 147; acquires power, 148; death, 148
Adyars, 20, 22, 23
Afghanistan, vi, 3, 11-13, 30, 131, 141, 164, 191, 196, 200, 235, 251, 252, 254, 264, 294n; Abdali recalled by internal disturbances, 156; Zaman

recalled, 190, 192, 195; Franco-Russian menace, 220, 221; Burnes' mission, 277, 287; Shah Shuja tries to recover his throne, 280-81, 287-88; Ranjit Singh apprehensive of British policy, 284; revised British policy, 287-88; see also Ahmed Shah Abdali, Barakzais, Jahan Khan, Saddozais, Shah Mahmud, Shah Shuja, Shah Zaman, Taimur, Azim Khan, Dost Mohammed, Fateh Khan
Africa, east, v, 21
Africa, south, v
Agra, 55, 71, 73, 94, 180, 191, 211, 310
Ahluwalia Misl, 132, 142, 147, 171, 182, 189; see also Jassa Singh
Ahmed Shah Abdali, 141, 152, 161n, 169, 170, 182, 187, 190, 205, 207n, 235, 237n; effect of invasions, vi, 128n; invited by Shah Nawaz, 130; first invasion 1747, 131, 133; second 1748, 135-36; third 1751, 137-39; Treaty of 1752, Kashmir annexed, 139; invited by Mughlani, 142; by the Mughal emperor and Najibuddaulah, 143; fourth invasion 1756, 143-45; enters Delhi, 143; takes Sirhind, 144; harassed by the Sikhs, 144-45, 151, 159-60; assigns the Punjab to Taimur, 145; blows up the Harimandir, 145, 154, 158; fifth invasion 1759, 149-51; battle of Panipat, 150; sixth invasion 1762, 153-56; Vada Ghallughara, 153-54; courts Marathas and Mughal emperor, recaptures Kashmir, 155; battle of Amritsar, 155-56; seventh invasion 1764, 157-60; honours Ala Singh of Patiala, 159; eighth invasion 1766, 163-66; offers subedari of Lahore to Lehna Singh, 164; gives Amar Singh of Patiala district of Sirhind, 165; ninth inva-

sion 1769, 167; achievements, 167-68

Ajit Singh, son of Gobind Singh and Mata Sundari, 51, 81, 90, 91

Ajit Singh, adopted son of Mata Sundari, 102n, 103n

Akalgarh, 199, 216n

Akalis, 215n, 229n, 294

Akal Takht, 63, 123

Akbar, *see* Mughal emperor

Akbar Shah, Syed, 262, 272

Akhnur, 217, 239

Ala Singh of Patiala, 124, 133, 144, 151, 154, 159

Alamgir II, *see* Mughal emperor

Alexander, 11

Alexander, Tsar, 220

Ali Makhdum Hujwiri, 27

Aligarh, 150, 172

Allah, 24, 26

Allahabad, 71, 169

Allard, Jean François, 258-60, 263, 272, 273

Alvars, 20, 22, 23, 175

Amar Das, 97n, 122n, 310; family tree, 51; character and achievements, 52-54; fixes first of Baisakh for annual gathering, 54; chooses Ram Das, 55; son passes collection of hymns to Arjun, 58, 304; hymns, 306, 358-60

Amar Singh of Patiala, 165, 173, 175

Amar Singh Thapa, 190, 214

Ambala, 142, 144, 225

Amherst, Lord, *see* governor general

Amir Khan, 211

Amritsar, 61n, 65, 67, 122, 133, 134, 148, 152, 154, 162, 196, 204, 209, 233, 310; new name given, 57; Arjun compiles Adi Granth, 58, 304; Lohgarh built, 63; Mughal garrison, 120; biennial meetings, 121; central Sikh fighting force billetted, 123; Zakarya Khan sends large force, 124; Khalsa resume pilgrimage, 126; Lakhpat Rai wreaks vengeance, 129; building of Ram Rauni, 130; important Baisakh gathering, 132; headquarters of

Dal Khalsa, 141-42; Afghan attacks, 145, 158, 164-65; battle of, 155-56; misl representatives appointed, 161; in the hands of the Bhangis, 171, 189; Shah Zaman's invasions, 192-93; meeting of Sikh chiefs hostile to Ranjit Singh, 197-98; capture of the city by Ranjit Singh, 206-7; Lake's pursuit of the Marathas, 211-12; Ranjit Singh's finances managed by banking house, 217; Malwai chiefs summoned by Ranjit Singh, 222; Metcalfe joins Ranjit Singh's camp, 226; commotion caused by Mohran, 227n; treaty of 1809 discussed and signed at, 229-30; clash between Shia Muslims and Akalis, 229; British delegation, 268; public works, 270; *see also* Hariman-dir, Gobindgarh, Ram Rauni

Anandpur, 73, 77n, 78, 79, 81, 314; built by Tegh Bahadur, 71; Tegh Bahadur's head cremated by his son, 74, 76; Gobind Singh builds chain of fortresses, 80; spends 12 years in intellectual activity, 80; baptism of the five chosen ones, 82-86; baptism of 20,000 Sikhs, 86, 89; encircled by hill chiefs, 90; besieged by Mughals, 91; Adina Beg Khan slays Sikh pilgrims, 139; taken by Mohkam Chand, 220; British concede Durbar claim, 279; Gobind Singh inserts his father's compositions in the Adi Granth, 305; most of the Dasam Granth compiled, 313, 315, 316

Angad, 44n, 53, 97n, 299-300, 301-6, 310; Nanak chooses Lehna and calls him Angad, 36, 49; character and achievements, 50, 52; hymns, 357

Anglo-Gurkha war, 248

Anglo-Sikh war, 207n, 218n

Anirodh Chand, 232, 269

Arabia, 17, 20; Arabian Sea, 249; Arabs, 13, 20, 21

Arjun, 28n, 63, 64, 77, 97n, 98, 302,

308, 311; family tree, 51; invested as fifth guru, 55-56; completes the building of Harimandir, 56; compiles the Adi Granth, 58, 301, 304-6, 309; meets Akbar, 59, achievements, 56-59, 62; pays homage to Khusrau, fined by Jehangir, 60; tortured and put to death, 60, 61, 312; hymns, 61, 361, 376; relationship with Gurdas, 310

army, British, 207, 221, 225, 227, 228n, 279, 288

army, Maratha, 149, 284

army, Punjabi, 219, 259; militias of dispossessed chieftains incorporated, 205; reorganisation, 207-9, 258, 260-62; Dallewalia forces incorporated, 216; call to arms during Metcalfe mission, 227; at Kangra, 232-33; Multan, 236, 250, 251; in Kashmir, 239, 240, 246, 247, 254, 255; battle of Attock, 242, 243; administration, 248; service offered to Gurkhas, 248; Ramgarhia forces taken over, 249; in the northwest, 253, 254, 257; battle of Naushera, 262-65; loss of Punjabi generals, 265-66; battle of Jamrud, 285-86; army of the Indus, 288, 295; estimate, 295

Aryans, 5, 10, 11, 13, 14n, 15, 18

Assam, 33, 37, 72

Ata Mohammed Khan, 236, 238, 240

Attariwalas, 261

Attar Singh Ahluwalia, 263

Attar Singh Dhari, 236

Attock, 236, 246, 251n, 252, 254; taken by the Bhangis, 171; fort handed over by Jahan Dad Khan, 240-41; battle of, 242-43

Attock, river, 196, 239, 253, 263

Auckland, Lord, see governor general

Aurangabad, 136, 141

Aurangzeb, see Mughal emperor

Avitabile, Paolo de, 260, 270

Azim Khan, Mohammed, 246, 247, 254, 262-64; family tree, 238, governor of Kashmir, 241; plot to invade Punjab, 244n; see also Barakzais

Azizuddin, Fakir, 202; sketch, 198; sent to Kasur, 215; Metcalfe mission, 224, 227; fort of Attock handed over by Jahan Dad Khan, 241; reception at Peshawar, 262; negotiates with Dost Mohammed Khan, 281-82; present at negotiations on Sindh, 284; British proposal to put Shah Shuja back on the throne, 287; on Ranjit Singh, 291, 294

Babar, see Mughal emperor

Bagarian family, 68n

Baghdad, 33, 34, 302

Baghel Singh, 173, 175, 177, 179, 180

Bahadur Shah, see Mughal emperor

Bahadur Singh Hindustani, 270

Bahawalpur, 169, 201, 225, 237n, 248, 252, 276; Dera Ghazi Khan assigned to the Nawab, 255-56

Bala Sandhu, 29n, 299-302, 312

Balbhadra, General, 263, 264

Baluchis, 12, 157, 158, 234

Baluchistan, vi, 3, 8, 21, 256

Banda, 59n, 120, 121, 122n, 162, 183, 312; charged by Gobind Singh to avenge his sons, 101-2; issues proclamation of protection, 103; takes Samana, 104; battle of Sirhind, 105-6; strikes new coins, 107; seizes Jullundur and Hoshiarpur, 108; revolt spreads over Majha, 109; retreats to the mountains, 110-11; Mukhlisgarh besieged, 112; besieged at Gurdaspur, 113-15; captured and sent to Delhi, 115-16; executed, 117; achievements, 117-19

Barakzais, 235, 237, 240, 241, 252, 278, 281, 282; family tree, 238

Bari Doab, 4n, 124, 129, 139

Barlow, Sir, George, see governor general

Basohli, 170, 217, 233

Bassawan, Colonel, Shaikh, vii, 288, 295

Batala, 30, 109, 111, 113, 140, 204, 256

Beas, river, 3, 4n, 5n, 68n, 133, 165, 194n; Arjun builds Sri Hargobindpur, 57; Darius' invasion, 11; Lake pursues Holkar, 211-12; territories of Sada Kaur's brother-in-law seized, 234

Benares, 33, 57, 71, 80, 311, 321

Bengal, 24, 33, 72, 120, 173n, 309

Bentinck, Lord Wm., see governor general

Bhag Singh of Jind, 228; joins the imperial forces and encircles Patiala, 175; letter from Perron, 210n; espouses cause of Nabha, 213; given Ludhiana, 214; delegation of Malwais visit Delhi, 222

Bhagavad Gita, 4n, 23

Bhakkar, 256, 257

Bhaktas, 23-29, 37, 39, 41, 43, 46, 53, 306, 307

Bhakti, 22, 23, 44

Bhanga Singh of Thanesar, 175, 180, 181

Bhangani, 78, 79, 317

Bhangi misl, 150, 160, 207n; Dal divided into misls, 132; takes Rechna and Chaj Doabs, 142; helps Marathas take Sirhind, 147; helps Sukerchakias take two doabs, 155; defeats Jahan Khan, 156; takes Lahore, 161; Multan taken, 169, 190; holds Multan, Lahore, and Amritsar, 171; Jammu bone of contention, 171, 182, 183; most powerful misl, Ranjit Singh decides to break them, 189; combines with other misls against Ranjit Singh, 197; promises Shah Zaman support, 199; Multan retaken, 205; all forts taken by Nuruddin, 234; see also Hari Singh, Gujjar Singh, Lehna Singh, Jhanda Singh, Ganda Singh, Gulab Singh

Bhani, daughter of Amar Das, 51, 53

Bharatpur, 14n, 162

Bhasin, village, 198, 206

Bhawani Das, 217

Bhim Chand, Raja, 78, 79, 90, 91, 111, 132

Bhimbar, 239, 248, 255

Bilaspur, 78, 79, 90, 91, 111; Raja of, 65, 67

Binod Singh, 114

Birbal Dhar, Pandit, 254

Bolan Pass, 3, 249

Bradford, Sir Thomas, 274

Brahma, 18, 85, 97n

Brahmins, 13, 19, 43, 46, 53, 54, 56n, 73n, 97, 289

Brindaban, 143

British policy: not to extend their power beyond the Ganges, 169, 178-79; give protection to the Nawab Wazir of Oudh, 178; Hastings keeps Sikhs and Marathas divided, 178-80; policy reversed, 191; decide to circumscribe Shah Zaman's influence, 199-200; not to make any more annexations, 212-220; steps taken to meet Franco-Russian menace, 221; Metcalfe mission, 221-31; Ranjit Singh's and the company's attitude to the Malwais, 219-31; Rajputs and Gurkhas, 232; the Multanis, 235; open negotiations with Sindh, 265; Fateh Singh seeks protection, 266-67; opening up of the Indus, 274-77; troops moved to Ferozepur, 279; the Afghans, 283-84, 287-88; see also East India Company

Buddha, Gautama the, 19

Buddha, Bhai, 63, 301, 302; proclaims Angad second guru, 49; invests Arjun as fifth, 55; shows Akbar the Adi Granth, 58; appointed first granthi, 58, 304; asked to instal Hargobind, 61; looks after the affairs of the community, 66, 311

Buddhism, 19, 20, 25, 29n, 33n; Buddhists, 13, 22, 41n

Budh Singh Sandhawalia, 272

Budh Singh Singhpuria, 234

Budh Singh Sukerchakia, 187, 188

Budha Dal, *see* Khalsa
Burma, v; Burmese, 265
Burnes, Alexander, 274-76, 287

Calcutta, 229, 231n, 278, 294n
Cambay, Gulf of, 20, 21
Canada, v
Central Asia, 206, 249
Ceylon, 33; king of, 33n
Chaj Doab, 3n, 142, 155
Chamba, 111, 170, 217, 233
Chamkaur, 91, 279
Chand Kaur, 27n
Chandu Shah, 61n
Charhat Singh Sukerchakia, 132, 161n; subdues Muslim tribes, 139; harasses Ahmed Shah Abdali, 145, 160; occupies Lahore, 150; invests Sialkot and defends Gujranwala, 152; defeats Jahan Khan, 156; achievements, 168; killed in Jammu, 182, 187; shifted headquarters to Gujranwala, 187; family tree, 188
Chenab, 3, 4n, 5, 133, 135, 147, 152, 167n, 197n
China, v, 255, 296
Chittagong, 72, 302
Christ, 10, 19, 33n; Christianity, 25, 33n, 34n
Cis-Sutlej, 4n, 170, 181, 216, 219-21, 225n, 231n, 237n, 268; *see also* Malwa, Malwais
Clive, Lord, 164n, 280
coinage issued by Banda, 152n, 153n; by the Sikhs, 161, 201
Collins, Resident, 196, 197n, 210n
Cornwallis, Lord, *see* governor general
court, general, 260
Cunningham, J. D., v, 14n, 30n, 67n, 68n, 74n, 314

Dacca, 72, 302
Dal Khalsa, *see* Khalsa
Dalip Singh, 188, 288n
Dal Singh, Ranjit Singh's uncle, 193n
Dal Singh, General, 239, 257

Dallewalia misl, 132, 142, 213, 216
Dam Dama, 93, 94, 95n, 305, 314
Dara Shikoh, 68
Darius, 11
Dasam Granth, 90n, 94, 305, 313-17
Data Ganj Baksh, *see* Ali Makhdum Hujwiri
Daulat Khan Lodhi, 31, 32
Daya Kaur, 257n
Deccan, 94, 95, 102, 107, 120, 150
Deep Singh, 132, 145, 146
Dehra Dun, 69n, 177
Delhi, 71, 74n, 76, 107-9, 111-12, 114, 127n, 128, 131, 134-36, 141-42, 147-50, 155, 163, 176, 178, 179, 191, 194, 197n, 210, 221, 227, 237n, 249, 272n; Aurangzeb summons Har Rai, 69; summons Hari Krishen, 70; Tegh Bahadur arraigned before the Kazi's court, 73; Banda in the vicinity, 102, 103; Bahadur Shah orders general mobilisation, 110; Banda captured and sent to, 115; becomes the centre of Sikh activity, 121; Nadir Shah plunders the capital, 125; Sikhs come to within 50 miles of the capital, 139; Afghans loot the capital, 143-44; Sikhs plunder in the vicinity of, 162, 166; administered by Najibuddaulah, 169; Marathas consolidate their hold, 170; Sikhs loot the suburbs, 174, 177; enter the capital, 175, 180; British become masters of, 211
Dera Baba Banda, 112
Dera Ghazi Khan, 201, 252, 255, 262, 280
Dera Ismail Khan, 201, 252, 256, 257, 262, 280
Desa Singh Majithia, 209, 233, 234, 263
Dewan Chand, Misr, 259, 261, 266; campaign in the southwest, 249; marches against Multan, 250-51; capture of Kashmir, 254-55; campaign in the west, 257; battle of Naushera, 262-64; death, 265

Dhian Singh, 267, 294; appointment as deorhidar, 252; chief of the Council of Ministers, 269; advises rejection of British proposal, 287; Kharak Singh's chief minister, 289

Dhirmal, 51, 67, 70, 71, 81, 122n; Dhirmaliyas, 51, 122n

Dick, General Sir Robert, 258n

Dina Nath, 248, 294

Dipalpur, 122, 234

Diwan Singh, 167

Dogras, 134, 161, 171, 252

Dost Mohammed Khan, 265; family tree, 238; expels Jahan Dad from Peshawar, 254; expresses loyalty to Ranjit Singh, 262; invests Jehangiria, 263; takes up the cry of jihad, 274; Shah Shuja routed by the Barakzais at Kandhar, 281; demands evacuation of the Khyber region, 281-82; battle of Jamrud, 285-86; demand for Peshawar rejected, 286-87; British negotiations, 287; proposal to depose him, 287; see also Barakzais

East India Company, 170, 174, 261, 262; protection of Oudh, 172, 175, 179, 181; deserters from the Company's regiments, 207-8, 258n; Perron's intrigue, 210; clash with the Marathas, Treaty of Lahore 1806, 210-12; Ochterlony at Kharak Singh's wedding, 237n; Shah Shuja seeks asylum, 245n; at war with the Gurkhas, 247-48; the Burmese, 265; Kharak Singh, 266; exchange of deputations, 268; Anirodh Chand seeks protection, 269; relations with the Lahore Durbar, 278; Lahore Durbar's claims to territory across the Sutlej, 279; see also British policy

Elphinstone, M., 221, 226, 235

Elahi Baksh, Shaikh, 208, 250, 294

Eminabad, formerly Saidpur, 9, 34, 157, 301

England, King of, 268, 274

famine, 178, 269

Farid Shakarganj, 28, 42n, 319

Faridkot, 224, 225

Farkhunda Bakht, Prince, 175

Farrukh Siyar, see Mughal emperor

Fateh Khan, Wazir, 235-42, 244, 245n, 250, 252, 254; see also Barakzais

Fateh Singh, son of Gobind Singh, 51, 81, 91, 92, 156, 308

Fateh Singh Ahluwalia, 123n, 189n, 198, 204, 205, 212, 263, 266, 267

Fateh Singh Kalianwala, 204, 216

Fatehgarh, fortress, 80; temple, 156

Ferozepur, 279, 287, 288; district, 216

Firoz Khan, 110

France, 220, 222; King Louis Phillippe, 259

French, 191, 222, 224, 228, 258, 259n; government, 223

Fyzullapuria misl, see Singhpuria misl

Gajpat Singh of Jind, 173, 176, 187

Gakkhars, 12, 139, 171

Ganda Singh Bhangi, 163, 171

Ganga Ram, 248

Ganges, 35, 85, 157, 169, 171, 172, 175, 177-79, 181, 191, 221n

Gangetic Doab, 166, 176, 177

Gangu Shahias, 122n

Gaya, 33, 71

Ghallughara, chota, 129; vada, 129n, 154, 155, 304

Ghammand Chand, Raja, 153

Ghaus Mohammed or Mian Ghausa, 208, 209, 246, 247, 294

Ghazis, 157n, 215, 250, 263, 264n, 273, 285, 286n

Ghaznis, 12, 288

Gobindgarh, 206, 207, 209, 227, 233

Gobind Singh, vi, 5n, 72, 73n, 98, 103, 104, 121, 122n, 133, 154n, 187, 215, 300, 304, 307, 312; family tree, 51; cremates his father's head, 74; hymns, 74, 75, 79, 87, 88, 92, 93, 96; at Paonta, 76; mission becomes clear, 77; battle of Bhangani, 78;

of Nadaun, 79; reorganises the community, 79-80; invests the guruship in the granth and panth, 81, 87, 95, 308; abolition of the masands, 82; baptism of five chosen ones, 82-84; codes of conduct, 84, 86; his address to the assembly, 85-86; did Gobind mean to change the faith of Nanak? 87-90; clash with Mughals, 90; besieged at Anandpur, 91; at Chamkaur, 91-92; death of two sons, 91; death of two younger sons and mother, 92; prepares an edition of the Granth at Dam Dama, 93, 305; collects hymns for Dasam Granth, 93-94, 305; communicates with Aurangzeb, 94; assists Bahadur Shah in the war of succession, 94; death, 95; character and achievements, 95-96; chooses Banda, 101; arms Banda, 102; coins issued, 107, 161; temple built, 178; description of Dasam Granth, 313-18; collects his father's hymns, 376-77

Gobindpur, 249

Godavari, river, 95, 101

Goindwal, 52n, 53-55, 59, 67, 311

governors general, 244n, 248; Amherst, Lord, 265, 268, 272n; Auckland, Lord, 284, 287, 288; Barlow, Sir George, 212n; Bentinck, Lord Wm., 274-77, 291; Cornwallis, Lord, 212; Hastings, Warren, 178, 180; Minto, Lord, 221-23, 225, 226, 229-31, 232n, 235, 239n; Mornington, Earl of (Wellesley), 197n, 199, 210n, 212, 220; see also British policy

Grand Trunk Road, 104, 176

Greeks, 11, 258

Guddun, Rani, 289

Gujarat, 9, 21, 136, 141, 163, 189, 193, 199, 217, 234, 257n, 260

Gujjars, 107, 108, 179

Gujjar Singh Bhangi, 160, 161, 164, 166, 171

Gujranwala, 9, 132, 152, 171, 187, 193, 196, 295

Gulab Raiyas, 51, 122n

Gulab Singh, 111

Gulab Singh Bhangi, 160, 198, 206

Gulab Singh Dallewalia, 132

Gulab Singh Dogra, 252

Gulbahar Begam, 295

Gurbaksh Singh of Khem Karan, 158

Gurdas, Bhai, 49n, 55, 61n, 300, 302; and Nanak, 38-39; Amar Das, 310; Arjun, 56, 310; Adi Granth, 58, 304, 305, 310, 311; community leader, 63, 66, 311; Vars, 299, 301, 312; his life, 310-12

Gurdaspur Nangal, 112, 113

Gurditta, 51, 66, 67

Gurkhas, 83n, 190, 191, 208, 214, 219, 232, 233, 247, 248, 264

Gurmata, 85n, 121

Gurmukhi, 52

Gwalior, 64, 73n, 311

Handaliyas, 122n

Hansi, 181, 189, 230

Hapur, 169n, 180

Harappa, 10, 171

Hardwar, 35, 181n, 221n

Hargobind, 68n, 70, 77, 78, 98, 305, 311; family tree, 51; Arjun's message, 61; achievements, 63; raises private army anew, 64; travels, clashes with the Mughals, 65; moves from Kartarpur to Kiratpur, 66; call to arms, 66; chooses Har Rai as seventh guru, 67; death, 67; contemporary with Muhsin Fani, 302; Gurdas' writings, 310

Hari Krishen, 51, 69, 70, 178, 305

Hari Singh Bhangi, 132; achievements, 129, 168; occupies Lahore, 150; relieves Gujranwala, 152; takes Kasur, 156; harasses Abdali, 160; death, 171

Hari Singh Nalwa, 209, 246, 257, 259, 263; the terror of the northwest tribes, 253; Ranjit Singh comes to his rescue, 271; attacked by Syed Ahmed, 273; builds forts near the Khyber Pass, 281; battle of Jamrud, 284-86; death, 286

Hariana, 4n, 14n, 124, 142, 221, 228; desert, 153

Harimandir or Golden Temple, 63, 97, 123, 164, 165, 193; foundation stone laid, 28n, 56; Arjun raises money, 57; Granth Sahib formally installed, 58, 304, 307, 310; Tegh Bahadur shut out of the temple, 71; Mani Singh entrusted with its care, 80n, 122, 124; desecrated by Massa Ranghar, 127n; tank fouled by Lakhpat Rai, 129; Kaura Mal assigns revenue, 137; blown up on the fourth Afghan invasion, 145; again desecrated, death of Deep Singh, 146; Afghan prisoners made to clean up pool, 148, 157n; blown up on sixth invasion, 154-55; again on seventh invasion, 158; rebuilt at considerable expense, 160; Ranjit Singh makes grant for rebuilding, 207; Holkar makes an offering, 211; Desa Singh Majithia assigned administration, 233n; Nizam of Hyderabad presents a bejewelled canopy, 279n

Haripur, 242, 246, 271

Harlan, Josiah, 260, 282

Har Rai, 51, 67-70, 305

Harsha, 11

Hassan Abdal, 190, 253

Hastings, Warren, see governor general

Hazara, 253, 256; hills, 273

Herat, 278, 287, 288

Himalayas, vi, vii, 3, 7, 12, 33, 65, 107, 125, 142, 157, 182, 234, 279, 295

Himmat Singh, 167

Hindu Kush, 3, 11

Hinduism, 28, 29n, 37; Nanak emphasises what is common with Islam, v, 17; Vedic Hinduism, 11; Jats refuse to submit to Brahmanical Hinduism, 15; definition, 17-18; most important aspect, 19; impact of Buddhism, 19; renaissance, 20; faces challenge of Islam, 20-22; Shankara provided debating points, 22; influence of the Bhaktas, 24; Islam's compromise, 25-26; rising tide of militant Hinduism, 149

Hindus, vii, 14, 48, 52-53, 57, 58, 60, 72, 73n, 119, 143, 184, 193, 202, 209, 247, 249; Jats, 14n; massacre of, 22; and Ramananda, 23; Kabir promotes Hindu/Muslim unity, 24; coming of the Sufis, 25-28; revert to the worship of idols and the wearing of caste marks, 29; and Nanak, 37; advocate three alternative paths to salvation, 43; Amar Das's innovations tend to break close affiliation with Sikhs, 54; four doors of Harimandir represent four castes, 56n; Arjun continues Nanak's mission, 62; influx into Sikh fold under Hargobind, 66; Tegh Bahadur looked upon as leader, 74n; most converts from the trading caste, 78; the Granth, 97; large number of converts, 98, 106; Bahadur Shah suspects most in sympathy with rebellion, 110n; large estates broken up into smaller holdings, 118; chiefs of Rajasthan appeal to Abdali to save them from the Marathas, 149; Sikhs rescue many women from Abdali, 151; Shah Zaman tries to alienate them from the Muslims, 194; Ranjit Singh stresses equality, 203; Holkar flatters Ranjit Singh as the only hope of Hindus, 211; many compelled to leave the Kashmir Valley, 254; consequence of influx into the Sikh fold, 289n, 308

Hira Singh, 132, 252, 269

Hissar, 4n, 14n, 182

Hola Mohalla, 89n, 139

Holkar, Jaswant Rao, 211, 212, 219

Honigberger, Dr., 260, 289
Hoshiarpur, 108, 132
Hukma Singh Chimni, 209, 234
Huns, Mongoloid, 11
Hussain, 204
Hyderabad, Amir of, 277
Hyderabad, Nizam of, 279

Ibrahim Lodhi, 12
Imad-ul-mulk, Wazir, 144
Imamuddin, Fakir, 198n, 268n, 294
Indri, 176
Indus, 3, 20, 171, 225, 280; excluded
    from rivers of the Punab, 5; ar-
    chaeological remains, 10; Pathans
    and Baluchis, 12; Nadir Shah
    harassed, 125; Abdali given all
    territory west of the river, 135;
    Afghans cross the river, 137, 143,
    149, 191; Abdali harassed, 145,
    151; Sikhs in control from the
    Sutlej, 153; from the Jumna, 157,
    170, 182n; Taimur holds his fa-
    ther's conquests west of the river,
    169; estates of Hafiz Ahmed Khan,
    256; fall of Mankera extends Pun-
    jab to the river, 257; opening up
    of the river to shipping, 274-75,
    277; Sindh, 282-84; Grand Army
    of, 288
Iraq, 37
Iskardu, 280
Islam, 21, 22, 28, 37, 59n, 106, 118,
    295; Nanak emphasises what is
    common with Hinduism, v, 17;
    challenge to Hinduism, 19-20; the
    Bhaktas, 24; compromise with
    Hinduism, 25-26; Hindu untouch-
    ables, 27; the Granth, 58, 311; Je-
    hangir plans to bring Arjun into
    the fold, 60; Tegh Bahadur exe-
    cuted on refusing conversion, 73n;
    Hindu resistance, 98; Banda of-
    fered pardon if he accepts Islam,
    117; Mani Singh executed on re-
    fusing conversion, 124; danger of
    militant Hinduism, 149
Itmad-ud-Daulah, 128n

Jabbar Khan, 238, 254, 255, 263
Jahan Dad Khan, 236, 240, 254
Jahan Khan, General, 135, 137, 138,
    145-47, 149, 150, 164
Jahandar Shah, see Mughal em-
    peror
Jai Singh Kanhaya, 129, 132, 150,
    152, 160, 182, 183, 188
Jains, 13, 22; Jainism, 19, 20
Jaipur, Raja of, 71n, 142, 162
Jalalabad, 108, 173
Jammu, 70, 187, 201; Kabuli Mal
    recruits Dogras, 161; bone of con-
    tention among misls, 171, 182-83,
    188; richest of the hill states, 182;
    Gurbaksh Singh Kanhaya killed,
    188; taken by Hukam Singh Chim-
    ni, 234; garrisoned, 239; given to
    Mian Singh, 269
Jammu, Raja of, 193; casts off Mu-
    ghal yoke, 133; relations with Ab-
    dali, 145, 155; family disputes,
    182-83; Ranjit Singh leads expe-
    dition against him, 198
Jamrud, 281, 285, 286
Jandiala, 127, 148, 153
Janjuas, 12, 171
Jasrota, 113, 217, 233, 260
Jassa Singh Ahluwalia, 189n; sketch,
    123; achievements, 129, 168, 183;
    defeats Adina Beg Khan, 131-32;
    commander of Dal Khalsa, 132-
    33; accepts one-fourth of the reve-
    nue of Patti, 134; helps Kaura Mal
    to take Multan, 137; calls on misl-
    dars to avenge the death of Deep
    Singh, 146; enters Lahore at the
    head of the army, 150, 152; rela-
    tions with Ala Singh, 151; at Guj-
    ranwala, 152; evacuates Lahore,
    153; plunders Jullundur Doab,
    155; defeats Bhikhan Khan, 156;
    harasses Abdali, 160; extends his
    hold along the Sutlej and occu-
    pies Kapurthala, 170; goes to the
    rescue of Patiala, 175; opposes the
    Mughals and Rohillas, 176
Jassa Singh Ramgarhia, 134, 140,
    160, 178, 179, 181

Jatpura, 92

Jats, 13-16, 57, 89, 93, 120, 159, 162, 169, 172, 291n, 292n

Jehangir, see Mughal emperor

Jehangiria, 253, 263

Jhanda Singh Bhangi, 160, 163, 171, 182

Jhang, 208, 249

Jhelum, 9; Punjab and Afghan armies leave for Kashmir, 240

Jhelum, river, 3, 5n, 12, 139, 155, 163, 167, 171, 187, 192, 254, 257; Durbar generals take Mangla, 234

Jind, 4n, 68n, 93, 139, 233, 237n; see also Bhag Singh, Gajpat Singh

Jindan, 288n

Jito, 51, 81

Jodh Singh, 167

Jodh Singh Kalsia, 246

Jujhar Singh, 51, 81, 91

Jullundur, 137, 146; liberated, 108; farmed by Adina Beg Khan, 141; joined to the Durbar, 234

Jullundur Doab, 9, 65, 118, 139, 140n, 147, 155, 159, 165, 170; Arjun raises Kartarpur, 57; doab liberated, 108; Adina Beg Khan governor, 130; offers over a lac protection money, 146; retaken by Jassa Singh Ahluwalia, 156

Jumna, river, 3-5, 13, 77, 80, 106-9, 157-62, 170-71, 174, 182n, 214; Gobind Singh spent many years at Paonta, 76; Sikh incursions across the river, 172, 174-76, 178-80; Ranjit Singh hopes to unify the Punjab up to its banks, 219-22, 226; British policy—no further than the Jumna, 220, 222; policy reversed, 231n

Jumna-Gangetic Doab, 174, 176, 181

justice, 198, 202, 270

Kabir, 23, 24, 37n, 306, 321

Kabul, vii, 128n, 183, 192, 206, 224, 235, 237n, 239, 262, 274, 281, 282, 288, 311; civil strife prevents Shah Zaman from invading India, 200; Elphinstone mission, 221, 223, 226; Shah Zaman negotiates for the restoration of the Saddozais, 236; Shah Mahmud owed his throne to Fateh Khan, 252; Muslims prefer to pay tribute to, 257; Russian agents, 287; victory parade, 295

Kabuli Mal, 156, 157, 161

Kahan Singh, 234

Kaithal, 68n, 104, 213, 222, 237n

Kalabagh, 171

Kalanaur, 109, 155

Kam Baksh, 95

Kamalia, 234

Kamran, Prince, 252

Kandhar, 68n, 167, 281, 288

Kanganwal, 122

Kangra, 170, 190, 194, 204, 214, 232-34, 237n, 256, 269; Valley, 248

Kanhaya misl, 150, 209, 217; inauguration, 132; takes over land between Amritsar and the Himalayas, 142; captures the fort of Kangra, 170; dispute over Jammu, 171, 182-83, 188; Sada Kaur new head, 189; suffers partial eclipse, 234; see also Jai Singh

Kapur Singh, 133, 187; recognised leader, 123; army commander, 124, 129; relinquishes leadership, 132; at Lahore, 135; achievements, 183

Kapurthala, 123n, 170

Karam Singh, 178

Karnal, 3, 4n, 9, 110, 125, 155, 162, 172, 221, 227, 228

Karora Singhia misl, 133

Kartarpur founded by Arjun, 57, 65-67, 146, 305

Kartarpur founded by Nanak, 34, 36, 49

Kashmir, 141n, 173, 201, 256, 257n, 262, 279; Ramanuja's travels, 23; visited by Hargobind, 65; annexed by Abdali, 139, 155; held by Taimur, 169, 190; Ata Mohammed governor, 236; Fateh Khan and Ranjit Singh's joint expedition, 237, 239-40; Azim Khan governor, 241, 244n; second Punjabi campaign, 246-48; Jabbar Khan governor, 254; captured by Punjabis, 254-55; Moti Ram governor, 255; violent earthquake and famine, 268-69; Muslims flock to Syed Ahmed's banner, 273

Kashmira Singh, 188, 257n

Kasur, 9, 219, 224; island of Mughal authority, 109; falls to Hari Singh Bhangi, 156, 171; district ruled by a Pathan family, 189-91; Nizamuddin Khan leads assault against the Sikhs, 194; recognises Ranjit Singh as sovereign, 204; fort again bombarded, 205, 215; Kutubuddin Khan given jagir at Namdot, 215; to be administered by Nihal Singh Attariwala, 215; garrisoned by Lahore Durbar, 279

Katoch, 113, 153, 183

Kaura Mal, 130, 134, 136, 139

Keane, Sir John, 288

Khadur, 49, 52n, 67

Khairpur, Amir of, 277

Khalsa, 8on, 89, 90, 96-97, 102n, 118, 124, 201, 206, 259; Gobind Singh selects five chosen ones to be the nucleus of a casteless community, the Khalsa or the pure, 83; five emblems prescribed, 84; Gobind Singh merges his entity in the Khalsa, 85; Gobind Singh vests the institution of guruship in the Granth and the Panth, 87; Aurangzeb orders the governors of Sirhind and Lahore to destroy the Khalsa, 91; many Jats of Malwa join the fraternity, 93; their sword inscribed on Banda's coins, 107; edict issued by the emperor to apprehend them, 120-21; bandai and Tat Khalsa divided, 121; bandai merge with the Tat Khalsa, 122; ordered to come out of their hideouts, 123; Budha Dal and Taruna Dal billetted at Amritsar, 123; plunder Nadir Shah, 125; resume pilgrimage to Amritsar, 126; suffer terrible hardship during Za-

karya Khan's tenure, 127; Lakhpat Rai's oath of vengeance, 129n; death of Mannu and end of another attempt to destroy their rising power, 140

Khalsa, Dal, 157, 163, 182; the army of the Khalsa, 123; divided into 11 misls, 132-33; estimated total force about 70,000 horse and foot, 133; headquarters at Amritsar, 141; military administration, 142; Afghans no longer strong enough to challenge them in the plains, 151; Jassa Singh Ahluwalia enters Lahore at their head, 152; go to the rescue of Patiala, 175; oppose an army of Mughals and Rohillas, 176

Khalsa, Sarbat, 130, 148-49; biennial meetings held at Amritsar on 1st Baisakh and at Divali come to be known as the Sarbat Khalsa, 121; appoints jathedars, 121; jathedars form small bands and take villages under their protection, 122; jathas reorganised: when the community in jeopardy unites to merge with the Dal Khalsa, 123; description of, 123; decide to merge the small jathas into 25 regiments of cavalry under Kapur Singh, 128-29; decide to have one army, the Dal Khalsa, divided into 11 misls, 132-33; decide to seize Lahore, 150, 152, 161; Harimandir rebuilt and misl representatives appointed, 160-61; becomes a snake with many heads, 170; considers the clash between the Marathas and the British, 211

Kharak Singh, 27n, 198; family tree, 188; jealousy of Sher Singh, 214n, 266; engaged to a Kanhaya, 217; wedding, 237; enters Srinagar, 255; in communication with the British, 266; ordered to punish the Mazaris, 282; invested with the title of Maharajah of the Punjab, 289

Kharkhauda, 162

Khattaks, 253, 262-64

Khem Karan, 158, 224

Khewra, 234

Khuda Yar, Tiwana Chief, 294

Khushab, 234, 257

Khushal Singh, 218, 252, 255, 257

Khusrau, Prince, 59, 60

Khyber Pass, vi, 3, 253, 262, 281, 285, 286, 288

Kiratpur, 65-69, 71, 90, 111, 219

Kishtwar, 279

Kohinoor, 125, 131n, 239n, 241, 242n, 244n

Koran, 26, 29, 48, 53, 93n, 282, 285, 294

Kot Kapura, 93

Krishna, 4n, 85, 317, 318

Kshatriyas, 13, 19, 56n, 291n

Kulu, 111, 233

Kup, village, 153, 154

Kurukshetra, 4n, 42n

Ladakh, 33, 279, 280

Lahore, vi, 4n, 11n, 28n, 56, 57, 68n, 90, 111, 115, 124-26, 131, 132, 134, 136, 141-44, 148, 154, 192, 199, 205, 206, 215, 221n, 227, 233, 239, 243, 244, 247, 248, 254, 258-60, 265-67, 279, 288n, 294, 305; seat of most governments, 8; Arjun tortured, 60; Mani Singh executed, 80n; district governor ordered to destroy the Khalsa, 91; island of Mughal authority, 109; Zakarya Khan governor, 122; Shahidganj, 127, 129, 140; Yahya Khan governor, 128; Shah Nawaz claims himself governor, 130; Kapur Singh occupies the city, 135; ceded to Abdali, 138-39; Jahan Khan orders general mobilisation, 145; Sikhs plunder suburbs, 142, 146-47; Sabaji Sindhia occupies it, 149; Sikhs withdraw, 150; gates thrown open to welcome Jassa Singh, 152; Abdali reoccupies the city, 153, 155; Kabuli Mal governor, 156; Sikhs invest the town,

156-57, 161; Lehna Singh proposed as governor, 164, 166; in the possession of the Bhangis, 171, 189; at the time of Shah Zaman, 191, 192, 194-95; Ranjit Singh invited to take the city, 196-98; reorganises administration, 202; Treaty of 1806, 212; of 1809, 230-32, 378-79; Shah Zaman in the city, 237; Shah Shuja, 241, 242n, 245; epidemic of cholera, 269; gardens laid out, 270; arrival of Burnes, 275; Wade obtains signature to commercial treaty, 277; envoys from Nepal, 278; Nao Nihal Singh's wedding, 285; Ranjit Singh dies 40 years after its conquest, 289

Lahore Durbar, 212, 233, 242, 246, 250, 251n, 266, 272, 289n, 292, 293, 295; Ranjit Singh's new title gives legal right to demand tribute, 201; Jhang and Ucch declare allegiance, 208; Lake asks them to expel Holkar, 211; action taken against rebels, 216-17; review of past decade, 219; territories of Tara Singh Gheba taken over, 220; Metcalfe mission, 221-31; Bhangi, Singhpuria, Nakkai and other territories taken, 234; Shah Shuja solicits aid, 235; army ordered to Multan, 235; allowance given Shuja and Zaman's families, 236; undertakes joint expedition to Kashmir with Fateh Khan, 237, 239-41; offer of Kohinoor, 237, 241; Shah Shuja's plot to overthrow the Durbar, 243-45; turns down approach from the Gurkhas and offers help to the East India Company, 247-48; offers service to disbanded Gurkhas, 248; Jhang, Ucch, Ramgarhia estates merged, 249; introduction of Dogras, 252; Khattaks pay tribute, 253; acquisition of Kashmir, 254-55; pacification of tribes remains major problem, 256-57;

Ventura and Allard engaged, 258; Yar Mohammed reinstated at Peshawar, 265; Sindh, 268, 275-78, 282-84; Dogras most powerful element, 269; acted with the Maharajah as the Supreme Court, 270; tribes of the northwest challenge their sovereignty, 271; undercurrent of hostility with British, 278; territories across the Sutlej, 279; garrisons Kasur, 279; Ladakh, 279-80; offers to put Shah Shuja back on the throne, 280; occupies Peshawar, 281; rejects Afghan demand for Peshawar, 287; Tripartite Treaty, 287-88

Lake, Lord, 211, 212n, 219, 220
Lakhmi Das, 31, 36, 50
Lakhpat Rai, 124, 129, 130
Landai, river, 262n, 263, 264
Langar, 43, 50, 52, 97, 107, 161
Lehna Singh Bhangi, 160, 161, 164, 166
Lehna Singh Majithia, 233n, 260, 261, 275, 293n
Lehna Singh Sandhawalia, 281, 285
Leiah, 256, 257
Leili, 273n
Lodhis, 12, 29
Lohgarh, 63, 80
Ludhiana, 9, 211n, 213, 242n, 244n, 275, 280, 281; given to Bhag Singh, 214; taken over by the British, 228; superseded by Ferozepur, 279

Machiwara, 92, 279
Macnaghten, Sir W., 287
Madhav Rao Peshwa, 169
Madho Lal, 28n, 204
Maha Singh, Commander at Jamrud, 281, 285
Maha Singh Sukerchakia, 183, 187, 188
Mahabharata, 4n, 15
Mahavira, 19
Mahmud of Ghazni, 11, 21, 243, 280
Majha, 4n, 109, 170, 182, 183; Punjabi nationalism, 14; Jat converts, 57

Majhails, 4n, 104-5, 175; expansion of misls, 170-71; break up of misls, 182; Jammu, 182-83; Shah Zaman, 194; Ranjit Singh reduces the misls, 219
Mala Singh, 200
Malabar, 21, 22, 33; King of, 21
Malaya states, v
Malcolm, Colonel, 221
Malerkotla, 104, 144, 156, 225; Nawab of, 228
Malhar Rao, 163n
Malwa, 4n, 124, 165, 170-74, 181, 182, 210, 213, 268; Jat converts, 93; Banda, 103, 105, 108, 110, 118; the Marathas, 149, 172, 180, 211; Mirza Shafi's expedition, 176; Ranjit Singh's tours, 213, 216, 224-26
Malwais, 4n, 104, 212; expansion of misls, 171-72; pillage the suburbs of Delhi, 173; Sikh-Rohilla alliance, 174; Najaf Khan sows seeds of discord, 175-76; Perron dictates terms, 181, 210; break up of misls, 182-83; Shah Zaman, 194; Yusuf Ali's mission, 199; Nabha/Patiala dispute, 213-14; Ranjit Singh and the British, 219-31
Mandi, 111, 170, 214, 234
Mani Majra hills, 165n, 166n
Mani Singh, 61n, 299, 315; Harimandir, 80n, 122; Adi Granth, 80n, 93, 305; Dasam Granth, 94, 305, 314, 316; looks after Sikh community, 121; Divali fair in Amritsar, 124; arrested and executed, 80n, 124; Bhagat Ratnavali, 301
Mankera, 171, 201, 249, 252, 256, 257, 262, 280
Manu, 4n
Marathas, 120, 155, 159, 170, 175, 219, 220, 222; relations with Adina Beg Khan, 134n, 147-48; the Sikhs, 149, 162, 180-81; battle of Panipat, 150-51, 167, 207n; Shah Alam

II, 169, 179; Najaf Khan, 174; Warren Hastings, 178-79; achievements since Panipat, 191; Shah Zaman, 192; invite the Afghans, 211; clash with the British, 211-12; Lahore Durbar, 230, 279

Mardana, 31, 32, 34, 307

Masands, 53, 57, 66, 68, 70, 71, 72n, 81, 82, 89

Mathura, 11n, 33, 143

Mauryas, 11

Mazaris, 282, 283

Mecca, 24, 27, 34, 36, 48, 57, 157n

Meerut, 180, 218

Meeth Singh Bharania, 246

Mehrauli, 117, 319

Mehrban, 81

Mehtab Kaur, 188, 214n, 256

Mehtab Singh, 127n

Mehta Kalian Das Bedi, 29, 30n

Menander, 11

Metcalfe, T., 239n, 241n, 256n; mission to Lahore, 221-30; report on Syed Ahmed, 272n

Mian Mir, 28n, 56, 59n, 61

Milkha Singh, 171

Minas, 51, 122n

Minto, Lord, see governor general

Mir Mannu, 128n, 131, 133-42

Mira Bai, 24, 306

Mirza Beg, General, 79

Mirza Shafi, 176

Misldari system, 184; inauguration, 132; advantages, 133, 142; begins to lack cohesion, 170; description, 172n; break up, 182-83; Ranjit Singh's decision, 189; factionalism, 190

Mithankot, 282

Mohammed, the Prophet, 21, 24-26, 59, 154, 262, 311

Mohammed Azim Khan, see Azim Khan

Mohammed-bin-Qasim, 21

Mohammed Shah, see Mughal emperor

Mohan, son of Amar Das, 58, 304

Mohar Singh, 196

Mohenjodaro, 10, 18

Mohkam Chand, Dewan, 246, 247n, 259, 265; administration of Dallewalia estates, 216; takes Pathankot, 217; takes Anandpur, 220; leader of the fight-the-British group, 227, 230; takes over Singhpuria estates, 234; Kashmir expedition, 239-41; battle of Attock, 243

Mohran, Bibi, 28n, 227n, 292, 295

Mongols, 13

Morinda, 156, 216

Mornington, Earl of, see governor general

Moti Ram, 217n, 255, 268

Mughal emperors, 139: Akbar, 3n, 53-55, 58, 59, 292, 311, 312; Akbar Shah II, 271; Alamgir II, 141, 143, 144; Aurangzeb, 68-70, 72-74, 77-79, 90-94, 313; Babar, 9n, 12, 29, 34, 301; Bahadur Shah, 79, 94, 95, 101, 102, 104, 107, 109-12, 115n, 117; Farrukh Siyar, 112, 120; Jahandar Shah, 110, 112; Jehangir, 59, 61, 63-65; Mohammed Shah, 144, 237n; Shah Alam II, 155, 163n, 169, 173, 174, 176, 178-80, 191, 210, 211; Shah Jahan, 64n, 65, 67n, 68

Mughals, 29, 34n, 78, 92, 120, 129, 139-41, 143-44, 148, 183, 198, 201, 215n, 222, 235; clashes with the Sikhs in the time of Hargobind, 65-66; of Gobind Singh, 79, 90, 91, 94, 101; Banda, 105-7, 109-15, 118-19; defeated by the Persians, 125; Mannu in command of the army, 131; Raja of Jammu casts off the Mughal yoke, 134; at Multan, 137; administration destroyed, 167; relations with the Malwais, 172-76; with Zabita Khan, 175, 77; army reorganised by Najaf Khan, 176; Kohinoor, 237n

Mughlani Begam, 136n, 141, 142-44

Mukhlis Khan, 65

Mukhlisgarh, 106, 107, 110-12

Multan, 8, 29, 34, 46n, 68n, 122, 133, 157, 163, 201, 211, 219, 225,

237n, 242, 255, 257n, 262, 280, 282, 296; Shah Nawaz governor, 128, 136; Kaura Mal ejects the Afghans, 134; Kaura Mal governor, 137; ceded to Abdali, 139, 141; Taimur takes it from the Bhangis, 169-71, 190; sketch, 205-6; taken by Lahore Durbar, 215, 235-36, 248-52; Shah Shuja cedes his right to, 380

Multana Singh, 188, 257n

Muslims, vii, 14, 48, 52, 57, 58, 60, 73n, 84, 137, 150, 153n, 157n, 184, 192, 209, 219, 248; coming of, 11; Jats, 14n; intermix, 21; invasions, 22; and Ramananda, 23; Kabir promotes understanding with Hindus, 24; coming of the Sufis, 25-28; and Nanak, 37; Arjun's influence, 59n, 62; and Gobind Singh, 78; Granth, 97; religious sentiment exploited, 98; and Banda, 105, 118, 119; converts, 106; northwest tribes, 139, 187; militant Hinduism, 149; Lahoris, 161, 164, 166; Sikhs regain confidence of the peasantry, 183; massacre at Gujarat, 193; Shah Zaman tries to alienate them from the Hindus, 194; Ranjit Singh sets up separate courts, 202; stresses equality, 203, 205, 249; raises infantry battalions, 208; Metcalfe's escort, 229; Shariat law, 270; Syed Ahmed recruits volunteers, 271, 273; at Jamrud, 286n; Ranjit Singh's funeral, 289; Kabul, 295; Hargobind's close association, 311

Mustafabad, 105, 176

Muzaffar Khan of Multan, 205, 206, 215, 235, 236, 248, 250, 251, 255

Muzaffargarh, 250

Muzaffarnagar, 174

Mysore, 192

Nabha, 68n, 93, 123n, 213, 222, 228, 237n

Nadaun, 79, 317

Nadir Shah, 125, 126, 127n, 128n, 130, 131, 135, 173n, 237n

Nahan, 111, 177; Raja of, 111

Najaf Khan, 173-77

Najibuddaulah, invites Afghans to India, 143; Abdali's representative at the Mughal court, 144; expelled from Delhi, 149; at Panipat, 150n; intercedes on behalf of Ala Singh, 154n; clashes with the Sikhs, 162-63, 165-66; administers Delhi, 169; death, 169n; advice to son, 172n

Nakkai misl, 132, 171, 189, 209, 234; see also Hira Singh, Kahan Singh

Nam Dev, 24, 306, 321

Nanak, vi, 35, 53, 65, 69, 77, 81, 85, 89, 96, 97, 108, 137, 195, 289n, 312, 313, 319; preaches the unity of Hinduism and Islam, v; description of countryside, 5-7, 38; ethnic pattern of the Punjab, 12-13; harnesses the spirit of tolerance, 14; describes his times, 29; birth, 29-30; childhood, marriage, birth of two sons, 30-31; first mystic experience, 31-32; message—there is no Hindu, there is no Mussulman, 32-33; travels, 33-34, 36; chooses Lehna and renames him Angad, 36, 49; death, 37; relations with Hindus and Muslims, 37; achievements, 37-39, 46-47; concept of God, 39-41; guruship, 41; ideal, 41-43; caste, 43; langar, 43; namamarga, 43-45; path of sahaj, 45-46; political aspect, 48; family tree, 50-51; Granth reflects his faith, 58; seed sown blossoms in Arjun's time, 62; similarities and differences between Gobind Singh's approach and his own, 87-88; coins struck in his name, 107, 161, 201; records of his life, 299-303; composition of Adi Granth, 304-9; hymns, 324-57

Nanaki, 30, 31, 50

Nanauta, 108, 173

Nanded, 95, 101n

Nand Lal Goya, 79n, 80n, 86n
Nankana Sahib, 30
Nao Nihal Singh, 198n, 267, 285
Napoleon Bonaparte, 220, 222n, 228, 258, 293
Naraingarh, 204n, 216
Nasir Khan of Kalat, 157, 159
Nasiruddin, 274, 283
Naudh Singh Sukerchakia, 129, 132, 187, 188
Naushera, 204, 207n, 271; battle of, 262-64
Nepal, 232, 247, 278; King of, 269
Nihal Singh Attariwala, 215, 236
Nihangs, 89n, 128n, 248, 255, 276; Ranjit Singh's front line troops, 207n, 250-51, 264, 286n; origin, 215; fracas with Metcalfe's escort, 229
Niranjanias, 122n, 127, 148, 153
Nishanwalia misl, 132, 142
Nizamuddin Khan, 191, 194, 198, 204, 205, 215
Nur Mohammed, 157-60
Nurpur, 170, 204, 233, 248, 260
Nuruddin Bamezei, 152
Nuruddin, Hakim, 198n, 202, 234, 294

Obed Khan, 152, 153
Ochterlony, Colonel, 226-28, 237n, 244n
Oms, Senor or Musa Sahib, 260
Oudh, vi, 108, 110
Oudh, Nawab Wazir of, 150, 164n, 169, 171, 173n, 174-76, 178, 179, 181n, 191, 192

Pahar Singh Man, 233
Painda Khan, 66, 238
Pakistan, v
Pak Pattan, 9, 28, 33, 34, 42n, 163, 319
Panchayat, 15, 81, 83, 270
Panipat, 155, 163, 167, 169, 175, 228; battle of 1526, 12; of 1761, 150-51, 191, 207n; invasion of large Sikh force, 172; Rahim Dad Khan governor, 173; Sikhs' right recognised to levy rakhi on lands between Panipat and Delhi, 177
Paonta, 76, 78, 96
Pasrur, 136, 141
Pathankot, 109, 217
Pathans, vi, 12, 92, 95, 265; Hargobind recruits mercenaries, 64; leader deserts, 66; 500 mercenaries nucleus of Gobind Singh's private army, 78; join the Mughals in fighting Banda, 110, 113; help to swell Nadir Shah's army, 131; join Abdali, 149; of Kasur, 171, 190, 194, 204, 215; Punjabis' first victory over them, 243; Punjabis enter Peshawar, 253; battle of Naushera, 263-64; join Syed Ahmed, 272-73; name of Nalwa, 281; join the Afghans in investing Jamrud, 285-86; Grand Army of the Indus, 288
Patiala, 4n, 144, 176, 224, 225, 228, 233, 237n; association with the Sikhs in the time of the gurus, 68n, 93; encircled by Mughals, 175; Marathas intercede in a quarrel with Singhpurias, 180; invite Ranjit Singh's arbitration, 213, 216; seek protection from the British, 222; Metcalfe receives them, 223; see also Ala Singh, Amar Singh, Sahib Singh
Patna, 71, 72, 76, 314
Perron, General, 181, 191, 210, 211
Persia, 8, 191, 220, 221, 224, 256, 287n
Persians, 5, 11, 13, 125, 126, 183, 200, 250, 287, 288
Peshaura Singh, 188, 257n
Peshawar, 131, 135, 235, 241, 257n, 263, 282; Persians rule for 100 years, 11; Yar Mohammed Khan governor, 253; Punjabis enter the city, 253-54; Jahan Dad Khan governor, 254; Dost Mohammed offers one lac a year, 254; Avitabile governor, 260; Yar Mohammed comes and goes, 262, 265,

271, 272; Ranjit Singh enters, 264; Syed Ahmed captures the city, 273; Sher Singh gives it to Sultan Mohammed Khan, 273; Shah Shuja asked to renounce his title to the city, 280, 283; Lahore Durbar removes Sultan Mohammed and garrisons the city, 281; Dost Mohammed's strategy, 285-87; Shah Shuja renounces his title to the city, 380

Phillaur, 213, 217, 227, 247n

Phoolkia misl, 133; *see also* Ala Singh

Phula Singh, 251n, 253, 266; Ranjit Singh takes him into his employ, 207n; fracas with Metcalfe's escort, 229; wanted Ranjit Singh to tear up the Treaty of 1809, 230; occupy forts at Multan, 248; battle of Naushera, 263-64; death, 264; *see also* Nihangs

Pindi Bhattian, 205

Pindi Gheb, 171

Pir Mohammed Khan, 238

Pir Panjal Range, 255

Poonch, 101n, 246; Poonchis, 247

Pothohar, 4n, 166, 205

Pottinger, Colonel, 274, 275n, 287n

Prithi Chand, 51, 55, 56, 58, 81, 122n, 310

Proclamation of August 22, 1811, 231

Purdah, 54

Qadir, Ghulam, 179, 180

Qamaruddin, Wazir, 128n, 130, 131

Raghu Nath Rao, 147

Rahim Dad Khan, Mullah, 173

Rahon, 108, 216

Rai Bular, 300, 312

Rai Singh Bhangi, 173, 175, 181n

Raj Kaur, Rani, 200n, 266

Rajasthan, 14n, 24, 28n, 33, 107, 112, 149

Rajauri, 101n, 239, 240, 246, 248, 254, 255

Rajputana, 94

Rajputs, 4n, 13, 80, 83n, 109, 110, 120, 156, 191, 204, 269; 1883 census, 14n, 15n; desert Gobind Singh, 58; in revolt against Bahadur Shah, 102; help Abdus Samad Khan against Banda, 113; Marathas come to their aid, 162; anarchy, 169; in conflict with the Malwais, 172; alliance with Sikhs, 183; position in Punjab, 190; no longer powerful, 219

Rakhi, 142, 148, 167, 172, 177, 178, 180

Ram Das, 97n, 130, 161, 304, 305; family tree, 51; builds town of Amritsar, 55; achievements, 55; hymns, 55, 306, 307, 360-61; chooses Arjun, 55-56; initiates Gurdas, 310

Ram Dyal, 217n, 246, 247, 256, 265

Ram Nagar, 192

Ram Rai, 51, 69-71, 81, 122n

Ram Raiyas, 51, 69n, 122n

Ram Rauni (later Ramgarh), 130, 133, 134, 137, 140, 148

Ram Singh, 218n, 242n

Ramananda, 23, 24, 306, 321

Ramanuja, 23

Ramgarhia misl, 133, 206; holds land between Amritsar and Himalayas, 142; helps the Marathas to take Sirhind, 147; levies tribute on hill states, 170; expelled from Majha, 182; invited back, 183; combination against Ranjit Singh, 197; estates taken over, 249; *see also* Jassa Singh Ramgarhia

Ranjit Singh, 56n, 162, 294; Forster's prophecy, 184; birth, ancestry, 187; family tree, betrothal, 188; marriage to Kanhaya heiress, 189; British estimate, 196; capture of Lahore, 196-97; administration of Lahore, 202; early administrative arrangements, 198; birth of sons, 200n, 214n, 288n; coronation and consequences, 200-2; land revenue, 202-3; unification of the Punjab, 189, 200-5, 216-17,

219-31, 233-34, 248-49; capture of Amritsar, 206-7; modernisation of the army, 207-9, 211n, 229n, 248, 258, 260; finance, 217-18; capture of Kangra, 232-33; Kohinoor, 237, 239n, 241, 242; Kashmir expeditions, 239-40, 246-47, 254-55; fall of Multan, 249-52; judicial reform, 270-71; claims territory across the Sutlej, 279; death and cremation, 289; character and achievements, 201, 291-96; relations with the British, 199-200, 210-12, 219-31, 265, 267, 268, 274-80, 283-84, 287-88; the Dogras, 269; Dost Mohammed, 254, 262-65, 274, 281-82, 284-87; Fateh Khan Barakzai, 239-43; Fateh Singh Ahluwalia, 189, 204, 266-67; France, 259; Gurkhas, 232-33, 247-48, 278; Kasurians, 204-5, 215; Ladakhis, 279-80; Malwais, 213-14, 216, 219-31; Marathas, 211-12, 230, 279; Muslims, 27n, 28n, 203-5, 208, 294, 295; Perron, 210; Rajputs, 204, 214, 232-33, 269; Rohillas, 230; Russians, 278; Sada Kaur, 256; Begam Samru, 230; Shah Shuja, 234-37, 240-45, 278, 280, 283, 287-88; Shah Zaman, 190-97, 236-37; Sindhians, 278, 282-83; campaigns in the northwest, 205, 240-43, 252-54, 256, 262-65, 271-74, 281; the west, 256-57; southwest, 205-6, 215, 235-36, 248-52; see also army, Punjabi, Lahore Durbar

Ratan Kaur, 257n

Ravi, river, 3, 4n, 109, 129, 133, 138, 147, 155, 187, 194, 249, 250, 269, 278; Nanak builds Kartarpur, 34; Arjun's end, 61; Khalsa build fort Dallewal, 126; expansion of Nakkais, 171

Rawalpindi, 9, 11, 166, 171, 236, 253

Rechna Doab, 4n, 142, 155

Red Fort, 169

Reinhardt, Walter, 173

revenue, 201, 248-49, 279; reorgani-
sation, 198; land revenue system, 202-3; system of collection in Amritsar, 206; from Dallewalia estates, 216; Singhpuria estates, 234; Ramgarhia estates, 249; Multan, 252; Peshawar, 254, 265; Kashmir, 255; Mankera, 257; effect of static revenue on army, 261; Ranjit Singh's instructions on collection, 293n; Punjab, 295

Rikab Ganj Gurdwara, 74n, 178n

Rohilkhand, 177

Rohillas, 120, 159, 230; join the Afghans, 150; Sikhs suffer reverse, 162, 163, 165n; anarchy, 169; in conflict with Malwais, 172; alliance with Sikhs, defeat imperial forces, 173-74; defeated by Najaf Khan, 174; desert Sikhs, 175; conflict with Dal Khalsa, 176, 179; take over imperial city, 180; defeated by the Nawab Wazir of Oudh, 181n; promise to side with Shah Zaman, 191-92; alliance with Marathas, 211

Rohtak, 4n, 14n

Rohtas, 190, 239, 253

Rojhan, 282, 284

Ropar, 105, 113, 276, 277

Russia, 220; Russians, 278, 287, 288

Sada Kaur, 199; inherits Kanhaya estates, 188; helps Ranjit Singh in the taking of Lahore, 196; Sansar Chand seizes villages, 204; relations with Ranjit Singh, 189, 193n, 214n, 266n; misl suffers partial eclipse, 234; estates sequestered, apprehended, death, 256

Sadashiv Rao Bhao, 150

Saddozais, 131n, 235, 252; family tree, 139

Sadhaura, 105, 112, 176

Sadhu Singh, 207n, 251

Safdar Jang, Wazir, 134-36, 173

Sahajdharis, 89, 98, 120, 121

Saharanpur, 107, 108

Sahib Devan, 51, 83, 121

Sahib Singh Bedi, 195, 199, 200

Sahib Singh Bhangi, 192, 193, 196n
Sahib Singh of Patiala, 181n, 210n,
    225; collaborates with Shah Za-
    man, 191; promises Shah Zaman
    to bring over the Malwais, 194;
    invites Ranjit Singh's mediation,
    213, 216; presents Metcalfe the
    keys, 223; receives Ochterlony, 228
Saidpur, see Eminabad
Samana, 104
Samru, Begam, 173, 230
Sansar Chand, 190, 193, 194, 204,
    214, 232, 233, 237n, 269, 289n
Sarbat Khalsa, see Khalsa
Sarfaraz Khan of Multan, 294
Sati, 54
Sawan Mal, 282
Scythians, 11, 14n
Seton, A., Resident at Delhi, 221n,
    222
Shabkadar, 281, 285, 286
Shahabad, 105, 110, 225
Shah Alam II, see Mughal emperor

Shahanchi Khan, 192; son, 193
Shaheed misl, 132; see also Deep
    Singh
Shahidganj, 127, 129, 140
Shah Ismail, 271
Shah Jahan, see Mughal emperor
Shah Mahmud, 139, 190, 192, 195,
    235-37, 239n, 244n, 245n, 252; see
    also Saddozais
Shah Nawaz, 128, 130, 131, 134n,
    136, 137
Shah Shuja, 242; family tree, 139;
    sketch, 235; sent in chains to
    Kashmir, 236; wife offers Ranjit
    Singh the Kohinoor, 237, 239n;
    Mohkam Chand takes him into
    custody, 240; surrenders the Koh-
    inoor, 241; plot to overthrow the
    Lahore Durbar, 243-45; escapes
    from Lahore, 245; Lahore Durbar
    and recovery of his throne, 278,
    280, 283; defeated by Dost Mo-
    hammed, 281; Tripartite Treaty,
    287-88; see also Saddozais

Shah Zaman, 196, 200, 217; family
    tree, 139; invasions, 190-95; rela-
    tions with Ranjit Singh, 197, 199;
    sketch, 235; returns to the Punjab,
    236-37; see also Saddozais
Shaikh Ibrahim or Farid Sani, 34,
    42n, 319
Shalamar Gardens, 147, 161, 292
Shankara, 22, 23
Shariat Law, 202, 270
Shastras, 35, 85, 86, 289
Sheikhupura, 9, 217
Sher Singh, 198n, 271; family tree,
    188; birth, 214n; relations with
    Kharak Singh, 214n, 266; given
    Batala, 256; besieged at Jehan-
    giria, 263; relations with his fa-
    ther, 266; kills Syed Ahmed, 273,
    274n
Shikarpur, 278, 282, 283
Shiva, 18, 20, 25, 97n, 120
Shivalik hills, 111, 177
Shujauddaulah, 150
Shupaiyan, 246, 247; battle of, 255
Sialkot, 9, 136, 141, 152, 156, 163,
    164, 217
Simla, 268, 275, 277n, 291
Sindh, vi, 3, 10, 28, 219-21, 231,
    271, 274-75, 278, 281, 288; com-
    merce with Punjab by river, 8,
    249; overrun by Mohammed-bin
    Qasim, 21; Taimur holds his
    father's conquests, 169; conquest
    of Multan opens up road, 252;
    Punjabi dreams of expansion, 265;
    question discussed with British,
    271, 276, 283-84; Syed Ahmed, 273;
    Durbar troops on threshold, 282
Sindh, Amirs of, 280, 283, 284;
    British mission, 220-21, 223; Brit-
    ish negotiations, 265; Burnes' ex-
    pedition, 274-75; sign treaties with
    the British, 278
Singh Sabha, 314
Sindh Sagar Doab, 3n, 257
Sindhia, D. R., 210, 211
Sindhia, Madhaji, 169, 179-81
Sindhia, Sabaji, 149, 150

Singhpuria misl, 132, 139, 142, 180, 187, 213; *see also* Kapur Singh, Budh Singh

Sirhind, 4n, 9, 90, 94, 115, 131, 142-43, 155, 164, 165, 229n; Wazir Khan governor 92n; battle of, 104-6; Banda introduces new calendar, 107; farmed by Adina Beg Khan, 141; taken by Abdali, 144; Marathas take the town, 147; Sikhs recapture it, 156, 159; Malwais clash with Marathas, 172

Sirhindi, Shaikh Ahmed, 59n, 73n, 118

Sirmoor, 67; Raja of, 216

Sis Ganj Gurdwara, 74n, 178n

Sitana, 271

Sobha Singh Kanhaya, 161, 164, 166

Sodhis, 55, 71n, 97n, 213

Sonepat, 104, 172

Spain, 228; Spanish, 258

Sri Chand, 30, 36, 49, 50, 55n

Sri Hargobindpur, 57, 65

Srinagar, 247, 255

Stuart, Lieutenant Colonel, 181

Sucha Nand, 92n, 105, 106

Suchet Singh, 252

Sufis, 25-29, 33, 34, 37, 41, 42n, 45n, 46, 59n, 306, 307

Sufism, 26, 28

Suhrawardiyas, 28

Sukerchak, village, 129, 132

Sukerchakia misl, 184, 233n; Dal Khalsa divided into misls, 132; subdues Muslim tribes, 139; takes over the Rechna and Chaj doabs, 142; helps Marathas in taking Sirhind, 147; at Lahore, 150; with Bhangis takes two doabs, 155; Zam Zama, 161n, 207n; Jammu, bone of contention, 171, 182; the Ramgarhias, 183; sketch, 187-89; Rohtas taken, 190; *see also* Charhat Singh, Maha Singh, Naudh Singh

Suket, 233, 234

Sulaiman, 3, 11

Sulakhni, 30, 50

Sultan Khan of Bhimbar, 239

Sultan Mohammed Khan, 238, 273, 281, 282

Sultanpur, 31, 170

Sundari, Mata, 51, 81, 103n, 121, 122, 123n, 315

Suraj Mal, 51, 67

Sutlej, 3, 4, 65, 80, 105, 106, 109, 124, 133, 139, 147, 151, 153, 159, 165, 211-15, 232, 237n, 249, 250, 265, 266, 268, 279, 280, 282-84, 296; Singhpurias and Ahluwalias, 142, 170; boundary question, 219, 220, 224, 226-30

Syed Ahmed, 271-74, 283

Taimur, the Lame, 12, 28, 249, 296

Taimur, Prince, 288

Taimur Shah, 144-47, 168, 169, 190, 237n; family tree, 139

Tara Singh, 188, 214n, 266n

Tara Singh Gheba, 155, 174, 175, 216, 220

Taran Taran, 57, 145, 204

Taru Singh, 127n

Taxila, 11

Tegh Bahadur, 66, 67, 98, 308; family tree, 51; chosen by Hari Krishen, 70; builds Anandpur, 71; travels, 71-72; birth of Gobind Singh, 72; advice of, 72; arrested, 73; executed, 74; Gobind Singh writes of his martyrdom, 74-75; two temples erected, 177-78; tablets in East Pakistan, 302; Gobind Singh includes his father's hymns in the Adi Granth, 304-5; hymns, 306, 376-77

Tej Singh, 218n

Thanesar, 110, 139, 175, 180, 181, 213

Thomas, George, 181, 189, 190, 210

Tibet, 66n, 255

Tippu Sultan, 192, 210n

Tonk, Nawab of, 271

Trans-Sutlej, 4n, 170

Treaty of Lahore 1806, 212; of 1809, 235, 268, 283, 378

Treaty with the Marathas, 180
Tripartite Treaty, 287, 380
Tripta, 30, 50
Trumpp, Dr., 68n, 300
Tughlaks, 12
Turanis, 134
Turks, 13

Ucch, 208; district, 249
Udai Singh, 91
Udasis, 50
United States, v
untouchables, 97
Upanishads, 19
Uttar Pradesh, 14n, 24, 65, 71, 110, 120, 309

Vairowal, 198
Van Cortlandt, General, 258n
Vardhana, 11
Vedas, 19, 22, 80n, 86, 97
Ventura, Jean Baptiste, 258, 259, 263, 266, 272, 273
Vishnu, 18, 20, 25, 97n

Wade, Captain, 275, 279n, 280, 288; delegation to Amritsar, 268; visits Lahore for signature of 1832

treaty, 277; Sindh, 283-84; Tripartite Treaty, 287
Wafa Begam, 237, 239n, 241, 242n, 244n, 245
Wazir Khan, 92n, 93, 94, 95n, 101, 104-6
Wazirabad, 9, 135, 147, 234, 241, 246, 254, 260
Wellesley, Lord, see Governor General
Whadni, 216
Wolff, Dr. Joseph, 276, 277n

Yahya Khan, 128-30
Yar Mohammed Khan, 238, 253, 262, 265, 271-73, 281
Yusuf Ali, Mir, 199
Yusufzais, 262-64, 272

Zabita Khan, 169n, 172-77, 179
Zakarya Khan, 112, 115, 122-28, 130
Zam Zama, 161n, 207, 236, 250, 251
Zebunnissa, 161
Zorawar Singh, son of Gobind Singh, 51, 156, 308
Zorawar Singh, General, vii, 81, 91, 92, 279, 280, 295
Zulfiqar, 294

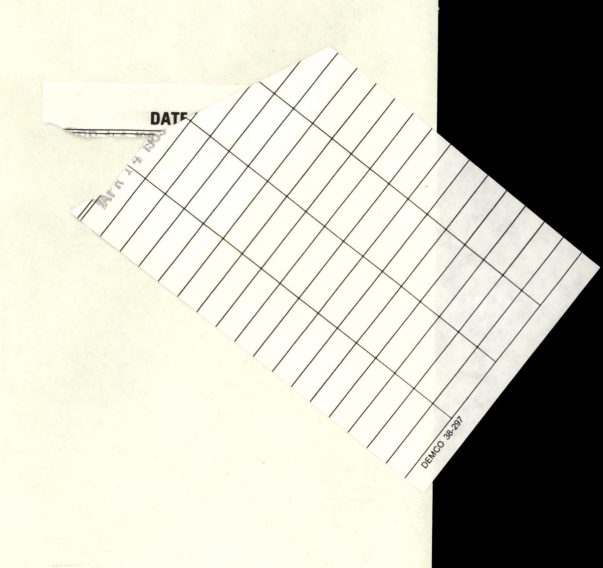